REAL WORLD
GLOBALIZATION

FIFTEENTH EDITION

A READER IN ECONOMICS, BUSINESS, AND POLITICS FROM
DOLLARS&SENSE

EDITED BY JAWIED NAWABI, ALEJANDRO REUSS, CHRIS STURR,

AND THE *DOLLARS & SENSE* COLLECTIVE

REAL WORLD GLOBALIZATION, 15th edition

ISBN: 978-1-939402-28-8

Published by: Economic Affairs Bureau, Inc. d/b/a *Dollars & Sense*

  89 South Street, LL02, Boston, MA 02111

  617-447-2177; dollars@dollarsandsense.org; www.dollarsandsense.org.

Real World Globalization is edited by the *Dollars & Sense* Collective, which also publishes *Dollars & Sense* magazine and books including *Microeconomics: Individual Choice in Communities, Real World Micro, Real World Macro, Current Economic Issues, The Economics of the Environment, Introduction to Political Economy, Labor and the Global Economy, Real World Banking and Finance, Real World Latin America, Real World Labor, Unlevel Playing Fields: Understanding Wage Inequality and Discrimination,* and *The Wealth Inequality Reader.*

The 2016 *Dollars & Sense* Collective:

Betsy Aron, Nancy Banks, Autumn Beaudoin, Sarah Cannon, Nina Eichacker, Peter Kolozi, John Miller, Jawied Nawabi, Kevin O'Connell, Alejandro Reuss, Dan Schneider, Zoe Sherman, Bryan Snyder, Chris Sturr, De'En Tarkpor, William Whitham, and Jeanne Winner.

Editors of this volume: Jawied Nawabi, Alejandro Reuss, and Chris Sturr

Production: Alejandro Reuss

Cover design: Alejandro Reuss

Cover photo: ptwo from Germany and UK - 1492, Illuminated globes, Frankfurt book fair 2012 in Germany, Creative Commons Attribution-Share Alike 2.0 Generic license.

Printed in U.S.A.

CONTENTS

DEFINING GLOBALIZATION

The concept of "globalization" can refer to a process, a system, an era, or a condition. Four characteristics of contemporary globalization stand out in mainstream analysis: 1) The increasing *multiplication and thickening* of social networks and activities which are able to overcome political, economic, cultural, and geographical boundaries, mainly because of revolutionary innovations in transportation. 2) The *intensification and acceleration* of cultural and social exchanges (increasing accessibility to movies, music, writing, etc., from all over the globe) because of revolutionary innovations in communications. 3) The *expansion and stretching* of international institutions, including inter-governmental and non-governmental organizations. 4) The sum of these effects has led to the *compression of time and space*, and as a result, a general global consciousness. This is manifested by the way people around the world increasingly speak in a discourse that is trans-national—whether they're speaking of human rights, the environment, the economy, etc. (Steger, pp. 7, 9-12).

These four characteristics give us an abstract and conceptual picture of what globalization is. More, they describe the positive side of globalization. However, whether the overall effects of capitalist globalization are, on balance, positive is a matter of controversy. Let us look at the more concrete disruptive aspects of globalization. The predominant motor of globalization is the capitalist mode of production—an economic system in which a minority own the principal means of production, employ others as wage workers, and offer the goods and services the latter produce for sale with the goal of private profit. There is abundant historical evidence that this system expands relentlessly, spreading its ethos of individualism and competition, tearing down the walls of other social systems whatever their particular traditional beliefs and ways of economic production—often with devastating consequences on entire ethnic groups and regions. Yet history also shows ample evidence of resistance against the expansion of the capitalist of mode of production, continuing to the present day.

When we survey the world today, there are indeed many positive developments—from new technological conveniences to life-saving medical advances. Yet, despite all the advances for which the world capitalist system receives accolades, there is the continuing growth of inequality within and between nations, the coexistence of extreme poverty and pauperization with the heights of luxury:

- Divide the world's income in half. The richest 8% of the world population takes one half and the other 92% gets the other half. Or, to look at it another way, three-fourths of the world's population gets just 20% of the total income, while the richest 1.7% also gets 20% (Yates, p. 9). Wealth is distributed even more unequally than income. In 2010, the richest 388 people in the world owned as much wealth as the poorest half of the world population. By 2011, it was down to the richest 177; by 2012, the richest 159; by 2013, 92; by 2014, 80; by 2015, only 62.

- In 1850, the rich countries of today accounted for 35% of the world's total income. By the 1980s, they accounted for 68%. The difference between the per capita incomes of the poor and rich countries increased from 70% in 1850 to more than 1000% in the 1980s. While there have been some countries, like China, India, and the so-called "Asian Tigers" (Hong Kong, Singapore, South Korea and Taiwan), that have moved towards the incomes of the developed countries, inequality between nations has remained very high (Yates p. 7; Gorringe, pp. 63-64; Cypher, pp. 17-18). Latin America had a decade of declining income, the "lost decade" of the 1980s, and the 1990s were not good either. Sub-Saharan Africa had declining income for *two* decades, the 1980s and 1990s. Only starting in 2000 did those two regions have growing incomes again. Excluding China and India, in fact, income inequality between the world's high-income developed regions and the developing regions may have increased rather than decreased since 1980.

- Polarisation between countries is accompanied moreover by increasing inequality within countries. Economist Arthur MacEwan describes, based on OECD and World Bank data, a "widespread rise of income inequality within countries, especially among high-income countries" since the 1980s. While the picture among low-income countries is mixed, in terms of income-inequality trends, the most populous low-income countries— China, India, and Indonesia—have also experienced rising inequality (Yates p. 10; Went, p. 35).

For all the fanfare about the positive and beneficial aspects of globalization, there are also disruptive and exclusionary dimensions of globalization. Neoliberalism, or "free market" economics, offers ideological justification for the latter. It frustrates attempts to regulate or socialize the material resources of nation-states. It drives for the elimination of any restrictions on the mobility of capital or its penetration of local economies. Old-style regulation, which smaller and less-developed nation-states once erected to promote their local industries, are derided as anachronistic and "inefficient." In the doctrine of neoliberalism, the notion of competition is central. Competition between nations, regions, firms, and of course between individuals is supposed to allocate all resources, whether physical, natural, human, or financial with the greatest possible efficiency. The results of this sort of competition is to commodify all aspects of human relations that were previously not within the logic of the capitalist mode of production.

What's in This Book

It is the aim of this book to explain and critically analyze the basic contours of globalization, focusing especially on the negative and disruptive aspects of corporate-led globalization. It also aims to outline alternatives to the current form of globalization, with the aim of eliminating poverty and hunger, extreme social and economic inequality, environmental destruction, and violence.

The book is made up of twelve chapters, each focusing on a particular aspect of the global economy.

Chapter 1: Critical Perspectives on Globalization

This chapter starts off the volume with several key questions about globalization today: Is the corporate controlled version of globalization inevitable? Are there possibilities of a more inclusive and sustainable globalization? Are the trends of growing inequality inevitable? Has globalization increased the potential for economic freedom and social mobility, while safeguarding our rights and opportunities for a dignified life?

Chapter 2: Corporate Power and the Global Economy

The articles in this chapter focus on the power of multinational corporations (MNCs). The models in mainstream ("neoclassical") economics textbooks assume that markets are competitive, with thousands of sellers offering consumers what they want at competitively determined prices. In other words, firms wield no real power and the consumer is "sovereign." In the real world, we find a handful of giant companies controlling an enormous share of world trade in each major industry. MNCs have immense power to influence the terms of trade in the world's food system, the monetary and fiscal policies of of developing countries, the legal language of international agreements, and the power structures of international institutions.

Chapter 3: International Trade and Investment

Despite differences among neoclassical economists on many theoretical and practical questions, one issue where there is unanimity is the gospel of free trade. The theory of comparative advantage, or at least the contemporary textbook version, purports to show that "free trade" will benefit all countries regardless of size and level of economic development. The articles in this chapter offer critical perspectives about both trade itself and the use of "free trade" as a justification for elimination of barriers to international movements of capital. It considers just what circumstances—what forms of integration into the world economy—are required for trade between countries to be genuinely beneficial to their populations.

Chapter 4: International Finance

The world of international finance may appear in standard textbooks as a benign sphere where people buy and sell the currencies of various countries, mainly in order to buy and sell the goods and services of those countries. However, the currency policies of large, high-income countries have profound effects on all countries. U.S. government policies maintaining the dollar as the primary reserve currency in the world, for example, help create financial pressures on developing countries to put away a large part of their savings—sometimes hundreds of billions of dollars—in in dollars or securities denominated in dollars. The deregulation of international finance, meanwhile, means that countries are exposed to destabilizing short-run, speculative movements of capital. Financial investment can rush into a country during a boom (making its currency more valuable), only to stampede out just as fast at the first hint of a downturn (potentially causing the currency to crash). As a result, instead of being able to engage in large-scale productive investment, developing countries instead have to use savings to defend their currency's stable exchange rate from possible speculative "attack." Instead of productive investment that could benefit lower-income people in developing countries, this structure concentrates wealth in the financial sectors of the United States and other high-income countries, a form of invisible imperialism, as the articles in this chapter will describe.

Chapter 5: International Institutions

The world needs international institutions as much as we need domestic institutions. Institutions regulate matters like product safety, resource depletion and environmental pollution, and conditions and compensation for labor. They create formal channels through which disputes between contracting parties can be resolved. Mainstream accounts often assume that existing international institutions are designed to bring about fair resolutions for these and other matters, based what is best for the global community or the majority of a the population. However, the articles in this chapter—on the International Monetary Fund (IMF), the World Bank, the World Trade Organization (WTO), the North American Free Trade Agreement (NAFTA), the European Union (EU), the Trans-Pacific Partnership (TPP), and the Transatlantic Trade and Investment Patnership (TTIP)—reveal an elite-controlled international financial architecture. These international institutions are decidedly of the wealthy, by the wealthy, and for the wealthy. As you read the articles in this chapter you will learn about the role of international institutions in "austerity" or "structural adjustment" programs—cutting back on basic public services like education and health care, shifting the tax burden onto lower-income people, and redistributing income upwards to the wealthy individuals and large corporations. Such policies benefit both ruling elites of developing countries and their counterparts in the core developed economies.

Chapter 6: Labor in the Global Economy

Where do the cheap goods which fill our malls come from? When we see commercials for the products that we eat or wear, should we wonder about the working conditions of the workers who make them? The articles in this chapter describe the condition of workers in an array of countries, such as Bangladesh, China, and Indonesia. They give a wide variety of examples, throughout the world, showing that globalization does not inevitably result in a "race to the bottom" on wages and working conditions. The power of workers' organizations, and laws and policies that set conditions for labor organization in different countries, sectors, and occupations, also matter.

Chapter 7: Migration

Donald Trump's proposals, as a candidate for U.S. president and as president-elect, for deporting millions of undocumented migrants from the United States has made immigration a hot topic. Around the world, there are nearly 250 million migrants living outside their home countries, primarily for economic reasons. The influx of immigrants to the United States and the EU has met with a right-wing populist backlash, depicting immigrants as criminals, terrorists, enemies of of native-born workers, and free-riders on public services. As the articles in this chapter reveal, immigrants bring their creative talents and immense productive energy, from which their new adopted countries and most native-born and longtime-resident workers benefit. Furthermore, not all migration is from the "third world" to the "first world." A substantial percentage of migration operates within individual developing countries, or goes from one developing country to another. This aspect of global migration gets too little attention in the mainstream media, but is highlighted in this chapter.

Chapter 8: Development and "Underdevelopment"

Does the development of one country or region come at the expense of other countries or regions? What does "development" actually measure? Why have the economic policies of the "Washington Consensus," formulated by the best trained economists from the top universities in the world, not been able to reduce poverty and misery in Latin America? Does China's economy and high growth offer a strong enough engine for the world's economy to continue growing and developing? What are the roles of such factors as the control of land and access to credit in economic development? These are some of the central questions in development economics that are addressed in this chapter, each in a concrete, present-day context.

Chapter 9: The Political Economy of Empire

This chapter, which focuses on the unequal relations of power (military, political, and economic) among countries, flows logically from the previous one. What is the relationship of neocolonialism to "underdevelopment" in today's world economy? Is Puerto Rico a colony, and how does its political status affect its economic development? Why does foreign aid from high-income countries have such a poor record on the economic development of countries which have received the most aid per capita? Is the main goal of U.S. military action globally to gain or maintain control of strategic resources, such as oil, and if so who benefits from this control?

Chapter 10: Natural Resources and the Environment

This chapter addresses key controversies in regard to natural-resource depletion and environmental degradation. Would it be costly, in terms of economic growth and jobs, to adopt more sustainable methods of production? Is the industrialization of the world's food system, and its control by a few large MNCs, the most productive and environmentally sustainable path for food production? Does the local food movement offer feasible alternatives to a globalized industrial food system? What are the disagreements between developed and developing countries on climate policy? Can climate policies actually benefit us today, or are these painful sacrifices that only benefit future generations?

Chapter 11: Crisis, Austerity, and Stagnation

Many economists and business reporters have argued that financial crises—such as those in Mexico, Argentina, Russia, and much of Asia in the 1980s and 1990s—are problems of developing economies with weak institutions. Developed economies, they assured us, were immune from such instability due to their developed financial markets and regulatory oversight. As the articles in this chapter reveal—with the financial crash in Iceland, the ongoing economic crises in Greece and Spain, Japan's two decades of stagnation, and generalized "secular stagnation" besetting the economies of the developed world—the "first world" has not proved immune after all. The financial sector detonated a global crisis which has caused massive economic hardship from unemployment and growing inequality. The conventional economic measures of fiscal austerity and further deregulation have only exacerbated the problem. The chapter concludes with selections proposing alternative approaches to get back to full employment and more widely shared benefits from rising productivity.

Chapter 12: Resistance and Alternatives

Are there alternatives to the present corporate-controlled globalization? If there are, how do we get there? The articles in this chapter are focused on ways that the international economic system can be reorganized to bring about better conditions for labor, reduced inequality, greater economic stability and security, and greater environmental sustainability. They offer not pie-in-the-sky fantasies but concrete and practical alternatives to corporate globalization, which people around the world are advocating and organizing today. Another World Is Possible!

—*Jawied Nawabi*

Sources: International Labor Organization, Global unemployment projected to rise in both 2016 and 2017, Jan. 19, 2016 (ilo.org); "Richest 62 people as wealthy as half of world's population, says Oxfam," *The Guardian*, Jan. 18, 2016; "244 million international migrants living abroad worldwide, new UN statistics reveal," United Nations, Jan. 12, 2016; James M. Cypher, *The Process of Economic Development*, 4th ed. (Routledge, 2014); Timothy Gorringhe, *Fair Shares: Ethics and the Global Economy* (Thames and Hudson, 1999); B. Manfred Steger, *Globalization: A Very Short Introduction* (Oxford University Press, 2003); Robert Went, *Globalization: Neoliberal Challenge, Radical Responses* (Pluto Press, 2000); Michael Yates, "Measuring Global Inequality," *Monthly Review*, November 2016.

Chapter 1

CRITICAL PERSPECTIVES ON GLOBALIZATION

Article 1.1

A GREAT FALL
The Origins and Crisis of Neoliberalism

BY DAVID M. KOTZ
November/December 2015

In the fall of 2008, a massive financial and economic crisis struck the United States and much of the world. The biggest American banks were suddenly insolvent and survived only thanks to government bailouts. A deep recession spread around the globe. The unemployment rate in the United States jumped up to 10%. Over the following five years, more than four million U.S. homeowners were tossed out of their homes due to foreclosure, as home values plummeted below the mortgage debt owed and unemployment cut household incomes. The economies of the United States, Europe, and much of the rest of the world have been stuck in stagnation or worse since 2008.

This condition is not something new in the history of capitalism. Capitalist economic systems—in which a small percentage of the population owns the enterprises, hires wage workers, and sells the products aiming for a profit—have brought economic growth but also periodic severe economic crises. To understand these recurring crises, we need to take account of the quite different forms of capitalism over time. While always having the key features noted above, capitalism has nevertheless not looked the same at all times. For several decades following World War II, the United States had a "regulated capitalism" in which government, trade unions, and other non-market institutions played major roles in regulating the economy. Since 1980, we have lived under "neoliberal capitalism," in which the government retreated from regulation of business and markets, and trade unions were marginalized. In the past, each form of capitalism has worked well on its own terms—fostering investment and economic growth—for a few decades, after which snowballing problems gave rise to severe economic crises such as today's.

The crisis of neoliberal capitalism has made it vulnerable to replacement by something else. Every past economic crisis of this severity has been followed by major changes in economic and political institutions. Earlier so-called "free-market" forms of capitalism have produced economic crises before in U.S. history—in the 1890s and the end of the 1920s. In each case, the crisis was followed by the construction of some kind of regulated capitalism, in response to the forces that had brought on the crisis. After 1900, Progressive Era reforms together with the rise of powerful Wall Street banks led to a corporate-dominated form of regulated capitalism. This lasted until the end of World War I, when another shift brought a decade of relatively unhindered pursuit of profit—the Roaring Twenties—that culminated in the 1929 crash. Eventually, a more thoroughly regulated capitalism, this time based on capital-labor compromise, emerged in the late 1940s. While history does not always repeat itself, there is good reason to expect that, if U.S. capitalism is to surmount the stagnation that has followed the crash of 2008, it will do so through another version of regulated capitalism, which can potentially address the problems that led to the current crisis.

Several big questions cry out for answers. Why did the last sea change, from regulated to neoliberal capitalism, take place—not just in the United States but in much of the world—around 1980? Why did a radically different form of capitalism emerge after decades of active state regulation and strong trade unions? Why did the post-1980 "neoliberal capitalism" eventually produce such a big economic crisis after 25 years of seemingly stable, if lackluster and unequally distributed, economic growth? And most immediately, what kind(s) of economic change are possible and likely today? The relative strength and determination of key economic classes has decided the direction of economic change in past crisis periods, and the current one is not likely to be an exception.

Big Business and the Origins of Regulated Capitalism

The post-World War II "regulated capitalism" emerged in the United States in the late 1940s, following a decade of labor militancy, the formation of strong industrial unions, and militant strikes and factory occupations in the 1930s. After the wartime no-strike pledge ended in 1945, labor militancy resumed. At that point, a decisive section of big business concluded that its long-standing effort to crush unions had failed and decided to strike a deal with the labor movement.

A threatening world pushed big business in that direction. Labor, Social Democratic, Socialist, and Communist parties were in power or contending for power in the UK, France, Italy, and Japan. Even in the United States there was a relatively strong Communist party. A suddenly enlarged and empowered bloc of states—encompassing some 35% of the world's population—was ruled by Communist parties. Despite the unsavory features of those regimes, which limited their appeal to workers in the West, big business feared that they lent credence to the possibility of a viable alternative to capitalism.

Not least, big business leaders (like many others) feared that, with the end of the huge public spending of World War II, the Great Depression would return. The Committee for Economic Development (CED), the leading big-business policy organization of that period, warned that another big depression might give rise to a "growing receptivity to futile or dangerous ideas that appear to promise relief from all ills"—that is, they feared a growing receptivity to socialism.

CED policy statements endorsed collective bargaining with unions, expansion of Social Security, and a Keynesian program of government spending and tax cuts to fend off another depression and keep the unemployment rate relatively low. Big business formed an informal coalition with organized labor that completed the construction of regulated capitalism, which had begun with the New Deal reforms of the 1930s.

Some analysts refer to a "capital-labor accord" after World War II, but that term suggests a more cordial relationship than the uneasy compromise actually hammered out. Big business leaders held their noses as they agreed to arrangements that legitimized unions and reduced management power in certain ways (employers accepted collective bargaining over wages, benefits, and conditions, contract grievance procedures, and so on). In return, unions accepted "management rights" clauses in collective bargaining agreements—leaving decisions over the production process, technology, product design, pricing, etc. as the employers' exclusive domain—and accepted responsibility to crack down against worker job actions like slowdowns or wildcat strikes outside of contract-negotiation periods. While this deal did deliver labor relations that were more stable in some ways, it did not eliminate class conflict at the workplace, as major strikes still occurred frequently during the 1950s and 1960s. The capital-labor accord, along with the other features of regulated capitalism, delivered relatively robust economic growth, with rising profits for business alongside increasing wages for workers—what some observers came to call the "Golden Age of Capitalism."

The Crisis of the Postwar System and the Big Business Response

No form of capitalism, however, works smoothly forever. In the late 1960s, the average rate of profit began to fall in the United States, the UK, and France. In the United States, it declined by more than half from 1966 to 1982 (see Figure 1), a development that big business spokespeople blamed on excessive wage gains. The aim of business is profit, and when profit falls for an extended period of time this tends to destabilize the economy. In the 1970s, the economy became increasingly unstable, with rising inflation and unemployment. The Bretton Woods international monetary system dating back to 1944—with fixed currency exchange rates based on the U.S. dollar—tottered and then collapsed in 1973.

For a decade, big business sought to solve its growing problems within the system of regulated capitalism. However, modest reform efforts failed to resolve the crisis, and by the late 1970s it had changed its position. The main big-business lobbying group of that period, the Business Roundtable, began to blame a strong labor movement for the decline in profits. Big business was also agitated by the victories, in alliance with organized labor, of the environmental, occupational-health, and consumer-product-safety movements, and the resulting expansion of government regulation of industry in the 1970s. Groups like the Business Roundtable grabbed onto neoliberal ideas and policies as the way to resolve the problems facing big business.

As big business deserted its previous coalition with organized labor, and allied with small business organizations that had never supported regulated capitalism, it was able to rapidly sweep away the institutions and dominant ideas of regulated capitalism. While organized labor was relatively strong at that time, it could not stop a determined push by a united business class to carry out economic restructuring at the expense of labor and the majority of the population. By the early 1980s, a new form of capitalism had emerged—the neoliberal capitalism that we still live under to the present day.

The end of regulated capitalism and the rise of neoliberalism brought with it a new orthodoxy in economics. Gone were the days when professors at America's leading universities taught that capitalist economies required close regulation by the government to avoid big depressions and high unemployment, and that trade unions played a positive role in reducing inequality. In its place arose a new worship of "free markets," rejecting any role for government or trade unions in improving economic outcomes.

Starting in the early 1980s the declining profit rate reversed and trended upward thereafter (see Figure 1). The neoliberal mantra of privatization, liberalization, and deregulation, as put into practice, served to crush organized labor and put employers in control. Liberalizing foreign trade and removing barriers to capital flight put American

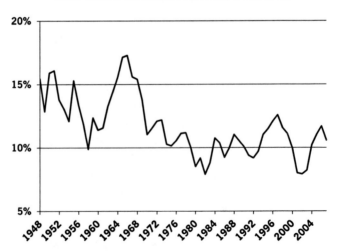

**FIGURE 1: RATE OF PROFIT OF U.S. NONFINANCIAL
CORPORATE BUSINESS SECTOR, 1948-2007**

Source: U.S. Bureau of Economic Analysis (2013), NIPA Table 1.14, Fixed Assets Table 4.1.

FIGURE 2: AVERAGE ANNUAL UNEMPLOYMENT RATE

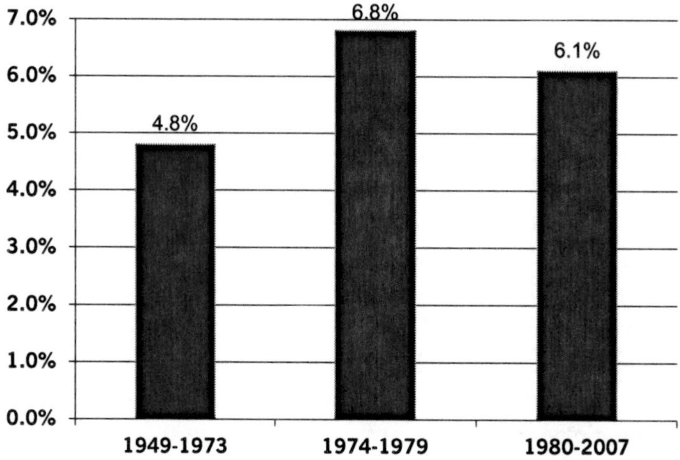

Source: U.S. Bureau of Labor Statistics (2013).

workers in more direct competition with low-wage labor in poor countries. Stopping Keynesian policies aimed at a low unemployment rate gave rise to a higher unemployment rate after 1980 than from the late 1940s to early 1970s (see Figure 2).

This weakened labor's bargaining power. Privatizing and cutting back social welfare programs, too, weakened workers' fallback position in bargaining with employers (see Figure 3).

Lax enforcement of labor law facilitated the corporate agenda of driving out unions and extracting huge wage concessions. Deregulation of basic industries resulted in cutthroat competition replacing the stable environment of government regulation—and relatively high-wage jobs won by unions gave way to rapidly declining pay and worsening working conditions.

Big business could not have effectively argued that wages must fall so that profits could rise, that welfare recipients were too rich while CEOs were too poor, that the unemployment rate should be driven up so that wages could be driven down, or that American workers should be forced into a "race to the bottom" with the poorest workers in the world. However, neoliberal restructuring of American and global capitalism achieved all those aims by promising great economic benefits for all citizens once the magic of the "free market" was unleashed.

Economic Foundations of Neoliberal Capitalism

For some 25 years, neoliberal capitalism in the United States produced long, if tepid, economic expansions with low inflation. Former Federal Reserve Chairman Ben Bernanke coined the term "The Great Moderation" to describe what neoliberal economists believed was a newly stabilized capitalism, a result of lifting the heavy hand of government from the back of big business, and the "grasping" hand of unions from its pockets. While the rich got richer at an astonishing and accelerating rate, the majority did not fare well. As long as neoliberal capitalism was delivering rising profits and growing riches for those at the top, however, it was difficult for critics to make much headway against it.

Beneath the surface, though, long-run trends guaranteed an unhappy ending down the road. Neoliberal capitalism brought three key developments that led to the crash of 2008.

The first was rapidly growing inequality. As neoliberal restructuring undermined labor's bargaining power, real wages stagnated (see Figure 4). This allowed profits to recover from their long decline. The big gap emerging, after 1979, between profit growth and wage and salary growth jumped sharply upward after 2000 (see Figure 5).

The second key development was the transformation of financial institutions and their role in the economy. Bank deregulation began in 1980-1982, and soon financial institutions began to create a raft of so-called "financial innovations"—new types of financial assets such as subprime mortgage-backed securities, collateralized debt obligations, and credit default swaps. The high profitability of such maneuvers pushed the profits of the financial sector from about 20% of all corporate profit to a remarkable 40% in the early 2000s. The term "financialization" arose to describe the expanding and changing role of the financial sector in contemporary capitalism.

The third development was a series of large asset bubbles—that is, the continuing rise in the prices of assets like real estate or corporate stocks, driven by speculative expectations of further price increases. The 1980s saw a bubble in southwestern commercial real estate, whose collapse sank a large part of the

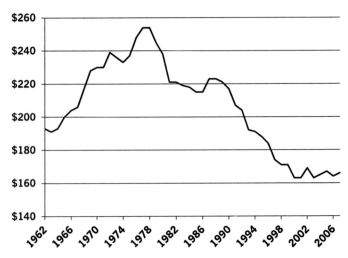

FIGURE 3: MONTHLY BENEFIT PER RECIPIENT UNDER AID TO FAMILIES WITH DEPENDENT CHILDREN OR TEMPORARY ASSISTANCE FOR NEEDY FAMILIES IN 2009 DOLLARS, 1962-2007

Source: U.S. Department of Health and Human Services (2013).

FIGURE 4: AVERAGE HOURLY EARNINGS OF NON-SUPERVISORY WORKERS IN 2011 DOLLARS, 1948-2007

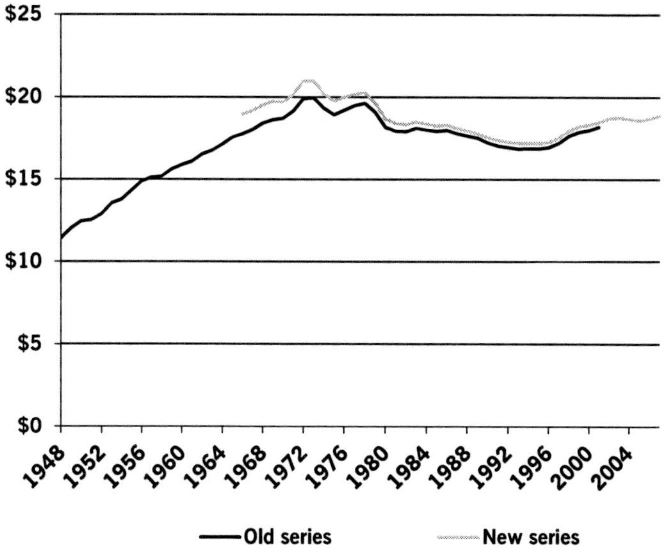

Old series ――― New series

Source: Economic Report of the President (1990, 2003, 2010).

Note: The Bureau of Labor Statistics revised the methodology for the series for average hourly earnings in 2004, adn so there is no single series available from 1948 to 2007.

savings-and-loan industry. In the second half of the 1990s, a giant stock market bubble arose. And in the 2000s, a still larger bubble engulfed the U.S. real estate market. The preceding period of regulated capitalism had no large asset bubbles. The rapidly rising flow of income into corporate profit and rich households exceeded the available productive investment opportunities, and some of that flow found its way into investment in assets. The eagerness of the deregulated financial institutions to lend for speculative purposes enabled incipient asset bubbles to grow larger and larger.

Neoliberal Capitalism and the Crisis of 2008

Growing inequality, the speculative financial sector, and the series of large asset bubbles all contributed to the long economic expansions in the U.S. economy during the neoliberal era—1982–1990, 1991–2000, and 2001–2007.

These trends, however, were unsustainable in the long run. From 1980 to 2007, household debt doubled relative to household income. Financial institutions, finding limitless profit opportunities in the wild financial markets of the period, borrowed heavily to pursue those opportunities. As a result, financial-sector debt increased from 21% of GDP in 1980 to 117% of GDP in 2007. At the same time, financial institutions' holdings of the new high-risk securities grew rapidly. In addition, unused resources in the industrial sector gradually crept upward over the period from 1979 to 2007, as consumer demand increasingly lagged behind the total productive capacity of the economy.

As long as a big asset bubble continued to inflate, people remained willing to borrow more and more, and financial institutions remained willing to lend to them. But every asset bubble eventually must burst. When the biggest one—the real estate bubble—started to deflate in 2007, the crash followed. As households lost the ability to borrow against their no-longer-inflating home values, consumer spending dropped at the beginning 2008, driving the economy into recession. Falling consumer demand meant more excess productive capacity, leading business to reduce its investment in plant and equipment. The deflating housing bubble also worsened investor expectations, further depressing investment. Finally, in the fall of 2008, the plummeting market values of the new-fangled financial securities, which had been dependent on real-estate prices, suddenly drove the highly indebted major commercial banks and investment banks into insolvency, bringing a financial meltdown.

Thus, the big financial and broader economic crisis that began in 2008 is explained by the way neoliberal capitalism worked. The very same mechanisms that brought 25 years of long expansions under neoliberal capitalism were bound to eventually give rise to this sort of "big bang" crisis.

Change: Reactionary, Reformist, or Radical?

So far, the powers that be, in the United States and elsewhere, have been pursuing "austerity policy" as a way of doubling down on neoliberalism, which has greatly rewarded the "one percent." However, continuing along that path promises only unending stagnation. Long-lasting stagnation is destabilizing to capitalism, tending to promote the growth of political movements—on the left and the right—demanding major political and economic change. This prods big business to consider some restructuring of capitalism to overcome stagnation and its dangerous consequences.

There is some evidence of the beginnings of big business consideration of economic alternatives. In January 2015, Lawrence Summers, a close ally of Wall Street who promoted bank deregulation in the 1990s as treasury secretary in the Clinton administration, coauthored a major report calling for significant institutional changes—including measures to reduce inequality and to redirect large corporations toward the pursuit of long-run gains instead of short-run profits.

Big business is not the only actor on the stage. If history is any guide, we can expect that various groups and classes will become increasingly active in the years ahead, pushing for changes that would further their own interests. While significant change seems highly likely, the precise outcome cannot be foretold in advance. Three possible directions of change can be identified—reactionary, reformist, and radical. Which one emerges will depend on the relative strength and determination of the potential beneficiaries of each kind of change. If labor and other popular movements remain relatively weak, as they have after several decades of demoralization and demobilization under neoliberalism, big business will likely drive change in the reactionary direction. This could take the form of a statist and nationalist form of capitalism without any capital-labor compromise.

FIGURE 5: ANNUAL GROWTH RATES OF WAGES AND SALARIES AND CORPORATE PROFIT

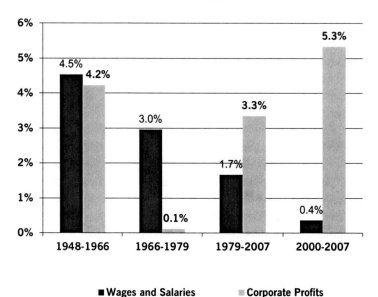

■ Wages and Salaries   ▨ Corporate Profits

Source: U.S. Bureau of Economic Analysis (2013), NIPA Table 1.14, 1.1.4; U.S. Bureau of Labor Statistics (2013).

The neoliberal labor market and the current weak position of labor would remain, while the underlying problem of inadequate growth of demand would be solved via growing state spending for military purposes and perhaps infrastructure and technological innovation. Nationalism is the likely dominant ideology of such a transformation, focusing the attention of the 99% on building national economic and military strength and away from the limited economic benefits for them of this reactionary direction of change. Two prominent right-wing intellectuals, Francis Fukuyama and William Kristol, have recently suggested a move in that direction. Such a reactionary program would not only spell continuing bad conditions for American workers but, with further military buildup and nationalist posturing, a growing danger of even greater inter-state conflict than we have seen in recent times.

If the labor movement, and other popular movements, gain in strength, then a second, reformist, direction of change would become possible. This might entail another capital-labor compromise. A form of capitalism like the previous regulated capitalism, of the post-World War II period, could potentially resolve the current economic crisis by bringing a more balanced growth of profits and wages. It would also likely include a growing state role focused on infrastructure, innovation, education, social provision, and environmental protection. However, change of that type has never come from a "forward-looking" big business class. It would become a serious possibility only if the labor and progressive movements revive and are able to force compromise on the capitalists. Unless big business sees a mortal threat to capitalism, it is not likely to be willing to compromise with labor.

A reformist direction of change, while better for the majority than the reactionary direction, would still pose serious problems. The previous capital-labor compromise of the 1940s to the 1960s left out some groups, notably many women and many African Americans, and it is not clear today if all of the 99% could be accommodated under a renewed compromise. Also, such a reformed capitalism is not a promising system for avoiding disastrous climate change. Reformed capitalism would require—and give rise to—relatively robust economic growth, which would make it difficult and perhaps impossible to avoid the looming climate-change tipping point. While reformed capitalism would likely include measures aimed at environmental protection, large private companies tend to be effective in resisting government measures that limit their freedom of action in pursuit of profit.

If labor and other popular movements gain strength, however, that would also open the possibility of a move beyond capitalism. Continuing stagnation, along with the other problems that derive from capitalism, are likely to lead many to question whether capitalism can any longer meet the needs of the majority and to consider whether an alternative system might able to do so. That would mean a renewal of interest in socialism, which is the only comprehensive alternative to capitalism. There is evidence of a possible shift in that direction in public opinion surveys since 2009, which have consistently found that, in the United States, between one-third and 45% of people under age 30 have a positive view of (an undefined) "socialism." The high level of popular support for Sen. Bernie Sanders (I-Vt.), a self-declared democratic socialist, in his campaign for the Democratic presidential nomination is also suggestive.

In Latin America, a number of countries, such as Venezuela, Bolivia, and Ecuador have elected leaders pledged to build some form of socialism. New leftist political movements in Europe, such as Syriza in Greece and Podemos in Spain, have been challenging the austerity policies that have generated mass unemployment (although the Syriza government elected in January 2015 has so far been unable to jettison the austerity program forced on Greece by the big powers in the European Union). Given the many negative features of twentieth-century Soviet-style socialism, advocates of a new socialism stress the need for democracy and widespread popular participation in both economic and political decision-making.

Change in this direction would be driven by the conviction that production for the profits of the minority can never adequately meet the needs of the majority, which instead requires an economy system that places the human needs of all at its center. Unlike capitalism of any variety, such a system in a highly developed country would not require a relentless increase in the production of goods, and therefore could build a sustainable relationship to nature. A socialism based on democracy, participation, cooperation, and sustainability could bring a promising future for all. Perhaps, in this period of pressure for institutional change, such an alternative path might emerge—but only if the 99% become active, organized, and determined to chart their own future. ❑

Article 1.2

IS RISING INCOME INEQUALITY INEVITABLE?

BY C.P. CHANDRASEKHAR AND JAYATI GHOSH

September 2014; Hindu Business Line

Rising inequality is now a concern on everyone's minds, even amongst the rich. Unequal societies are actually more unpleasant and dangerous for everyone, not just for those deprived by the system. High and rising inequality can be dysfunctional for the economy: for example, many now argue that growing inequality and the suppression of wage incomes combined with the effects of financial deregulation to generate the global financial crisis of 2008, and that the subsequent poor performance of most economies is related to the slow and limited recovery of labor incomes. Policy makers seem to recognize that addressing inequalities is important not only for justice and social cohesion, but also for continued material progress.

This may partly explain the recent proliferation of academic studies on global and national inequalities, as well as the numerous reports on the subject that have come from UN organizations and other multilateral organizations. The huge media attention devoted to one academic study—French economist Thomas Piketty's *Capital in the Twenty-First Century*—is a sign of the times. The spotlight that is shone on the rising share of incomes of the rich and the substantial empirical data that have been brought to bear on establishing this are indeed welcome. But that book, like many other recent analyses of inequality, tends to ascribe some sort of inevitability to the process, as the result of the working of some inexorable economic forces.

Piketty, for example, argues that there is a general tendency for wealth and income inequalities to increase because the rate of return on capital tends to exceed the rate of growth of the economy. There are various analytical concerns with this formulation, which relies on assumptions of full employment over the process of economic expansion and returns to factors like capital being determined by their marginal productivity (itself a problematic concept that is also impossible to measure).

The general increase in inequality in most countries over the past two decades—as indicated in Figure 1 that covers both developed and developing countries—can clearly be related to declining shares of wages in national income. (The data for the charts and table are taken from the United Nations Development Programme (UNDP) report *Humanity Divided: Confronting Inequality in Developing Countries* (2014).) Various analysts have attributed this trend of falling wage shares to the impact of labor-saving technological change, as well as the globalization of trade and production, both of which have dramatically reduced the bargaining power of labor relative to capital. Technological change has also increased wage dispersion in many instances, thereby generating more wage inequalities as well. Some observers have pointed to the effects of financialization in increasing the share of rentier incomes and enabling policies that serve financial interests rather than those of society at large.

FIGURE 1: GINI INDEX OF HOUSEHOLD INEQUALITY

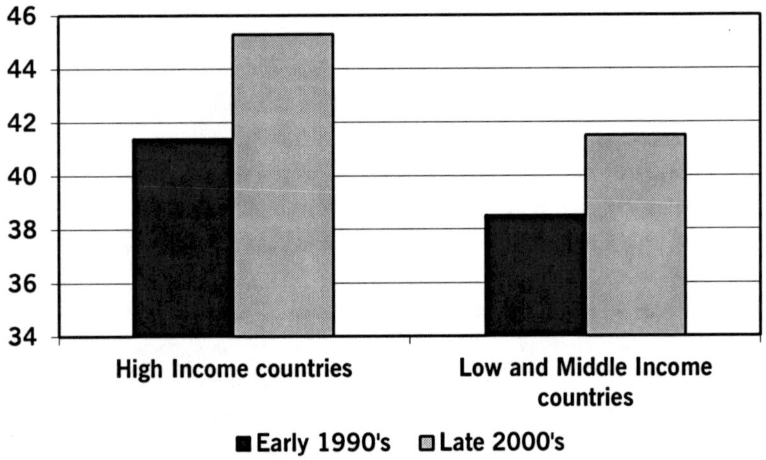

■ Early 1990's □ Late 2000's

However, these shifts cannot be ascribed purely to economic forces, since domestic social and political forces and policies also play important roles. Indeed, the last point highlights the important role of policy and the political economy that determines policies that affect income and asset distribution. In the developed countries, the declining emphasis on welfare states has been associated with the weakening of institutions and regulations that could protect workers and therefore the labor share of incomes. In developing countries, the perceived need to provide incentives to large private capital for generating investment and thereby growth, as well as drives for fiscal stabilization, have also operated in the same way.

But the important point is that not all countries show the same trends and not all governments have behaved the same way. Figure 2 shows that the aggregate measure of inequality the Gini index has moved in different ways in the various major regions of the developing world. In two major regions—Africa and Latin America and the Caribbean—the recent period has in fact witnessed a significant *decline* in inequality, though it is to be noted that these were the regions with higher inequality to start with. By contrast, there have been very significant increases in inequality in the transition economies of Europe as well as in Asia.

Even looking at regions is obviously too broad given the huge diversity within these large geographical spaces. Table 1 provides a further disaggregation, indicating the number of countries where inequality has increased or decreased and the

FIGURE 2: GINI INDEX BY REGION

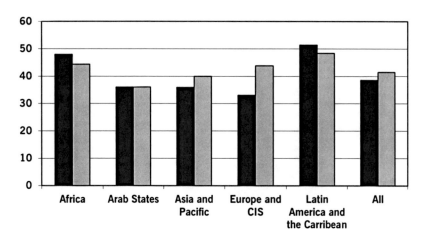

■ Early 1990's   ▣ Late 2000's

average rate of change across these. Latin America particularly stands out in terms of number of countries experiencing significant reduction of inequality. Some of the policies followed in countries of Latin America (and now some in Africa as well) are therefore worth noting. Fiscal policies operated to reduce inequality through progressive income taxation and highly redistributive social transfers targeting education and health spending as well as public child and old-age benefits. There were

TABLE 1: CHANGES IN INEQUALITY BY REGION

Region	Falling inequaliy		Inequality un-changed		Rising inequality		All countries	
	Number of coun-tries	%age point change in Gini	Number of coun-tries	%age point change in Gini	Number of coun-tries	%age point change in Gini	Number of coun-tries	%age point change in Gini
Africa	16	-15	3	-1	7	10	26	-7
Arab states	3	-5	1	1	2	12	6	0
Asia/ Pacific	5	-19	2	2	6	19	13	13
Europe and CIS	2	-11	1	11	16	43	19	35
Lat Am/ Carib	8	-10	5	-2	7	9	20	-5
All	34	-14	12	1	38	20	84	11

increases in formal employment, led by significant increases in public employment, through the expansion of and improvement of quality in public services in areas such as health and education, as well as through "in-sourcing" activities that were earlier outsourced to private companies by governments. Wage gaps between skilled and unskilled workers were reduced by increases in educational access and enrollment, and this contributed to the recent drop in income inequality. Legal minimum wages rose through most of the 2000s, and in some countries like Brazil they more than doubled in real terms. Incidentally this also reduced gender wage gaps, since women workers tend to be clustered in the lower end of the wage distribution, at and around the minimum wage. Reviving institutions and regulations such as labor unions, employment protection, minimum wages, unemployment benefits and regulation with respect to firing played an important role in moderating wage inequalities and improving wage shares of national income. So even in heavily "globalized" economies operating broadly within market capitalism, domestic policies can still be effective in shaping patterns of inequality and bringing about some decline. Rising inequality is therefore not inevitable—it is a political choice. ❏

Article 1.3

INEQUALITY IN THE WORLD

BY ARTHUR MacEWAN
November/December 2014

Dear Dr. Dollar:
I had thought that neoliberal globalization was making the world more unequal. But recently I have seen claims that the distribution of income in the world has become more equal. Is this true?
—*Evan Swinerton, Brookline, Mass.*

The answer to these questions depends on what you mean by "in the world." In many countries in the world—including most of the high-income countries and the most populous lower-income countries—the distribution of income has become more unequal. If we look at the income differences among countries, however, the situation has become more equal because per capita income has generally increased more rapidly in lower-income countries than in higher-income countries—though with important exceptions. And if we look at income distribution among all the people in the world—accounting for inequality both within and between countries—it seems that in recent decades the very high degree of inequality has remained about the same. (Before proceeding, please see the warning in the box below.)

Warning!

There are many problems in determining the extent of income inequality. The results can differ depending on which measure of inequality we use. Also, there are data difficulties. While some of these difficulties arise from poor reporting, plenty arise from the complexity of the issues. Also, different countries collect income data in different ways and do so in different years. With one exception (explained below), I will not detail the difficulties here, but readers should keep in mind that such difficulties exist.

How we compare incomes in different countries, where relative prices differ, currencies differ, and exchange rates (e.g., the number of Mexican pesos it takes to buy a dollar) often do not tell us accurately the buying power of income in different countries. The income data here are reported in terms of purchasing power parity (PPP) and reported in relation to the U.S. dollar. Comparing incomes in different countries using the PPP method gives us a comparison of the real buying power of income in the different countries. Calculating PPP data is complex and not precise, but the PPP figures are the best we have.

**FIGURE 1: INCOME RATIO, TOP 10% TO BOTTOM 10%,
SELECTED HIGH-INCOME COUNTRIES**

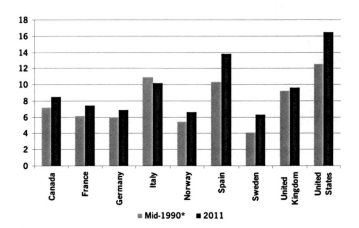

Source: OECD. *For the U.K. the figure is for 1999; for Spain the figure is for 2004; for France the figure is for 1996. For all others the earlier figures are for 1995. The later U.S. figure is for 2012.

Distribution *Within* Countries

Take a look at Figures 1 and 2, which show the changes in the distribution of income within selected countries, several high-income and several low- or middle-income, over roughly the last two decades. The measure of income distribution used in these graphs is the ratio of the total income of the highest-income tenth of the population to the total income of the lowest-income tenth of the population.

The first thing that stands out in Figure 1 is that the U.S. income distribution is substantially more unequal than those of any of the other countries. Also, the absolute increase by this measure of inequality is greatest in the United States. However, with the sole exception of Italy, all the countries in Figure 1 experienced *rising income inequality.*

Things are different in Figure 2, which includes the ten most populous lower-income countries (ten of the twelve most populous countries in the world, the United States and Japan being the other two). The degree of inequality is quite high in some of the countries in the graph. Brazil is the extreme case. However, Brazil and most of the other countries in Figure 2 experienced a *reduction of inequality* in this period—though several are still highly unequal. The most populous countries in Figure 2—China, India, and Indonesia—though, experienced rising inequality. These countries are the first, second, and fourth most populous countries in the world (with the United States third).

The data in Figures 1 and 2 illustrate the widespread rise of income inequality *within* countries, especially among high-income countries. Among lower-income countries, the picture is mixed. Although Brazil remains highly unequal, the reduction of inequality in Brazil is important because it has been achieved, at least in part, by policies directed at reducing poverty. Brazil's redistributive policies represent a trend in many Latin American countries—a backlash against the neoliberal policies of preceding decades.

FIGURE 2: INCOME RATIO, TOP 10% TO BOTTOM 10%, MOST POPULOUS LOW- AND MIDDLE-INCOME COUNTRIES

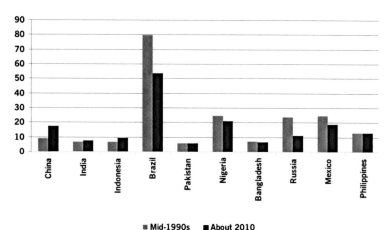

Source: World Bank. *Note:* These countries along with the United States and Japan are the twelve most populous countries in the world. The combined population of these ten accounts for 55% of the world's population in 2014.

FIGURE 3: PER CAPITA GDP, MOST POPULOUS LOW- AND MIDDLE-INCOME COUNTRIES, AS PERCENTAGE OF U.S. GDP (PPP)

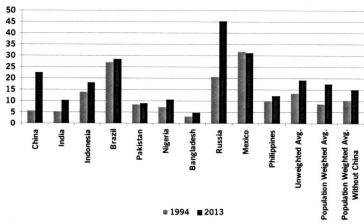

Source: World Bank.

Distribution *Among* Countries

Figure 3 illustrates what has been happening to income distribution *among* countries and indicates that the situation has become more equal because, in general, lower-income countries have grown more rapidly during the last two decades than have higher-income countries. For 1994 and 2013, the two columns in Figure 3 show Gross Domestic Product (GDP) per capita in the ten most populous low- and middle-income countries (listed by population) compared to GDP per capita in the United States. The comparison is in terms of purchasing power parity (PPP).

For nine of these ten countries—Mexico is the exception—GDP per capita rose more rapidly than in the United States. Taken as a group and using an average weighted by population, these ten countries in 1994 had an average GDP per capita 9% of that in the United States, but by 2013 this figure had risen to 17%. The basic result is not due simply to the remarkably rapid economic growth in China. When China is removed from the group, the weighted average still increases over this time period, from 10% to 15%. (This general phenomenon is certainly not a universal phenomenon; several very low-income countries have fallen further and further behind.)

So, if countries are our units of observation, Figure 3 illustrates how things have become more equal since the early 1990s. Going back further in time, comparing countries' incomes weighted by population shows inequality dropping pretty much continuously since 1960, and especially sharply since the early 1990s. But if the average is not weighted by population—thus removing the dominance of China, India, and some other very populous countries—the situation among countries only started to become more equal from 2000. Nonetheless, many low-income countries have been left behind in this period, most notably several countries of Africa. The dominant trend is not the exclusive trend.

Global Distribution Among People

To obtain a truly global estimate of the distribution of income, it is necessary to compare the incomes of people (or families or households) in the world. Availability of data (as well as other data problems) makes such an estimate rough, but useful nonetheless. Branko Milanovic, perhaps the leading expert on these issues, has shown that, from the mid-1980s to 2011, global inequality remained roughly constant, with a slight decline toward the end of this period—likely explained by the greater slowdown of high-income countries compared to low-income countries in the Great Recession. The relative stability of income distribution would seem to result from a rough balance between the reduction of inequality among countries (Figure 3) and the rise of inequality within countries (Figure 1 and the most populous countries of Figure 2).

Milanovic's estimate uses the Gini coefficient, a standard measure of income inequality. The Gini takes account of incomes of the whole population, unlike the measure used in Figures 1 and 2, which focuses on extremes. The Gini can vary from 0 (everyone has the same income) to 1 (all the income goes to one person). For income distribution in almost all countries, the Gini ranges from about 0.27 (Norway) to about 0.65 (South Africa).

For the global population, over the period of Milanovic's estimates, the Gini varies around 0.70—a higher figure, showing a more unequal distribution, than for any single country. However, if inequality were measured by a comparison of extremes, it is likely that inequality would be rising. There remains a large share of the world's population that continues to live in extreme poverty, while incomes at the very top have sky-rocketed in recent years. But whether the measure is the Gini or a comparison of extremes, the distribution among people in the world is very unequal.

What Matters?

Each of these measures of income inequality "in the world" matters in one way or another. For example, to understand political conflicts within countries, the changes in the distribution within countries is probably most important. To understand how the changing structures of the global economy have affected people's lives in various parts of the world, it is useful to consider all of these measures. And to understand the dynamics of international politics, the measures that focus on inequalities among countries are probably paramount.

The measurements show both some positive and negative changes in the world. On the one hand, the rapid growth of several low-income and middle-income countries has, in spite of the high (and sometimes rising) level of inequality in these countries, pulled many people out of abject poverty. On the other hand, we know that rising inequality within a country tends to undermine social cohesion and generate stress at virtually all levels of society—with damaging effects on health, education, the natural environment, and crime. Even in this era of increased globalization, it is in the national context that inequality has the primary impact on people's behavior and how they judge their well-being.

And no matter how we look at the situation, the world has long been and remains a very unequal place. ❑

Sources: Branko Milanovic, *Worlds Apart: Measuring International and Global Inequality*, Princeton University Press, 2005; Branko Milanovic, *Global Income Inequality by the Numbers: in History and Now—An Overview*, The World Bank, Development Research Group, Poverty and Inequality Team, November 2012; Christoph Lakner and Branko Milanovic, *Global Income Distribution: From the Fall of the Berlin Wall to the Great Recession*, The World Bank, Development Research Group, Poverty and Inequality Team, December 2013, WPS6719; Richard Wilkinson and Kate Pickett, *The Spirit Level: Why Greater Equality Makes Societies Stronger*, Bloomsbury Press, 2009.

Article 1.4

MAXIMUM "ECONOMIC FREEDOM": NO CURE-ALL FOR OUR ECONOMIC ILLS

BY JOHN MILLER
March/April 2005

> We are the party of maximum economic freedom and the prosperity freedom makes possible.
>
> Our vision of an opportunity society stands in stark contrast to the current Administration's policies that expand entitlements and guarantees, create new public programs, and provide expensive government bailouts. That road has created a culture of dependency, bloated government, and massive debt.
>
> —2012 Republican Platform, "We Believe in America"

> The decline in economic freedom in the United States has been more than three times greater than the average decline found in the OECD [Organisation for Economic Cooperation and Development]. … Unless policies undermining economic freedom are reversed, the future annual growth of the US economy will be only about half its historic average of 3%.
>
> —James Gwartney, Robert Lawson, and Joshua Hall, *Economic Freedom of the World: 2015 Annual Report*, The Fraser Institute

The Republican Party no doubt will once again in 2016 claim that it is the "party of maximum economic freedom" and that the presidential election will once again offer a choice between free enterprise, an opportunity society, and prosperity versus "a culture of dependency, bloated government, and massive debt."

Just in case the boilerplate of their platform is not enough to convince you that maximum "economic freedom" is the key to prosperity, two free-market think tanks, the Canada-based Fraser Institute and the Washington, D.C.-based Cato Institute, have the numbers to prove it—or so they say.

Their Economic Freedom Index of the World (EFW), its latest edition published just this fall, purports to show that economic freedom in the United States is on the decline, and as economic freedom has plummeted, economic growth has slowed, inequality has worsened, and political rights and civil liberties have been curtailed. The same, according to the EFW report, holds true for countries across the globe—those that are "more free" economically enjoy better economic outcomes and more civil liberties and political rights.

But even a quick glance at the EFW country rankings makes clear that there is something seriously amiss with its numbers.

That Can't Be Right—and It Isn't

The EFW provides an objective-looking list that ranks 157 countries and territories from the "most free" (Hong Kong and Singapore) to the "least free" (The Republic of the Congo and Venezuela). Their assessment of economic freedom uses 24 separate measures to score each country on five major areas: the size of government, the legal system and property rights, sound money, freedom to trade internationally, and regulation.

So what's wrong with the numbers? To begin with, the rankings seem to have little to do with political freedom. Consider the two city-states, Hong Kong and Singapore, which have repeatedly topped their list of free countries. Freedom House, which the *Wall Street Journal* has called "the Michelin Guide to democracy's development," classifies Hong Kong and Singapore as only "partially free." Freedom House, however, classifies some 89 other countries, almost half of the countries in its rankings, as "free." Hong Kong receives low marks from Freedom House for its restrictions on press freedom and freedom of assembly, especially limiting protests, and for the Chinese government's limits on the candidates who can be nominated for Hong Kong's executive elections. Likewise, the organization reports that Singapore's press is "not free," while the Internet is only "partially free" there. Also, in Singapore, rights to demonstrate are limited; films, TV, and the like are censored; and preventive detention is legal.

In addition to its rankings, the EFW report comes with accompanying charts. They purport to show that the "most free" quartile of the countries in their rankings average higher levels of per capita income, faster economic growth rates, less inequality, longer life expectancies, and more political rights and civil liberties than the other three "less free" quartiles of countries.

But these correlations are too facile to be credible. For instance, instead of arranging countries by their EFW ranking, let's group them by their score on just one of the five major areas of the index, the size of government. Because the EFW size-of-government index never recognizes that government programs such as Social Security have improved the life chances of citizens and enlarged the choices available to them, countries with the smallest government and lowest tax rates score the highest on "freedom." If the correlations between the EFW and prosperity, well-being, and political freedom have meaning, then the countries with the smallest governments should be associated with better outcomes than those being crushed by an outsized public sector.

But that's not case. The economies of the EFW's ten best-scoring countries on size of government (from first to tenth: Hong Kong, Bangladesh, Honduras, Madagascar, the Philippines, Nepal, Haiti, Guatemala, Nicaragua, and Pakistan), on average, did grow more quickly than those of the ten countries that did worst by that measure (from 148th to 157th: Finland, Algeria, Netherlands, Denmark, Belgium, France, Timor-Leste, the Republic of Congo, Burundi, and Finland). But the average income per capita for the EFW's worst ten countries was more than four times as great as for the EFW's best ten countries on the government-size measure. Also, the overall levels of income inequality (according to the standard measure, the Gini coefficient) were lower and the income share of the poorest 10% of the population was larger. In

SIZE OF GOVERNMENT AND ECONOMIC PERFORMANCE: THE ECONOMIC FREEDOM INDEX OF THE WORLD

Size of gov't (EFW rank)	Growth rate 1992-2014	GDP per capita	Gini coefficient	Income share, bottom 10%	Life expectancy at birth	Political rights, civil liberties
Top ten (smallest gov't)	3.14%	$8,633	43.4	2.36%	70.8	3.9
Bottom ten (largest gov't)	2.60%	$26,946	30.8	3.42%	73.8	2.6

Note: The conventional preferable score (higher growth, higher GDP, greater equality/lower inequality, higher life expectancy, greater political rights and civil liberties) is shaded in the table.

Definitions and Sources: Size of government: *Economic Freedom of the World: 2015 Annual Report*; Economic growth rates: Annual average 1992-2014, source: UNCTADstat; Gross Domestic Product per capita: Purchasing Power Parity, constant 2011 dollars, source: World Bank, 2014; Gini coefficient: lower number means greater equality, source: World Bank, latest year available 2009-2013; Income share of bottom or poorest 10% of the population: larger share means greater equality, source: World Bank, latest year available 2006-2013; Life expectancy: number of years a person can expect live at birth, source: World Bank, 2013; Political rights and civil liberties: average of Freedom House civil liberties and political rights scores, lower score indicates greater political rights and civil liberties, source: *Freedom of the World 2015*, Freedom House.

addition, the average lifespans in the countries the EFW ranked worst were three years longer than for those living in the countries the EFW ranked best. Finally, according to Freedom House, political rights and civil liberties are greater in the countries with the largest-size governments than in those with the smallest-size governments.

If the goal is a more prosperous nation with greater equality, longer lifespans, and more political rights and civil liberties, then a proper reading of EFW is that quite a large government is called for. That's hardly the message the EFW is intending to send, and one more likely to appear on the Bernie Sanders website than in the Republican Party platform.

U.S. Stagnation and "Unfreedom"

The EFW report also claims to show that that deteriorating economic freedom is at the heart of U.S. economic stagnation and worsening inequality. Since 2000, the United States has fallen in the EFW rankings from third to sixteenth. In addition, the drop in the U.S. economic freedom score was more than three times that of the OECD average score. (The Organisation for Economic Cooperation and Development (OECD) includes most high-income countries.) "Unless policies undermining economic freedom are reversed," warns the EFW report, "the future annual growth of the U.S. economy will be only about half its historic average of 3%."

But before you dust off your copy of Ayn Rand's *Atlas Shrugged* and join some "maximum economic freedom" movement, consider this: As the U.S. EFW score dropped three times faster than that of the average OECD country, the U.S. economy grew more quickly (1.6% a year) than the OECD average (1.4% a year) from

2000 to 2014. Last year, the U.S. economy grew at an annual rate of 2.4%—considerably above the OECD average of 1.8%, but still well below its 3.0% historical average. But the specific factors driving the decline of the U.S. EFW rating don't support the case that deteriorating economic freedom is what lies behind continued economic stagnation in the United States.

Since 2000, the U.S. ratings have fallen in all five areas of the EFW index. For instance, the U.S. size of government score got worse as government spending, consumption, and transfers increased, especially in the wake of the Great Recession. The U.S. score on "sound money" also slipped after the Great Recession, as the Federal Reserve (the "Fed") pushed interest rates to near zero by accelerating the growth of the money supply. But the additional government spending, though falling far short of what was needed, did more to revive economic growth than to inhibit it. Likewise, without the Fed's lax monetary policy, the less-than-robust economic growth since the Great Recession would have been yet more feeble.

But the largest declines in the U.S. EFW score came in three other areas: the legal system and the protection of property rights, freedom to trade internationally, and regulation. The EFW report allows that several factors could lie behind the drop in the U.S. scores in these areas, including some serious infringements on civil liberties.

But the EFW report goes on to ask if Sarbanes-Oxley (a 2002 law that seeks to improve corporate accounting practices and to make CEOs responsible for their corporations' profit reports), or the Affordable Care Act (which expands healthcare coverage), or Dodd-Frank (which attempts to curb some of the worst practices of a reckless financial industry), or the auto-industry bailout (that revived a failing industry and saved millions of jobs) "could be seen as a threat to property rights." The fact that the EFW report would single out those government interventions makes clear that what counts in their index is the economic freedom of only a tiny segment of the U.S. population, not that of workers, consumers, or even, in some cases, stockholders.

Despite its objective appearance, the EFW fails to make the case that a lack of economic freedom is the root cause of our economic ills, or that its brand of maximum "economic freedom" will cure them. Rather the EFW stands in the way of policies that might resolve our economic problems and improve the life chances of most people, as it protects the economic freedom and prerogatives of elites. ❏

Sources: "We Believe in America: 2012 Republican Platform"; James Gwartney, Robert Lawson, and Joshua Hall, *Economic Freedom of the World: 2015 Annual Report* (Fraser Institute, 2015); Freedom House, "Discarding Democracy: Return to the Iron Fist—Freedom in the World 2015" (freedomhouse.org); Robert Lawson, "Economic Freedom in the United States and Other Countries," in Donald Boudreaux, ed., *What America's Decline in Economic Freedom Means for Entrepreneurship and Prosperity* (Fraser Institute, 2015); James Gwartney, Randall Holcombe, and Robert Lawson, "Institutions and the Impact of Investment on Growth," *Kyklos*, 59(2), 2006; Greg Leichty, "'Economic Freedom?' Professor, Your Bias Is Showing," Progress Louisville, Oct. 15, 2015; Daniel Mitchell, "Economic Freedom in America is Declining Mostly Because of Creeping Protectionism and the Loss of Rule of Law and Property Rights," Aug. 25, 2015 (finance.townhall.com).

Article 1.5

TRUMP AND "NATIONAL NEOLIBERALISM"

BY SASHA BREGER BUSH
January/February 2017

Many writers and pundits are currently framing Trump's election in terms of a dispossessed and disenfranchised white, male working class, unsatisfied with neoliberal globalization and the insecurity and hardship it has unleashed—particularly across regions of the United States that were formerly manufacturing powerhouses (like the Rust Belt states of Pennsylvania, Michigan, Ohio and Wisconsin, four states believed to have cost Hillary Clinton the election). While there is much truth to this perspective and substantial empirical evidence to support it, it would be a mistake to see Trump's election wholly in these terms.

Trump's election is in some ways a neoliberal apex, an event that portends the completion of the U.S. government's capture by wealthy corporate interests. While in my opinion Trump's election does not signal the beginning of a rapid descent into European-style fascism, it appears to be a key stage in the ongoing process of American democratic disintegration. American democracy has been under attack from large and wealthy corporate interests for a long time, with this process accelerating and gaining strength over the period of neoliberal globalization (roughly the early 1970s to the present). This time period is associated with the rise of powerful multinational corporations with economic and political might that rivals that of many national governments.

In terms of the political consequences of these trends in the U.S., certain thinkers have argued that the U.S. political system is not democratic at all, but rather an "inverted totalitarian" system. Political commentator Chris Hedges notes: "Inverted totalitarianism is different from classical forms of totalitarianism. It does not find its expression in a demagogue or charismatic leader but in the faceless anonymity of the corporate state." Citing the American political theorist Sheldon Wolin, Hedges argues that our inverted totalitarian system is one that retains the trappings of a democratic system—e.g. it retains the appearance of loyalty to "the Constitution, civil liberties, freedom of the press, [and] the independence of the judiciary"—all the while undermining the capacity of citizens to substantively participate and exert power over the system.

In my view, what Trump's election has accomplished is an unmasking of the corporate state. Trump gives inverted totalitarianism a persona and a face, and perhaps marks the beginning of a transformation from inverted totalitarianism to totalitarianism proper. By this I mean that I think we are entering a period in which our political system will come to look more obviously totalitarian, with ever fewer efforts made to conceal its true nature and with the demagoguery that we typically associate with this form of politics. In spite of this, it makes no sense to me to call the system toward which we are heading (that is, if we do not stand up and resist with all our might right this second) "fascism" or to make too close comparisons to the Nazis. The European fascists put their faith in the power of the state to remake society. I do not see this on the horizon for the liberal-capitalist US, where feelings of hatred and distrust towards an oversized federal government helped to elect Trump. Whatever totalitarian nightmare is on our horizon, it will be uniquely American: a kind of "corporate" or "market-based" totalitarianism that is unique in world history. With its orientation towards the needs of the marketplace and big business, it will resemble in many ways the system that we've been living under for decades. If the pre-Trump system of inverted totalitarianism solidified in the context of global neoliberalism, the period of corporate totalitarianism that we are entering now seems likely to be one characterized by what I call "national neoliberalism."

Trump's Election Doesn't Mean the End of Neoliberalism

Trump's election represents a triumph of neoliberal thinking and values. Perhaps most importantly, we should all keep in mind the fact that Americans just elected a businessman to the presidency. In spite of his Wall Street background and billionaire status, Trump successfully cast himself as the "anti-establishment" candidate. This configuration—in which a top-one-percenter real estate tycoon is accepted as a political "outsider"—is a hallmark of neoliberal thinking. The fundamental opposition between market and government is a central dichotomy in the neoliberal narrative. In electing Trump, American voters are reproducing this narrative, creating an ideological cover for the closer connections between business and the state that are in store moving forward. (Indeed, Trump is already using the apparatus of the U.S. federal government to promote his own business interests). As states and markets further fuse in coming years, this representation of Trump and his administration—as being anti-government—will help immunize his administration from accusations of too-cozy relationships with big business. Trump's promises to "drain the swamp" by imposing Congressional term limits and constraints on lobbying activities by former political officials will also help to hide this relationship. (Has anyone else noticed that Trump only addresses half of the "revolving door," i.e., he plans to limit the lobbying of former politicians, but not the political roles of businessmen?)

Trump's Contract with the American Voter, his plan for the first 100 days in office, discusses policies and programs many of which are consistent with neoliberal thinking. (I interpret the term "neoliberalism" to emphasize at its core the importance of private property rights, market-based social organization, and the dangers of government intervention in the economy.) Trump's plan redirects the activities of the U.S. government along the lines touted by neoliberal "market fundamentalists" like Milton Friedman, who advocate limiting government's role to market-supportive functions like national defense (defense stocks are doing very well since the election) and domestic law and order (Trump's proposals have a lot to do with altering immigration policy to "restore security"). Trump also plans to use government monies to revitalize physical infrastructure and create jobs. Other government functions, for example, health care provision and education as well as protecting the environment and public lands, are open for privatization and defunding in Trump's agenda. Under Trump, the scope of federal government activities will narrow, likely to infrastructure, national defense, and domestic policing and surveillance, even if overall government spending increases (as bond markets are predicting).

Trump also seems content to take neoliberal advice in regard to business regulation (less is best) and the role of the private sector in regulating itself (industry insiders understand regulatory needs better than public officials). Trump's plan for the first 100 days specifies "a requirement that for every new federal regulation, two existing regulations must be eliminated." As of the time of this writing, his selection of cabinet appointees illustrate a broad willingness to appoint businesspeople to government posts. As of mid-December 2016, a Goldman Sachs veteran, Steven Mnuchin, has been appointed Secretary of the Treasury; billionaire investor Wilbur Ross, Secretary of Commerce; fossil-fuel-industry supporter and Oklahoma Attorney General Scott Pruitt, EPA administrator; fast-food mogul Andrew Puzder, Secretary of Labor; Exxon-Mobil CEO Rex Tillerson, Secretary of State. Trump's business council is staffed by the CEOs of major U.S. corporations including JP Morgan Chase, IBM, and General Motors. To be fair, the "revolving door" between government and industry has been perpetuated by many of Trump's predecessors, with Trump poised to continue the tradition. But this is not to say that neoliberalism will continue going in a "business as usual" fashion. The world is about to get much more dangerous, and this has serious implications for patterns of global trade and investment.

Trump's Election Does Mean the End of Globalism

The nationalism, xenophobia, isolationism, and paranoia of Donald Trump are about to replace the significantly more cosmopolitan outlook of his post-WWII predecessors. While Trump is decidedly pro-business and pro-market, he most certainly does not see himself as a global citizen. Nor does he intend to maintain the United States' extensive global footprint or its relatively open trading network. In other words, while neoliberalism is not dead, it is being transformed into a geographically more fragmented and localized system (this is not only about the U.S. election, but also about rising levels of global protectionism and Brexit, among other anti-globalization trends around the world). I expect that the geographic extent of the U.S. economy in the coming years will coincide with the new landscape of U.S. allies and enemies, as defined by Donald Trump and his administration.

Trump's Contract with the American Voter outlines several policies that will make it more expensive and riskier to do business abroad. All of these need not occur; I think that even one or two of these changes will be sufficient to alter expectations in business communities about the benefits of certain cross-border economic relationships. Pulling the United States out of the TPP, along with threats to pull out of the Paris Climate Agreement and attempts to renegotiate NAFTA, is already signaling to other countries that the new administration will not be interested in international cooperation. A crackdown on foreign trading abuses will prompt retaliation. Labelling

China a currency manipulator will sour relations between the two countries and prompt retaliation by China. As Trump goes forward with his anti-immigration and anti-Muslim rhetoric and policies, he will alienate the United States' traditional allies in Europe (at least until Europe elects its own nationalist and xenophobic leaders) and communities across the Global South. The U.S. election has already undermined performance in emerging markets, and bigoted rhetoric and policy will only increase anti-American sentiment in struggling economies populated largely by people of color. Add to this the risk of conflict posed by any number of the following: his antagonizing China, allying with Russia, deploying ground troops to stop ISIS, and pulling out of the Korean DMZ, among other initiatives that seem likely to contribute to a more confrontational and violent international arena. All of this is to say that Trump will not have to intervene directly in the affairs of business in order to make it less international and more national. The new global landscape of conflict and risk, combined with elevated domestic spending on infrastructure and security, will bring U.S. business and investment back home nonetheless.

National Neoliberalism and State-Market Relations

Fascist states are corporatist in nature, a state of affairs marked by a fusion of state and business functions and interests. In the fascist states on the European continent in the 1930s and 1940s—systems that fall under the umbrella of "national socialism"—the overwhelming power of the state characterized this relationship. Political theorist Sheldon Wolin writes in Democracy, Inc., in regard to Nazi Germany and Fascist Italy (as well as Stalinist Russia), "The state was conceived as the main center of power, providing the leverage necessary for the mobilization and reconstruction of society."

By contrast, in Trump's America—where an emergent "national neoliberalism" may be gradually guiding us to a more overt and obvious corporate totalitarian politics—we can expect a similar fusion of state and market interests, but one in which the marketplace and big business have almost total power and freedom of movement. State and market in the U.S. will fuse further together in the coming years, leading some to make close parallels with European fascism. But it will do so not because of heavy handed government dictates and interventions, but rather because domestic privatization initiatives, appointments of businessmen to government posts, fiscal stimulus, and the business community's need for protection abroad will bring them closer. Corporate interests will merge with state interests not because corporations are commanded to, but rather because the landscape of risk and reward will shift and redirect investment patterns to a similar effect. This may be where a budding U.S. totalitarianism differs most starkly from its European cousins.

Of course, it helps that much of the fusion of state and market in the United States is already complete, what with decades of revolving doors and privatization initiatives spanning the military, police, prison, healthcare and educational sectors, among others. It will not take much to further cement the relationship. ❏

Sources: Associated Press, "Trump's foreign policy plan includes boots on the ground against ISIS," PBS Newshour, Aug. 16, 2016 (pbs.org); Kristen Bellstrom, "Trump's Pick for Secretary of Labor: 'Ugly' Women Don't Sell Burgers," *Fortune*, Dec. 9, 2016 (fortune.com); Jackie Calmes, "What is Lost by Burying the Trans-Pacific Partnership?" *New York Times*, Nov. 11, 2016 (nytimes. com); Szu Ping Chan, "From Brexit to the rise of protectionism: is the world facing an era of permanent low-growth?" *The Telegraph*, Oct. 10, 2016 (telegraph.co.uk); Shawn Donnan, "WTO Warns on Rise of Protectionist Measures by G20 Economies," *Financial Times*, June 21, 2016 (ft. com); Ben Geier, "Even the IMF Now Admits Neoliberalism Has Failed," *Fortune*, June 3, 2016 (fortune.com); Chris Hedges, "Sheldon Wolin and Inverted Totalitarianism," Common Dreams, Nov. 2, 2015 (commondreams.org); Michael Hirsh, "Why Trump and Sanders Were Inevitable," Politico, Feb. 28, 2016 (politico.com); Ben Jacobs and Martin Pengelly, "Donald Trump on North Korea going to War: 'Good luck, enjoy yourself folks'," *The Guardian*, April 2, 2016 (theguardian. com); Jake Johnson, "Blame the Neoliberals," Nov. 10, 2016 (commondreams.org); Rich Lowry, "The Anti-Establishment Front-Runner," Politico, Oct. 21, 2015 (politico.com); Gene Marcial, "Trump Victory Boosts Demand for Trump Stocks," *Forbes*, Nov. 13, 2016 (forbes.com); Nolan D. McCaskill, "Trump transition website promotes his brand," Politico, Nov. 10, 2016 (politico.com); Chris Mooney, Brady Dennis, and Steven Muffson, "Trump names Scott Pruitt, Oklahoma attorney general suing EPA on climate change, to head EPA," *Washington Post*, Dec. 7, 2016 (washingtonpost. com); Steven Muffson and Brady Dennis, "Trump Victory Reverses US Energy and Environmental Priorities," *Washington Post*, Nov. 9, 2016 (washingtonpost.com); Damian Paletta; Carol E. Lee; and Jeremy Page, "Donald Trump's Message Sparks Anger in China," *The Wall Street Journal*, Dec. 5, 2016 (wsj.com); Sally Pipes, "Under Trump, Americans Can Finally Put Obamacare Behind Us," *Forbes*, Nov. 14, 2016 (forbes.com); Mercedes Schnelder, "Donald J. Trump's 'Vision' for Education," Nov. 13, 2016 (huffingtonpost.com); Michael Shear, et. al., "Trump Unveils High-Powered and Well-Heeled Business Council, and Invites Filipino Strongman to White House," *New York Times*, Dec. 2, 2016 (nytimes.com); Jeffery Smith, "This Is the Most Important Market Reaction to Donald Trump's Victory," *Fortune*, Nov. 9, 2016 (fortune.com); Karin Strohecker, "Emerging Markets-Strong dollar, higher US yields make stocks, currencies suffer," Reuters, Nov. 14, 2016 (reuters.com); Steven Swinford and Ben Riley-Smith, "Trump-Putin Alliance Sparks Diplomatic Crisis as British Ministers Demand Assurances from US over Russia," *The Telegraph*, Nov. 12, 2016 (telegraph.co.uk); Donald Trump, "Donald Trump's Contract with the American Voter: 100-day Action Plan to Make America Great Again," DonaldJTrump.com, 2016; Sheldon Wolin, *Democracy Inc: Managed Democracy and the Specter of Inverted Totalitarianism* (Princeton University Press, 2008); John Ydstie, "Trump Picks Steve Mnunchin to Lead Treasury Department," NPR, Nov. 30, 2016 (npr.org); Jim Zarroli. "Trump Taps Billionaire Investor Wilbur Ross for Commerce Secretary," NPR, Nov. 30, 2016 (npr.org).

Chapter 2

CORPORATE POWER AND THE GLOBAL ECONOMY

Article 2.1

MONOPOLY CAPITAL AND GLOBAL COMPETITION

BY ARTHUR MacEWAN
September/October 2011

Dear Dr. Dollar:
Is the concept of monopoly capital relevant today, considering such things as global competition?

—*Paul Tracy, Oceanside, Calif.*

In 1960, the largest 100 firms on *Fortune* magazine's "annual ranking of America's largest corporations" accounted for 15% of corporate profits and had revenues that were 24% as large as GDP. By the early 2000s, each of these figures had roughly doubled: the top 100 firms accounted for about 30% of corporate profits and their revenues were over 40% as large as GDP.*

The banking industry is a prime example of what has been going on: In 2007 the top ten banks were holding over 50% of industry assets, compared with about 25% in 1985.

If by "monopoly capital" we mean that a relatively small number of huge firms play a disproportionately large role in our economic lives, then monopoly capital is a relevant concept today, even more so than a few decades ago.

---

* The profits of the top 100 firms (ranked by revenue) were quite low in 2010, back near the same 15% of total profits as in 1960, because of huge losses connected to the financial crisis incurred by some of the largest firms. Fannie Mae, Freddie Mac, and AIG accounted for combined losses of over $100 billion. Also, the revenues of all firms are not the same as GDP; much of the former is sales of intermediate products, but only sales of final products are included in GDP. Thus, the largest firms' revenues, while 40% as large as GDP, do not constitute 40% of GDP.

Global competition has certainly played a role in reshaping aspects of the economy, but it has not altered the importance of very large firms. Even while, for example, Toyota and Honda have gained a substantial share of the U.S. and world auto markets, this does not change the fact that a small number of firms dominate the U.S. and world markets. Moreover, much of the rise in imports, which looks like competition, is not competition for the large U.S. firms themselves. General Motors, for example, has established parts suppliers in Mexico, allowing the company to pay lower wages and hire fewer workers in the states. And Walmart, Target, and other large retailers obtain low-cost goods from subcontractors in China and elsewhere.

Economics textbooks tell us that in markets dominated by a few large firms, prices will be higher than would otherwise be the case. This has generally been true of the auto industry. Also, this appears to be the case in pharmaceuticals, telecommunications, and several other industries.

Walmart and other "big box" stores, however, often do compete by offering very low prices. They are monopsonistic (few buyers) as well as monopolistic (few sellers). They use their power to force down both their payments to suppliers and the wages of their workers. In either case—high prices or low prices—large firms are exercising their market power to shift income to themselves from the rest of us.

Beyond their operation within markets, the very large firms shift income to themselves by shaping markets. Advertising is important in this regard, including, for example, the way pharmaceutical firms effectively create "needs" in pushing their products. Then there is the power of large firms in the political sphere. General Electric, for example, maintains huge legal and lobbying departments that are able to affect and use tax laws to reduce the firm's tax liability to virtually nothing. Or consider the success of the large banks in shaping (or eliminating) financial regulation, or the accomplishments of the huge oil companies and the military contractors that establish government policies, sometimes as direct subsidies, and thus raise their profits. And the list goes on.

None of this is to say that everything was fine in earlier decades when large firms were less dominant. Yet, as monopoly capital has become more entrenched, it has generated increasingly negative outcomes for the rest of us. Most obvious are the stagnant wages and rising income inequality of recent years. The power of the large firms (e.g., Walmart) to hold down wages is an important part of the story. Then there is the current crisis of the U.S. economy—directly a result of the way the very large financial firms were able to shape their industry (deregulation). Large firms in general have been prime movers over recent decades in generating deregulation and the free-market ideology that supports deregulation.

So, yes, monopoly capital is still quite relevant. Globalization does make differences in our lives, but globalization has in large part been constructed under the influence and in the interest of the very large firms. In many ways globalization makes the concept of monopoly capital even more relevant. ❏

Article 2.2

NO FRIENDSHIP IN TRADE
Farmers face modern-day robber barons.

BY SASHA BREGER BUSH
March/April 2015

Presiding over monopolies in shipping and railroads, U.S. robber baron Cornelius Vanderbilt once said that "there is no friendship in trade." During the 19th century, railroad magnates like Vanderbilt used their concentrated power to increase the price of freight, creating financial hardships for farmers who needed to ship their produce. Likewise, bankers like J.P. Morgan squeezed farmers, who were reliant on credit to get through the growing season, with high interest rates. By the latter part of the century, farmers "found the prices for their produce going down, and the prices of transportation and loans going up," wrote historian Howard Zinn, "because the individual farmer could not control the price of his grain, while the monopolist railroad and the monopolist banker could charge what they liked." The market dynamics set in motion by the robber barons ushered in decades of conflict between farmers and the railroad magnates, motivating populist movements and calls for government regulation of monopolies.

Biographer T.J. Stiles notes that a "blood-chilling ruthlessness infused all [of Vanderbilt's] actions." He continues, "Although Vanderbilt habitually dressed in the simple black-and-white outfit of a Protestant clergyman, his only religion was economic power." This religion of economic power is alive and well in today's global food system and farmers trade with the new robber barons of the global food system at their peril.

The small farmers and laborers who grow and process most of the world's food—who provide one of the few things we cannot live without—are themselves often hungry and poor. That is the simple, central paradox of the global food system.

Much of the explanation for this state of affairs focuses on processes of "unequal exchange." Unequal exchange results from trading relationships between parties with unequal levels of power, between powerful monopolies on the one hand and people who struggle in more competitive markets on the other. Unequal exchange is a mechanism for *exploitation* in the food system; that is, it siphons wealth away from farmers and workers and enriches multinational food and finance corporations.

Power, Inequality, and Unequal Exchange

Beginning in the 16th century, colonization, industrialization, and globalization have worked to undermine locally self-sufficient systems of food production, gradually replacing them with a system of global food interdependence. In this new system, food production, processing, distribution, and consumption are divided up among lots of different people and communities performing different food-related tasks, often in different parts of the world. In other words, there is now a "global division of labor" in food, and the people within this division of labor (who, these days, represent most of the global population) are dependent upon one another for the food they need to survive.

This new system is hierarchically ordered, with large multinational food and agriculture corporations controlling many aspects of production, processing, distribution, and consumption. Multi-national corporations' (MNCs) dominance over the global food system owes in large part to their *market power.* "Market power" refers to a firm's ability to influence the terms of trade—such as prices, but also quality and production standards—in a given market.

Today's food monopolies have consolidated their power thanks both to changes in national and international laws and regulations and to the policies of international institutions like the World Trade Organization (WTO), World Bank, and International Monetary Fund (IMF), among others. Of course, the capital- and technology-intensive nature of food processing, distribution, and retail these days—a key part of the process of food industrialization—also results in high barriers to entry in these markets. These barriers reduce competition for companies in the food industry.

The global food system is riddled with monopolistic markets, markets in which, on one side, stand only one or a few multinational corporate juggernauts, while on the other side there are many people jockeying for position. Inequalities in market power are magnified by geographical inequalities (e.g., between the global North and the global South), gender inequalities, racial inequalities, and inequalities in standards of living.

The U.S. Poultry Economy

The U.S. poultry chain is a good example. In the United States, three companies—Tyson, Perdue, and Pilgrim's Pride—control more than 50% of the market in broiler chickens. These large, industrial poultry companies are called "integrators," a reference to the "vertically integrated" poultry chain where big companies own and control almost every stage of the poultry production process. One recent commentator notes: "In fundamental ways, the meat business has returned to the state where it was 100 years ago, a time when just four companies controlled the market with a shared monopoly."

Poultry producers working in Arkansas, Mississippi, Georgia, or Kentucky compete with one another like dogs for scraps from the integrator's table, and thus end up with low incomes, low standards of living, and large debts. Poultry producers are largely "contract growers," meaning that they produce at the behest of the integrators and must accept whatever price the integrators offer for their chickens. In fact, the chickens themselves are actually owned by the integrator, with the "integrated out growers" (poultry producers) owning only the expensive chicken houses that chicks are raised in. The chicken houses are often purchased from the integrators on credit, burdening producers with large debts. Poultry producers also risk injury on the job, income losses associated with dead birds, antibiotic resistance and allergy (stemming

---

Monopolies, Monopsonies, Oligopolies, Oligopsonies: A Note on Terminology

In a **perfectly competitive** marketplace, no single participant can influence prices because there are so many buyers and sellers, each of which represents only a very small portion of the total marketplace.

By contrast, a **monopoly** is a type of uncompetitive market in which there is only one seller. The classic textbook example is the post-WWII diamond monopoly held by the DeBeers company.

A **monopsony** is a type of uncompetitive market in which there is only one buyer. The classic example is a labor market in a one-factory town; the relationship Walmart has with many of its suppliers is another good example.

An **oligopoly** is an uncompetitive market with only a few sellers (like the U.S. markets for airline tickets), while an **oligopsony** is an uncompetitive market with only a few buyers (like the U.S. market for published books which is dominated by Amazon and Barnes & Noble, or the global market for unroasted coffee beans).

As a shorthand, I refer to all of types of uncompetitive markets as "monopolies," and those companies that enjoy market power as "monopolists." Some economics textbooks technically define an "oligopoly" as a market in which the 50% of the market is controlled by four or fewer firms, while others employ the looser definition noted above.

---

from their regular contact with the antibiotics used to treat sick birds), among other serious risks. While the most risky and costly stage of the process—growing out the birds—is left to poultry producers, the integrators enjoy absolute control, massive profits and minimal competition in virtually every other stage of production. The integrators even operate under a "gentlemen's agreement" of sorts, with each integrator agreeing not to employ the growers contracted by the others, limiting competition among integrators and constraining poultry producers even further.

This trading relationship—between monopolistic integrators on the one hand and poultry producers facing high competition, serious risk, and large production costs on the other—is a stark example of unequal exchange and has concrete implications for the well-being of producers.

In an interview with the *American Prospect* magazine, Mike Weaver, who heads up a West Virginia poultry producer association, describes the tenuous financial position of producers in the United States. Weaver notes that "chicken farmers in his area are settling for almost an entire cent less per pound of meat *than they did in 1975*—when the median household income [in the United States] was around $11,800. ... The number of companies buying livestock from farmers has declined, and the surviving companies have grown bigger by acquiring the smaller firms. For growers, that often means doing business with only one firm."

The inequalities and injustices apparent in the poultry chain are replicated within the corporate hierarchy of integrators like Tyson: there is a dangerous division of labor between those who must compete to survive and those who do not need to do so. Highly paid executives, who are engaged in management work and are secure in their positions, lord over low-paid, interchangeable employees who work with their hands capturing chickens one-by-one at night in the chicken houses or performing dangerous work in slaughterhouses. Most of these managers are white men, while many of the workers that actually capture and slaughter the chickens are people of color, often with insecure immigration status. The Food Empowerment Project notes that workers in meat processing are mostly people of color from low-income communities. Historically populated by African Americans, this workforce has recently witnessed an influx of Latin American workers, with some 38% of workers in meat processing today hailing from outside of the United States.

The Global Coffee Economy

The power dynamics, inequalities and unequal exchanges apparent in the U.S. poultry chain are replicated in a variety of global food production systems. Take, for example, the global coffee economy, a chain connecting different parts of the global division of coffee labor to one another, taking us downstream from the green coffees harvested in the field by farmers, through various traders and processors, to the cups of roasted coffee consumed by final consumers.

International traders and roasters operate in a very uncompetitive market setting—they are monopolists. The six largest coffee trading companies control over 50% of the marketplace at the trading step along the coffee chain (Neumann Kaffee Gruppe from Germany and ED&F Man based in London are the largest international traders). The roasting stage of coffee production is even more concentrated, with only two companies (Nestle and Phillip Morris) controlling almost 50% of the market. Market power gives these modern-day robber barons influence over prices and other terms of trade, allowing them to place downward pressure on prices they pay to farmers, and upward pressure on the prices they charge to consumers.

This inequality in market power introduces inequalities in incomes and standards of living between different actors in the coffee economy. Unsurprisingly, farmers operating in the shadow of the big traders and roasters have relatively low incomes and standards of living. By contrast, owners, managers, and some workers

---

Coffee: A Story of Market Power

The global coffee economy is marked by severe inequalities in wealth and power.

Coffee farmers along with small-scale traders and processors, operate in a competitive market environment. Located primarily in the global South, they sell their coffees onward, down the supply chain, to international traders and roasters. The traders and roasters operate in a relatively uncompetitive market environment and are located primarily in the global North. These inequalities in market power result in lower standards of living for coffee farmers and other marginalized actors in producing countries.

Consumers (most of whom are from the global North) also have little negotiating power, when it comes to purchasing coffee from big retailers (supermarkets and corporate café chains like Starbucks). By contrast, the northern monopolies in trading, roasting, and retail earn high profits associated with their disproportionate market power.

Monopolists thus push prices for growers down and prices for consumers up, capturing the super-profits generated in between.

at the big coffee monopolies enjoy relatively high incomes and standards of living. There are also race and gender dimensions to consider: coffee farmers are disproportionately women of color, while owners and managers in the big coffee monopolies are generally white men. There is also a strong North-South dimension to this power inequality—coffee farmers from Latin America, Africa, and Asia compete fiercely with one another, their incomes undermined by the pricing power of monopolies headquartered in Europe and the United States.

Twenty-five million coffee farming families from Latin America, sub-Saharan Africa, South Asia, and Southeast Asia compete globally with one another to sell coffee to a handful of international coffee trading companies. Similar to the situation of poultry producers, there are in practice usually only one or two potential buyers for a farmer's coffee crop. Lacking the transport and information resources to effectively market their crops, many coffee farmers sell to whomever comes to the farm gate. Unsurprisingly, things do not usually go well for our coffee farmers.

The graph below illustrates the distribution of income in the global coffee economy. Only a small percentage of total income is retained by those—growers, small-scale traders who transport coffee from the farm gate, and petty processors who transform dried coffee cherries into green beans in producing countries—who operate in competitive markets. Most of the income is appropriated in consuming countries, mainly by the coffee monopolists in trading and roasting, but also

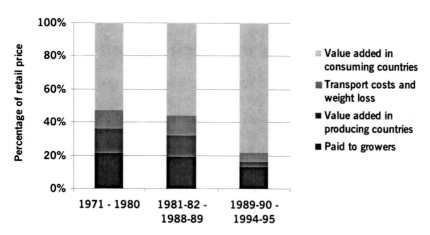

DISTRIBUTION OF INCOME IN THE GLOBAL COFFEE ECONOMY (% OF INCOME)

Source: John M. Talbot, "Where Does Your Coffee Dollar Go? The Division of Income and Surplus along the Coffee Commodity Chain," *Studies in Comparative International Development*, Vol. 32, No. 1 (1997), Tables 1 and 2.

Note: Data for 1971–1980 are for calendar years. Data for 1981–82 to 1988–89 and for 1989–90 to 1994–95 are for "coffee years" (Oct. 1–Sept. 30). Percentages of total retail price (reported by Talbot (1997)) for calendar years (1971–1980) or coffee years (1981–82 to 1988–89 and 1989–90 to 1994–95) were used to calculate means for intervals shown. Figures calculated did not add exactly to 100.0% due to rounding (in all cases between 99.9% and 100%). Bar graphs show each income category as percentage of sum of four income categories.

The Farmer and the Supplier

Unequal exchange is also common for farmers looking to purchase supplies for their businesses. In conventional farming systems, farmers and livestock growers regularly purchase seeds, young animals, feed, pesticides, or fertilizers from large multinational corporations like Tyson, Monsanto, and Cargill. In this unequal exchange, multinational giants charge farmers small fortunes for the supplies they need.

The farmers receive overpriced goods that often fail to work as advertised. In the case of expensive genetically modified seeds, farmers often end up with lower-than-promised yields and rising costs for fertilizers, pesticides, and water. Fertilizers and pesticides, for their part, erode the long-term health of the soil and increase irrigation requirements. Worse still, as farmers rack up these huge input costs, the prices that international traders offer them for their crop often fails to cover the rising costs of production. Farmers are thus "squeezed" between two monopolies, with unequal exchange ensuring that farmers pay too much for their inputs and receive too little for their crop. This trading mechanism thus works to rob especially small and peasant farmers of wealth and redistributes it to the monopolies.

The outcome for farmers is bleak and frequently results in rising debt. In India, the debts that result from this financial squeeze have led more than 200,000 peasant farmers to commit suicide, according to author Vandana Shiva. Agricultural laborers in rural areas also often suffer in this context, as temporary workers are laid off by small farmers experiencing hardship.

---

by large retailers (e.g., supermarkets and corporate café chains like Starbucks). The position of coffee growers deteriorated between the 1970s and 1990s. Expanded global trade in coffee since the late 1980s, with "free trade" increasing the market leverage of multinational traders and roasters over coffee farmers and final consumers, has led to decreasing relative income of growers.

Promoting Justice and Equity in the Global Food System

As the coffee and chicken examples suggest, unequal exchange is commonplace between farmers and producers on the one hand, and multinational, monopolistic middlemen (food traders, processors, and supermarkets) on the other. While larger corporate coffee farms may have some leverage in negotiating prices with these big middlemen, smaller and peasant farms have virtually no negotiating power. If a coffee farmer does not want to sell to the Neumann Kaffee Gruppe (NKG) at the price NKG offers, then NKG will simply move on until it finds a farmer who will. Similarly, if a poultry producer does not want to sell to Tyson at the company's offered price, the producer risks being cut out of the chain all together. Tyson will just move on to the next farm. In both cases, the market power of the monopolists also allows them to set conditions such as product quality and the specific technologies used in the production process. The same basic relationship holds for cattle ranchers and cocoa farmers selling to Cargill, pork producers selling to Smithfield (now owned by the China-headquartered WH Group), soy farmers selling to Archer Daniels Midland, vegetable producers selling to Walmart and Tesco, and orange producers selling to Coca-Cola Co. (to make Fanta Orange and Minute Maid juices), among many other global examples.

Unequal exchange helps to explain inequalities in wealth and power in the global food system, and how trade relationships work to facilitate exploitation—the unjust redistribution of wealth from people with less to people with more market power, from poor to rich, from black and brown to white, from women to men, from the global South to the global North. In answer to the question posed at the outset—how is it that the people who produce our food are themselves so often poor and hungry?—I answer simply: Because they engage in unequal exchange with powerful food monopolies, and there is no friendship in this trade.

A variety of policies, programs, and alternatives could help to make the global food system more equitable and fair. These include, but are certainly not limited to, anti-trust enforcement, public commodity price management, and producer unionization. In 1890, the U.S. Congress passed the Sherman Anti-Trust Act, a piece of legislation aimed at breaking up some of the large monopolies that dominated the U.S. economy at the time. Among the targets of the new anti-trust enforcers were the big meatpackers. The Supreme Court's 1905 decision in *Swift & Co. v. United States* found the Chicago "meat trust" to be engaging in price-fixing for meat and shipping rates. The case set the stage for more stringent government regulation of monopolies. Since the early 1980s, starting with the Reagan administration, anti-trust enforcement in the U.S. has waned. According to Barry Lynn, the author of *Cornered: The New Monopoly Capitalism and the Economics of Destruction*, this is partly due to increasingly pro-big business ideologies and political interests of public officials, like Reagan. Yet, the Sherman Act remains on the books and could be revived as a tool to break up the new meat trusts in the U.S. food system.

Historically, governments have also intervened in food markets to set and stabilize prices. While the system was not perfect, the International Coffee Agreement that regulated global coffee trading from 1962 to 1989 did indeed help many coffee farmers obtain better prices for their crops. A system of import and export quotas at the international level was complemented by public institutions at the national level that were responsible for purchasing coffee from producers at fixed prices and then exporting the coffee into the global market according to the quota arrangement. While the system was a mechanism for exploiting farmers in some cases (as in Uganda in the 1970s), in other cases (like in Mexico) public commodity price management helped farmers earn more money and stabilize their incomes. With the eruption of the global food crisis in 2006–7, global interest in such institutions has been revived, perhaps creating a political opening for new public price management programs.

As with most economic cases in which individuals are overpowered by large companies—be they integrators, coffee roasters, or employers—organization and unionization can help them increase their market leverage and bargaining power. In Colombia, some three quarters of the country's coffee farmers are organized under the umbrella of a single union. The union advocates for farmers in various

political forums, and negotiates coffee prices with exporters and traders, often securing higher prices for farmers than they could obtain on their own. Support for
such organizations, as well as related farmer cooperatives and producer associations,
could help to empower and organize producers.

Such policies and programs are not mutually exclusive. Further, anti-trust
enforcement, public price management, and producer unionization could be complemented by a wide variety of other mechanisms for promoting justice and equity
in the global food system. For example, programs that support national and local
food self-sufficiency, crop and income diversification, and organic farming techniques can potentially reduce producer reliance on global monopolists for income,
financing and production inputs, among many other benefits. ❏

Sources: Oscar Farfan, "Understanding and Escaping Commodity Dependency: A Global Value
Chain Perspective," World Bank, 2005; Food Empowerment Project, "Slaughterhouse Workers,"
Food Empowerment Project, 2015 (foodispower.org); Michael Kazin, "Ruthless in Manhattan,"
New York Times, May 7, 2009; Christopher Leonard, "How the Meat Industry Keeps Chicken
Prices High," March 3, 2014 (slate.com); Barry Lynn, "Killing the Competition: How the New
Monopolies are Destroying Open Markets," *Harper's Magazine*, February 2012; National Chicken
Council, "Vertical Integration," 2015 (nationalchickencouncil.org); Stefano Ponte, "The Latte
Revolution," *World Development*, 2002; Monica Potts, "The Serfs of Arkansas," *The American
Prospect*, March 5, 2011; Vandana Shiva, "From Seeds of Suicide to Seeds of Hope," Huffington
Post, May 29, 2009; Howard Zinn, *A People's History of the United States* (Harper, 2005).

Article 2.3

CRONY CAPITALISM, OR PLAIN OLD CAPITALISM?

BY ARTHUR MacEWAN
September/October 2014

> Dear Dr. Dollar:
>
> Congressional Republicans and the Heritage Foundation are making a big deal about the Export-Import Bank, calling it "crony capitalism." Are they right? Does the ExIm Bank serve a useful purpose, or is it just propping up the profits of trans-national corporations? —*Arnie Alpert, Canterbury, N.H.*

The Export-Import Bank, created in 1934, is a federal government agency that supplies loans or guarantees loans to foreign firms to finance their purchases of U.S. exports. Its supporters argue that it strengthens the U.S. economy and creates jobs in the United States by bolstering demand abroad for goods produced here.

For the Export-Import Bank to stay in existence, Congress must reauthorize it by the end of September. Its existence, however, has come under attack by the anti-big-government forces of the right. They claim that there is no justification for the government to provide this support for U.S. firms. If the buyers abroad of U.S. goods cannot get financing for the purchases from regular banks—i.e., in the "free market"— the U.S. exporters must be charging prices that are too high. That is, the U.S. firms are not effectively competing in the "free market," and it is not the job of government to subsidize their inefficient operations.

These critics of the Export-Import Bank claim it is simply "crony capitalism," where well-connected firms are able to get handouts from the government. This, they argue, is not the way "real capitalism" should and can function. For example, in a June 25 editorial titled "The Ex-Im Bank: Crony Capitalism in Action" at the National Review Online, the editors wrote that the Bank "hands out generous loans and credit guarantees to a select number of corporations [and] is corrupt and poorly managed. …The bank has a long history of dealing with dodgy firms and doling out suspiciously large amounts of loans to certain companies."

The Export-Import Bank has long been supported by the establishment of both the Republican and Democratic parties. Helping business sell goods abroad, they have argued, is a good way to create jobs in the country. The Bank's supporters argue that foreign governments provide similar subsidies to their firms, and thus we must provide subsidies to our firms so they can effectively compete. They frequently cite the support that European governments provide to Air Bus, the primary competitor of the U.S. firm Boeing. (Back to Boeing in a moment.)

The Export-Import Bank also touts itself as a supporter of small business. Yet its support in fact goes mostly to a few large firms. In 2013, the Bank made loan guarantees totaling $12.2 billion, of which $8 billion, 65%, were for purchases of goods from a single company, Boeing; another 8.2% of the guarantees went to finance the exports of the giant engineering firm Fluor.

Of the $6.9 billion in direct loans that the Bank provided in 2013, 81% went for purchases from just five firms—Bechtel, General Electric, Applied Materials, Fluor, and Komatsu America. The total direct loans and guarantees of about $19 billion is tiny (less than 1%) compared to the United States' total 2013 exports of about $2.3 trillion. Still, they are important for Boeing and these other firms.

But the Export-Import Bank's support for these large firms is not "crony capitalism." The firms are not getting support because their CEO's relatives or friends sit in Congress. They are getting support in the same way very large firms always get support: by spending money to influence elections and gain access to government officials and by using their power to create the belief that what's good for their profits is good for the economy. Whether it is via this Bank or through U.S. ambassadors around the world and various government-led "trade missions," the U.S. government has long promoted sales by U.S. firms abroad.

Rather than "crony capitalism," this is "real capitalism," the way the system regularly works. Consider, for example, lax regulation of financial firms, subsidies to fossil-fuel firms, or patent rules that treat pharmaceuticals so favorably. The right-wing arguments against the Export-Import Bank could just as well be applied in these and many other cases. The so-called "crony capitalism" of the Bank cannot be so easily carved out from the operation of real capitalism.

The right-wing attack on the Export-Import Bank focuses attention on the way real capitalism works. It also reveals the division among conservatives. The Republican establishment has long ballyhooed the "free market," while making sure the government has provided plenty of support for big business. There are, however, many conservatives who seem to be true believers in the "free market." These two groups have long managed to stay together, promoting a common rhetoric. For better or for worse, the crack in the conservative political bloc represented by the Export-Import Bank dispute may portend some major political changes. ❑

Article 2.4

INVERSION ACCELERATION

More and more U.S. corporations are sending their headquarters offshore to reap immense tax savings.

BY ROGER BYBEE
May/June 2016

Corporate "inversions"—the fast-accelerating phenomenon of major U.S. firms moving their official headquarters to low-tax nations through complex legal maneuvers—are causing an annual loss of about $100 billion in federal tax revenues.

But new rules imposed in early April by the U.S. Treasury Department scuttled the mammoth $162 billion deal between pharmaceutical giant Pfizer and Allergan, based on relocating the official headquarters to low-tax Ireland. The Treasury rules are designed to inhibit "serial inverters"—corporations that repeatedly shift their official headquarters to cut U.S. taxes—and to discourage "earnings stripping," where firms use loans between their American units and foreign partners to reduce U.S. profits subject to federal taxation. The collapse of the Pfizer-Allergan inversion suggests that the Treasury regulations may constitute a major barrier to some future inversions. However, with firms like Johnson Controls and Tyco moving ahead with their inversion plans, stronger measures will clearly be needed to halt the tide.

U.S. corporations have pulled off about 60 inversions over the last two decades, according to *Fortune*. In the last five years alone, corporations have executed 40 inversions, the *New York Times* stated.

This fast-rising dimension of corporate globalization has immense implications for Americans. The industrial powerhouse Eaton Corp. (#163 on the Fortune 500), Medtronic, Accenture (formerly the consulting wing of Arthur Andersen), Burger King, and AbbVie (the world's 11th-largest drug maker) are among the firms that have repudiated their U.S. nationality and shifted their official headquarters to low-tax nations. The annual toll to the U.S. Treasury from corporate inversions is about $100 billion, based on the studies of Reed College economist Kimberly Clausing. This impact is likely to worsen significantly in the near future. Another dozen or more inversions are currently under consideration, according to conservative *New York Times* business columnist Andrew Ross Sorkin.

Fortune senior writer Allan Sloan, who has been outraged by inversions despite his overall pro-corporate stance, points to powerful vested interests who stand to gain: "There's a critical mass of hedge funds, corporate raiders, consultants, investment bankers, and others who benefit from inversions." (The collapse of the Pfizer-Allergan deal could cost just the major banks as much as $200 million, the *New York Times* reported.) These interests and their political allies have incessantly claimed that American-based multinational corporations are driven to repudiate their U.S. nationality in order to escape "burdensome" U.S. corporate tax rates that they call "the world's highest."

In reality, actual federal corporate taxes on 288 profitable corporations —as distinguished from the official 35% rate almost all firms easily avoid—were actually only 19.4% in the 2008-2012 period, a 2014 Citizens for Tax Justice (CTJ) report revealed. This placed the United States 8th lowest among the advanced nations in the Organization for Economic Cooperation and Development (OECD), the CTJ found (see sidebar).

A just-released CTJ study went further in its scope and included state and local taxes as well as federal levies in comparing the United States with other OECD countries. It found combined U.S. corporate taxes at 25.7%, ranking 4th lowest in the OECD, based on U.S. Treasury figures. The OECD average is 34.1%. Only Chile, Mexico, and South Korea had a lower total burden as a share of GDP.

Incessant Talk of 35% Tax "Burden" Diverts Focus from Minimal Taxes

Elite debate about corporate taxes is dominated by the notion that U.S. corporations are afflicted by the highest official corporate tax rate in the world. In fact, the 35% official rate is easily avoided by almost all corporations. *Effective* U.S. corporate taxes—what corporations actually end up paying—are among the lowest in the advanced world. This represents a huge drain on the U.S. Treasury's revenues needed for public services.

- A 2014 study by Citizens for Tax Justice found an *effective* average tax rate of only 19.4% for major, consistently profitable corporations. This places the United States at 8th-lowest among the 34 OECD nations in terms of the effective federal tax rate.

- The most recent study on corporate taxes by the CTJ, released in April 2016, went further in its scope and included state and local taxes as well as federal levies. It found combined U.S. corporate taxes at 25.7%, ranking 4th-lowest in the OECD (above only Chile, Mexico, and South Korea). The OECD average is 34.1%.

- Strategies for tax avoidance have been particularly effective for the very largest members of the Fortune 500. Corporations studied by CTJ included 26—such as Boeing, General Electric, Priceline.com, and Verizon—that paid no federal income tax whatsoever over the five-year period.

- Boeing, which depends heavily on federal contracts, had an effective federal tax rate of negative 2%, despite earning $26.4 billion in profits 2008-2013. It also collected a record $13.2 billion in state-level tax breaks and subsidies in 2013. About one-third of the corporations—93 of the 288 studied by CTJ—paid an effective tax rate of less than 10% between 2008 and 2013. And contrary to claims that U.S. corporate taxes are far higher than those facing their foreign competitors, two-thirds of those corporations with significant offshore profits paid higher corporate tax rates to foreign governments for their overseas operations than they paid in the United States on their U.S. profits.

Source: Citizens for Tax Justice, "The Sorry State of Corporate Taxes," 2014 (ctj.org).

Despite this reality of low corporate taxes, a growing number of large multinational firms have concluded that repudiating their U.S. "citizenship" and inverting is the most effective means of cutting their tax burdens, avoiding possible reforms that could potentially hike their tax bills, and most importantly, gaining direct and unregulated access to untaxed "offshore" funds.

The 35% Myth

The fundamental realities of U.S. taxes on multinational corporations are obscured by an elite debate fixated on the official statutory rate of 35%, which is relentlessly cited as a barrier to U.S. competitiveness.

House Republican James Sensenbrenner (R-Wisc.), for example, wrote in a recent *Milwaukee Journal Sentinel* opinion piece, "The current rate paid by American companies is 35 percent—the highest corporate tax rate among developed countries."

This narrative—endlessly recited by leading corporate and media elites, along with virtually all Republicans and a number of Democrats, has come to dominate much of the national dialogue. Robert Pozen, a senior fellow at the liberal Brookings Foundation, urgently called for a sharp cut in the 35% statutory rate, claiming broad bi-partisan support in Congress. "If there's one policy agreement between Republicans and Democrats, it's that the 35% corporate tax rate in the United States should be reduced to 28% or 25%," he asserted. "The current rate, highest in the advanced industrial world, disincentivizes investment and encourages corporations to relocate overseas."

Even President Barack Obama, while an outspoken foe of inversions, perversely weakened his own case against them by speaking of "companies that are doing the right thing and choosing to stay here, [and] they get hit with one of the highest tax rates in the world. That doesn't make sense," as he told a Milwaukee audience in a typical comment.

Obama has thus inadvertently reinforced the conventional wisdom among U.S. elites that is used to justify inversions, as outlined by John Samuels of the International Tax Foundation. "Today, with most of their income and almost all of their growth outside the United States, U.S. companies have a lot more to gain by relocating their headquarters to a foreign country with a more hospitable tax regime," declares Samuels. "And conversely they have a lot more to lose by remaining in the United States and having their growing global income swept into the worldwide U.S. tax net and taxed at a 35% rate."

Why Inversions?

The crucial motive in transferring corporations' "nationality" and official headquarters to low-tax nations is that inversions shield the "foreign" profits of U.S. corporations from federal taxation and ease access to these assets. This protects total U.S. corporate profits held outside the United States—a stunning $2.1 trillion—from any U.S. corporate taxes until they are "repatriated" back to the United States.

Major corporations benefit hugely from the infinite deferral of taxes purportedly generated by their foreign subsidiaries. "If you are a multinational corporation, the federal government turns your tax bill into an interest-free loan," wrote David Cay Johnston, Pulitzer-Prize winning writer and author of two books on corporate tax avoidance. Thanks to this deferral, he explained, "Apple and General Electric owe at least $36 billion in taxes on profits being held tax-free offshore, Microsoft nearly $27 billion, and Pfizer $24 billion."

Nonetheless, top CEOs and their political allies constantly reiterate the claim that the U.S. tax system "traps" U.S. corporate profits overseas and thereby block domestic investment of these funds. But these "offshore" corporate funds are anything but trapped outside the United States. "The [typical multinational] firm ... chooses to keep the earnings offshore simply *because it does not want to pay the U.S. income taxes it owes*," explains Thomas Hungerford of the Economic Policy Institute. "This is a very strange definition of 'trapped'."

In fact, these offshore profits can be, and are, routed back into the United States through the use of tax havens. (Tax havens, where corporations and super-rich individuals place an estimated $7.6 trillion, were thrust into the international spotlight with the recent release of the Panama Papers. See William K. Black, "Business Press Spins Elite Tax Fraud as 'Good News'," p. 5.) "'Overseas' profits are neither overseas nor trapped," explained Kitty Rogers and John Craig. "It is true that for accounting purposes, multinational corporations keep these dollars off of their U.S. books. But in the real world, the money is often deposited in U.S. banks, circulating in the U.S."

However, the "overseas" profits come with some significant constraints on their use, pointed out David Cay Johnston. "The funds can only be accessed for short-term loans back to the U.S., and are not useful for major investments like new factories or long term R&D, or for investment outside the U.S.," said Johnston. But inversions eliminate these restrictions on how SUCH funds can be used. "By inverting and then using a variety of tax avoidance schemes, the firms can have access to these earnings virtually free of U.S. taxes," notes Hungerford. "This is undoubtedly the primary motivation to invert."

The inversion route is not the only means for U.S. corporations to radically slash their U.S. taxes and gain access to offshore earnings. Any particular company's tax-avoidance strategy is dependent on the specific conditions it faces. As tax expert Johnston notes, "Every company has its own unique issues so it will decide what works for it."

Some giant multinational corporations, like Apple, Microsoft, and Google, have chosen to bypass inverting. Instead, they utilize immensely complex shifts of their revenue to minimize their taxes and maintain access to their offshore earnings. These maneuvers have gained exotic names like "Double Dutch Irish Sandwich," reflecting the multiple transfers of capital that they employ. The corporations involved are able to avoid the public backlash brought on by jettisoning their U.S. nationality. On the other hand, such ploys require careful planning and execution, compared to the simple, direct step of inverting.

Corporate inversions also head off the possibility of higher rates being imposed in the United States, an idea with very broad public support as shown by polling. But in addition to the vast political resources that corporations bring to any fight in Congress on corporate taxes, inversions remind U.S. public officials that their policies can be undermined by CEOs' unilateral decisions to relocate anywhere on the globe. Companies use this trump card to weaken the push for increases in corporate taxes and instead build momentum for further federal concessions.

Johnson Controls: The Ugly Truth

The most recent inversion deal, orchestrated by Johnson Controls—called the "latest and quite possibly the most brazen tax-dodger" in a *New York Times* editorial—explodes the myths underlying the standard rationale for inversions. Johnson Controls, which has been based in the Milwaukee area for 131 years, is the 66th largest firm in the United States.

Much media coverage has focused on the $149 million in annual tax savings that Johnson Controls will purportedly reap by jettisoning its U.S. identity and moving its official "domicile" to Ireland, where the tax rate is 12.5%. This is a tidy sum, but not because Johnson Controls was victimized by paying the statutory rate of 35%.

On the contrary, Johnson Controls has already been benefitting handsomely from a U.S. tax system that is remarkably generous to major corporations. As Matthew Gardner of the Institute on Tax and Economic Policy pointed out, "Between 2010 and 2014, Johnson Controls reported just over $6 billion in U.S. pretax income, and it paid a federal income tax rate averaging just 12.2 percent over this period." Significantly, "This is actually *lower* than the 12.5 percent tax rate Ireland applies to most corporate profits."

Far more central to Johnson Controls' inversion is the virtually tax-free status that it will gain over its vast pile of profits accumulated offshore, Gardner argues. Digging beneath the surface, Gardner found, "At the end of 2014, Johnson Controls disclosed holding $8.1 billion of its profits as permanently reinvested foreign income, profits it has declared it intends to keep offshore indefinitely."

The tax stakes for Johnson Controls are therefore much higher than the annual savings so often cited. "Reincorporating abroad would allow Johnson Controls to avoid ever paying a dime in U.S. income tax on profits currently stashed in tax havens," Gardner stated.

Johnson Controls is using the common inversion strategy of arranging for a smaller corporation based in a low-tax nation to purchase a much larger firm operating in the United States. In this case, the Ireland-based Tyco International (itself an inverted firm which had long been based in the United States) is buying Johnson Controls. Tax expert Edward Kleinbard describes this as a "minnow swallowing a whale" scenario that characterizes many inversions.

The Johnson Controls-Tyco deal qualifies as a so-called "super inversion," as *Fortune* put it, because it evades a number of new ownership regulations set by the

U.S. Treasury Department to discourage inversions. "Tyco shareholders will own 44% of the deal after it is done, avoiding any penalties the Treasury Department has tried to impose on these deals," *Fortune* reported. "The Treasury Department had set an ownership requirement in 2014 of 40% for foreign firms involved in inversion deals with U.S. corporations, in an effort to discourage inversions."

The deal with Tyco will change virtually nothing for Johnson Controls International except for its slightly modified name—"Johnson Controls plc."—and its ability to manipulate the U.S. tax system. The company's new domicile will officially be Cork, Ireland, but it will retain its real operating headquarters in its present site near Milwaukee. It will continue to be listed on the S&P 500 stock index. Johnson Controls will still be protected by the vast legal architecture safeguarding U.S. firms, like those on securities, intellectual property, and patents.

The corporation's CEO Alex Molinaroli insists that the firm is simply acting to best serve its shareholders: "It would be irresponsible for us as a company to not take advantage of the opportunities that come along." The inversion will also provide some advantages to the CEO himself, with *Fortune* observing, "Molinaroli will receive at least $20.5 million and as much as $79.6 million for doing the deal over the next 18 months."

Johnson Controls also stands to retain other advantages. It will remain eligible for U.S. government and state contracts under current law, as have Accenture and other firms which have staged inversions. Between 2010 and 2014, Johnson and its subsidiaries received more than $1 billion in federal contracts—more than $210 million a year, according to ITEP's Gardner. Furthermore, Johnson Controls' ability to gain federal and state tax incentives for job creation will apparently continue.

The Pushback

In an age of fast-eroding economic security, corporate inversions have stirred vast public anxieties and outrage over corporations that seem both rootless and ruthless. Public anger over inversions is mounting, as household incomes continue to fall for tens of millions of Americans and worry about the offshoring of capital and jobs becomes more widespread. An August 2014 poll by Americans for Tax Fairness revealed that more than two-thirds of likely voters disapprove of corporate inversions—86% of Democrats, 80% of independents, and 69% of Republicans.

Surprisingly, one of the loudest voices to emerge against inversions has been *Fortune*'s Allan Sloan. Sloan penned a cover story titled "Positively Un-American," warning, "We have an emergency, folks, with inversions begetting inversions." Even though Sloan advocates long-term changes that would tilt the tax system further in a pro-corporate direction, he called for immediate action by the Congress and President Obama to stem the tide of inversions. "I still think we need to stop inversions cold right now," he wrote, "to keep our tax base from eroding beyond repair."

Besides the drain to the U.S. tax base, Sloan expressed concern about the impact of inversions on Americans' view of corporate America: "It also threatens to undermine the American public's already shrinking respect for big corporations."

The recently announced Johnson Controls inversion dealt a major blow to public trust in America's largest corporations, reflected in calls by Democratic presidential candidates Bernie Sanders and Hillary Clinton for stiff regulation on inversions.

Johnson Controls' announcement gave Sanders and Clinton a chance to tap a strong vein of public sentiment. Lashing out at the company in a January 25 media release, Sanders called it and its new partner Tyco "corporate deserters." Sanders declared, "Profitable companies that have received corporate welfare from American taxpayers should not be allowed to renounce their U.S. citizenship to avoid paying U.S. taxes."

Clinton blasted Johnson Controls on January 27 at an Iowa campaign stop, stating "I will do everything I can to prevent this from happening, because I don't want to see companies that thrive, use the tax code, the gimmicks, the shenanigans ... to evade their responsibility to support our country." She also began using a TV commercial aired in Michigan and elsewhere, showing her speaking in front of the Johnson Controls headquarters to denounce the corporation's inversion.

A Cure Worse Than the Disease

Up until now, conservative Republicans' control of the House of Representatives has blocked even modest legislation from gaining any traction, despite public outrage against inversions. Using the standard Republican soundbite about the high corporate tax rate driving U.S. firms and jobs overseas, Sensenbrenner, wrote in an op-ed in the *Milwaukee Journal Sentinel*: "Despite the negative effects the departures of these companies are having on the American economy, it is difficult to blame corporate leaders when you crunch the numbers."

Similarly, influential hedge-fund tycoon Carl Icahn, although acknowledging the dislocation and insecurity generated by inversions, exempted corporations from any obligation to the United States and laid the blame at the feet of Congress for failing to cut corporate taxes. "Chief executives have a fiduciary duty to enhance value for their shareholders," he argued in a *New York Times* opinion piece. "The fault does not lie with them but with our uncompetitive international tax code and with our dysfunctional Congress for not changing it."

Icahn expressed hope that the public's sense of urgency about stopping inversions could be shunted away from its current anti-corporate trajectory and instead stampede Congress into lowering corporate tax rates this year. He wrote in the *New York Times*, "How will representatives and senators, with an election year approaching, explain to their constituents why they are out of work because their employers left the country, when it could so easily have been avoided?"

In pressing for lower corporate taxes in the name of heading off more inversions, corporate and financial figures like Icahn and Republicans are backed by some influential Democrats and self-described liberals who share an elite consensus on corporations' absolute "right" to switch their nationalities and to offshore jobs and capital. *New York Times* business columnist Jeffrey Sommer summarized this consensus in 2014, inadvertently illustrating the vast gulf between elite opinion and majority sentiment. "At this stage of globalization," Sommer declared, "… most American consumers, investors and politicians have tacitly accepted that if a company is profitable, doesn't violate the law and produces appealing products and services, it can operate wherever and however it likes."

Treating corporate investment decisions as sacrosanct regardless of their impact on the public welfare, key Democratic figures like Sen. Charles Schumer (D-N.Y.) and Senate Minority Leader Harry Reid (D-Nev.) are calling for a "tax holiday" on the foreign profits of U.S. corporations. They essentially seek to replicate the holiday declared in 2004 to encourage corporations to "repatriate" foreign profits to the United States by giving them a radically discounted tax rate.

The "tax holiday" idea is a particularly counter-productive measure. First, tax holidays reinforce corporations' use of tax deferrals as they create an incentive for the companies to wait for Congress to capitulate and offer discounted tax rates. Second, these top Democrats' backing of a new corporate-tax holiday is particularly indefensible given the disastrous outcome of the 2004 holiday. "Advocates said it would create 660,000 new jobs," pointed out David Cay Johnston. "Didn't happen. Pfizer brought home the most, $37 billion, escaping $11 billion in taxes. Then Pfizer fired 41,000 workers."

A Real Solution

If corporate tax avoidance is to be stopped, the most immediate step is ending corporations' ability to endlessly defer taxes on income which they claim to have generated overseas.

Offshore tax havens enable corporations to routinely engage in a practice called "profit-stripping." With this practice, taxable earnings in the United States are stripped—with costs allocated to the U.S. units and earnings attributed to firms' foreign subsidiaries. "This kind of accounting alchemy actually works, turning the black tax ink of profit into red ink of debt," Johnston explained. "You appear as a pauper to government but valuable to investors."

"Most of America's largest corporations maintain subsidiaries in offshore tax havens," reported Citizens for Tax Justice. "At least 358 companies, nearly 72 percent of the Fortune 500, operate subsidiaries in tax haven jurisdictions as of the end of 2014."

This means a loss of an additional $90 billion to the Treasury, according to Citizens for Tax Justice, apart from the cost of inversions.

It is relatively easy to envision reforms that would give the U.S. tax code a badly needed updating—suited to the current era dominated by the global operations of multinational corporations—to foreclose maneuvers like inversions and the deferral of taxes on foreign earnings.

But serious action on inversions and major loopholes will likely prove impossible as long as our political democracy continues to be eroded by a torrent of campaign contributions from the multinational corporations exploiting the existing tax system.

Until that link—between those who write the big campaign checks and those who write our laws and tax code—is irrevocably broken, our political system will remain impervious to majority sentiment for stiffer taxes and restrictions on corporations' inversions and the offshoring of capital and jobs. ❑

Sources: Matt Gardner, "Johnson Controls Attempts a Snow Job," Tax Justice Blog, Jan. 26, 2016 (taxjusticeblog.org); Citizens for Tax Justice "The Sorry State of Corporate Taxes," 2014 (ctj.org); Citizens for Tax Justice, "Offshore Shell Games," Oct. 5, 2015 (ctj.org); Jesse Drucker and Zachary R. Mider, "Tax Inversion: How U.S. Companies Buy Tax Breaks," BloombergView QuickTake, Nov 23, 2015 (bloombergview.com); David Cay Johnston, "Corporate Deadbeats: How Companies Get Rich Off Of Taxes," *Newsweek*, Sept. 4, 2014; Andrew Ross Sorkin, "A Tidal Wave of Corporate Migrants Seeking (Tax) Shelter," Dealbook, *New York Times*, Jan. 26, 2016; David Cay Johnston, "The Shocking Numbers Behind Corporate Welfare: Boeing and Its Stockholders Fly High on Tax Dollars,"

Article 2.5

THE OTHER COLOMBIA
The Economics and Politics of Depropriation

BY PATRICIA M. RODRIGUEZ
November/December 2010

It has rained for days, and the swampy ocean waters that surround this community of displaced fishermen in northern Colombia rise at their own whim, flooding people's houses and making life even harder than usual. Yet most of the families living in this tiny makeshift encampment in Boca de Aracataca in the Magdalena province of Colombia have gathered under a tarp to eloquently tell a group of activists from Witness for Peace, a Washington-based social justice organization, about their problems. "[The foreign companies] kicked us out of our land. We do not have water, electricity, food, nor any help from the government... we need to be respected, we need to be treated as people, and not as animals," says Alicia Camargo, who has been displaced three times already, once very violently, along with family and neighbors.

As it turns out, the source of the problems in this community—and others nearby—is the presence of multinational corporations. In this particular case, it involves a new port expansion project along the Caribbean coast near the otherwise-idyllic city of Santa Marta. The construction of this mega-port has been funded by foreign coal companies that have operated practically unrestrictedly in Colombia for nearly 15 years. When it is finished in 2013, the port will allow U.S.-based company Drummond and Swiss-based Glencore to ship an extra 30 to 60 million tons of coal per year to global markets, in addition to the nearly 69 million tons they already export. The Colombian government allegedly receives a royalty of 10% of this total export profit, but only a handful of people see this money. A large portion of the money is never transferred to the communities that are most impoverished and environmentally affected by corporate presence. Still, foreign direct investment is embraced wholeheartedly by Colombian elites who equate corporate ventures in the agricultural, mineral, and industrial sectors with growth and prosperity.

It is not uncommon to hear about how corporations bring investment to developing countries and even their "willingness" to address problem areas such as environmental contamination and child labor practices. It is sometimes said that corporations' business practices are completely socially responsible and that corporations give back to the communities in which they operate. The media give much less attention to stories about how corporations destroy local lives, directly and indirectly. Yet it happens, and in some cases it leaves a trail of unimaginable destruction and violence. In this Caribbean region of Colombia, to talk of displacement of communities by corporations does not do justice to the reality; rather, locals speak of depropriation, or the takeover of property and livelihoods with complete impunity.

In this corner of the world, multinational corporations in the coal industry like Drummond and Glencore, and in the banana sector, like Dole and Chiquita Brands (among others), are not just operating on the basis of government-granted licenses to exploit natural resources. Through alliances with authorities, legal and otherwise, these companies have crafted what amounts to an informal ownership of the region. They own a large part of the railroads, highways, ports, and mines, and they have little concern for how communities feel about their presence there.

But what is it about the nature of these enterprises and the context in which they operate that make for such dominance, and what facilitates their exploitation of workers and communities? How have local people resisted these infractions, and to what degree, considering the widespread corruption of their political representatives? To answer both these questions, it helps to understand more about the region. Whether due to its strategic location, its natural resources, or its distance from the centers of power in the capital city, Bogotá, this region is often referred to as "the other Colombia." It is an allusion both to its potential and to its stigma as something of a no man's land.

Free Reign in the "Other Colombia"

Multinational companies began to arrive in the Magdalena and Cesar provinces in large part because the location offers such natural advantages. Surrounded in the east by the Sierra Nevada mountains, several municipalities in Magdalena province have direct access to the rivers that originate in these slopes. This makes the land well suited for banana plantations and other kinds of large-scale agriculture, and therefore for elite and corporate interests. It comes as no surprise that one of the U.S.-based companies with most presence throughout Latin America, the United Fruit Company (UFCO), operated in Magdalena since the beginning of the 20th century. As with its operations elsewhere, UFCO labor practices in Colombia were exploitative and repressive. During a strike by UFCO banana workers on December 6, 1928, in which they asked for better treatment and working conditions, an indefinite number of workers were massacred by company and police security forces in Ciénaga. The Nobel Prize-winning Colombian writer Gabriel García Márquez wrote a fictional account of this massacre in One Hundred Years of Solitude. Though UFCO left the Magdalena region in 1950s and moved to other regions of Colombia, it continued subcontracting with local growers.

In the mid to late 1980s, Chiquita Brands (formerly UFCO) and Dole rediscovered the Zona Bananera, or the Caribbean Banana Zone, at a time when local landowners had already been paying a "security fee" to rebel guerrilla groups that operated from the largely uninhabited Sierra Nevada, like the National Liberation Army (ELN). Noticing the potential for exclusive control of land and/or lucrative contracts with local large-scale banana growers, Chiquita and Dole officials negotiated economic deals with the landowners and security deals with the guerrillas. Their aim was to guarantee the companies' unrestricted access to highways and railroads leading to the coastal ports. In just a few years, however, small private security gangs began brutal confrontations with guerrillas in the mountains and the cities. Aware of their stronger firepower, the companies began to pay these small groups for protection instead of the guerrillas. By the late 1990s, these gang-style private security groups multiplied and fought each other for control of the territory (and for the substantial payments from landowners and multinational companies). A handful of gang leaders emerged victorious, and soon formed more structured paramilitary organizations like the powerful United Self-Defense Forces of Colombia (AUC). AUC and other paramilitary groups are known to have solid ties to drug lords as well as to military and high-level state authorities.

One of the AUC leaders in the Caribbean region is Rodrigo Tovar, popularly known as Jorge 40. He was a former army official and comes from one of a handful of powerful traditional families in the region. In the mid 1990s, Jorge 40 began to work under the command of the Castaño family, who founded the AUC when the patriarch Jesús Castaño was kidnapped and assassinated in the mid 1990s by another guerrilla group, the Revolutionary Armed Forces of Colombia (FARC). To garner control, Jorge 40 was known to carry out "cleansings" of local communities in Magdalena and Cesar provinces, targeting anyone suspected of ties to ELN or FARC. In 2000, after a guerrilla attack on a group of business and mafia leaders in the town of Nueva Venezia, Jorge 40 ordered the massacre of 70 people from this community. According to witnesses, the armed paramilitaries then played soccer with victims' severed heads to show the community that they were in complete control. There are several others like Jorge 40 who have ties to the different landowning families and to different companies.

In 2007, Chiquita Brands admitted in federal court that it paid nearly $2 million to paramilitary death squads over a period of seven years. On its end, Drummond is currently being sued in a United States court under the Alien Tort Claims Act for having contracted paramilitary forces to kill three union leaders. The violence in the region is widespread, and largely tied to corporate interest in acquiring lands and controlling the regions' vast resources. Between 1997 and 2007, 4,000 people died and at least 500 were disappeared. Moreover, during the height of the violence in between 2003 and 2006, 43,300 families from the region suffered forced displacement from their communities.

On their end, the companies suffered no major consequences from the bloodbath, other than occasionally having to rearrange their deals with different paramilitary leaders. As long as they kept scheduled payments, the companies enjoyed complete control over vast lands. By 2002 Chiquita and Dole decided to divvy up the 10,000 hectares of land in the Zona Bananera: the medium-to-large farms that grew bananas for Dole had their main houses painted red and white, and those that grew bananas for Chiquita were painted blue and white. They also happily shared the railroad. On the other hand, small farms that for one or another reason do not have contracts with these companies have hardly survived. Many peasants have agreed to sell their lands, only to lose most of their money to criminal and paramilitary gangs that extorted them shortly after the sale. Others, out of fear, have simply never returned after their violent displacement by paramilary groups. In the near future, these corporations are likely to continue to buy lands in the region, especially with the impending passage of the free trade agreement (FTA) between the United States and Colombia. While former president Alvaro Uribe championed the push for the FTA deal with the United States, current president Juan Manuel Santos, a former defense minister and a millionaire who has solid ties to many traditional elite Colombian families, is likely to deepen the open-borders approach.

The free reign of foreign coal companies reflects a similar history. The mountainous terrain in neighboring Cesar province contains some of the biggest coal mines in Latin America. Drummond, Prodeco (a subsidiary of Glencore), and now Brazilian-owned Vale, have capitalized on this by buying part of the national railroad company Fenoco, so as to have unrestricted access to the approximately 300 miles of railroad line between the mines and the port of Ciénaga, near Santa Marta. The port installations now cover four kilometers (of a total twelve kilometers) of the coastal shores in Magdalena, but the mega-port currently under construction would extend them by another two kilometers. When the project got under way in 2008, several communities living in the swamps, or ciénaga, near the port were forcibly displaced by armed gunmen, and many ended in the encampment in Boca de Aracataca. The port expansion work has prevented the fishermen from being able to access close-by waters and they now have to fish in far away waters, if their boats are solid enough to make it there.

The damage extends far beyond access. For years, the companies have been dumping millions of tons of coal onto communities where the railroad crosses, and into coastal waters. This is due to negligence, as residuals "accidentally" fall out when the coal is carried uncovered or dumped into the shipping containers. This has resulted in severe erosion and environmental contamination of local flora and fish. As if that did not suffice, Drummond was recently conceded the rights to Rio Toribio, including control over the station that supplies clean water to local communities. According to the fishermen, Drummond uses the water to wet down the coal so that it does not ignite in the containers on the way to global markets. This has generated the contamination of river water with coal dust, and has caused a variety of skin and respiratory diseases among the local population.

State Complicity

This depropriation and destruction occurs under the protective eye of the Colombian state. Though laws exist which delimit any alterations to the agro-ecological balance in much of the coastal area, the government blatantly disregards the laws. In December 2007 the national Ministry of Transportation declared that the entire municipality was a public interest zone for purposes of national development, paving the way for the expansion of the port. Though Drummond and Prodeco appear to have followed all the legal steps to begin the expansion project, the process has certainly faltered in many aspects. According to a report prepared by local community leaders, the companies and municipal authorities did not adequately consult local community groups about worrisome environmental and socio-economic effects. Though the royalties for mining concessions and banana profits by law should remain in the communities for social and infrastructural investment, a majority of this money is simply distributed privately to national and municipal authorities. As a community leader from Ciénaga states, "what we have here is a case of mafia triangulation, with companies, the central government, and local authorities keeping the municipal funds for themselves, and thereby diffusing any responsibility that they should have towards communities."

The foreign companies do as they please, with impunity. When unionized coal workers organize to demand respect for their labor rights, or to ask for appropriate paid sick time for work injuries, the companies fire them. Such is the case of Moisés Padilla, a former Drummond employee who belongs to the Sintraminergética (National Union of Industry and Energy Workers) union. He worked for 50 years as a welder (25 at Drummond), and is now incapacitated due to severe respiratory and heart conditions. The company has successfully resisted any outside intervention, despite legal efforts of the union. In a letter to Moisés Padilla, a company representative stated that it was not company policy to consent to third-party involvement, in this case a committee of independent and state officials that could evaluate his injury claims.

Union workers have less and less job security especially since the company has recently created its own union, Sintradrummond. Although the practice was previously prohibited, a recent judicial decision has opened a loophole for companies to begin organizing their own unions. Anibal Perez, another injured worker from Sintraminergética, affirms that "for us to belong to our union is considered by the state practically a crime…the state does not give us the tools and protections to make our voices heard, and the result is that we have communities full of widows, orphans, and sick workers." The union has had five of its leaders killed since 2001, and several others now live in exile after being threatened by paramilitaries.

The companies are also quick to hold on to the façade of being socially and environmentally responsible. One example: Drummond trains a certain number of people from the community to be mine workers, but rarely hires local trainees. Some think this is because it is cheaper for the company to hire migrants from other regions. Similarly, national companies like Augura (Association of Banana Workers of Colombia) organize some of their own workers in seemingly beneficial cooperatives. Though independent on paper, Augura does business strictly with Dole, and prices are arranged between top level managers from Augura and Dole. So even if cooperative workers would truly get a fair trade price for their bananas, the lack of liberty to make autonomous decisions within the company-run cooperatives is problematic at best.

Not that state intervention would do any good. For one thing, much of the state funding for social programs for local communities is channeled to the companies themselves, such as the Augura-run cooperatives. So while the state has funds that it invests in social programs, these are mostly captured by the companies. Secondly, other state-funded social programs deliver subsidies as if community members were clients. The community at large, whether they belong to the category of low-income families, displaced families, or relatives and victims of violence, barely has access to a program that distributes about $40 every two months; most do not have enough of a connection with municipal authorities to receive even this small benefit. Thirdly, though the laws exist on paper to make the state more responsible and responsive, implementation is a problem. For instance, Colombia has had a Labor Statute since 1991, but the mechanisms for its implementation have not yet been discussed in Congress. Besides, corruption pervades the state. In 2009, a national scandal erupted over a government program aimed at helping struggling farmers, the Agro Ingreso Seguro (AIS) program. The funding (partly from the U.S. Agency for International Development) began in 2006 as part of an effort to ease concern over a potential negative impact of an impending FTA with the United States, but small farmers were not the ones benefiting; the bulk of AIS' $630 million per year was discovered to be going to rich landowners, narco-traffickers, and mobsters.

Organizing an Effective Resistance

Considering the pervasiveness of corporate interests, violence, and state complicity, what can the handful of community leaders, human rights defenders, and union workers do to organize effective resistance? The truth is that they cannot organize freely; their lives are threatened constantly. Despite the threats, is not so hard to understand why those who are still alive publicly denounce the companies, the Colombian government, and the United States for trampling on their dignity. "Our denunciations make us very public personas, and since we do not have money to pay for private security guards, speaking out publicly and internationally ironically gives us some sense of security," says Edgardo Alemán, a local human rights defender.

And so they do challenge, collectively when possible. One of the small victories of the sintramienergética union and other allied groups has been the Collective Labor Agreement signed between the union and Drummond, for the years 2010-2013. Even at quick glance, it is easy to find the voice of the workers, and their concern for community. Article 7 states that when a job opens at Drummond, the company will give preference to skilled members of the local community; upon the death of a worker, the company commits to hiring a family member of the victim. Union leaders concur that the agreement feels more like "our list of demands" than an actual commitment by Drummond representatives. Yet many insist that a more effective interaction between the communities and the companies is the only solution. "We need to guarantee a way to capture the resources, to have a social development policy that favors our communities. If we go through the politicians, we will get nothing," says local activist and economist, Luís Eduardo Rendón.

If the state's lack of responsiveness is any indication, negotiating with the companies might in fact be a viable approach. But the success of that strategy does not depend on the amount of pressure Colombian workers and community leaders exert. In this sense, the context (and place) in which they operate limits their impact. For their voice to mean anything in a system dominated by elite power in Bogotá and abroad, it will take the U.S. government and global citizens en masse to press the companies (American companies!) and the Colombian state to be honest, and to practice their activities legally, with true social responsibility. Perhaps then there can begin to be justice for these communities in the other Colombia. ❏

Sources: Luis E. Barranco, "Como el gobierno nacional convirtió una zona agroecológica en zona de interés público para fines portuarios," *EDUMAG*, Ciénaga, Colombia, 2010; Marcelo Bucheli, *Bananas and Business: The United Fruit Company in Colombia, 1899-2000* (New York University Press, 2005); Peter Chapman, *Bananas: How the United Fruit Company Shaped the World* (Canongate, 2007); Aviva Chomsky, Garry Leech, and Steve Striffler, *Bajo el manto del carbon: Pueblos y multinacionales en las minas de El Cerrejón* (Casa Editorial Pisando Callos, 2007).

Article 2.6

HOW GOLDMAN SACHS CAUSED A GREEK TRAGEDY

BY JIM HIGHTOWER
March 2010

Another Greek-based cargo ship and its crew was recently hijacked by Somalian pirates, costing the Greek owners an undisclosed amount in ransom.

Such ongoing acts of brazen piracy off the coast of Somalia have riveted the establishment media's attention. But the same news hawks have missed (or ignored) a much more brazen, longer-running and far larger robbery in Greece by Gucci-wearing thieves who are more sophisticated than common pirates—but lack a pirate's moral depth.

I refer to—who else?—Wall Street financiers. Specifically, Goldman Sachs.

Goldman, a global financial conglomerate and America's largest banking fiefdom, is notorious in our country for its arrogant, anything-goes corporate ethic that is astonishingly avaricious, even by Wall Street's dissolute standards. The firm is villainous enough that it could be its own reality TV show, perhaps titled, "Bankers Behaving Badly." A few highlights:

- During the past decade, Goldman's wizards were particularly inventive monkey-wrenchers, devising much of the investment gimmickry that enriched crafty Wall Streeters like them, even as it led to the wrecking of our economy.

- In 2006, Goldman's CEO was considered such a whiz that he was elevated to treasury secretary and soon was handed the task of fixing the very economic mess he had helped create. His "fix" was the cockamamie, self-serving, multitrillion-dollar taxpayer bailout that did save Wall Street ... but has left our economy in shambles.

- Rather than apologizing for their failures and using their bailout funds to rush loans to America's credit-starved businesses, Goldman's debauched financiers immediately went back to playing the same old global game of high-risk craps that caused America's crash, this time rolling the dice with the backing of our tax dollars.

- Juiced by an infusion of federal funds, Goldman executives declared a profit this year and promptly lavished more than $16 billion in bonus payments on themselves.

- To keep the fun rolling, Goldman is now lobbying furiously in Washington to kill regulatory and consumer bills that could rein in its destructive greed.

- Moving from mere greed to naked narcissism, Goldman's current CEO, Lloyd Blankfein, has proclaimed that his bonus bonanza is warranted because he is "doing God's work."

Perhaps he was referring to one of the Greek gods. It turns out that, for the past decade, Goldman has also been practicing its ethical flim-flammery in Greece, a nation long mired in a sea of debt.

In 2001, Goldman's financial alchemists formulated a scheme to allow the Greek government to hide the extent of its rising debt from the public and the European Community's budget overseers. Under this diabolical deal, Goldman funneled new capital from super-wealthy investors into the government's coffers.

Fine. Not so fine, though, is that, in exchange, Greek officials secretly agreed that the investors would get 20 years' worth of the annual revenue generated by such public assets as Greece's airports. For its part, Goldman pocketed $300 million in fees paid by the country's unwitting taxpayers.

The financial giant dubbed its airport scheme "Aeolus," after the ancient Greek god of the wind—and, sure enough, any long-term financial benefit for Greece was soon gone with the wind. By hiding the fact that the government's future revenues had been consigned to secret investors, Goldman bankers made the country's balance sheet look much rosier than it was, allowing Greek officials to keep spending like there was no tomorrow.

Last month, however, tomorrow arrived. Greece's crushing debt has exploded into a full-blown crisis, with its leaders disgraced and the country on the precipice of the unthinkable: the default of a sovereign nation.

So, who is getting punished for the finagling of Greek politicos and Goldman profiteers? The people, of course—just like here! Greeks now face deep wage cuts, rising taxes and the elimination of public services just so their government can pay off debts the people didn't even know it had. Meanwhile, Greece's financial conflagration is endangering the stability of Europe's currency and causing financial systems worldwide (including ours) to wobble again. All of this to enrich a handful of global speculators.

Thanks, Goldman Sachs. ❏

By permission of Jim Hightower and Creators Syndicate, Inc.

Chapter 3

INTERNATIONAL TRADE AND INVESTMENT

Article 3.1

THE GOSPEL OF FREE TRADE
The New Evangelists

BY ARTHUR MacEWAN
November 1991, updated July 2009

Free trade! With the zeal of Christian missionaries, for decades the U.S. government has been preaching, advocating, pushing, and coercing around the globe for "free trade."

As the economic crisis emerged in 2007 and 2008 and rapidly became a global crisis, it was apparent that something was very wrong with the way the world economy was organized. Not surprisingly, as unemployment rose sharply in the United States, there were calls for protecting jobs by limiting imports and for the government to "buy American" in its economic stimulus program. Similarly, in many other countries, as unemployment jumped upwards, pressure emerged for protection—and some actual steps were taken. Yet, free trade missionaries did not retreat; they continued to preach the same gospel.

The free-traders were probably correct in claiming that protectionist policies would do more harm than good as a means to stem the rising unemployment generated by the economic crisis. Significant acts of protectionism in one country would lead to retaliation—or at least copying—by other countries, reducing world trade. The resulting loss of jobs from reduced trade would most likely outweigh any gains from protection.

Yet the argument over international economic policies should not be confined simply to what should be done in a crisis. Nor should it simply deal with trade in goods and services. The free-traders have advocated their program as one for long-run economic growth and development, yet the evidence suggests that free trade is not a good economic development strategy. Furthermore, the free-traders preach the virtue of unrestricted global movement of finance as well as of goods and services. As it turns out, the free flow of finance has been a major factor in bringing about and spreading the economic crisis that began to appear in 2007—as well as earlier crises.

The Push

While the U.S. push for free trade goes back several decades, it has become more intense in recent years. In the 1990s, the U.S. government signed on to the North American Free Trade Agreement (NAFTA) and in 2005 established the Central American Free Trade Agreement (CAFTA). Both Republican and Democratic presidents, however, have pushed hard for a *global* free trade agenda. After the demise of the Soviet Union, U.S. advisers prescribed unfettered capitalism for Eastern and Central Europe, and ridiculed as unworkable any move toward a "third way." In low-income countries from Mexico to Malaysia, the prescription has been the same: open markets, deregulate business, don't restrict international investment, and let the free market flourish.

In the push for worldwide free trade, the World Trade Organization (WTO) has been the principal vehicle of change, establishing rules for commerce that assure markets are open and resources are available to those who can pay. And the International Monetary Fund (IMF) and World Bank, which provide loans to many governments, use their financial power to pressure countries around the world to accept the gospel and open their markets. In each of these international organizations, the United States—generally through the U.S. Treasury—plays a dominant role.

Of course, as with any gospel, the preachers often ignore their own sermons. While telling other countries to open their markets, the U.S. government continued, for instance, to limit imports of steel, cotton, sugar, textiles, and many other goods. But publicly at least, free-trade boosters insist that the path to true salvation—or economic expansion, which, in this day and age, seems to be the same thing—lies in opening our market to foreign goods. Get rid of trade barriers at home and abroad, allow business to go where it wants and do what it wants. We will all get rich.

Yet the history of the United States and other rich countries does not fit well with the free-trade gospel. Virtually all advanced capitalist countries found economic success through heavy government regulation of their international commerce, not in free trade. Likewise, a large role for government intervention has characterized those cases of rapid and sustained economic growth in recent decades—for example,

Japan after World War II, South Korea in the 1970s through the 1990s, and China most recently.

Free trade does, however, have its uses. Highly developed nations can use free trade to extend their power and control of the world's wealth, and business can use it as a weapon against labor. Most important, free trade can limit efforts to redistribute income more equally, undermine social programs, and keep people from democratically controlling their economic lives.

A Day in the Park

At the beginning of the 19th century, Lowell, Massachusetts became the premier site of the U.S. textile industry. Today, thanks to the Lowell National Historical Park, you can tour the huge mills, ride through the canals that redirected the Merrimack River's power to those mills, and learn the story of the textile workers, from the Yankee "mill girls" of the 1820s through the various waves of immigrant laborers who poured into the city over the next century.

During a day in the park, visitors get a graphic picture of the importance of 19th-century industry to the economic growth and prosperity of the United States. Lowell and the other mill towns of the era were centers of growth. They not only created a demand for Southern cotton, they also created a demand for new machinery, maintenance of old machinery, parts, dyes, *skills*, construction materials, construction machinery, *more skills*, equipment to move the raw materials and products, parts maintenance for that equipment, *and still more skills*. The mill towns also created markets—concentrated groups of wage earners who needed to buy products to sustain themselves. As centers of economic activity, Lowell and similar mill towns contributed to U.S. economic growth far beyond the value of the textiles they produced.

The U.S. textile industry emerged decades after the industrial revolution had spawned Britain's powerful textile industry. Nonetheless, it survived and prospered. British linens inundated markets throughout the world in the early 19th century, as the British navy nurtured free trade and kept ports open for commerce. In the United States, however, hostilities leading up to the War of 1812 and then a substantial tariff made British textiles relatively expensive. These limitations on trade allowed the Lowell mills to prosper, acting as a catalyst for other industries and helping to create the skilled work force at the center of U.S. economic expansion.

Beyond textiles, however, tariffs did not play a great role in the United States during the early 19th century. Southern planters had considerable power, and while they were willing to make some compromises, they opposed protecting manufacturing in general because that protection forced up the prices of the goods they purchased with their cotton revenues. The Civil War wiped out the planters' power to oppose protectionism, and from the 1860s through World War I, U.S. industry prospered behind considerable tariff barriers.

Different Countries, Similar Experiences

The story of the importance of protectionism in bringing economic growth has been repeated, with local variations, in other advanced capitalist countries. During the late 19th century, Germany entered the major league of international economic powers with substantial protection and government support for its industries. Likewise, in 19th-century France and Italy, national consolidation behind protectionist barriers was a key to economic development.

Britain—which entered the industrial era first—is often touted as the prime example of successful development without tariff protection. Yet, Britain embraced free trade only after its industrial base was well established; as in the U.S., the early and important textile industry was erected on a foundation of protectionism. In addition, Britain built its industry through the British navy and the expansion of empire, hardly prime ingredients in any recipe for free trade.

Japan provides an especially important case of successful government protection and support for industrial development. In the post-World War II era, when the Japanese established the foundations for their economic "miracle," the government rejected free trade and extensive foreign investment and instead promoted its national firms.

In the 1950s, for example, the government protected the country's fledgling auto firms from foreign competition. At first, quotas limited imports to $500,000 (in current dollars) each year; in the 1960s, prohibitively high tariffs replaced the quotas. Furthermore, the Japanese allowed foreign investment only insofar as it contributed to developing domestic industry. The government encouraged Japanese companies to import foreign technology, but required them to produce 90% of parts domestically within five years.

The Japanese also protected their computer industry. In the early 1970s, as the industry was developing, companies and individuals could only purchase a foreign machine if a suitable Japanese model was not available. IBM was allowed to produce within the country, but only when it licensed basic patents to Japanese firms. And IBM computers produced in Japan were treated as foreign-made machines.

In the 20th century, no other country matched Japan's economic success, as it moved in a few decades from a relative low-income country, through the devastation of war, to emerge as one of the world's economic leaders. Yet one looks back in vain to find a role for free trade in this success. The Japanese government provided an effective framework, support, and protection for the country's capitalist development.

Likewise, in many countries that have been late-comers to economic development, capitalism has generated high rates of economic growth where government involvement, and not free trade, played the central role. South Korea is a striking case. "Korea is an example of a country that grew very fast and yet violated the canons of conventional economic wisdom," writes Alice Amsden in *Asia's Next Giant: South Korea and Late Industrialization*, widely acclaimed as perhaps the most important analysis of the South Korean economic success. "In Korea, instead of the market mechanism allocating resources and guiding private entrepreneurship, the government made most of the pivotal investment decisions. Instead of firms operating in a competitive market structure, they each operated with an extraordinary degree of market control, protected from foreign competition."

Free trade, however, has had its impact in South Korea. In the 1990s, South Korea and other East Asian governments came under pressure from the U.S. government and the IMF to open their markets, including their financial markets. When they did so, the results were a veritable disaster. The East Asian financial crisis that began in 1997 was a major setback for the whole region, a major disruption of economic growth. After extremely rapid economic growth for three decades, with output expanding at 7% to 10% a year, South Korea's economy plummeted by 6.3% between 1997 and 1998.

Mexico and Its NAFTA Experience

While free trade in goods and services has its problems, which can be very serious, it is the free movement of capital, the opening of financial markets that has sharp, sudden impacts, sometimes wrecking havoc on national economies. Thus, virtually as soon as Mexico, the United States and Canada formed NAFTA at the beginning of 1994, Mexico was hit with a severe financial crisis. As the economy turned downward at the beginning of that year, capital rapidly left the country, greatly reducing the value of the Mexican peso. With this diminished value of the peso, the cost of servicing international debts and the costs of imports skyrocketed—and the downturn worsened.

Still, during the 1990s, before and after the financial crisis, free-traders extolled short periods of moderate economic growth in Mexico —3% to 4% per year—as evidence of success. Yet, compared to earlier years, Mexico's growth under free trade has been poor. From 1940 to 1990 (including the no-growth decade of the 1980s), when Mexico's market was highly protected and the state actively regulated economic affairs, output grew at an average annual rate of 5%.

Most important, Mexico's experience discredits the notion that free-market policies will improve living conditions for the masses of people in low-income countries. The Mexican government paved the way for free trade policies by reducing or eliminating social welfare programs, and for many Mexican workers wages declined sharply during the free trade era. The number of households living in poverty rose dramatically, with some 75% of Mexico's population below the poverty line at the beginning of the 21st century.

China and Its Impact

Part of Mexico's problem and its economy's relatively weak performance from the 1990s onward has been the full-scale entrance of China into the international economy. While the Mexican authorities thought they saw great possibilities in NAFTA, with the full opening of the U.S. market to goods produced with low-wage Mexican labor, China (and other Asian countries) had even cheaper labor. As China also gained access to the U.S. market, Mexican expectations were dashed.

The Chinese economy has surely gained in terms of economic growth as it has engaged more and more with the world market, and the absolute levels of incomes of millions of people have risen a great deal. However, China's rapid economic growth has come with a high degree of income inequality. Before its era of rapid growth, China was viewed as a country with a relatively equal distribution of income. By the beginning of the new millennium, however, it was much more unequal than any of the other most populace Asian countries (India, Indonesia, Bangladesh, Pakistan), and more in line with the high-inequality countries of Latin America. Furthermore, with the inequality has come a great deal of social conflict. Tens of thousands of "incidents" of conflict involving violence are reported each year, and most recently there have been the major conflicts involving Tibetans and Ouigers.

In any case, the Chinese trade and growth success should not be confused with "free trade." Foundations for China's surge of economic growth were established through state-sponsored infra-structure development and the vast expansion of the country's educational system. Even today, while private business, including foreign business, appears to have been given free rein in China, the government still plays a controlling role—including a central role in affecting foreign economic relations.

A central aspect of the government's role in the county's foreign commerce has been in the realm of finance. As Chinese-produced goods have virtually flooded international markets, the government has controlled the uses of the earnings from these exports. Instead of simply allowing those earnings to be used by Chinese firms and citizens to buy imports, the government has to a large extent held those earnings as reserves. Using those reserves, China's central bank has been the largest purchaser of U.S. government bonds, in effect becoming a major financer of the U.S. government's budget deficit of recent years.

China's reserves have been one large element in creating a giant pool of financial assets in the world economy. This "pool" has also been built up as the doubling of oil prices following the U.S. invasion of Iraq put huge amounts of funds in the pockets of oil-exporting countries and firm and individuals connected to the oil industry. Yet slow growth of the U.S. economy and extremely low interest rates, resulting from the Federal Reserve Bank's efforts to encourage more growth, limited the returns that could be obtained on these funds. One of the consequences—through a complex set of connections—was the development of the U.S. housing bubble, as financial firms, searching for higher returns, pushed funds into more and more risky mortgage loans.

It was not simply free trade and the unrestricted flow of international finance that generated the housing bubble and subsequent crisis in the U.S. economy. However, the generally unstable global economy—both in terms of trade and finance—that has emerged in the free trade era was certainly a factor bringing about the crisis. Moreover, as is widely recognized, it was not only the U.S. economy and U.S. financial institutions that were affected. The free international flow of finance has meant that banking has become more and more a global industry. So as the U.S. banks got in trouble in 2007 and 2008, their maladies spread to many other parts of the world.

The Uses of Free Trade

While free trade is not the best economic growth or development policy and, especially through the free flow of finance, can precipitate financial crises, the largest and most powerful firms in many countries find it highly profitable. As Britain preached the loudest sermons for free trade in the early 19th century, when its own industry was already firmly established, so the United States—or at least many firms based in the United States—find it a profitable policy at the beginning of the 21st century. The Mexican experience provides an instructive illustration.

For U.S. firms, access to foreign markets is a high priority. Mexico may be relatively poor, but with a population of 105 million it provides a substantial market. Furthermore, Mexican labor is cheap relative to U.S. labor; and using modern production techniques, Mexican workers can be as productive as workers in the United States. For U.S. firms to obtain full access to the Mexican market, the United States has to open its borders to Mexican goods. Also, if U.S. firms are to take full advantage of cheap foreign labor and sell the goods produced abroad to U.S. consumers, the United States has to be open to imports.

On the other side of the border, wealthy Mexicans face a choice between advancing their interests through national development or advancing their interests through ties to U.S. firms and access to U.S. markets. For many years, they chose the former route. This led to some development of the Mexican economy but also—due to corruption and the massive power of the ruling party, the PRI—huge concentrations of wealth in the hands of a few small groups of firms and individuals. Eventually, these groups came into conflict with their own government over regulation and taxation. Having benefited from government largesse, they came to see their fortunes in greater freedom from government control and, particularly, in greater access to foreign markets and partnerships with large foreign companies. National development was a secondary concern when more involvement with international commerce would produce greater riches more quickly.

In addition, the old program of state-led development in Mexico ran into severe problems. These problems came to the surface in the 1980s with the international debt crisis. Owing huge amounts of money to foreign banks, the Mexican government was forced to respond to pressure from the IMF, the U.S. government, and large international banks which sought to deregulate Mexico's trade and investment. That pressure meshed with the pressure from Mexico's own richest elites, and the result was the move toward free trade and a greater opening of the Mexican economy to foreign investment.

Since the early 1990s, these changes for Mexico and the United States (as well as Canada) have been institutionalized in NAFTA. The U.S. government's agenda since then has been to spread free trade policies to all of the Americas through more regional agreements like CAFTA and ultimately through a Free Trade Area of the Americas. On a broader scale, the U.S. government works through the WTO, the IMF, and the World Bank to open markets and gain access to resources beyond the Western Hemisphere. In fact, while markets remain important everywhere, low-wage manufacturing is increasingly concentrated in Asia—especially China—instead of Mexico or Latin America.

The Chinese experience involves many of the same advantages for U.S. business as does the Mexican—a vast market, low wages, and an increasingly productive labor force. However, the Chinese government, although it has liberalized the economy a great deal compared to the pre-1985 era, has not abdicated its major role in the economy. For better (growth) and for worse (inequality and repression), the Chinese government has not embraced free trade.

Who Gains, Who Loses?

Of course, in the United States, Mexico, China and elsewhere, advocates of free trade claim that their policies are in everyone's interest. Free trade, they point out, will mean cheaper products for all. Consumers in the United States, who are mostly workers, will be richer because their wages will buy more. In Mexico and China, on the one hand, and in the United States, on the other hand, they argue that rising trade will create more jobs. If some workers lose their jobs because cheaper imported goods are available, export industries will produce new jobs.

In recent years this argument has taken on a new dimension with the larger entrance of India into the world economy and with the burgeoning there of jobs based in information technology—programming and call centers, for example. This "out-sourcing" of service jobs has received a great deal of attention and concern in the United States. Yet free-traders have defended this development as good for the U.S. economy as well as for the Indian economy.

Such arguments obscure many of the most important issues in the free trade debate. Stated, as they usually are, as universal truths, these arguments are just plain silly. No one, for example, touring the Lowell National Historical Park could seriously argue that people in the United States would have been better off had there been no tariff on textiles. Yes, in 1820, they could have purchased textile goods more cheaply, but in the long run the result would have been less industrial advancement and a less wealthy nation. One could make the same point with the Japanese auto and computer industries, or indeed with numerous other examples from the last two centuries of capitalist development.

In the modern era, even though the United States already has a relatively developed economy with highly skilled workers, a freely open international economy does not serve the interests of most U.S. workers, though it will benefit large firms. U.S. workers today are in competition with workers around the globe. Many different workers in many different places can produce the same goods and services. Thus, an international economy governed by the free trade agenda will tend to bring down wages for many U.S. workers. This phenomenon has certainly been one of the factors leading to the substantial rise of income inequality in the United States during recent decades.

The problem is not simply that of workers in a few industries—such as auto and steel, or call-centers and computer programming—where import competition is an obvious and immediate issue. A country's openness to the international economy affects the entire structure of earnings in that country. Free trade forces down the general level of wages across the board, even of those workers not directly affected by imports. The simple fact is that when companies can produce the same products in several different places, it is owners who gain because they can move their factories and funds around much more easily than workers can move themselves around. Capital is mobile; labor is much less mobile. Businesses, more than workers, gain from having a larger territory in which to roam.

Control Over Our Economic Lives

But the difficulties with free trade do not end with wages. In both low-income and high-income parts of the world, free trade is a weapon in the hands of business when it opposes any progressive social programs. Efforts to place environmental restrictions on firms are met with the threat of moving production abroad. Higher taxes to improve the schools? Business threatens to go elsewhere. Better health and safety regulations? The same response.

Some might argue that the losses from free trade for people in the United States will be balanced by gains for most people in poor countries—lower wages in the United States, but higher wages in Mexico and China. Free trade, then, would bring about international equality. Not likely. In fact, as pointed out above, free trade reforms in Mexico have helped force down wages and reduce social welfare programs, processes rationalized by efforts to make Mexican goods competitive on international markets. China, while not embracing free trade, has seen its full-scale entrance into global commerce accompanied by increasing inequality.

Gains for Mexican or Chinese workers, like those for U.S. workers, depend on their power in relation to business. Free trade or simply the imperative of international "competitiveness" are just as much weapons in the hands of firms operating in Mexico and China as they are for firms operating in the United States. The great mobility of capital is business's best trump card in dealing with labor and popular demands for social change—in the United States, Mexico, China and elsewhere.

None of this means that people should demand that their economies operate as fortresses, protected from all foreign economic incursions. There are great gains that can be obtained from international economic relations—when a nation manages those relations in the interests of the great majority of the people. Protectionism often simply supports narrow vested interests, corrupt officials, and wealthy industrialists. In rejecting free trade, we should move beyond traditional protectionism.

Yet, at this time, rejecting free trade is an essential first step. Free trade places the cards in the hands of business. More than ever, free trade would subject us to the "bottom line," or at least the bottom line as calculated by those who own and run large companies. ❑

Article 3.2

COMPARATIVE ADVANTAGE

BY RAMAA VASUDEVAN
July/August 2007

Dear Dr. Dollar:

When economists argue that the outsourcing of jobs might be a plus for the U.S. economy, they often mention the idea of comparative advantage. Free trade, they say, would create higher-paying jobs than the ones that would be outsourced. But is it really true that free trade leads to universal benefits?

—*David Goodman, Boston, Mass.*

You're right: The purveyors of the free trade gospel do invoke the doctrine of comparative advantage to dismiss widespread concerns about the export of jobs. Attributed to 19th-century British political-economist David Ricardo, the doctrine says that a nation always stands to gain if it exports the goods it produces *relatively* more cheaply in exchange for goods that it can get *comparatively* more cheaply from abroad. Free trade would lead to each country specializing in the products it can produce at *relatively* lower costs. Such specialization allows both trading partners to gain from trade, the theory goes, even if in one of the countries production of *both* goods costs more in absolute terms.

For instance, suppose that in the United States the cost to produce one car equals the cost to produce ten bags of cotton, while in the Philippines the cost to produce one car equals the cost to produce 100 bags of cotton. The Philippines would then have a comparative advantage in the production of cotton, producing one bag at a cost equal to the production cost of 1/100 of a car, versus 1/10 of a car in the United States; likewise, the United States would hold a comparative advantage in the production of cars. Whatever the prices of cars and cotton in the global market, the theory goes, the Philippines would be better off producing only cotton and importing all its cars from the United States, and the United States would be better off producing only cars and importing all of its cotton from the Philippines. If the international terms of trade—the relative price—is one car for 50 bags, then the United States will take in 50 bags of cotton for each car it exports, 40 more than the 10 bags it forgoes by putting its productive resources into making the car rather than growing cotton. The Philippines is also better off: it can import a car in exchange for the export of 50 bags of cotton, whereas it would have had to forgo the production of 100 bags of cotton in order to produce that car domestically. If the price of cars goes up in the global marketplace, the Philippines will lose out in relative terms—but will still be better off than if it tried to produce its own cars.

The real world, unfortunately, does not always conform to the assumptions underlying comparative-advantage theory. One assumption is that trade is balanced.

But many countries are running persistent deficits, notably the United States, whose trade deficit is now at nearly 7% of its GDP. A second premise, that there is full employment within the trading nations, is also patently unrealistic. As global trade intensifies, jobs created in the export sector do not necessarily compensate for the jobs lost in the sectors wiped out by foreign competition.

The comparative advantage story faces more direct empirical challenges as well. Nearly 70% of U.S. trade is trade in similar goods, known as *intra-industry trade*: for example, exporting Fords and importing BMWs. And about one third of U.S. trade as of the late 1990s was trade between branches of a single corporation located in different countries (*intra-firm trade*). Comparative advantage cannot explain these patterns.

Comparative advantage is a static concept that identifies immediate gains from trade but is a poor guide to economic development, a process of structural change over time which is by definition dynamic. Thus the comparative advantage tale is particularly pernicious when preached to developing countries, consigning many to "specialize" in agricultural goods or be forced into a race to the bottom where cheap sweatshop labor is their sole source of competitiveness.

The irony, of course, is that none of the rich countries got that way by following the maxim that they now preach. These countries historically relied on tariff walls and other forms of protectionism to build their industrial base. And even now, they continue to protect sectors like agriculture with subsidies. The countries now touted as new models of the benefits of free trade—South Korea and the other "Asian tigers," for instance— actually flouted this economic wisdom, nurturing their technological capabilities in specific manufacturing sectors and taking advantage of their lower wage costs to *gradually* become effective competitors of the United States and Europe in manufacturing.

The fundamental point is this: contrary to the comparative-advantage claim that trade is universally beneficial, nations as a whole do not prosper from free trade. Free trade creates winners and losers, both within and between countries. In today's context it is the global corporate giants that are propelling and profiting from "free trade": not only outsourcing white-collar jobs, but creating global commodity chains linking sweatshop labor in the developing countries of Latin America and Asia (Africa being largely left out of the game aside from the export of natural resources such as oil) with ever-more insecure consumers in the developed world. Promoting "free trade" as a political cause enables this process to continue.

It is a process with real human costs in terms of both wages and work. People in developing countries across the globe continue to face these costs as trade liberalization measures are enforced; and the working class in the United States is also being forced to bear the brunt of the relentless logic of competition. ❑

Sources: Arthur MacEwan, "The Gospel of Free Trade: The New Evangelists," *Dollars & Sense*, July/August 2002; Ha-Joon Chang, *Kicking Away the Ladder: The Real History of Fair Trade*, Foreign Policy in Focus, 2003; Anwar Shaikh, "Globalization and the Myths of Free Trade," in *Globalization and the Myths of Free Trade: History, Theory, and Empirical Evidence*, ed. Anwar Shaikh, Routledge 2007.

Article 3.3

DO TRADE AGREEMENTS FORECLOSE PROGRESSIVE POLICY?

BY ARTHUR MacEWAN
May/June 2016

Dear Dr. Dollar:

Doesn't the increasing liberalization of U.S. international economic policies foreclose the possibilities for progressive policies in this country? Don't these policies undercut the effectiveness of fiscal policy efforts to stimulate employment and output? And don't they virtually rule out many progressive reforms, such as a single payer health care system or new environmental regulations?
—*Anonymous, by voicemail*

The simple answer to this set of questions is: yes and no. But let's step back for a minute.

From the North American Free Trade Agreement (NAFTA), adopted in the early 1990s, to the Trans-Pacific Partnership (TPP) and the Transatlantic Trade and Investment Partnership (TTIP) being advanced today, criticism has focused on the negative impacts of these agreements on employment in many U.S. industries. These negative impacts are real and are one factor contributing to the decline of manufacturing in the United States, to the stagnation of wages, and to the hollowing out of the "middle class."

Yet, another impact of these agreements generally gets ignored—namely their negative impacts on progressive economic and social policies. Here too the impacts are real, but they are not absolute.

Take the issue of fiscal stimulus—that is, when the government runs a budget deficit, spending more to increase output and create jobs than it is taking in as taxes. In 1970, imports of goods and services were only 6.3% as large as GDP, but in 2014, imports were equal to 18.2% of GDP. This implies that in the earlier era, of a dollar spent on goods and services in general, only 6.3% would go towards imports. Today, as liberalization of trade has brought about the larger role for imports in GDP, a much larger share would go for the stimulation of jobs and output abroad. That is, the impact would in part "leak" out of the U.S. economy.

However, stimulus spending need not be spending "in general." If the government focused its spending on physical infrastructure (roads, bridges, public transport systems) and early childhood education, for example, less of the impact would "leak" out of the country. And certainly there are great needs for spending on infrastructure and early childhood education. (There would still be "leakage" in the later rounds of spending, as those who received the government funds—for example, construction companies and workers, preschools and early-childhood teachers—spent what they had received.)

To an extent, the American Recovery and Reinvestment Act of 2009 (ARRA) did focus spending on infrastructure investment. And, while there is controversy regarding its impact, it did seem to have a positive, though limited impact (it wasn't big enough) in contributing to the recovery from the severe recession of 2007–2008.

The constraints that the decades of liberalization of U.S. international economic activity places on social programs is related to investment, not trade. Various agreements—like NAFTA, TPP, and TTIP—incorporate provisions that derive from the General Agreement on Trade in Services (GATS), a treaty of the World Trade Organization (WTO) that came into force in 1995. These agreements allow firms from outside a country to sue the government of that country if it imposes "over-burdensome" regulations or policies that undermine the firm's profits. (See Robin Broad, "Remembering the 'Tokyo No': Fifty Years Later," pp. 327-329)

For example, a mining firm based in one country could sue the government of another county in which it is operating if environmental protection regulations are put in place that harm the firm's profits. Or, for a second example, a private health care firm based abroad could sue if the establishment of a single-payer health care system were established in the United States, harming the firm's profits. The threat of such suits could deter the government form implementing these sorts of programs. It might seem, then, that the government's hands would be tied, preventing the enactment of progressive programs.

But let's not forget what government we are talking about here. These profit-protecting provisions of the WTO and particular international economic agreements have been largely the creation of the world's most powerful government—i.e., the U.S. government. If the U.S. government wanted to change those provisions—that is, if it wanted to clear the way for progressive programs—it would not have great problems in doing so. If it is not unrealistic to believe that a U.S. government would want to create a single-payer health care system or a strong set of environmental

NAFTA, UPS, and Canada: It's All about Money

In 2000, under provisions in NAFTA, the U.S. courier company UPS sued Canada Post (Canada's public postal service), claiming $230 million in lost profits. UPS argued that Canada Post had an unfair advantage because it used the public postal system to support its own courier business. In 2007, UPS finally lost its suit, leading the president of Canada Post to comment: "This dispute was all about money. The United Parcel Service of America is attempting to force postal administrations around the world out of the parcel and courier business in order to increase their market share."

Source: "Canada Post claims victory at NAFTA over UPS," CBC News, Jan. 13, 2007 (cbc.ca).

protection regulations, it is not unrealistic to believe that it could also abrogate or get around those profit-protecting provisions.

The example described in the box shows the real threat to public services that is created by the provisions in trade agreements. It also shows how in a relatively rich country—Canada in this case—with the resources and expertise to fight such a threat, a government can prevail. The situation of less-powerful, low-income countries is very different.

So, yes, the liberalization of U.S. international commerce does create constraints on progressive economic policies and social programs. But, no, these constraints are by no means absolute. Ultimately, the constraints are political, not technical constraints of economic agreements. ❏

Sources: "The Trans-Pacific Partnership clause everyone should oppose," Elizabeth Warren, *Washington Post*, February 25, 2015 (washingtonpost.com); "The Economic Impact of the American Recovery and Reinvestment Act Five Years Later," Final Report to Congress, Executive Office of the President, Council of Economic Advisers, February 2014 (whitehouse.gov).

Article 3.4

OUTSIZED OFFSHORE OUTSOURCING

The scope of offshore outsourcing gives some economists and the business press the heebie-jeebies.

BY JOHN MILLER
September/October 2007

At a press conference introducing the 2004 *Economic Report of the President*, N. Gregory Mankiw, then head of President Bush's Council of Economic Advisors, assured the press that "Outsourcing is probably a plus for the economy in the long run [and] just a new way of doing international trade."

Mankiw's comments were nothing other than mainstream economics, as even Democratic Party-linked economists confirmed. For instance Janet Yellen, President Clinton's chief economist, told the *Wall Street Journal*, "In the long run, outsourcing is another form of trade that benefits the U.S. economy by giving us cheaper ways to do things." Nonetheless, Mankiw's assurances were met with derision from those uninitiated in the economics profession's free-market ideology. Sen. John Edwards (D-N.C.) asked, "What planet do they live on?" Even Republican House Speaker Dennis Hastert (Ill.) said that Mankiw's theory "fails a basic test of real economics."

Mankiw now jokes that "if the American Economic Association were to give an award for the Most Politically Inept Paraphrasing of Adam Smith, I would be a leading candidate." But he quickly adds, "the recent furor about outsourcing, and my injudiciously worded comments about the benefits of international trade, should not eclipse the basic lessons that economists have understood for more than two centuries."

In fact Adam Smith never said any such thing about international trade. In response to the way Mankiw and other economists distort Smith's writings, economist Michael Meeropol took a close look at what Smith actually said; he found that Smith used his invisible hand argument to favor domestic investment over far-flung, hard-to-supervise foreign investments. Here are Smith's words in his 1776 masterpiece, *The Wealth of Nations*:

> By preferring the support of domestic to that of foreign industry, he [the investor] intends only his own security; and by directing that industry in such a manner as its produce may be of the greatest value, he intends only his own gain, and he is in this, as in many other cases, led by an invisible hand to promote an end, which was no part of his intention.

Outsized offshore outsourcing, the shipping of jobs overseas to take advantage of low wages, has forced some mainstream economists and some elements of the business press to have second thoughts about "free trade." Many are convinced that the painful transition costs that hit before outsourcing produces any ultimate benefits may be the biggest political issue in economics for a generation. And some recognize, as Smith did, that there is no guarantee unfettered international trade will leave the participants better off even in the long run.

Keynes's Revenge

Writing during the Great Depression of the 1930s, John Maynard Keynes, the pre-eminent economist of the twentieth century, prescribed government spending as a means of compensating for the instability of private investment. The notion of a mixed private/government economy, Keynes's prosthesis for the invisible hand of the market, guided U.S. economic policy from the 1940s through the 1970s.

It is only fitting that Paul Samuelson, the first Nobel Laureate in economics, and whose textbook introduced U.S. readers to Keynes, would be among the first mainstream economist to question whether unfettered international trade, in the context of massive outsourcing, would necessarily leave a developed economy such as that of the United States better off—even in the long run. In an influential 2004 article, Samuelson characterized the common economics wisdom about outsourcing and international trade this way:

> Yes, good jobs may be lost here in the short run. But ...the gains of the winners from free trade, properly measured, work out to exceed the losses of the losers. ... Never forget to tally the real gains of consumers alongside admitted possible losses of some producers. ... The gains of the American winners are big enough to more than compensate the losers.

Samuelson took on this view, arguing that this common wisdom is "dead wrong about [the] *necessary* surplus of winning over losing" [emphasis in the original]. In a rather technical paper, he demonstrated that free trade globalization can sometimes give rise to a situation in which "a productivity gain in one country can benefit that

---

Offshored? Outsourced? Confused?

The terms "offshoring" and "outsourcing" are often used interchangeably, but they refer to distinct processes:

Outsourcing—When a company hires another company to carry out a business function that it no longer wants to carry on in-house. The company that is hired may be in the same city or across the globe; it may be a historically independent firm or a spinoff of the first company created specifically to outsource a particular function.

Offshoring or *Offshore Outsourcing*—When a company shifts a portion of its business operation abroad. An offshore operation may be carried out by the same company or, more typically, outsourced to a different one.

country alone, while permanently hurting the other country by reducing the gains from trade that are possible between the two countries."

Many in the economics profession do admit that it is hard to gauge whether intensified offshoring of U.S. jobs in the context of free-trade globalization will give more in winnings to the winners than it takes in losses from the losers. "Nobody has a clue about what the numbers are," as Robert C. Feenstra, a prominent trade economist, told *BusinessWeek* at the time.

The empirical issues that will determine whether offshore outsourcing ultimately delivers, on balance, more benefits than costs, and to whom those benefits and costs will accrue, are myriad. First, how wide a swath of white-collar workers will see their wages reduced by competition from the cheap, highly skilled workers who are now becoming available around the world? Second, by how much will their wages drop? Third, will the U.S. workers thrown into the global labor pool end up losing more in lower wages than they gain in lower consumer prices? In that case, the benefits of increased trade would go overwhelmingly to employers. But even employers might lose out depending on the answer to a fourth question: Will cheap labor from abroad allow foreign employers to out-compete U.S. employers, driving down the prices of their products and lowering U.S. export earnings? In that case, not only workers, but the corporations that employ them as well, could end up worse off.

Bigger Than A Box

Another mainstream Keynesian economist, Alan Blinder, former Clinton economic advisor and vice-chair of the Federal Reserve Board, doubts that outsourcing will be "immiserating" in the long run and still calls himself "a free-trader down to his toes." But Blinder is convinced that the transition costs will be large, lengthy, and painful before the United States experiences a net gain from outsourcing. Here is why.

First, rapid improvements in information and communications technology have rendered obsolete the traditional notion that manufactured goods, which can generally be boxed and shipped, are tradable, while services, which cannot be boxed, are not. And the workers who perform the services that computers and satellites have now rendered tradable will increasingly be found offshore, especially when they are skilled and will work for lower wages.

Second, another 1.5 billion or so workers—many in China, India, and the former Soviet bloc—are now part of the world economy. While most are low-skilled workers, some are not; and as Blinder says, a small percentage of 1.5 billion is nonetheless "a lot of willing and able people available to do the jobs that technology will move offshore." And as China and India educate more workers, offshoring of high-skill work will accelerate.

Third, the transition will be particularly painful in the United States because the U.S. unemployment insurance program is stingy, at least by first-world standards, and because U.S. workers who lose their jobs often lose their health insurance and pension rights as well.

How large will the transition cost be? "Thirty million to 40 million U.S. jobs are potentially offshorable," according to Blinder's latest estimates. "These include scientists, mathematicians and editors on the high end and telephone operators, clerks and typists on the low end."

Blinder arrived at these figures by creating an index that identifies how easy or hard it will be for a job to be physically or electronically "offshored." He then used the index to assess the Bureau of Labor Statistics' 817 U.S. occupational categories. Not surprisingly, Blinder classifies almost all of the 14.3 million U.S. manufacturing jobs as offshorable. But he also classifies more than twice that many U.S. service sector jobs as offshorable, including most computer industry jobs as well as many others, for instance, the 12,470 U.S. economists and the 23,790 U.S. multimedia artists and animators. In total, Blinder's analysis suggests that 22% to 29% of the jobs held by U.S. workers in 2004 will be potentially offshorable within a decade or two, with nearly 8.2 million jobs in 59 occupations "highly offshorable."

Mankiw dismissed Blinder's estimates of the number of jobs at risk to offshoring as "out of the mainstream." Indeed, Blinder's estimates are considerably larger than earlier ones. But these earlier studies either aim to measure the number of U.S. jobs that will be outsourced (as opposed to the number at risk of being outsourced), look at a shorter period of time, or have shortcomings that suggest they underestimate the number of U.S. jobs threatened by outsourcing.

Global Arbitrage

Low wages are the reason U.S. corporations outsource labor. Computer programmers in the United States make wages nearly *ten times* those of their counterparts in India and the Philippines, for example. Today, more and more white-collar workers in the United States are finding themselves in direct competition with the low-cost, well-trained, highly educated workers in Bangalore, Shanghai, and Eastern and Central Europe. These workers often use the same capital and technology and are no less productive than the U.S. workers they replace. They just get paid less.

This global labor arbitrage, as Morgan Stanley's chief economist Stephen Roach calls it, has narrowed international wage disparities in manufacturing, and now in services too, by unrelentingly pushing U.S. wages down toward international norms. ("Arbitrage" refers to transactions that yield a profit by taking advantage of a price differential for the same asset in different locations. Here, of course, the "asset" is wage labor of a certain skill level.) A sign of that pressure: about 70% of laid-off workers in the United States earn less three years later than they did at the time of the layoff; on average, those reemployed earn 10% less than they did before.

And it's not only laid-off workers who are hurt. A study conducted by Harvard labor economists Lawrence F. Katz, Richard B. Freeman, and George J. Borjas finds that every other worker with skills similar to those who were displaced also loses out. Every 1% drop in employment due to imports or factories gone abroad shaves 0.5% off the wages of the remaining workers in that occupation, they conclude.

Global labor arbitrage also goes a long way toward explaining the poor quality and low pay of the jobs the U.S. economy has created this decade, according to Roach. By dampening wage increases for an ever wider swath of the U.S. workforce, he argues, outsourcing has helped to drive a wedge between productivity gains and wage gains and to widen inequality in the United States. In the first four years of this decade, nonfarm productivity in the United States has recorded a cumulative increase of 13.3%—more than double the 5.9% rise in real compensation per hour over the same period. ("Compensation" includes wages, which have been stagnant for the average worker, plus employer spending on fringe benefits such as health insurance, which has risen even as, in many instances, the actual benefits have been cut back.) Roach reports that the disconnect between pay and productivity growth during the current economic expansion has been much greater in services than in manufacturing, as that sector weathers the powerful forces of global labor arbitrage for the first time.

Doubts in the Business Press?!

Even in the business press, doubts that offshore outsourcing willy-nilly leads to economic improvement have become more acute. Earlier this summer, a *BusinessWeek* cover story, "The Real Cost of Offshoring," reported that government statistics have underestimated the damage to the U.S. economy from offshore outsourcing. The problem is that since offshoring took off, *import* growth, adjusted for inflation, has been faster than the official numbers show. That means improvements in living standards, as well as corporate profits, depend more on cheap imports, and less on improving domestic productivity, than analysts thought.

Growing angst about outsourcing's costs has also prompted the business press to report favorably on remedies for the dislocation brought on by offshoring that deviate substantially from the non-interventionist, free-market playbook. Even the most unfazed pro-globalization types want to beef up trade adjustment assistance for displaced workers and strengthen the U.S. educational system. But both proposals are inadequate.

More education, the usual U.S. prescription for any economic problem, is off the mark here. Cheaper labor is available abroad up and down the job-skill ladder, so even the most rigorous education is no inoculation against the threat of offshore outsourcing. As Blinder emphasizes, it is the need for face-to-face contact that stops jobs from being shipped overseas, not the level of education necessary to perform them. Twenty years from now, home health aide positions will no doubt be plentiful in the United States; jobs for highly trained IT professionals may be scarce.

Trade adjustment assistance has until now been narrowly targeted at workers hurt by imports. Most new proposals would replace traditional trade adjustment assistance and unemployment insurance with a program for displaced workers that offers wage insurance to ease the pain of taking a lower-paying job and provides for portable health insurance and retraining. The pro-globalization research group McKinsey Global Institute (MGI), for example, claims that for as little as 4% to 5% of the amount they've saved in lower wages, companies could cover the wage losses of all laid-off workers once they are reemployed, paying them 70% of the wage differential between their old and new jobs (in addition to health care subsidies) for up to two years.

While MGI confidently concludes that this proposal will "go a long way toward relieving the current anxieties," other globalization advocates are not so sure. They recognize that economic anxiety is pervasive and that millions of white-collar workers now fear losing their jobs. Moreover, even if fears of actual job loss are overblown, wage insurance schemes do little to compensate for the downward pressure offshoring is putting on the wages of workers who have not been laid off.

Other mainstream economists and business writers go even further, calling for not only wage insurance but also taxes on the winners from globalization. And globalization has produced big winners: on Wall Street, in the corporate boardroom, and among those workers in high demand in the global economy.

Economist Matthew Slaughter, who recently left President Bush's Council of Economic Advisers, told the *Wall Street Journal*, "Expanding the political support for open borders [for trade] requres making a radical change in fiscal policy." He proposes eliminating the Social Security-Medicare payroll tax on the bottom half of workers—roughly, those earning less than $33,000 a year—and making up the lost revenue by raising the payroll tax on higher earners.

The goal of these economists is to thwart a crippling political backlash against trade. As they see it, "using the tax code to slice the apple more evenly is far more palatable than trying to hold back globalization with policies that risk shrinking the economic apple."

Some even call for extending global labor arbitrage to CEOs. In a June 2006 *New York Times* op-ed, equity analyst Lawrence Orlowski and New York University assistant research director Florian Lengyel argued that offshoring the jobs of U.S. chief executives would reduce costs and release value to shareholders by bringing the compensation of U.S. CEOs (on average 170 times greater than the compensation of average U.S. workers in 2004) in line with CEO compensation in Britain (22 times greater) and in Japan (11 times greater).

Yet others focus on the stunning lack of labor mobility that distinguishes the current era of globalization from earlier ones. Labor markets are becoming increasingly free and flexible under globalization, but labor enjoys no similar freedom of movement. In a completely free market, the foreign workers would come here to do the work that is currently being outsourced. Why aren't more of those workers coming to the United States? Traditional economists Gary Becker and Richard Posner argue the answer is clear: an excessively restrictive immigration policy.

Onshore and Offshore Solidarity

Offshoring is one of the last steps in capitalism's conversion of the "physician, the lawyer, the priest, the poet, the man of science, into its paid wage laborers," as Marx and Engels put it in the *Communist Manifesto* 160 years ago. It has already done much to increase economic insecurity in the workaday world and has become, Blinder suggests, the number one economic issue of our generation.

Offshoring has also underlined the interdependence of workers across the globe. To the extent that corporations now organize their business operations on a global scale, shifting work around the world in search of low wages, labor organizing must also be global in scope if it is to have any hope of building workers' negotiating strength.

Yet today's global labor arbitrage pits workers from different countries against each other as competitors, not allies. Writing about how to improve labor standards, economists Ajit Singh and Ann Zammit of the South Centre, an Indian non-governmental organization, ask the question, "On what could workers of the world unite" today? Their answer is that faster economic growth could indeed be a positive-sum game from which both the global North and the global South could gain. A pick-up in the long-term rate of growth of the world economy would generate higher employment, increasing wages and otherwise improving labor standards in both regions. It should also make offshoring less profitable and less painful.

The concerns of workers across the globe would also be served by curtailing the ability of multinational corporations to move their investment anywhere, which weakens the bargaining power of labor both in advanced countries and in the global South. Workers globally would also benefit if their own ability to move between countries was enhanced. The combination of a new set of rules to limit international capital movements and to expand labor mobility across borders, together with measures to ratchet up economic growth and thus increase worldwide demand for labor, would alter the current process of globalization and harness it to the needs of working people worldwide. ❑

Sources: Alan S. Blinder, "Fear of Offshoring," CEPS Working Paper #119, Dec. 2005; Alan S. Blinder, "How Many U.S. Jobs Might Be Offshorable?" CEPS Working Paper #142, March 2007; N. Gregory Mankiw and P. Swagel, "The Politics and Economics of Offshore Outsourcing," Am. Enterprise Inst. Working Paper #122, 12/7/05; "Offshoring: Is It a Win-Win Game?" McKinsey Global Institute, August 2003; Diane Farrell et al., "The Emerging Global Labor Market, Part 1: The Demand for Talent in Services," McKinsey Global Institute, June 2005; Ashok Bardhan and Cynthia Kroll, "The New Wave of Outsourcing," Research Report #113, Fisher Center for Real Estate and Urban Economics, Univ. of Calif., Berkeley, Fall 2003; Paul A. Samuelson, "Where Ricardo and Mill Rebut and Confirm Arguments of Mainstream Economists Supporting Globalization," *J Econ Perspectives* 18:3, Summer 2004; Alan S. Blinder, "Free Trade's Great, but Offshoring Rattles Me," *Wash. Post,* 5/6/07; Michael Mandel, "The Real Cost of Offshoring," *BusinessWeek,* 6/18/07; Aaron Bernstein, "Shaking Up Trade Theory," *BusinessWeek,* 12/6/04; David Wessel, "The Case for Taxing Globalization's Big Winners," *WSJ,* 6/14/07; Bob Davis, "Some Democratic Economists Echo Mankiw on Outsourcing," *WSJ;* N. Gregory Mankiw, "Outsourcing Redux," gregmankiw.blogspot.com/2006/05/outsourcing-redux; David Wessel and Bob Davis, "Pain From Free Trade Spurs Second Thoughts," *WSJ,* 3/30/07; Ajit Singh and Ann Zammit, "On What Could Workers of the World Unite? Economic Growth and a New Global Economic Order," from *The Global Labour Standards Controversy: Critical Issues For Developing Countries,* South Centre, 2000; Michael Meeropol, "Distorting Adam Smith on Trade," *Challenge,* July/Aug 2004.

Article 3.5

INADVERTENT PRAISE FOR CHINA

BY MARK WEISBROT

September 2016; The Hill

President Obama's speech at the UN last week was mostly a defense of the world's economic and political status quo, especially that part of it that is led or held in place by the U.S. government and the global institutions that Washington controls or dominates. In doing so, he said some things that were exaggerated or wrong, or somewhat misleading. It is worth looking at some of the things that media reports on this speech missed.

"Over the last 25 years, the number of people living in extreme poverty has been cut from nearly 40 percent of humanity to under 10 percent." This is roughly true, according to World Bank data, but the story of how it happened goes against his whole speech—which argues that this progress is a result of the "globalization" that Washington leads and supports wherever it has influence in the developing world. In fact, the majority of the reduction in extreme poverty during this period (more than 1.1 billion people worldwide) took place in China. But during this period China was really the counterexample to the "principles of open markets" with which Obama insists "we must go forward, not backward."

China's historically unprecedented economic growth in the past 25 years (or 35 years, or even more) was accomplished with state-owned enterprises and banks dominating the economy. State control over investment, technology transfer, and foreign exchange was vastly greater than in other developing countries. China rejected the neoliberal policies of an "independent central bank," indiscriminate opening to international trade and investment, and rapid privatization of state companies. Instead, it chose a gradual transition, over 35 years, from an overwhelmingly planned economy to a mixed economy in which the state still plays a leading role. Even today, China expanded the investment of state-owned enterprises by 23.5 percent in the first six months of 2016 (as compared to the same period in 2015), to help boost the economy.

If we go back a bit more and look at 1981-2012, China accounted for even more of the reduction of the world population in extreme poverty, about 70 percent. This would indicate that other parts of the developing world increased their economic and social progress during the 21st century, relative to China, and indeed many developing countries did (as compared to the last two decades of the 20th century). But China played an increasingly large role in reducing poverty in other countries during this period. It was so successful in its economic growth and development—by far the fastest in world history—that it became the largest economy in the world, and pulled up many developing countries through its imports. Chinese imports went from a negligible 0.1 percent of other developing countries' exports to

3 percent, from 1980-2010. China also provided hundreds of billions of dollars in investment, loans, and aid to low- and middle-income countries in the 21st century. (In the last few years, Chinese growth has slowed, along with that of most countries, and that has contributed—although perhaps not as much as Europe has—to the global slowdown since 2011.)

Of course, the "principles of open markets" that Obama refers to is really code for "policies that Washington supports." Some of them are the exact opposite of "open markets," such as the lengthening and strengthening of patent and copyright protection included in the Trans-Pacific Partnership (TPP) agreement. President Obama also made a plug for the TPP in his speech, asserting that "we've worked to reach trade agreements that raise labor standards and raise environmental standards, as we've done with the Trans-Pacific Partnership, so that the benefits [of globalization] are more broadly shared." But the labor and environmental standards in the TPP, as with those in previous U.S.-led commercial agreements, are not enforceable; whereas if a government approves laws or regulations that infringe on the future profit potential of a multinational corporation—even if such laws or regulations are to protect public health or safety—that government can be hit with billions of dollars in fines. And they must pay these fines, or be subject to trade sanctions.

In his defense of a world economic order ruled by Washington and its rich country allies, President Obama also asserted that "we have made international institutions like the World Bank and the International Monetary Fund more representative." But that is a gross exaggeration: the most recent reform of IMF voting shares left the United States with an unchanged 16.7 percent share, enough to veto many important decisions (that require an 85 percent majority) by itself; and it left Washington and its traditional rich-country allies with a solid majority of more than 60 percent of votes. Of course, it is the developing countries, especially poorer ones, that are most subject to IMF decisions. But the IMF is—by a gentleman's agreement among the rich country governments—headed by a European, and the World Bank by an American. It should not be surprising if these institutions do not look out for the interests of the developing world.

"We can choose to press forward with a better model of cooperation and integration," President Obama told the world at the UN General Assembly. "Or we can retreat into a world sharply divided, and ultimately in conflict, along age-old lines of nation and tribe and race and religion."

But the rich country governments led by Washington are not offering the rest of the world any better model of cooperation and integration than the failed model they have been offering for the past 35 years. And that is a big part of the problem. But fortunately, their influence is diminishing. ❑

Article 3.6

THE "TRADE DEAL" SCAM

BY DEAN BAKER
June 2013; Truthout

As part of its overall economic strategy, the Obama administration is rushing full speed ahead with two major trade deals. On the one hand, it has the Trans-Pacific Partnership, which includes Japan and Australia and several other countries in East Asia and Latin America. On the other side, there is an effort to craft a U.S.-EU trade agreement.

There are two key facts people should know about these proposed trade deals. First, they are mostly not about trade. Second, they are not intended to boost the economy in a way that will help most of us. In fact, it is reasonable to say that these deals will likely be bad news for most people in the United States. Most of the people living in our partner countries are likely to be losers too.

On the first point, traditional trade issues, like the reduction of import tariffs and quotas, are a relatively small part of both deals. This is the case because these barriers have already been sharply reduced or even eliminated over the past three decades.

As a result, with a few notable exceptions, there is little room for further reductions in these sorts of barriers. Instead both deals focus on other issues, some of which may reasonably be considered barriers to trade, but many of which are matters of regulation that would ordinarily be left to national, regional, or even local levels of government to set for themselves. One purpose of locking regulatory rules into a trade deal is to push an agenda that favors certain interests (e.g., the large corporations who are at the center of the negotiating process) over the rest of society.

Both of these deals are likely to include restrictions on the sorts of health, safety, and environmental regulations that can be imposed by the countries that are parties to the agreements. While many of the regulations that are currently in place in these areas are far from perfect, there is not an obvious case for having them decided at the international level.

Suppose a country or region decides that the health risks posed by a particular pesticide are too great and therefore bans its use. If the risks are in fact small, then those imposing the ban will be the primary ones who suffer, presumably in the form of less productive agriculture and higher food prices. Is it necessary to have an international agreement to prevent this sort of "mistake"?

As a practical matter, the evidence on such issues will often be ambiguous. For example, does the natural-gas extraction technique of hydraulic fracturing (better known as "fracking") pose a health hazard to the surrounding communities? These agreements could end up taking control of the decision as to whether or not to allow fracking away from the communities who would be most affected.

In addition to limiting local control in many areas, these trade deals will almost certainly include provisions that make for stronger and longer copyright and patent protection, especially on prescription drugs. The latter is coming at the urging of the U.S. pharmaceutical industry, which has been a central player in all the trade agreements negotiated over the last quarter century. This is likely to mean much higher drug prices for our trading partners.

This is, of course, the opposite of free trade. Instead of reducing barriers, the drug companies want to increase them, banning competitors from selling the same drugs. The difference in prices can be quite large. Generic drugs, with few exceptions, are cheap to produce. When drugs sell for hundreds or thousands of dollars per prescription, it is because patent monopolies allow them to be sold for high prices.

If these trade deals result in much higher drug prices for our trading partners, the concern should not just be a moral one about people being unable to afford drugs. The more money people in Vietnam or Malaysia have to pay Pfizer and Merck for their drugs, the less money they will have to spend on other exports from the United States. This means that everyone from manufacturing workers to workers in the tourist sector can expect to see fewer job opportunities because of the copyright and patent protection rules imposed through these trade deals.

To see this point, imagine someone operating a fruit stand in a farmers' market. If the person in the next stall selling meat has a clever way to short-change customers, then his scam will come at least partly at the expense of the fruit stand. The reason is that many potential fruit stand customers will have their wallets drained at the meat stand and won't have any money left to buy fruit.

The drug companies' efforts to get increased patent protection, along with the computer and entertainment industries efforts to get stronger copyright protection, will have the same effect. Insofar as they can force other countries to pay them more in royalties and licensing fees or directly for their products, these countries will have less money to spend on other goods and services produced in the United States. In other words, the short-change artist in the next stall is not our friend and neither are the pharmaceutical, computer, or entertainment industries.

However, these industries all have friends in the Obama administration. As a result, these trade deals are likely to give them the protections they want. The public may not have the power to stop the high-powered lobbyists from getting their way on these trade pacts, but it should at least know what is going on. These trade deals are about pulling more money out of their pockets in order to make the rich even richer. ❑

Chapter 4

INTERNATIONAL FINANCE

Article 4.1

LESSONS FROM ICELAND'S FINANCIAL CRISIS

BY NINA EICHACKER
March/April 2016

In a span of just three days in 2008—between October 7 and October 9—Iceland's three largest banks, Landsbanki, Glitnir, and Kaupthing, all failed. The banks' debts amounted to over 15 times Iceland's GDP at the time. Iceland residents, British and Dutch account holders, bank shareholders, and, soon, the rest of the world learned that those banks were completely insolvent, and that the Icelandic government could not afford to bail them out (at an estimated price tag of $300 billion).

Following these events, the people of Iceland began the "Kitchenware Revolution," gathering in front of parliament while banging pots and pans. They successfully demanded the resignation of the ruling right-wing Independence Party, which had implemented the financial deregulation that had led to the implosion of Iceland's financial system. In addition, they laid the groundwork for the rejection in a national referendum of the next government's plan to pay loan guarantees, for one of the country's three big banks, to the governments of the UK and the Netherlands. In December 2008, the Icelandic government created the Special Inquiry Commission, which produced an exhaustive report of the causes and consequences of the financial crisis. The government authorized a special prosecutor to investigate and bring charges against guilty parties—including prominent political figures such as the former minister of finance, financial figures including the president and CEO of Glitnir, the president and chairman of Kaupthing, and the president and managing director of Landsbanki.

The crisis, years in the making, was a consequence of the Icelandic government's rapid deregulation and privatization of Iceland's banking system back in the 1990s and early 2000s, and of the banks' embrace of large-scale and risk-heavy investment banking. With little or no supervision, and relying on the widespread belief globally in the integrity of Iceland's government and financial system, bankers got away with murder—until the fall of the U.S. investment bank Lehman Brothers in 2008, after which Iceland's banks could no longer rely on cheap and easy credit from U.S. investment banks.

Foreseeable, But Not Foreseen

Policymakers, academics, and business reporters should have seen it coming. By 2006, Icelandic banking and economic data described an overheating financial sector and overall economy. Foreign banks' lending to Iceland increased from just over 50% of Icelandic GDP in 1999 to nearly 80% in 2003 to over 400% in 2007. Icelandic credit intermediation—the share of loans held by financial corporations compared to borrowing by non-financial firms, the general government, households, and non-profits—also increased in this period, from 64% in 2004 to 80% in 2007. This trend of a rapidly growing financial sector relative to the "real" sector of the economy was by no means unique to Iceland, but the scale was. Financial firms' debt rose from less than four times Iceland's GDP in 2003, to over nine times in 2007, to over 15 times in 2008. The net negative financial worth of Iceland's financial corporations rose from 4% of GDP in 2003, to 147% in 2007, to 649% in 2008.

Economist Anne Sibert and finance expert Gudrun Johnsen have written about "love-letters"—debt securities issued by Icelandic banks and then used as collateral for borrowing from other Icelandic banks, the Central Bank of Iceland, and even the European Central Bank. Icelandic banks' developed this fraudulent practice as they found it more difficult to borrow in global capital markets from 2006 onward. Economist and former banking regulator William K. Black has argued that the rapid acceleration of the banks' debts just before the collapse of Iceland's banking system was the result, not of desperate attempts to resurrect the banks, but of fraud: bank officers were trying to loot as much money as possible while they still could. In the years that Icelandic banks engaged in these practices, Frederic Mishkin (Columbia University), Richard Portes (London Business School), and Fridrik Baldursson (Reykjavik University) all wrote reports celebrating the integrity of the Icelandic financial system.

Perhaps as a consequence of these reports, top Icelandic officials, like the then prime minister and head of the central bank, were still surprised by the onset of the country's financial crisis, as were reporters with major media outlets like the *New York Times*, *Fortune*, and *BusinessWeek*. Top economists who had promoted the Icelandic strategy of financial deregulation, like Arthur Laffer (formerly economic advisor in the Reagan administration), Mishkin, Portes, and Baldursson were quiet in the immediate aftermath.

These events point to the dominance of neoliberal theories about the necessity of financial deregulation, and an assumption that a northern European country would have the institutional sophistication to avoid financial crises like those observed in developing countries that had rapidly deregulated. Neoclassical economists with outsize faith in the efficiency of financial markets and integrity of the Icelandic state believed that little could go wrong in Iceland—the crisis in October of 2008 proved otherwise. A wider understanding of the theories of economists John Maynard Keynes and Hyman Minsky would have helped policymakers and other observers foresee Iceland's crisis, and to prevent future such episodes. Keynes and Minsky understood—as Icelandic government officials, academic economists, and the financial press did not—that financial actors will engage in risky behavior in the pursuit of profits, making financial crises inevitable in the absence of regulation to prevent such behavior. Governments therefore must regulate financial sectors for the greater economic good.

Underproduction of Criticism, Overproduction of Praise

The lack of financial-market transparency was one integral reason that Iceland's crisis went unforeseen. Organizations that could have reported on the conditions of the Icelandic financial marketplace and the state of the Icelandic economy simply did not. The Icelandic state threatened to defund public institutions and agencies that published reports contradicting the narrative of a robust financial infrastructure and growth.

Iceland's Chamber of Commerce paid economists, like Columbia University's Mishkin, hundreds of thousands of dollars to write favorable reports—including one titled "Financial Stability in Iceland"—about the country's financial sector and overall economic growth prospects. Mishkin would later become infamous, in the documentary "Inside Job," for that report and for changing its title to "Financial Instability in Iceland" on his curriculum vitae after Iceland's collapse.

The Icelandic news media consistently underpublicized reports critical of the Icelandic financial sector, while publishing many stories that praised Iceland's big three banks. Iceland's center-right party historically had large ownership stakes in several Icelandic media companies; the shared interest of Iceland's right and center-right parties in promoting the financial sector explains some of the media's lack of coverage of financial malfeasance.

Another cause of this disparity was the cross-ownership of media company shares by Icelandic financial actors and institutions, and financial-corporation shares by Icelandic media institutions. The chair of the board of directors of Baugur Group, a large stakeholder in Kaupthing Bank, also owned 365—parent company of *Frettabladid*, Iceland's largest-circulation daily newspaper—as well as DV, another large media company. Björgólfur Guðmundsson, the former majority owner and chairman of Landsbanki, acquired Arvakur, the company that publishes *Morgunbladid*, the other major Icelandic newspaper, only to sell in 2009 after declaring bankruptcy. The interconnectedness of these industries created conflicts of interest for all involved.

Credit-rating agencies, meanwhile, also contributed to the notion that Iceland's financial markets were safer than they were. The sub-prime mortgage crisis of 2007 revealed a host of problems with how the three largest global credit-rating agencies—Moody's, Standard & Poor's, and Fitch—operate. It used to be that parties interested in investing in a particular class of assets paid for reports evaluating their riskiness.

Since the 1970s, however, the setup as shifted, to one in which institutions issuing securities paid for ratings. This gave the agencies an incentive to rate securities as safer than they were. In other words, it created huge conflicts of interest.

In 2007, Fitch, the smallest of the big three rating agencies, downgraded Iceland's credit rating on the basis of its overextension. But Moody's, one of the two bigger agencies, upgraded it, on the premise that Iceland was so financially leveraged that its central bank would, as the lender of last resort, bail out the big three banks. This move paradoxically increased broad confidence in Icelandic financial stability, despite the fact that the rationale for the improved rating was the excessive leverage of Iceland's financial sector. This further lulled international investors and retail banking customers into trusting Icelandic financial actors with their money and spurred still greater leverage and risky behavior. The feedback effects increased the scale of the financial system relative to the Icelandic economy as a whole, placed more and more actors throughout Iceland at risk in the likely event of failure, and increased the severity of the imminent collapse of Iceland's financial system.

In short, the underproduction of criticism and the overproduction of praise for Iceland's banks skewed public understanding of the country's financial sector.

Governments and International Institutions

The Icelandic Central Bank's decision to change from stability-promoting to inflation-targeting monetary policy led to rising interest rates, precipitous increases in capital inflows, and asset bubbles in the housing market.

Prior to the early 1990s, the Icelandic Central Bank had pursued economic stability above all else. It charged very low interest rates in order to promote lending to local banks, and to hedge against possible bank failures at the local level. Bank employees at all levels were compensated in ways that would not encourage risky behavior.

The shift to inflation-targeting monetary policy resulted in a rapid increase in Icelandic interest rates. Inflation targeting is designed to prevent an increase in the price level, typically through high interest rates, which make it more difficult for banks and other institutions to borrow. High interest rates, however, attracted capital flows from investors in the United States and Western Europe, two financial markets with low interest rates in the early 2000s. This, in turn, had the perverse consequence of raising the value of the Icelandic krona relative to other global currencies. As the krona grew stronger, Iceland's exports fell and its imports rose, leading to a large trade deficit. The financial inflows also provided Icelandic bankers with a ready source of funding for financial speculation. The government's promotion of non-financial firms' and households' purchase of shares in the banks created perverse incentives for them to raise share prices, and increased the scope of losses in the event of the banks' failure. Bank employees now had motivation to boost share prices by whatever means; households with little understanding of the activities of the banking sector would be increasingly vulnerable to the fate of the banks' performance.

Global financial institutions, meanwhile, seemed to forget that Argentina and Chile had liberalized their financial markets in the 1970s and 1980s with bad results: banks became more risk-taking, without becoming more efficient. Argentina's Central Bank offered guarantees on bank deposits, which encouraged more capital inflows. Though Chile's government initially stated that it would not insure deposits, its Central Bank ultimately guaranteed them after several panics early in the liberalization process. The big banks that had been privatized in the 1970s had to be re-nationalized during the crisis of the early 1980s, despite the "free market" views of the University of Chicago economists (or "Chicago Boys") who made economic policy for Chile's military dictatorship.

Foreign governments' economic and political pressure for governments and central banks to insure their investments guaranteed what economists call "moral hazard" problems: if businesses and banks trust that a government will bail them out in times of crisis, they will likely engage in riskier behavior, since they will profit more in the event of success, and not pay as much (or perhaps not pay anything) in the event of failure. Private financial institutions around the world, but particularly in Europe, trusted in Iceland's supposedly robust financial governance, despite Iceland's short history of financial liberalization. Many followed the advice of economists like Mishkin and Portes, who argued that Iceland should not be assumed to have the same financial risks as developing economies, despite the newness of its supercharged financial system. Outside investors' continued willingness to lend to Iceland increased the leveraged state of Icelandic banks and the scope of the eventual financial crisis.

Heading Off the Next Crisis

Iceland's crisis reveals the inherent instability created by rapid financialization. When a country deregulates banks, encourages international capital inflows, and promotes wide-scale acquisition of those financial institutions' securities (by households, non-financial firms, government, and other banks), financial firms appear to be artificially profitable. Conflicts of interest develop that weaken the stability of the financial sector and the economy as a whole.

Mainstream economists failed to recognize this. However, this was well understood by heterodox figures like Keynes and Minsky, who argued that financial systems without adequate regulatory apparatuses are inherently prone to crisis. A number of current scholars, absorbing the lessons of Keynes and Minsky, argued that Iceland's financial sector was due for a collapse given the changes that had occurred in banking practices and economic orientation of the country. These processes increased Icelandic instability and the costs of the inevitable crisis.

Irrational exuberance and moral hazard overcame the ample evidence that Iceland was dangerously over-leveraged. Investors had access to data demonstrating the risks of investing in Iceland's financial system and economy, yet turned headlong into the storm. National and international unwillingness to compare Iceland's policy actions and history to that of developing economies like Argentina and Chile reflected the faulty assumption that Icelandic institutions were ready for the job of supervising a radically transformed financial sector. The Icelandic government's repression of data demonstrating instability, and the Icelandic media's unwillingness to publish unflattering stories, gave the lie to the notion that western European states' financial institutions and governments were robust enough for highly liberalized financial sectors.

Iceland's crisis demonstrates the need for radically different policies: States and social movements must promote widespread financial literacy, so that ordinary people are aware of changes in the financial landscape and better able to protect themselves. If it is to be undertaken, financial deregulation, like cigarette packages, should come with large and impossible-to-miss warnings about its inherent dangers. These warnings should alert the public to the risks of purchasing large shares in globally active banks or other under-regulated financial products, and should warn less sophisticated financial intermediaries like pension funds about the riskiness of different financial assets. In Iceland, as in the United States, the financial system's default setting was to push households into excessive risk-taking; a public counterweight that prioritizes stability over risk would be valuable. "Nudges" encouraging safer approaches to personal wealth management—like insured deposits, defined-benefit retirement plans, and manageable mortgage loans—would still allow financially savvy or risk-loving individuals to engage in riskier transactions, while protecting the broader public. Stability-minded monetary policy is another means to ensuring greater financial and economic well-being. Greater regulatory vigilance against the excesses of financialization and shadow banking, too, would benefit most.

More broadly, given Iceland's experiences and those of other countries before it, states should reject financial deregulation and finance-led growth strategies. The costs of financialization, in the presence of moral hazard and irrational exuberance, expand rapidly in the absence of meaningful oversight. Iceland's experience illustrates this to the rest of the world. The country's policy responses to the crisis—starting with a systematic inquiry and prosecution of guilty bankers—also provide a worthy model for the world. Other countries would be wise to follow its example: The renationalization of banks that could have bankrupted the Icelandic government and central bank, implementation of capital controls (regulations on international capital flows) to stabilize an out-of-control financial system, and enforcement of new financial regulations to protect banks, firms, and households from the consequences of another financial bubble. ❏

Sources: Robert Aliber, "Monetary Turbulence and the Icelandic Economy," in Robert Aliber and Gylfi Zoega, eds., *Preludes to the Icelandic Financial Crisis* (Palgrave MacMillan, 2011); Anna Andersen, "The Watchdog That Didn't Bark," Reykjavik Grapevine, October 2010 (grapevine.is); Daniel Chartier, *The End of Iceland's Innocence: The Image of Iceland in the Foreign Media During the Financial Crisis* (University of Ottawa Press, 2011); V. Corbo and J. De Melo, "Lessons from the Southern Cone Policy Reforms." *The World Bank Research Observer*, 2(2), 1987; Jon Danielsson and Gylfi Zoega, "The Collapse of a Country," Working Paper 09:03, Institute of Economic Studies (hhi.hi.is); C. Diaz-Alejandro, "Good-Bye Financial Repression, Hello Financial Crash." *Journal of Development Economics*, 19(1), 1985; Gudrun Johnsen, Bringing Down the Banking System (Palgrave MacMillan, 2014); John Maynard Keynes, "National Self-Sufficiency," *The Yale Review* 22, 1933; Charles Kindleberger and Robert Aliber, *Manias, Panics, and Crashes: A History of Financial Crises* (Wiley, 2005); E. G. Mendoza and M.E. Terrones, *An Anatomy of Credit Booms and Their Demise* (No. w18379), National Bureau of Economic Research, 2012 (nber.org); Hyman Minsky, *Stabilizing An Unstable Economy* (McGraw-Hill, 2008); Hyman Minsky, "The Financial Instability Hypothesis," The Levy Institute, Working Paper No. 74, May 1992 (levyinstitute. org); Hyman Minsky, *Can 'It' Happen Again? Essays on Instability and Finance* (M.E. Sharpe, Inc., 1982); Frederic Mishkin and Tryggvi Herbertsson, "Financial Stability in Iceland," Iceland Chamber of Commerce Publication, 2006 (vi.is); F. S. Mishkin, *Inflation Targeting in Emerging Market Countries* (No. w7618), National Bureau of Economic Research (nber.org); D. Rodrik, "Growth Strategies," in P. Aghion and S.N. Durlauf, eds., *Handbook of Economic Growth*, Volume 1 (Elsevier, 2005); Throstur Sigurjonsson, "Privatization and Deregulation: A Chronology of Events," in Robert Aliber and Gylfi Zoega, eds., *Preludes to the Icelandic Financial Crisis* (Palgrave Macmillan, 2011); Robert Wade, "Iceland as Icarus," *Challenge* 52, 2009; Robert Wade and Silla Sigurgeirsdottir, "Lessons from Iceland," *New Left Review* 65, 2010; Robert Wade and Silla Sigurgeirsdottir, "Iceland's Rise, Fall, Stabilization, and Beyond," *Cambridge Journal of Economics* 36, 2011; Gylfi Zoega, "A Spending Spree," in Robert Aliber and Gylfi Zoega, eds., *Preludes to the Icelandic Financial Crisis* (Palgrave Macmillan, 2011).

Article 4.2

INFLATION TARGETING AND NEOLIBERALISM

BY GERALD EPSTEIN
May 2016

I n recent decades, central banks in both high-income ("developed") and lower-income ("developing") countries have turned increasingly towards "inflation targeting" monetary policy—the emphasis on very low inflation, to the exclusion of other policy objectives. In this interview, Gerald Epstein, a professor of economics at UMass-Amherst and a founding co-director of the Political Economy Research Institute (PERI) explains the causes behind the rise of inflation targeting, its effects in practice, and possible alternative approaches. —Eds.

Dollars & Sense: When we talk about central banks and monetary policy, what precisely is meant by the phrase "inflation targeting"? And how does that differ from other kinds of objectives that central banks might have?

Gerald Epstein: Inflation targeting is a relatively new but very widespread approach to central bank policy. It means that the central bank should target a rate of inflation—sometimes it's a range, not one particular number, but a pretty narrow range—and that should be its only target. It should use its instruments—usually a short-term interest rate—to achieve that target and it should avoid using monetary policy to do anything else.

So what are some of the other things that central banks have done besides try to meet an inflation target? Well, the United States Federal Reserve, for example, has a mandate to reach two targets—the so-called "dual mandate"—one is a stable price level, which is the same as an inflation target, and the other is high employment. So this is a dual mandate. After the financial crisis there's a third presumption, that the Federal Reserve will look at financial stability as well. Other central banks historically have tried to promote exports by targeting a cheap exchange rate. Some people have accused the Chinese government of doing this but many other developing countries have targeted an exchange rate to keep an undervalued exchange rate and promote exports. Other countries have tried to promote broad-based development by supporting government policy. So there's a whole range of targets that, historically, central banks have used.

D&S: Has inflation targeting gone hand-in-hand not only with prioritizing price stability over other kinds of objectives, but also an emphasis on very low rates of inflation?

GE: That's right. In practice, what inflation-targeting advocates have argued for is an extremely low rate of inflation. For example, the European Central Bank has a 2% target, or to keep inflation in fact just below 2%, and typically what is called for is inflation in the low single digits. In developing countries, targets have ranged from 4% to 8%. So these are targets for inflation that are very low compared to broad historical experience. These days, very low inflation and indeed the threat of deflation in some countries have raised all kinds of issues about this inflation targeting approach.

I see this as part of a whole neoliberal approach to central banking. That is, the idea that the economy is inherently stable, it will inherently reach full employment and stable economic growth on its own, and so the only thing that the macro policymakers have to worry about is keeping a low inflation rate and everything else will take care of itself. Of course, as we've seen, this whole neoliberal approach to macroeconomic policy is badly mistaken.

D&S: Why have we seen inflation targeting become more prevalent in monetary policy making, both in high-income and lower-income countries, in recent years? What are the key arguments that are made by advocates of inflation targeting in favor of that approach? And what might be some underlying political and economic causes, even apart from those arguments?

GE: It's been a real revolution in central bank policy and, as I said earlier, it's in my view part and parcel of the whole neoliberal trend in macroeconomic policy. The essential thing underlying this, in my view, is to try to reduce the power of government and social forces that might exercise some power within the political economy—workers and peasants and others—and put the power primarily in the hands of those dominating in the markets. That's often the financial system, the banks, but also other elites.

The idea of neoliberal economists and policymakers is that you don't want the government getting too involved in macroeconomic policy. You don't want them promoting too much employment because that might lead to a raise in wages and, in turn, to a reduction in the profit share of the national income. So, sure, this might increase inflation, but inflation is not really the key issue here. The problem, in their view, is letting the central bank support other kinds of policies that are going to enhance the power of workers, people who work in agricultural areas, and even sometimes manufacturing interests. Instead, they want to put power in the hands of those who dominate the markets, often the financial elites.

That is, of course, not what the advocates of inflation targeting say publicly. What the advocates say is, "Look, inflation is harmful. We've got to keep a low and stable rate of inflation in order to promote economic growth." They build on the neoclassical, New Keynesian, or even New Classical approaches to macroeconomic policy that say the market economy is stable in and of itself, so government intervention can only mess things up. So there's only one thing left to do—there's only one thing on the "to do" list for macroeconomic policy—and that is to keep a stable inflation rate, so let's assign the central bank to do that and not to do anything else, and the capitalist economy will take care of itself.

This approach, I think, really has contributed to enormous financial instability. Notice that this inflation targeting targets commodity inflation. But what about asset bubbles, that is, asset inflation? There's no attempt to reduce asset bubbles like we had in subprime or in real estate bubbles in various countries. That is another kind of inflation that could have been targeted.

Of course, we know that the capitalist economy does not achieve full employment on its own. So why not target higher employment? In South Africa, for example, they have unemployment rates of 25 or 26%. They have an inflation-targeting regime to keep inflation in the low single digits, rather than targeting employment. It makes no sense at all.

The other argument that inflation-targeting advocates make is a government failure argument. Even if you concede that the economy won't do perfectly on its own, any time the government gets involved in the market economy they just mess it up. So, they argue, let's just have a minimalist kind of government intervention and at least the government will do no harm. I think this is a common argument as well. But as we know, there have been many successful government interventions in South Korea and China and elsewhere where governments working with a financial system and other actors in the economy have played a crucial role in economic development. The government-failure arguments, I think, have now been shown to be pretty fallacious. Olivier Blanchard, who was the chief economist at the IMF said we had this beautiful illusion that all we needed is one target, that is low inflation, and one interest rate, that is a short-term interest-rate, and everything would be OK. Well, after the crisis, we now know that we need multiple targets and we need multiple tools to achieve our goals.

D&S: Hasn't it been a central concern on the part of elites in capitalist countries, at least in those where there is representative government, that the majority could impose its will and force policymakers to prioritize full employment and wage growth (as opposed to, say, "sound money")? Has the transition toward inflation targeting been accompanied by institutional changes to "wall off" monetary policy from those kinds of popular pressures?

GE: Yeah, I think that's a very important point here. Inflation targeting ideas have also been often accompanied by the idea that central banks should be "independent"—that is, independent from the government. I think you'll find that these two things go hand-in-hand.

If you look at the whole list of central bank rules that the International Monetary Fund (IMF) and others have advocated for developing countries, the argument goes like this: You want to have an independent central bank. Well, what should this independent central-bank do? It should target inflation. Well, isn't this anti-democratic? No, what we're really saying is that central bankers should have instrument independence, that is, the ability to decide how they'll achieve their target. The government should set the target, but what should target be? Well, the consensus is that the target should be a low rate of inflation. So that's a nice little package designed to prevent the central bank from doing such things as helping to finance government infrastructure investment or government deficits. It's designed to prevent the central bank from keeping interest rates "too low," which might actually contribute to more rapid economic growth or more productivity growth, but might lead to somewhat higher inflation.

Where do they get this low inflation rate from? There's no economic evidence, in fact—and there have been lots of studies—to demonstrate that an inflation rate in the low single digits is optimal for economic growth in most countries, certainly not in developing countries. Some early studies—and this has been replicated many times—have suggested that inflation rates of up to 15%, even 20%, as long as they're relatively steady, don't harm economic growth. They might even contribute to it. So this is a kind of straitjacket that these forces are trying to put the central bank in, in order to prevent them from making policies in the interest of a broader part of the economy. And it's just one plank in the macroeconomic neoliberal straitjacket. The other plank, of course, is no fiscal deficits. So you limit what government can do—no fiscal deficits or low fiscal deficits—you limit what the central bank can do—only target low inflation—and you've pretty much made it impossible for the government to engage in macroeconomic policy that's going to have a broad-based supportive effect on the economy.

D&S: What is the record of inflation targeting policy in practice, in terms of economic outcomes we can actually observe, in both developing and so-called developed countries?

GE: The first thing to realize, I think, is that inflation-targeting approaches have been devastating in the reaction to the financial crisis of 2007-2008, particularly in Europe. There you had, an extreme case where the European Central Bank (ECB) mandate was to target inflation—period—and nothing else. And indeed to keep inflation in the low single digits, less than 2%. And what this did—along with other rules, other problems in Europe, not just this—was give the ECB the cover to do very little in terms of fighting the crisis when it hit, to in fact raise interest rates within the first year after the crisis hit. And it took the ECB several years before it finally realized the disaster that had befallen Europe and, when Mario Draghi finally came in as president of the ECB in 2011, to do whatever it takes to keep the euro going. It took a break from this kind of orthodoxy for them to begin to turn around Europe. (As we can now see Europe is still in terrible shape.)

Second, the single-minded focus on inflation in Europe and in other countries made them ignore the financial bubble, the asset bubbles that were occurring. Central bankers said, "Well, you know, that's not my department. I'll just worry about commodity inflation. I won't worry about other kinds of inflation because that's not my mandate." They had this tunnel vision, not seeing what else was going on around them in the economy.

In developing countries, there's pretty strong evidence that real interest rates have been higher than they would have been otherwise. There's some evidence that economic growth is lower in a number of developing countries than it would have been otherwise, because real interest rates have been so high. And there is some evidence that this has contributed to a redistribution of income towards the rentiers, that is, to the bankers and the financiers, and away from others because real interest rates have been so high and inflation has been relatively low. Most of the evidence suggests that it has had a negative consequence for working people and others in developing countries as well.

In the end, the negative impacts have been mitigated to some extent by the fact that a lot of central banks, in developing countries particularly, claim to be following a very strict inflation-targeting regime but in fact they've been "cheating." Almost all of them target exchange rates to some extent because they know they can't let their exchange rates get too overvalued or otherwise that is going to hurt their exports and cause other problems. They've been fiddling with the inflation data, or exactly what kind of inflation target they use, etc. In some ways it's a bit of a ruse. For developing countries, it's saying to the IMF, "OK, we're doing what you're telling us." Saying to the global financial markets, to the global investors, "OK we're doing this orthodox thing, but (wink wink) if we really did this all the time in a strict way it would be suicide so we're not going to really do this completely." So they're finally is a recognition, I think, that inflation targeting is a very destructive practice.

D&S: In your view, then, what would be a preferable approach to central bank policy—what priorities should central banks have and how should they go about achieving these aims?

GE: Central banks should be free and open, in conjunction with their governments, to identify the key problems facing their own countries, the key obstacles to social and economic development, and developing tools and targets that are appropriate to dealing with those problems. And these are going to differ from country to country. So, for example, in South Africa, my colleagues Bob Pollin, James Heintz, Leonce Ndikumana, and I did a study a number of years ago: We proposed an employment-targeting regime for the central bank. The Reserve Bank of South Africa, in conjunction with the government of South Africa, would develop a set of policies and tools—such as credit allocation policies, subsidized credit, lower interest rates, capital controls to keep the capital in the country, more expansionary and targeted fiscal policy—so that monetary policy and fiscal policy would work hand-in-hand to lower the massively high unemployment rate in South Africa. That's an example of an alternative structure for monetary policy and one that has worked for other developing countries. So, for example, in South Korea in the 1950s ,1960s, and 1970s, the central bank supported the government's industrial policy—by lending to development banks that would lend to export industries, by subsidizing credit for export industries, and they would do this as part of the government plan to develop the economy. I call this developmental central banking, that is, central banking that in combination with the government is oriented to developing the country using a variety of tools—interest rates, credit allocation tools, etc.

Not all countries would do the same thing. It not only depends on the country, but also on the problems of the historical conjuncture. So take the United States for example. Right now we do have for the Federal Reserve a dual mandate, which some Republicans are trying to get rid of, for high employment and stable prices. But the financial intermediation system is broken because of what happened in the crisis. Interest rates are down to zero but banks aren't lending to the real economy. People aren't able to borrow from banks for small businesses and so forth. The Federal Reserve, through quantitative easing, bought a lot of financial assets but it's probably time for the Fed to develop new tools, to give direct credit to small businesses, for infrastructure development, etc.

It is the case now, with the crisis and with negative interest rates, or very low interest rates, central banks are being much more experimental trying to develop new tools, new approaches. But they're all doing it under the guise of inflation targeting. European central bankers were doing all these wild monetary experiments, but their goal was really just to get inflation up to 2%. In fact, what's happening is that this inflation targeting is no longer the guiding post for central banks. They need to have much broader sets of tools and targets to get out of this terrible slump that most of these economies are in. ❏

Article 4.3

DOLLAR DOMINANCE

BY ARTHUR MacEWAN
January/February 2015

> Dear Dr. Dollar:
> What does it mean that the dollar is the "dominant" global currency? Why does this situation exist? And how does it matter? —*Anonymous*

Suppose that, when you paid for things with checks, all the recipients of those checks believed that you were a very responsible person, that you would keep plenty of money in the bank to honor those checks. Moreover, not only did the check recipients believe in you, but people in general had this same opinion.

Under these circumstances, the people holding your checks wouldn't have to cash them in. Those checks could simply be used as money. The checks themselves would be acceptable in transactions among all those people who believed you were so responsible.

This situation would be nice for you because you could write plenty of checks and not worry about those checks being cashed in against your account. Extra buying power for you. At the same time, the people who used your checks as money would have an easier time with transactions, having your checks as a widely acceptable form of currency—i.e., they would have more "liquidity." Also, holding onto your checks—keeping them "in reserve"—would be a safe way for people to store money for when they needed it.

Fiction and Reality

To a large extent, this fictional situation with your checks is analogous to the real situation of the U.S. dollar in global commerce. With people and banks around the world using dollars and holding dollars, not "cashing them in" for U.S. goods, the United States— primarily its government and businesses—is able to spend more abroad without giving up so much in goods and services produced in the United States. Governments, businesses, and people around the world have more liquidity than they would otherwise, and they have more confidence than they would otherwise in the value of the currency (dollars) they are using and holding in reserve

Like you in the fictional scenario, the U.S. government in the real scenario is viewed as "responsible." An important part of the U.S. government being viewed as "responsible" is that it would keep the value of the dollar relatively stable—i.e., not much inflation (at least compared to other currencies). This organization of the global finance system, with the dollar in this special, or dominant, position has an interesting history—and some powerful implications.

Where Did This System Come From?

The crucial formal step in creating the dollar-dominated system came at the end of World War II, with the United States in an extremely strong economic position. Indeed, the high level of government spending on the war had brought the U.S. economy out of the Great Depression, while other high-income countries (and many low-income countries) had had their economies physically decimated by the war. Combined with this economic power, the United States had extreme military power. Thus, the era following World War II came to be called "The American Century" (Of course it was not really a full century, but let's not quibble.)

As the end of the war was coming into sight, in July 1944, representatives of the U.S. government and of 43 allied governments (over 700 delegates in all) met over three weeks at the Mt. Washington Hotel in Bretton Woods, N.H. The purpose of this conference was to set up the arrangements for the operation of the global economy in the postwar era. Although the Soviet Union and China were both represented at the Bretton Woods conference, in subsequent years they did not take part in the arrangements. (Today you can go to Bretton Woods and, at the entrance to the hotel's driveway, see the sign commemorating this conference, but you have to pay an entrance fee to actually get onto the hotel grounds.)

Unsurprisingly, given the relative economic and political power of the allied governments, the U.S. government basically dictated the conference outcomes, arrangements by which commerce among capitalist countries would be organized in the decades following World War II—the "Bretton Woods era." The central feature of these arrangements was that the dollar would be at the core of global commerce. Other countries' currencies would be "pegged" to the dollar, which meant that each government would set the value of its currency in terms of the dollar. For example, in 1949 the French franc was pegged at $0.37 and the British pound at $2.80. The dollar itself was set in relation to gold: $34 to the ounce. Other countries' banks could redeem their dollars for gold at this rate, but, as with your checks, they generally didn't do so. When the gold-redemption promise was terminated in 1971, it turned out not to make much difference—more on that in a moment.

Of course, economies change in relation to one another. In the postwar era, different rates of inflation and different rates of productivity growth meant that the values of the currencies in terms of the dollar had to be changed from time to time. For example, if France was running a trade deficit with the rest of the world (importing more than it was exporting), this meant that the value of its franc was too high in relation to the dollar—i.e., in terms of dollars, the cost of French goods was too high and France's exports would be low, while the cost for France of goods from elsewhere would be too low and France's imports would be high. Moreover, with French exports not paying for its imports, France would necessarily build up a foreign debt to pay for the excess imports.

One could look at this franc-dollar relationship another way: instead of the franc being too high, one could say that the dollar was too low. But the rules that were established at Bretton Woods excluded the dollar from having to adjust. In this example, it was the French who would have to adjust the value of their currency—i.e., France would have to devalue its currency. And, importantly, it would have to borrow to cover the foreign debt it had built up. The U.S. economy, on the other hand, was protected from the disruption that would have been caused by changing the value of the dollar.

The International Monetary Fund (IMF) was established at Bretton Woods to provide countries in this kind of situation with the loans they needed. The IMF provided these loans, but with various conditions—in particular that the county taking the loans would have to take steps to reorganize their economies, generally in ways that opened them to more foreign commerce, trade and investment.

While the IMF did play a role in European adjustments, its actions became especially important in lower-income countries, where it used its loan conditions to push countries towards a greater openness to international investment and trade—very much in the interests of multinational firms based in the richer countries. (The World Bank was also created at Bretton Woods, but its role is not a central part of the story here.)

Change Without Change

The Bretton Woods rules of the game worked fairly well for twenty-five years. In fact, from the perspective of the United States one might say they worked too well. While the Bretton Woods system promoted U.S. commerce, opening up trade and investment opportunities around the (capitalist) world, it also provided a stability in global affairs in which firms based elsewhere—in Japan and Europe—were able to also expand and ultimately challenge the dominant position of U.S firms.

A critical juncture in global commercial arrangements then came in 1971: the Bretton Woods system fell apart. A combination of heavy spending abroad by the U.S. government (on the Vietnam War), the economic challenge from other rich countries, and inflation in the United States led the U.S. government to drop its promise of redeeming dollars for gold. Yet, while the system fell apart, there was surprisingly little change in international trade and investment. The relative economic and military power of the United States, though not as extreme as it had been in the immediate post-World War II era, continued. And the perceived threat of the Soviet Union served as a glue, binding the world's major capitalist powers in Europe and Asia to the United States, and leading them to accept continued U.S. economic, as well as military, dominance.

After 1971, various new arrangements were put in place—for example, a system of partially managed "pegs" was established. Yet the dollar remained the central currency of global commerce. Prices of internationally traded goods—most importantly oil—continued to be set in dollars, and countries continued to hold their reserves in dollars.

Although 1971 marked the beginning of a new era in international financial arrangements, the dollar retained its dominant position. Regardless of the various economic problems in the United States, the dollar has remained both relatively stable and in sufficient supply to grease the wheels of international commerce. Indeed, an ironic example of the continuing role of the dollar came in the Great Recession that began in 2008. Even while the U.S. economy was in the doldrums, businesses and governments elsewhere in the world were buying U.S. government bonds—a principal means of holding their reserves in dollars—since they still considered these the safest assets available.

Power and a Symbol of Power

In years leading up to the Great Recession, China had entered the global for-profit economy and was exporting at a high rate, exceeding its imports. The Chinese government used the extra money that China was obtaining from its trade surplus to heavily invest in U.S. government bonds. That is, China built up extensive reserves in dollars. In effect, China was loaning money to the United States—loans which filled both the federal budget deficit and the U.S trade deficit. What many observers decried as a dangerous situation—We are becoming indebted to the Chinese! Horror!—in fact served both the U.S. and Chinese governments quite well.

The international role of the dollar is a symbol of U.S. power and is based on that power. At the same time, the dollar's role works to enhance that power, giving the U.S. government and U.S. business the liquidity needed for carrying out global operations—everything from wars to benign commerce.

There are problems with the system. The continued role of the dollar depends to a large extent on the avoidance of significant inflation in the United States. Yet restraints on inflation—e.g., the Federal Reserve raising interest rates—generally work against expanding employment. So maintaining the role of the dollar can come at the expense of most people in the country.

Also, there is always the risk of change. Just as the position of the dollar supports U.S. power in world affairs, if that position is undermined, U.S. power would suffer. In recent years, there has been some threat that other governments would challenge the dollar with their own currencies. China, in particular, has attempted to establish its own positon in world affairs, which, if successful, could ultimately undercut the dominance of the dollar. Indeed, the fear associated with China holding reserves in dollars (i.e., as U.S. government bonds) is to some extent based on concern about the potential implications of China shifting out of dollars (or threatening to do so). Yet, especially with the recent weakening of the Chinese economy, this particular challenge does not appear likely in the near future.

Over the last several decades, the role of the dollar in world affairs has become like the role of the English language. Both developed as a consequence of the extreme power of the United States. in the global economy, and both give advantages to the U.S. government, to U.S. firms, and to any individuals engaged in international activities. Most important, the roles of both the dollar and the English language have become thoroughly entrenched. Even as the power of the United States weakens, then, those roles are likely to continue for some time to come. ❑

Article 4.4

IS CHINA'S CURRENCY MANIPULATION HURTING THE U.S.?

BY ARTHUR MacEWAN
November/December 2010

> Dear Dr. Dollar:
>
> Is it true that China has been harming the U.S. economy by keeping its currency "undervalued"? Shouldn't the U.S. government do something about this situation?
>
> —*Jenny Boyd, Edmond, W.Va.*

The Chinese government, operating through the Chinese central bank, does keep its currency unit—the yuan—cheap relative to the dollar. This means that goods imported *from* China cost less (in terms of dollars) than they would otherwise, while U.S. exports *to* China cost more (in terms of yuan). So we in the United States buy a lot of Chinese-made goods and the Chinese don't buy much from us. In the 2007 to 2009 period, the United States purchased $253 billion more in goods annually from China than it sold to China.

This looks bad for U.S workers. For example, when money gets spent in the United States, much of it is spent on Chinese-made goods, and fewer jobs are then created in the United States. So the Chinese government's currency policy is at least partly to blame for our employment woes. Reacting to this situation, many people are calling for the U.S. government to do something to get the Chinese government to change its policy.

But things are not so simple.

First of all, there is an additional reason for the low cost of Chinese goods— low Chinese wages. The Chinese government's policy of repressing labor probably accounts for the low cost of Chinese goods at least as much as does its currency policy. Moreover, there is a lot more going on in the global economy. Both currency problems and job losses involve much more than Chinese government actions— though China provides a convenient target for ire.

And the currency story itself is complex. In order to keep the value of its currency low relative to the dollar, the Chinese government increases the supply of yuan, uses these yuan to buy dollars, then uses the dollars to buy U.S. securities, largely government bonds but also private securities. In early 2009, China held $764 billion in U.S. Treasury securities, making it the largest foreign holder of U.S. government debt. By buying U.S. government bonds, the Chinese have been financing the federal deficit. More generally, by supplying funds to the United States, the Chinese government has been keeping interest rates low in this country.

If the Chinese were to act differently, allowing the value of their currency to rise relative to the dollar, both the cost of capital and the prices of the many goods imported from China would rise. The rising cost of capital would probably not be a serious problem, as the Federal Reserve could take counteraction to keep interest rates low. So, an increase in the value of the yuan would net the United States some jobs, but also raise some prices for U.S. consumers.

It is pretty clear that right now what the United States needs is jobs. Moreover, low-cost Chinese goods have contributed to the declining role of manufacturing in the United States, a phenomenon that both weakens important segments of organized labor and threatens to inhibit technological progress, which has often been centered in manufacturing or based on applications in manufacturing (e.g., robotics).

So why doesn't the U.S. government place more pressure on China to raise the value of the yuan? Part of the reason may lie in concern about losing Chinese financing of the U.S. federal deficit. For several years the two governments have been co-dependent: The U.S. government gets financing for its deficits, and the Chinese government gains by maintaining an undervalued currency. Not an easy relationship to change.

Probably more important, however, many large and politically powerful U.S.-based firms depend directly on the low-cost goods imported from China. Walmart and Target, as any shopper knows, are filled with Chinese-made goods. Then there are the less visible products from China, including a power device that goes into the Microsoft Xbox, computer keyboards for Dell, and many other goods for many other U.S. corporations. If the yuan's value rose and these firms had to pay more dollars to buy these items, they could probably not pass all the increase on to consumers and their profits would suffer.

Still, in spite of the interests of these firms, the U.S. government may take some action, either by pressing harder for China to let the value of the yuan rise relative to the dollar or by placing some restrictions on imports from China. But don't expect too big a change. ❑

Article 4.5

$2 LOST FOR EVERY $1 GAINED

How the Global Financial System Fails Developing Countries

BY JESSE GRIFFITHS

December 2014; Triple Crisis Blog

This will make you angry. After six months crunching all the best data from international institutions, here's what we found: for every dollar developing countries have earned since 2008, they have lost $2.07. In fact, lost resources have averaged over 10% of their Gross Domestic Product (GDP).

We're not talking about all flows of money out of developing countries, just the lost resources: money that should have been invested to support their development, but instead was drained out. Twice as much is leaking—or rather flooding—out than the combined inflows of aid, investment, charitable donations, and migrant remittances.

Losses vs. Inflows

The graphic below shows the proportionate losses of resources compared to one dollar of inflows. The figures are in U.S. cents, and are based on the average inflows and losses between 2008 and 2011. The four main lost resources shown in the graphic point to the problems, but also the solutions.

Loss one: Corporate tax dodging.

The biggest loss was illicit financial flows—money that was illegally earned, transferred or used—which cost developing countries 4.3% of their GDP ($634 billion) in 2011. Most of this was due to illegal corporate tax evasion. As there is currently no way of estimating how much more is lost through aggressive tax avoidance, the real figure lost to corporate tax dodging is likely to be much higher.

Part of the solution is corporate transparency. Companies: tell us who owns you, how you're structured, and where you make your money and employ your staff so the public—and tax authorities—can check that you're paying your fair share. The European Union made some initial progress last year, forcing banks to open up their books, but much remains to be done. Another solution is to stop the "race to the bottom" that sees governments giving up on taxing corporations—corporate tax rates have been on the slide for years. The U.N. should take a lead and tackle all these issues head-on in a new global body.

Loss two: Foreign investors making a killing.

The second biggest loss is the profits extracted from developing countries by foreign investors: totaling 2.3% of their GDP ($486 billion) in 2012. In fact, since 2008, foreign investors have been taking more profits out of developing countries than new investments have been coming in. Foreign investment can provide major benefits to the countries that receive it, but only if it is carefully managed, so that it brings with it skills training, new ideas, and doesn't push out domestic investment (which, by the way, is several times larger than foreign investment in developing countries). The scale of the outflows suggests something is seriously wrong.

That's why we've called for a focus on the quality of foreign investment. We need to support developing countries to insist that investors obey social, environmental and human rights standards, to push investors to go where investment is really needed, and to prevent chaos when investors pull money out too rapidly.

Loss three: Lending to rich countries (yes, really).

The third biggest loss is the money that developing countries are lending rich countries—mainly the United States—which totaled 1.2% of their GDP ($276 billion) in 2012 (though it has been much higher in previous years, which is why it comes out as a bigger loss in the graphic above). Developing countries have been building very large reserves to protect their economies from external shocks. These reserves take the form of dependable assets, largely the bonds of rich countries. Every time a developing country buys a U.S. Treasury bond it is lending money—at a low interest rate—to the United States.

In theory, developing countries could borrow from the International Monetary Fund (IMF) in times of crisis, but the IMF remains dominated by western countries, and continues to insist on damaging austerity as a condition of lending. Again, there are solutions on the table. In addition to allowing developing countries to regulate foreign money more tightly, the UN has proposed a form of global quantitative easing, issuing $250 billion new reserve assets every year, with the majority going to developing countries.

Loss four: Paying interest on debts rather than receiving aid.

The fourth biggest loss for developing countries is interest repayments on foreign debt, totaling 0.8% of their GDP ($188 billion) in 2012. Let's leave aside the fact that developing countries would not have had to borrow so much if rich countries had met their promise to devote 0.7% of national income to foreign aid (only five countries have).

The central problem is that there is no mechanism to deal with unsustainable, unfair, or unpayable debts of developing countries. The solution is elegant, and currently on the table at the United Nations: an independent insolvency regime for states to help reduce their debts in a rapid, orderly, and fair manner.

A Call to Action

It's clear that the global economic system has been failing developing countries, and the evidence could not be clearer: lost resources are double new inflows, and have been for some years. Many of the solutions are on the table: it's time to put them into action. ❑

Article 4.6

CAPITAL FLIGHT FROM AFRICA
What Is to Be Done?

BY JAMES K. BOYCE
November 2015

I am old enough to remember when the subject of illicit financial flows was not discussed in polite company. The topic was relegated to the shadows of official discourse. It is gratifying to see this important issue moving squarely onto the agenda
of the international community.

The terms "capital flight" and "illicit financial flows" sometimes are used
interchangeably, but they are distinct concepts. Capital flight is usually defined as
unrecorded capital outflows and measured as the missing residual in the balance of
payments, after corrections for underreported external borrowing and trade misin-
voicing. All capital flight is illicit, but not all illicit financial flows are capital flight.
Capital flight is illicit by virtue of illegal acquisition, illegal transfer, illegal holding
abroad, or some combination of the three.

Illicitly acquired capital is money obtained through embezzlement, bribes, extor-
tion, tax evasion, or criminal activities. Wealth acquired by these means is often
transferred abroad clandestinely in an effort to evade legal scrutiny as to its origins.

Illicitly transferred funds are outflows not reported to government authorities. Mechanisms include smuggling of bank notes, clandestine wire transfers, and
falsification of trade invoices.

Illicitly held funds are assets whose earnings are not declared as income to
national authorities of the owner's country. The concealment of foreign holdings
may be motivated by the desire to evade prosecution for illicit acquisition of the
funds, or may be for taxation evasion, or both.

The broader universe of illicit financial flows includes not only capital flight but also
payments for smuggled imports, transactions connected with illicit trade in narcotics
and other contraband, outflows of illicitly acquired funds that were domestically laun-
dered before flowing overseas through recorded channels, and transfer pricing by the
corporate sector. These, too, are illicit, but they are not the same as capital flight.

Capital Flight and External Debt

Countries often experience external borrowing and capital flight simultaneously. At
first glance this may seem anomalous. Why would we observe large capital flows in
both directions at once? External borrowing implies that both lenders and borrowers expect attractive investment returns. Yet capital outflows appear to signal higher
returns elsewhere. In practice, the two phenomena may not only co-exist but also
be causally linked. External borrowing can lead to capital flight, and capital flight

can lead to external borrowing. Understanding these linkages is important for the formulation of appropriate policy responses.

In debt-fueled capital flight, external borrowing finances private wealth accumulation outside the borrowing country. On the borrower side, the government contracts loans in the name of the public. Officials and other politically connected individuals then siphon part or all of the money into their own pockets—via kickbacks, padded procurements contracts, and diversion of funds—and stash part or all of the proceeds abroad for safekeeping. On the lender side, loan officers are rewarded for simply "moving the money," creating myopic incentives to turn a blind eye to these risks.

In flight-fueled external borrowing, flight capital finances external loans. A private individual illicitly parks funds abroad and then "borrows" them back. A key motive for such round tripping is concealment of the origins of the funds. The borrower reaps further illicit gains if, as often happens, liability for repaying the loan ultimately passes to the government by virtue of public guarantees in the event of default. Such transactions are attractive to bankers because they generate fees and commissions on both sides.

Econometric analysis indicates that for each new dollar of external borrowing by African countries, as much as 60 cents exits Africa as capital flight in the same year. The tight year-to-year correlation between external borrowing and capital flight suggests that debt management is important in addressing the problem of capital flight. Of course, not all flight capital originates in external borrowing. Statistical analysis shows that natural resource extraction, for example, is also strongly correlated with capital flight.

Stolen asset recovery

Let me now turn to policy responses, starting with efforts to recover and repatriate stolen assets. Some success has been scored on this front. For example, $700 million held in Swiss bank accounts by Nigeria's former military ruler Sani Abacha and his family has been recovered and repatriated. To be sure, the amounts recovered are modest compared to the total magnitude of capital flight, but they are not inconsequential. An added benefit of such recoveries is their demonstration effect, which may help to deter future capital flight.

Over the past two decades the international community has begun building institutional infrastructure to assist in stolen asset recovery. The United Nations Convention against Corruption includes articles on asset recovery and mutual legal assistance. The Stolen Asset Recovery Initiative, launched in 2007 by the United Nations Office on Drugs and Crime and the World Bank, provides technical assistance in tracing stolen wealth, asset seizure and confiscation, and enlisting international cooperation. Many countries have established Financial Intelligence Units to investigate transactions related to criminal activity, and anti-money laundering legislation requires banks and other financial institutions to file reports on suspicious transactions.

A key feature of this emerging international architecture is that when investigators identify substantial foreign holdings of politically exposed persons and others

U.S. Banks and the Dirty Money Empire

Every instance of capital flight must involve parties abroad, to receive the funds. In 2001, author James Petras (in a longer article excerpted here) detailed the culpability of leading U.S. banks in facilitating hundersds of billions in capital flight. As he put it, "The money laundering business ... is carried out by the United States' most important banks. The bank officials involved in money laundering have backing from the highest levels of the banking institutions. These are not isolated offenses perpetrated by loose cannons." —Eds.

Washington and the mass media have portrayed the United States as being in the forefront of the struggle against narcotics trafficking, drug-money laundering, and political corruption. The image is of clean white hands fighting dirty money from the Third World (or the ex-Communist countries). The truth is exactly the opposite. U.S. banks have developed an elaborate set of policies for transferring illicit funds to the United States and "laundering" those funds by investing them in legitimate businesses or U.S. government bonds. The U.S. Congress has held numerous hearings, provided detailed exposés of the illicit practices of the banks, passed several anti-laundering laws, and called for stiffer enforcement by public regulators and private bankers. Yet the biggest banks continue their practices and the sums of dirty money grow exponentially. The $500 billion of criminal and dirty money flowing annually into and through the major U.S. banks far exceeds the net revenues of all the information technology companies in the United States. These yearly inflows surpass the net profits repatriated from abroad by the major U.S. oil producers, military industries, and airplane manufacturers combined. Neither the banks nor the government have the will or the interest to put an end to practices that provide such high profits and help maintain U.S. economic supremacy internationally. ...

Hundreds of billions of dollars have been transferred, through the private-banking and correspondent-banking systems, from Africa, Asia, Latin America, and Eastern Europe to the biggest banks in the United States and Europe. In all these regions, liberalization and privatization of the economy have opened up lucrative opportunities for corruption and the easy movement of booty overseas. Authoritarian governments and close ties to Washington, meanwhile, have ensured impunity for most of the guilty parties. Russia alone has seen over $200 billion illegally transferred out of the country in the course of the 1990s. The massive flows of capital out of these regions—really the pillaging of these countries' wealth through the international banking system—is a major factor in their economic instability and mass impoverishment. The resulting economic crises, in turn, have made these countries more vulnerable to the prescriptions of the International Monetary Fund and the World Bank, including liberalized banking and financial systems that lead to further capital flight. — *James Petras*

Sources: "Private Banking and Money Laundering: A Case Study of Opportunities and Vulnerabilities," Permanent Subcommittee on Investigations of the Committee on Governmental Affairs, United States Senate, One Hundred Sixth Congress, November 9-10, 2000; "Report on Correspondent Banking: A Gateway to Money Laundering," Minority Staff of the U.S. Senate Permanent Subcommittee on Investigations, February 2001.

suspected of criminal activity, asset holders can be required to prove that the wealth was acquired legitimately. Pending the outcome of the legal proceedings, the assets can be restrained or seized.

Selective Debt Repudiation

Debts that fuel capital flight can be considered "odious" under international law. Selective repudiation of odious debt—which is distinct from across-the-board default—can prevent the diversion of scarce public resources into debt service payments on loans from which the public derived no benefit. Repudiation of odious debts also would change the incentive structure for creditors, encouraging due diligence and helping to improve the quality of future lending.

Odious debts are liabilities contracted by governments without the consent of the people, from which the people did not benefit, in circumstances where creditors knew or should have known these conditions to hold. They include funds stolen by corrupt individuals and money used to maintain the power of authoritarian regimes. Determining which loans served bona fide development purposes and which are odious is a challenging task. Systematic audits can help to establish which debts are legitimate and which offer objective grounds for repudiation. Where there is evidence of systematic misuse of borrowed funds, the burden of proof can be placed upon creditors to demonstrate that their loans were used for legitimate purposes, much as the burden of proof can be placed upon politically exposed persons to prove the legitimacy of foreign assets held in their names.

In this arena, there is scope for innovations in international governance. An impartial body for arbitration of odious debt disputes is sorely needed. A United Nations commission chaired by Nobel laureate Joseph Stiglitz called in 2009 for the creation of an international bankruptcy court that could consider, "where appropriate, partial debt cancellation." The IMF has noted that such a body could be charged with adjudicating claims of odious debts. The creation of such a forum could do much to curb debt-fueled capital flight and flight-fueled external borrowing.

Regulatory Reforms in International Banking

Further efforts are also needed to increase transparency in international banking. Most flight capital is domiciled in what are commonly referred to as offshore financial centres. The most important of these are not tropical islands, but rather New York, London, and other international banking centers. Improved transparency requires strengthening the enforcement of existing banking regulations and closing loopholes arising from the inadequate harmonization of banking regulations across countries.

An important piece in efforts to improve financial transparency is cross-country exchange of information on investment income, including interest, dividends, and capital gains. This necessitates information on beneficial ownership so that the recipients cannot conceal their identities behind shell companies and trusts. Banks and other financial institutions, including brokers and insurance companies, should be required to report this information to their governments, who can then share the information with the governments of income recipients.

Recent years have seen some progress on this front. In 2009, the exchange of information upon request became the international standard, monitored by the Global Forum on Exchange of Information and Transparency for Tax Purposes. This gave tax authorities access to information on offshore investment income, although it put the onus on them to identify specific individuals or firms in order to request this information. In 2013, the G20 Finance Ministers and Central Bank Governors endorsed the automatic exchange of information—rather than exchange upon request—as the new international standard. Bilateral agreements are now laying the foundation for multilateral cooperation to implement this policy.

Conclusion

Capital flight occurs for a variety of reasons. Two important motives are the desire to conceal funds that have been illicitly acquired and the desire to evade taxation. Individuals who engage in capital flight are aided and abetted in illicit transfers of funds by officers in banks and other financial institutions who are in a position to profit from these transactions as long as they are not detected and subjected to penalties. Foreign borrowing and extractive resource revenues are important correlates of capital flight, suggesting that these are significant sources for the illicit acquisition of private wealth.

Growing recognition of these problems is spurring international efforts to mitigate the consequences of past capital flight and to reduce its recurrence in future years. These include efforts to recover stolen assets, relieve external debt burdens, and promote transparency and due diligence in international banking. The creation of an impartial body to adjudicate cases of odious debts would further strengthen this international architecture. If well designed and implemented, these initiatives will help to curtail malfeasance, improve incentive structures, and contribute to a more efficient and equitable international financial architecture. ❑

Sources: J-P. Brun, et al., *Asset Recovery Handbook: A Guide for Practicioners*, Stolen Asset Recovery Initiative, World Bank and United Nations Office on Drugs and Crime, 2011; J. King, *The Doctrine of Odious Debt in International Law*, 2015; International Monetary Fund, *Sovereign Debt Restructuring—Recent Developments and Implications for the Fund's Legal and Policy Framework*, 2013; L. Ndikumana, J.K. Boyce, and A.S. Ndiaye, "Capital Flight from Africa: Measurement and Drivers," in I. Ajayi and L. Ndikumana (eds.), *Capital Flight from Africa: Causes, Effects and Policy Issues*, 2015; Organization for Economic Cooperation and Development, *Action Plan on Base Erosion and Profit Shifting*, 2013; N. Shaxson, *Treasure Islands: Tax Havens and the Men Who Stole the World*, 2011; United Nations, *Recommendations of the Commission of Experts of the President of the United Nations General Assembly on Reforms of the International Monetary and Financial System*, 2009.

Chapter 5

INTERNATIONAL INSTITUTIONS

Article 5.1

THE INTERNATIONAL MONETARY FUND AND WORLD BANK

BY THE *DOLLARS & SENSE* COLLECTIVE

March/April 2000, last revised December 2016

The basic structure of the postwar international capitalist economy was created in 1944, at an international conference in Bretton Woods, New Hampshire. While the Bretton Woods conference included high-level negotiations between representatives of the U.S. and British governments, the Americans dominated the outcome.

The British delegation (including the legendary economist John Maynard Keynes) argued for an international currency for world trade and debt settlements. The Americans insisted on the U.S. dollar being the de facto world currency (with the dollar's value fixed in terms of gold and the values of other currencies fixed in relation to the dollar). The British wanted countries that ran trade surpluses and those that ran trade deficits (and became indebted to the "surplus" countries) to share the costs of "adjustment" (bringing the world economy back into balance). The United States insisted on a system in which the "deficit" countries would have to do the adjusting, and a central aim would be making sure that the debtors would pay back their creditors at any cost.

Among the institutions coming out of Bretton Woods were the World Bank and the International Monetary Fund (IMF). For this reason, they are sometimes known as the "Bretton Woods twins." Both institutions engage in international lending. The IMF was established to lend to countries facing current-account deficit problems, so that they could continue international trade without interruption, and avoid defaulting on debts, which would disrupt world economic stability. So the IMF primarily acts as a "lender of last resort" to countries (usually, but not always, lower-income countries) that have become heavily indebted and cannot get loans elsewhere. The World Bank, officially called the International Bank for Reconstruction and Development, was initially tasked to help rebuild post-World War II Europe through infrastructure lending. In the years since, it has continued to engage primarily in longer-term "development" lending, though its focus has moved to the developing world.

At both the World Bank and the IMF, the number of votes a country receives is closely proportional to how much capital it contributes to the institution, so the voting power of rich countries like the United States is disproportionate to their numbers. Eleven rich countries, for example, account for more than 50% of the voting power in the IMF Board of Governors. At both institutions, eight powerful countries—the United States, China, France, Germany, Japan, Russia, Saudi Arabia, and the United Kingdom—get their own representatives on the institution's executive board, with the rest of the directors (16-17) elected by the rest of the 180-odd member countries. The president of the World Bank is elected by the Board of Executive Directors, and traditionally nominated by the U.S. representative. The managing director of the IMF is traditionally a European.

The IMF and the World Bank wield power vastly greater than the share of international lending they account for because private lenders follow their lead in deciding which countries are credit-worthy. The institutions have taken advantage of this leverage—and of debt crises in Latin America, Africa, Asia, and even Europe—to push a "free-market" (or "neoliberal") model of economic development.

The IMF

The IMF was a key part, from the very start, of the "debtor pays" system the U.S. government had insisted on at Bretton Woods. When a country fell heavily into debt, and could no longer get enough credit from private sources, the IMF would step in as the "lender of last resort." This made it possible for the debtor to continue to pay its creditors in the short run. The typical IMF adjustment program, however, demanded painful "austerity" or "shock therapy"—elimination of price controls on basic goods (such as food and fuel), cuts in government spending, services, and employment, and "devaluation" of the country's currency. All of these austerity measures hit workers and poor people the hardest, the first two for fairly obvious reasons. The impact of currency devaluation, however, requires a little more explanation.

Devaluation meant that the currency would buy fewer dollars—and fewer units of every other currency "pegged" to the dollar. This made imports to the country more expensive. (Suppose that a country's peso had been pegged at a one-to-one ratio to the dollar. An imported good that cost $10 would cost 10 pesos. If the currency was devalued to a two-to-one ratio to the dollar, an imported good that cost $10 would now cost 20 pesos.) Devaluation caused domestic prices to rise, both because imports became more expensive and because domestic producers faced less import competition and so could more readily raise their own prices. Meanwhile, it made the country's exports less expensive to people in other countries. The idea was that the country would export more, earn more dollars in return, and—this is the key—be able to pay back its debts to U.S. and European banks. In other words, the people of the country (especially workers and the poor) would consume less of what they produced, and send more of it abroad to "service" the country's debt.

It is the poor who are hurt the most by devaluation. For instance, if a county's devalues its currency by 50%, then the poor will lose about half the purchasing power on their money savings (which they hold overwhelmingly in the national currency). However, the rich and ruling elite hold the bulk of their financial wealth abroad in other currencies. Once a devaluation has been carried out, they can use their foreign currency holdings to buy their country's currency, now at a more favorable rate due to the devaluation.

For many years, austerity measures like these were the core of IMF "adjustment" plans. Starting in the 1970s, however, the IMF broadened its standard program to include deeper "structural" changes to debtor countries' economies. "Structural adjustment programs" (SAPs) included not only the austerity measures described above, but also the elimination of trade barriers and controls on international investment, the privatization of public enterprises, and the "deregulation" of labor markets (including elimination of minimum wage laws, hours laws, occupational safety and health regulations, and protections for unions).

These were the basic ingredients for overturning "regulated" (or "interventionist") forms of capitalism in many lower-income countries, and replacing it with "free-market" (or "neoliberal") capitalism. Austerity, privatization, and deregulation kept the same elite-dominated government and bureaucratic institutions in place, while moving the epicenter of economic decisionmaking away from public institutions and into private hands. The fact that economic development was now under the control of private corporations—with their power over basic resources such as water, food, and energy—meant that the populations of these countries had still *less* way to hold elites accountable than they had before.

Structural adjustment also prepared the ground for the system of globalized production—making it easier for multinational companies to locate operations in affected countries (thanks to the removal of restrictions on foreign investment), employ a relatively cheap and controllable workforce (thanks to the removal of labor regulations), and export the goods back to their home countries or elsewhere in the world (thanks to the elimination of trade barriers). Structural adjustment programs became the lance-point of "free-market" reform, especially in Latin America during the 1980s debt crisis, but also in other low-income regions.

The World Bank

In its early years, just after World War II, the World Bank mostly loaned money to Western European governments to help rebuild their war-ravaged economies. This was an important factor in the postwar reconstruction of the world capitalist economy. European reconstruction bolstered demand for exported goods from the United States, and ultimately promoted the reemergence of Western Europe as a global manufacturing powerhouse.

During the long period (1968-1981) that former U.S. Defense Secretary Robert

S. McNamara headed the World Bank, however, the bank turned toward "development" loans to lower-income countries. McNamara brought the same philosophy to development that he had used as a chief architect of the U.S. war against Vietnam: big is good and bigger is better. The World Bank came to favor large, expensive projects regardless of their appropriateness to local conditions, and with little attention to environmental and social impacts. The Bank became especially notorious, for example, for supporting large dam projects that flooded wide areas, deprived others of water, and uprooted the people living in affected regions. The Bank's support for large, capital-intensive "development" projects has also been a disguised way of channeling benefits to large global companies. Many of these projects require inputs—like high-tech machinery—that are not produced in the countries where the projects take place. Instead, they have to be imported, mostly from high-income countries. Such projects may also create long-run dependencies, since the spare parts and technical expertise for proper maintenance may only be available from the companies that produced these inputs in the first place.

While the Bank's main focus is long-term "development" lending, it has also engaged in "structural adjustment" lending. The Bank's structural adjustment policies, much like those from the IMF, have imposed heavy burdens on workers and poor people. In the 1980s and 1990s, during its "structural adjustment era," the Bank went so far as to advocate that governments charge fees even for public primary education. (Predictably, in countries that adopted such policies, many poor families could not afford the fees and school enrollment declined.) The Bank has since then publicly called for the abolition of school fees. Critics argue, however, that the shift is at least partly rhetorical. Katarina Tomasevski, founder of the organization Right to Education, argues that the Bank presents itself as opposing fees, but does not oppose hidden charges, as for textbooks, school uniforms, and other costs of attending school.

The World Bank has also made development loans conditional on the adoption of "free-market" policies, like privatization of public services. Most notoriously, the Bank has pushed for the privatization of water delivery. Where privatization of water or other public services has not been possible, the Bank has urged governments to adopt "cost-recovery" strategies—including raising fees on users. Both privatization and cost-recovery strategies have undermined poor people's access to water and other essentials.

Recent developments

Since the 1990s, opposition to World Bank and IMF policies have shaken the two institutions' credibility and economic policy influence—especially in Latin America, the world region to which "neoliberalism" came first and where it went furthest. This is part of a broader backlash against neoliberal policies, which opponents (especially on the Latin American left) blame for persistent poverty and rising inequality in the region. The last decade or so has seen a so-called "pink tide" in Latin America, with "center-left" parties coming to power in Argentina, Bolivia, Brazil, Chile, Ecuador, and Venezuela. (The center-left has since lost and then regained the presidency in Chile, and has recently lost the presidencies of Argentina and Brazil.) Different governments have adopted different policies in power, some staying close to the neoliberal path, others veering sharply away from it. Venezuela has, along with several other countries, withdrawn from the World Bank-affiliated International Centre for the Settlement of Investment Disputes (ICSID). Several South American governments, including those of Argentina, Brazil, and Venezuela, have also jointly formed a new regional lending institution, the Bank of the South, which aims to act as an alternative lender (for both long-term development and short-term "liquidity crises") to the IMF and World Bank.

On the other hand, the IMF has emerged, surprisingly, as a powerful influence in Western Europe. For many years, acute debt crises seemed to be confined to lower-income economies, and most observers did not dream that they could happen in Europe or other high-income regions. (For this reason, the IMF was widely criticized as a hammer that high-income countries used on low-income countries.) During the current economic crisis, however, several Western European countries have fallen deeply into debt. The IMF has stepped in as part of "bailout" programs for Greece, Iceland, and Ireland. True to its origins, it has also pushed for austerity—especially cuts in public spending—in highly indebted countries. Many economists—especially proponents of "Keynesian" views—have argued that weakness in total demand is the main cause of the current economic crisis in Europe and the rest of the world. Under these conditions, they argue, cuts in government spending will only reduce total demand further, and likely cause the crisis to drag on. ❑

Sources: International Monetary Fund, "IMF Members' Quotas and Voting Power, and IMF Board of Governors" (www.imf.org); International Monetary Fund, "IMF Executive Directors and Voting Power" (www.imf.org); World Bank, "Executive Directors and Alternates" (www. worldbank.org); World Bank, "Cost Recovery for Water Supply and Sanitation and Irrigation and Drainage Projects (www.worldbank.org); Zoe Godolphin, "The World Bank as a New Global Education Ministry?" Bretton Woods Project, January 21, 2011 (www.brettonwoodsproject.org); Katerina Tomasevski, "Both Arsonist and Fire Fighter: The World Bank on School Fees," Bretton Woods Project, January 23, 2006 (www.brettonwoodsproject.org); Katerina Tomasevski, "Six Reasons Why the World Bank Should Be Debarred From Education," Bretton Woods Project, September 2, 2006 (www.brettonwoodsproject.org).

Article 5.2

THE WORLD TRADE ORGANIZATION

BY THE *DOLLARS & SENSE* COLLECTIVE
March/April 2000, last revised December 2016

If the World Trade Organization (WTO) is famous for one thing, it is the "Battle in Seattle." Over 50,000 people went to Seattle in 1999 to say no to the WTO's corporate agenda, successfully shutting down the first day of the ministerial meeting. African, Caribbean, and other least-developed country representatives, in addition, walked out of the meeting. But what is the WTO? Where did it come from? And what does it do?

Where did it come from?

Starting in the 1950s, government officials from around the world began to meet irregularly to hammer out the rules of a global trading system. Known as the General Agreements on Trade and Tariffs (GATT), these negotiations covered, in excruciating detail, such matters as what level of taxation Japan could impose on foreign rice, how many American automobiles Brazil could allow into its market, and how large a subsidy France could give its vineyards. Every clause was carefully crafted, with constant input from business representatives who hoped to profit from expanded international trade.

The GATT process, however, was slow, cumbersome and difficult to monitor. As corporations expanded more rapidly into global markets they pushed governments to create a more powerful and permanent international body that could speed up trade negotiations as well as oversee and enforce provisions of the GATT. The WTO arose from the 1986-1994 GATT negotiations, known as the Uruguay Round. The new organization, formed out of the ashes of GATT, was formally established in 1995. It now occupies a central position in the world as an organization for trade negotiations.

Following the shocking demonstrations in Seattle, the WTO held its 2001 ministerial meeting in Doha, Qatar, safe from protest. The WTO initiated a new round of trade talks that it promised would address the needs of developing countries. The Doha Development round, however, continued the WTO's pro-corporate agenda. Two years later "the Group of 20 developing countries" at the Cancún ministerial refused to lower their trade barriers until the United States and EU cleaned up their unfair global agricultural systems. By the summer of 2006, five years after it began, the Doha round had collapsed and the WTO suspended trade negotiations.

What does it do?

The WTO functions as a sort of international court for adjudicating trade disputes. Each of its 164 member countries has one representative, who participates in negotiations over trade rules. The heart of the WTO, however, is not its delegates, but its dispute resolution system. With the establishment of the WTO, corporations now have a place to complain to when they want trade barriers—or domestic regulations that limit their freedom to buy and sell—overturned.

Though corporations have no standing in the WTO—the organization is, officially, open only to its member countries—the numerous advisory bodies that provide technical expertise to delegates are overflowing with corporate representation. The delegates themselves are drawn from trade ministries and confer regularly with the corporate lobbyists and advisors who swarm the streets and offices of Geneva, where the organization is headquartered. As a result, the WTO has become, as an anonymous delegate told the *Financial Times,* "a place where governments can collude against their citizens."

Lori Wallach and Michelle Sforza, in their book *The WTO: Five Years of Reasons to Resist Corporate Globalization*, point out that large corporations are essentially "renting" governments to bring cases before the WTO, and in this way, to win in the WTO battles they have lost in the political arena at home. Large shrimping corporations, for example, got India to dispute the U.S. ban on shrimp catches that were not sea-turtle safe. Once such a case is raised, the resolution process violates most democratic notions of due process and openness. Cases are heard before a tribunal of "trade experts," generally lawyers, who, under WTO rules, are required to make their ruling with a presumption in favor of free trade. The WTO puts the burden squarely on governments to justify any restriction of what it considers the natural order of things. There are no amicus briefs (statements of legal opinion filed with a court by outside parties), no observers, and no public records of the deliberations.

The WTO's rule is not restricted to such matters as tariff barriers. When the organization was formed, environmental and labor groups warned that the WTO would soon be rendering decisions on essential matters of public policy. This has proven absolutely correct. The organization ruled against Europe for banning hormone-treated beef and against Japan for prohibiting pesticide-laden apples. Also WTO rules prohibit selective purchasing laws, even those targeted at human rights abuses. In 1998 the WTO court lodged a complaint against the Massachusetts state law that banned government purchases from Burma in an attempt to punish its brutal dictatorship. Had the WTO's rules been in place at the time at the time of the anti-Apartheid divestment movement, laws barring trade with or investment in South Africa would have violated them as well.

Why should you care?

At stake is a fundamental issue of popular sovereignty—the rights of the people to regulate economic life, whether at the level of the city, state, or nation. The U.S. does not allow businesses operating within its borders to produce goods with child labor, for example, so why should we allow those same businesses—Disney, Gap, or Walmart—to produce their goods with child labor in Haiti and sell the goods here? ❏

Article 5.3

NAFTA AND CAFTA

From "The ABCs of Free-Trade Agreements and Other Regional Economic Blocs"

BY THE *DOLLARS & SENSE* COLLECTIVE
January/February 2001, last revised December 2016

In the early 1990s, as the North American Free Trade Agreement (NAFTA) was under consideration in Canada, Mexico, and the United States, supporters of the pact argued that both business owners and workers in all three countries would gain from the removal of trade and investment barriers. For example, the argument went, U.S. firms that produce more efficiently than their Mexican counterparts would enjoy larger markets, gain more profits, generate more jobs, and pay higher wages. The winners would include information technology firms, biotech firms, larger retailers, and other U.S. corporations that had an advantage because of skilled U.S. labor or because of experience in organization and marketing. On the other hand, Mexican firms that could produce at low cost because of low Mexican wages will be able to expand into the U.S. market. The main examples were assembly plants or *maquiladoras*.

Critics of the agreement, meanwhile, focused on problems resulting from extreme differences among the member countries in living standards, wages, unionization, environmental laws, and social legislation. The options that NAFTA would create for business firms, the critics argued, would put them at a great advantage in their dealings with workers and communities.

As it turned out, NAFTA was approved by the governments of all three countries, and went into effect on January 1, 1994. The agreement eliminated most barriers to trade and investment among the United States, Canada and Mexico. For some categories of goods—certain agricultural goods, for example—NAFTA promised to phase out restrictions on trade over a few years, but most goods and services were to be freely bought and sold across the three countries' borders from the start. Likewise, virtually all investments—financial investments as well as investments in fixed assets such as factories, mines, or farms (foreign direct investment)—were freed from cross-border restrictions.

The agreement, however, made no changes in the restrictions on the movement of labor. Mexican—and, for that matter, Canadian—workers who wish to come to the United States must enter under the limited immigration quotas, or illegally. Thus NAFTA gave new options and direct benefits to those who obtain their income from selling goods and making investments, but the agreement included no parallel provision for those who make their incomes by working.

For example, U.S. unions were weakened because firms could more easily shut down domestic operations and substitute operations in Mexico. With the government suppressing independent unions in Mexico, organization of workers in all three countries was undermined. (Actually, the formal Mexican labor laws are probably as good or better than those in the United States but they are usually not enforced.) While NAFTA may mean more jobs and better pay for computer software engineers in the United States, manufacturing workers in the United States, for example, have seen their wages stagnate or fall. Similarly, the greater freedom of international movement that NAFTA affords to firms has given them greater bargaining power over communities when it comes to environmental regulations. One highly visible result has been severe pollution problems in Mexican *maquiladora* zones along the U.S. border.

An additional and important aspect of NAFTA is that it creates legal mechanisms for firms based in one country to contest legislation in the other countries when it might interfere with their "right" to carry out their business. Thus, U.S. firms operating in Mexico have challenged stricter environmental regulations won by the Mexican environmental movement. In Canada, the government rescinded a public-health law restricting trade in toxic PCBs as the result of a challenge by a U.S. firm; Canada also paid $10 million to the complaining firm, in compensation for "losses" it suffered under the law. These examples illustrate the way in which NAFTA, by giving priority to the "rights" of business, has undermined the ability of governments to regulate the operation of their economies in an independent, democratic manner.

Finally, one of NAFTA's greatest gifts to business was the removal of restrictions on the movement of financial capital. The immediate result for Mexico was the severe financial debacle of 1994. Investment funds moved rapidly into Mexico during the early 1990s, and especially after NAFTA went into effect. Without regulation, these investments were able to abandon Mexico just as rapidly when the speculative "bubble" burst, leading to severe drops in production and employment.

CAFTA: Extending the Free Trade Agenda

After the implementation of NAFTA, it looked like the Americas were on a fast track to a hemisphere-wide free-trade zone. In 1994, then-President Bill Clinton proposed to have the world's largest trading block in place by 2005. Instead, the Free Trade Area of the Americas (FTAA) stalled in its tracks when, in 1997, Congress denied Clinton "fast-track" negotiating authority. President George W. Bush revived the fast-track push in 2001 and succeeded in getting fast-track legislation through both the House of Representatives and the U.S. Senate in 2002. Nonetheless, the entire decade of the 2000s came and went without the FTAA.

The NAFTA model, however, has been extended into Central America and the Caribbean through the Central American Free Trade Agreement (CAFTA). CAFTA is now in effect for trade between the United States and six other countries (five Central American, one Caribbean): Costa Rica, El Salvador, Guatemala, Honduras, Nicaragua, and the Dominican Republic. Economic size alone assures that U.S. interests dominate the agreement. The combined economic output of the countries in Central America is smaller than the total income of just two U.S.-based agribusiness companies that will benefit from the accord: Cargill and Archer Daniels Midland.

CAFTA, modeled after NAFTA, shares all of its shortcomings. It will do as much to hamper sustainable development and no more to further human rights or end labor abuses in Central America than NAFTA has in Mexico. A report from the "Stop CAFTA Coalition" documented the problems evident just one year after the agreement. First, CAFTA did not appear to be creating the promised regional textile complex to offset competition from China. Central American garment exports continued to lose market share to their Asian competitors. In addition, CAFTA contributed to making difficult conditions in the Central American countryside yet worse. For instance, imports of fresh beef, poultry, and dairy products from the United States increased dramatically, displacing local producers. (As in Mexico after NAFTA, the effect was to force people to migrate out of the hard-hit rural areas, either traveling to already-crowded cities or risking a treacherous journey to the United States.) Finally, CAFTA did nothing to improve human rights or extend labor rights in Central America.

And CAFTA poses yet another danger. Rules buried in the technical language of the agreement's investment chapter makes it more difficult for the Central American and Caribbean nations to formulat independent monetary policies focused at developing their national economies. This only makes it harder for them to escape heavy debt burdens or recover from a debt crisis. ❑

Article 5.4

THE EUROPEAN UNION AND THE EUROZONE

BY THE *DOLLARS & SENSE* COLLECTIVE
January/February 2001, last revised December 2016

The European Union (EU) forms the world's largest single market—larger than the United States or even the three NAFTA countries together. From its beginnings in 1951 as the six-member European Coal and Steel Community, the association has grown both geographically (now including 28 countries) and especially in its degree of unity. All national border controls on goods, capital, and people were abolished between member countries in 1993. And seventeen of the EU's members now share a common currency (the euro), collectively forming the "eurozone."

The EU and the "Social Charter": Promises Unkept

At first glance, open trade within the EU seemed to pose less of a threat for wages and labor standards than NAFTA or the WTO. Even the poorer member countries, such as Spain, Portugal, and Greece, were fairly wealthy and had strong unions and decent labor protections. Moreover, most EU countries, including top economic powers like France, Germany, Italy, and the United Kingdom, had strong parties (whether "socialist," social democratic, or labor) with roots in the working-class movement. This relationship had grown increasingly distant over time; still, from the perspective of labor, the EU represented a kind of best-case scenario for freeing trade. The results are, nonetheless, cautionary.

The main thrust of the EU, like other trade organizations, has been trade and investment. Labor standards were never fully integrated into the core agenda of the EU. In 1989, 11 of the then-12 EU countries signed the "Charter of the Fundamental Social Rights of Workers," more widely known as the "Social Charter." (Only the United Kingdom refused to sign.) Though the "Social Charter" did not have any binding mechanism—it is described in public communications as "a political instrument containing 'moral obligations'"—many hoped it would provide the basis for "upward harmonization," that is, pressure on European countries with weaker labor protections to lift their standards to match those of member nations with stronger regulations. The years since the adoption of the "Social Charter" have seen countless meetings, official studies, and exhortations but few appreciable results.

Since trade openness was never directly linked to social and labor standards and the "Social Charter" never mandated concrete actions from corporations, European business leaders have kept "Social Europe" from gaining any momentum simply by ignoring it. Although European anti-discrimination rules have forced countries like Britain to adopt the same retirement age for men and women, and regional funds are dispersed each year to bring up the general living standards of the poorest nations, the social dimension of the EU has never been more than an appendage for buying off opposition. As a result, business moved production, investment, and employment in Europe toward countries with lower standards, such as Ireland and Portugal.

The EU also exemplifies how regional trading blocs indirectly break down trade regulations with countries outside the bloc. Many Europeans may have hoped that the EU would insulate Europe from competition with countries that lacked social, labor, and environmental standards. While the EU has a common external tariff, each member can maintain its own non-tariff trade barriers. EU rules requiring openness between member countries, however, made it easy to circumvent any EU country's national trade restrictions. Up until 1993, member states used to be able to block indirect imports through health and safety codes or border controls, but with the harmonization of these rules across the EU, governments can no longer do so. Since then, companies have simply imported non-EU goods into the EU countries with the most lax trade rules, and then freely transported the goods into the countries with higher standards. (NAFTA similarly makes it possible to circumvent U.S. barriers against the importation of steel from China by sending it indirectly through Mexico.)

EU members that wished to uphold trade barriers against countries with inadequate social, labor, and environmental protections ended up becoming less important trading hubs in the world economy. This led EU countries to unilaterally abolish restrictions and trade monitoring against non-EU nations. The logic of trade openness seems to be against labor and the environment even when the governments of a trading bloc individually wish to be more protective.

The Eurozone: Caught in a Bind

The process of European economic integration culminated with the establishment of a common currency (the euro) between 1999 and 2002. The creation of the euro seemed to cap the rise of Europe, over many years, from the devastation of the Second World War. Step by step, Western Europe had rebuilt vibrant economies. The largest "core" economy, Germany, had become a global manufacturing power. Even some countries with historically lower incomes, like Ireland, Italy, and Spain, had converged toward the affluence of the core countries. The euro promised to be a major new world currency, ultimately with hundreds of millions of users in one of the world's richest and seemingly most stable regions. Some commentators viewed the euro as a potential rival to the dollar as a key currency in world trade, and as a "reserve" currency (in which individuals, companies, and national banks would hold financial wealth).

Of the 28 European Union (EU) member countries, only 19 have adopted the euro as their currency (joined the "eurozone"). One of the most important EU economies, the United Kingdom, for example, retained its own national currency (the pound). The countries that did adopt the euro, on the other hand, retired their national currencies. There is no German deutschmark, French franc, or Italian lira anymore. These currencies, and the former national currencies of other eurozone countries, stopped circulating in 2001 or 2002, depending on the country. Bank balances held in these currencies were converted to euros. People holding old bills and coins were also able to exchange them for euros.

The adoption of the euro meant a major change in the control over monetary policy for the eurozone countries. Countries that have their own national currencies generally have a central bank (or "monetary authority") responsible for policies affecting the country's overall money supply and interest rates. In the United States, for example, the Federal Reserve (or "the Fed") is the monetary authority. For eurozone countries, monetary policy is made not by a national central bank, but by the European Central Bank (ECB). ECB policy is made by 25-member "governing council," including the six members of the bank's executive board and the directors of each of the 19 member countries' central banks. The six executive-board members, meanwhile, come from various eurozone countries.

While all countries that have adopted the euro are represented on the governing council, Germany has a much greater influence on European monetary policy than other countries. Germany's is the largest economy in the eurozone. (France's economy is just over two-thirds the size of Germanys; Italy's, just over half; Spain's, just over one-third; the Netherlands', less than one-fourth.) German policymakers, meanwhile, have historically made very low inflation rates their main priority (to the point of being seen as "inflation-phobic"). Even during the current crisis, as economist Paul Krugman puts it, "what we're seeing is an ECB catering to German desires for low inflation, very much at the expense of making the problems of peripheral economies much less tractable."

For countries, like Germany, that were hit less hard by the global Great Recession, the "tight money" policy did not prevent a fairly quick return to normal levels of unemployment. For the harder-hit countries, however, the results have been disastrous. These countries are mired in a deep economic crisis, in heavy debt, and unable to adopt a traditional "expansionary" monetary policy on their own (since the eurozone monetary policy is set by the ECB). For them, a looser monetary policy could stimulate demand, production, and employment, even without causing much of an increase in inflation. In Europe today, however, there are vast unused resources—including millions of unemployed workers—so more demand could stimulate the production of more goods, and need not result in rising inflation.

Somewhat higher inflation, moreover, could actually help stimulate the harder-hit European economies. Moderate inflation can stimulate demand, since it gives people an incentive to spend now rather than wait and spend later. It also reduces the real burdens of debt. Countries like Greece and Spain are drowning in debt, both public and private. These debts are generally specified in nominal terms—as a particular number of euros. As the price level increases, however, it reduces the real value of a nominal amount of money. Debts can be paid back in euros that are worth less than when the debt was incurred. As real debt burdens decrease, people feel less anxious about their finances, and may begin to spend more freely. Inflation also redistributes income from creditors, who tend to be wealthier and to save more of their incomes, to debtors, who tend to be less wealth and spend most of theirs. This, too, helps boost demand.

The Crisis of the EU

The current crisis has led many commentators to speculate that heavily indebted countries, like Greece or Spain, might decide to abandon the euro and leave the EU. (Greece has appeared the most likely candidate to go that route. A possible Greek exit from the euro and the EU is widely referred to as "Grexit." This need not mean that they would repudiate (refuse to pay) their public debt altogether. They could, instead, convert their euro debts to their new national currencies. The resoration of monetary-policy sovereignty would give them more freedom to pursue an expansionary policy. Increasing the money supply could lower interest rates, stimulate spending, and boost economic growth and employment. To the extent that monetary expansion resulted in somewhat higher inflation, it would also reduce the real debt burden.

So far, neither Greece, nor Spain, nor any other hard-hit country has moved to exit the EU. The only country that has, ironically, is the UK, which is not even a member of the eurozone, and so is not subject to the loss of monetary-policy sovereignty that makes such a move, arguably at least, a serious coniseration in eurozone countries. Rather, the vote in the July 2016 referendum, which narrowly went in favor of "Brexit," appears to have been heavily influenced by anti-immigrant sentiment. (See Reuss, "Globalization, Nativism, and the Brexit Vote," pp. 182-183.)

The current crisis, some economists argue, shows how the euro project was misguided from the start. Paul Krugman, for example, argues that the common currency was mainly driven by a political (not economic) aim—the peaceful unification of a region that had been torn apart by two world wars. It did not make much sense economically, giiven the real possibility for divergent needs of different national economies. Today, it remains a real possibility that the eurozone, or even the EU itself, could come apart again. ❑

Sources: Paul Krugman, "European Inflation Targets," *New York Times* blog, January 18, 2011 (krugman.blogs.nytimes.com); European Central Bank, Decision-making, Governing Council (www.ecb.int/); European Central Bank, Decision-making, Executive Board (www.ecb.int/); Federal Statistical Office (Statistisches Bundesamt Deutschland), Federal Republic of Germany, Short-term indicators, Unemployment, Consumer Price Index (www.destatis.de); Paul Krugman, "Can Europe Be Saved?" *New York Times*, January 12, 2011 (nytimes.com).

Article 5.5

TRANS-PACIFIC PARTNERSHIP: CORPORATE POWER UNBOUND

BY JOHN MILLER
July/August 2015

The Trans-Pacific Partnership (TPP), a proposed multilateral "trade-and-investment" agreement that promised to be the next leap forward in corporate globalization, now seems like it's dead in the water. President-elect Donald Trump has vowed to pull the United States out of the deal, and without the United States there is no TPP. The critique presented here, however, reamins highly relevant. It shows that strong criticism of the TPP and similar agreements has also come from progressive quarters. And it suggests that an "unrigging" of the world economy need not follow the nationalistic and xenophobic paths of Trump and others like him, but can be rooted in a spirit of inclusiveness and solidarity —Eds.

The case [for opposing the Trans-Pacific Partnership] put forth by a showboating Sen. Elizabeth Warren is almost worse than wrong. It is irrelevant.

Less than 10 percent of the AFL-CIO's membership is now in manufacturing. It's undeniable that American manufacturing workers have suffered terrible job losses. We could never compete with pennies-an-hour wages. Those low-skilled jobs are not coming back.

Some liberals oddly complain that American efforts to strengthen intellectual property laws in trade deals protect the profits of U.S. entertainment and tech companies. What's wrong with that?

Then we have Warren stating with a straight face that handing negotiating authority to Obama would "give Republicans the very tool they need to dismantle Dodd-Frank."

—Froma Harrop, "The Left Is Wrong on Fast-Track Trade Issue," *Spokesman Review*, May 16, 2015.

The Trans-Pacific Partnership (TPP) sounds more like an international consortium of corporate law firms than a trade deal. That's for good reason. TPP is less about trade than about corporate-dominated globalization.

But that's all a mystery to Froma Harrop, liberal columnist, business writer, and robotic Obama supporter. (Obama has pushed hard for the TPP.) Why should the AFL-CIO, with so few members in manufacturing, oppose this trade deal, Harrop asks? And what so wrong with protecting corporate profits by enforcing intellectual property rights, as the TPP would?

The answer is plenty. And that's especially true now that the Obama administration and both Republicans and corporate Democrats in Congress have engineered the passage of the "fast-track authority," guaranteeing an up or down vote for the TPP.

The TPP Is Not About Trade

The TPP is surely marketed as a trade deal. And economist after economist supporting TPP has touted it as a giant step toward free trade that will bestow benefits on all nations in just the way every student learns it will in introductory economics.

But what economists have to say about the virtues of free trade, as flawed as that may be, has little to do with the TPP. The TPP is not about free trade or even principally about the gains from trade.

The TPP would be the largest regional "trade" agreement ever. It involves 12 countries: the United States, Australia, Brunei, Canada, Chile, Japan, Malaysia, Mexico, New Zealand, Peru, Singapore, and Vietnam. Those dozen countries collectively produce 40% of global output (GDP).

But if trade is the hype, it is not the substance of the deal. To begin with, the TPP would do little to reduce barriers to trade in these countries, which are already quite low. The average tariff level in each of the 12 countries is lower than the world average (6.8% in 2012) and far lower than global tariff rates two decades ago. In addition, Australia, Canada, Chile, Mexico, Peru, and Singapore are already members of other free trade agreements with the United States. In 2014, nearly three-quarters (74%) of U.S. goods traded with the TPP group was with those six nations. As tariff levels have dropped, so have potential gains from further lowering tariffs, as envisioned by those who have drunk the free trade Kool-Aid served up by economists.

For instance, the Peterson Institute for International Economics, a Washington-based pro-free trade thinktank, estimates that the TPP would add $77.5 billion of income to the U.S. economy by 2025, a figure the Obama administration uses to make the case for the TPP. That number might sound impressive, but those gains would add just 0.38% to U.S. GDP over the next ten years. And it is undoubtedly an overestimate, for it relies on the assumption that the U.S. economy and the economies of its trading partners will be at full employment during those years.

The Obama Administration claims that the TPP would create 650,000 new jobs in the next decade. They get that number by dividing the $77.5 billion income gain from the TPP in the Peterson report by the average cost to a company when it hires an additional worker. But nowhere in its report does the Peterson Institute project that the TTP would create jobs. Rather, the position of the Peterson Institute, according to Fred Bergsten, its founder, is that "a trade agreement does not on balance, create, or destroy jobs, it alters the composition of the workforce."

Nor would the meager income gains produced by the TPP be widely shared. In a Center for Economic and Policy Research (CEPR) report, economist David Rosnick estimates that just the top 10% of U.S. workers would see real wage gains, if the Trans-Pacific Partnership were enacted. Worse yet, the real wages of a broad swath of middle-income U.S. workers (from the 35th percentile to the 80th percentile) would fall, even under Rosnick's most conservative assumptions about the likely effect of the TPP on inequality.

Losses from trade agreements have been visited upon the same groups, especially manufacturing workers, time and time again. For instance, labor economists Avraham Ebenstein, Ann Harrison, Margot McMillan, and Shannon Phillips have found that, between 1983 and 2002, globalization forced U.S. workers out of manufacturing into lower-paying jobs, reducing their real wage by 12% to 17%.

TPP is About Corporate Power

Why would the labor movement go all out to defeat the TPP with so few of its members in manufacturing, and with lost manufacturing jobs unlikely to return to the United States?

Economic journalist Robert Kuttner gave perhaps the best answer: "The labor movement is not motivated just by the loss of factory jobs but by the entire ideological assault on the security of ordinary wage earners and consumers." That's also what lies behind the complaints about how the TPP would protect corporate profits in what Nobel Prize winning economist Joseph Stiglitz calls a "secret corporate takeover."

At the heart of the TPP is an Investor-State Dispute Settlement (ISDS) process that would give corporations yet more power to make the economic rules that govern our lives. The settlement process would allow investors who think that a country's laws have reduced their profits to take their case before a "tribunal" of three private attorneys; that is, to sidestep the country's own legal system. Unlike national courts, which can order corporations to be compensated for losses of actual assets, ISDS tribunals would be empowered to order taxpayers to compensate corporation for losses of expected profits—even those projected decades into the future.

These are not just hypothetical concerns. In other free trade agreements, the ISDS process has enabled:

- Phillip Morris to sue Australia and Uruguay, arguing that warnings required on cigarette packages are cutting their profits.
- Nuclear power operator Vattenfall to sue Germany for $3.7 billion in lost future profits over the German government's decision to phase out nuclear power after the Fukushima nuclear disaster.
- The oil and gas company Lone Pine Resources Inc. to sue the Province of Quebec for $250 million (in Canadian dollars) after Quebec imposed a fracking moratorium.
- Veolia, French waste management company, to sue Egypt because the country raised the minimum wage, increasing Veolia's costs.
- A Dutch subsidiary of a Japanese bank to sue the Czech Republic, arguing that the country had violated its rights by extending its bailout program only to "too big to fail" banks.

Defenders of the ISDS process maintain that it will have little effect in the United States with its corporate friendly legal system that they call the "good rule of law." The U.S. government, they hasten to point out, has not lost an ISDS case. And President

Obama, as Harrop emphasizes, has vehemently denied that he would ever sign an agreement that would threaten the Dodd-Frank financial reforms. But Obama's assurances are nearly meaningless. While he would have control over appointments to the ISDS tribunals, he would not be able to control what decisions his appointees reach, or who the Presidents who follows him appoint to the tribunals. And the "good rule of law" has not prevented Canada from having to pay out six ISDS claims brought by corporations. But whatever the ramifications for the United States, ISDS provisions shrink the "policy space" for other countries less inclined to have their governments constrained by what would pass muster with an ISDS tribunal.

Other TPP provisions would actually limit trade, not prompt it. Its provisions to enforce "intellectual property rights," which Harrop praises, would strengthen patents restricting the availability of prescription drugs. While a boon to big phrama, those provisions would drive up the cost of already expensive drugs to fight cancer and other diseases. Public health researchers Hazel Moir, Brigitte Tenni, Deborah Gleeson, and Ruth Lopert estimate that it would cut in half the share of Vietnam's AIDS patients who have access to life-saving antiretroviral drugs.

Not For Industry Alone

Just before the passage of fast track in June, Senator Elizabeth Warren (D-Mass.)—who led the fight against TPP in the Senate—warned against enacting more "trade agreements that offer gold-plated enforcement for giant corporations and meaningless promises for everyone else."

But TPP surely would do just that. Worse yet, it would exacerbate inequality and compromise democracy, as it exempts corporations from environmental and labor standards, or whatever laws interfere with their accumulation of profits.

Now that's not about the "good rule of law." It's about corporations using their power to evade the rule of law. ❑

Sources: Elizabeth Warren, "Trade agreements should not benefit industry only," *Boston Globe*, June 23, 2015; Robert Kuttner, "The Real Meaning of Obama's Trade Deal," *Huffington Post*, June 16, 2015; Joseph Stiglitz, "The Secret Corporate Takeover," Project Syndicate, May 13, 2015; Kevin Gallagher, "Saving Obama from a Bad Trade Deal," *The American Prospect*, March 4, 2015; Peter Petri and Michael Plummer, "The Trans-Pacifc Parternship and Asia-Pacific Integration," Peterson Institute for International Economics, June 2012; David Rosnick, "Gains from Trade?" Center for Economic and Policy Research, September 2013; Glen Kessler, "The Obama administration's illusionary job gains from the Trans-Pacific Partnership," *Washington Post*, Jan. 30, 2015; Peter Evans, "Our Delegation Stood Up to Bad Trade Deal," *Santa Fe New Mexican*, June 26, 2015; Avraham Ebenstein, Ann Harrison, Margaret McMillan, and Shannon Phillips, "Estimating the Impact of Trade and Offshoring on American Workers using the Current Population Surveys," *The Review of Economics and Statistics*, October 2014; Hazel Moir, Brigitte Tenni, Deborah Gleeson, and Ruth Lopert, "Assessing the impact of alternative patent systems on the cost of health care: the TPPA and HIV treatment in Vietnam," Asia-Pacific Innovation Conference, University of Technology Sydney, 27-29 November 2014.

Article 5.6

TRANSATLANTIC TRADE AND INVESTMENT PARTNERSHIP: IT'S NOT ABOUT TRADE

BY DEAN BAKER
February 2014; Atlantic-Community

The most important fact to know about the Transatlantic Trade and Investment Partnership (TTIP) is that promoting trade is not really the purpose of the deal. With few exceptions, traditional trade barriers, in the form of tariffs or quotas, between the United States and European Union (EU) are already low. No one would devote a great deal of effort to bringing them down further; there is not much to be gained.

The pursuit of free trade is just a cover for the real agenda of the TTIP. The deal is about imposing a regulatory structure to be enforced through an international policing mechanism that likely would not be approved through the normal political processes in each country. The rules that will be put in place as a result of the deal are likely to be more friendly to corporations and less friendly to the environment and consumers than current rules. And, they will likely impede economic growth.

In a wide variety of areas, the EU has much stronger protections for consumers and the environment than in the United States. For example, the United States has a highly concentrated mobile phone industry that is allowed to charge consumers whatever it likes. The same is true for Internet access. As a result, people in the United States pay far more for these services.

Fracking for oil and natural gas has advanced much more in the United States than in Europe in part because it is largely unregulated. In fact, the industry got a special exemption from laws on clean drinking water, so that the companies don't even have to disclose the chemicals they are using in the fracking process. As a result, if they end up contaminating ground water and drinking water in areas near a fracking site, it will be almost impossible for the victims to prove their case.

These are the sorts of regulatory changes that industry will be seeking in the TTIP. It is unlikely the governments of individual European countries or the EU as a body would support the gutting of consumer and environmental regulations. Therefore the industry groups want to use a "free trade" agreement to circumvent the democratic process.

However, the worst part of the TTIP is likely to be in its rules on patents and copyright. The United States has a notoriously corrupt patent system. A major food manufacturer once patented a peanut butter sandwich and of course Amazon was able to get a patent on "one-click shopping." These frivolous patents, which are common in the United States, raise prices and impede competition. Europeans will likely see more of such patents as a result of the TTIP.

The deal is likely to have even more consequences for the cost and availability of prescription drugs. The United States pays roughly twice as much for its drugs as Europe. This is due to the unchecked patent monopolies granted to our drug companies. A major goal of the pharmaceutical industry is to be able to get similar rules imposed in the EU so that companies can charge higher prices.

There is an enormous amount of money at stake in this battle. The United States spends close to $350 billion a year on drugs that would sell for around one-tenth this price in a free market. The difference is almost 2% of GDP, or more than 25% of after-tax corporate profits. This amounts to a huge transfer from the public at large to the pharmaceutical industry.

The enormous gap between the patent-protected price and production costs gives drug companies an incentive to mislead the public about the safety and effectiveness of their drugs, which they do with considerable regularity. In short, an outcome of the deal can be much higher drug prices and lower-quality health care.

None of the models used to project economic gains from the TTIP even try to estimate the economic losses that would result from higher drug prices or other negative consequences of stronger patent protection. For this reason these models do not provide a useful guide to the likely economic impact of the TTIP.

The notion that the TTIP will provide some quick boost to the economies of the EU and the United States is absurd on its face. The public should scrutinize whatever comes out of the negotiating process very carefully. If politicians demand a quick yes or no answer, then the obvious answer must be "no." ❑

Chapter 6

LABOR IN THE GLOBAL ECONOMY

Article 6.1

THE GLOBALIZATION CLOCK

BY THOMAS PALLEY
May/June 2006

Political economy has historically been constructed around the divide between capital and labor, with firms and workers at odds over the division of the economic pie. Within this construct, labor is usually represented as a monolithic interest, yet the reality is that labor has always suffered from internal divisions—by race, by occupational status, and along many other fault lines. Neoliberal globalization has in many ways sharpened these divisions, which helps to explain why corporations have been winning and workers losing.

One of these fault lines divides workers from themselves: since workers are also consumers, they face a divide between the desire for higher wages and the desire for lower prices. Historically, this identity split has been exploited to divide union from nonunion workers, with anti-labor advocates accusing union workers of causing higher prices. Today, globalization is amplifying the divide between people's interests as workers and their interests as consumers through its promise of ever-lower prices.

Consider the debate over Walmart's low-road labor policies. While Walmart's low wages and skimpy benefits have recently faced scrutiny, even some liberal commentators argue that Walmart is actually good for low-wage workers because they gain more as consumers from its "low, low prices" than they lose as workers from its low wages. But this static, snapshot analysis fails to capture the full impact of globalization, past and future.

Globalization affects the economy unevenly, hitting some sectors first and others later. The process can be understood in terms of the hands of a clock. At one o'clock is the apparel sector; at two o'clock, the textile sector; at three, the steel sector; at six, the auto sector. Workers in the apparel sector are the first to have their jobs shifted to lower-wage venues; at the same time, though, all other workers get price reductions. Next, the process picks off textile sector workers at two o'clock. Meanwhile, workers from three o'clock onward get price cuts, as do the apparel workers at one o'clock. Each time the hands of the clock move, the workers taking the hit are isolated. In this fashion, globalization moves around the clock, with labor perennially divided.

Manufacturing was first to experience this process, but technological innovations associated with the Internet are putting service and knowledge workers in the firing line as well. Online business models are making even retail workers vulnerable—consider Amazon.com, for example, which has opened a customer support center and two technology development centers in India. Public-sector wages are also in play, at least indirectly, since falling wages mean falling tax revenues. The problem is that each time the hands on the globalization clock move forward, workers are divided: the majority is made slightly better off while the few are made much worse off.

Globalization also alters the historical divisions within capital, creating a new split between bigger internationalized firms and smaller firms that remain nationally centered. This division has been brought into sharp focus with the debate over the trade deficit and the overvalued dollar. In previous decades, manufacturing as a whole opposed running trade deficits and maintaining an overvalued dollar because of the adverse impact of increased imports. The one major business sector with a different view was retailing, which benefited from cheap imports.

However, the spread of multinational production and outsourcing has divided manufacturing in wealthy countries into two camps. In one camp are larger multinational corporations that have gone global and benefit from cheap imports; in the other are smaller businesses that remain nationally centered in terms of sales, production and input sourcing. Multinational corporations tend to support an overvalued dollar since this makes imports produced in their foreign factories cheaper. Conversely, domestic manufacturers are hurt by an overvalued dollar, which advantages import competition.

This division opens the possibility of a new alliance between labor and those manufacturers and businesses that remain nationally based—potentially a potent one, since there are approximately 7 million enterprises with sales of less than $10 million in the United States, versus only 200,000 with sales greater than $10 million. However, such an alliance will always be unstable as the inherent labor-capital conflict over income distribution can always reassert itself. Indeed, this pattern is already evident in the internal politics of the National Association of Manufacturers (NAM), whose members have been significantly divided regarding the overvalued dollar. As one way to address this division, the group is promoting a domestic "competitiveness" agenda aimed at weakening regulation, reducing corporate legal liability, and lowering employee benefit costs—an agenda designed to appeal to both camps, but at the expense of workers.

Solidarity has always been key to political and economic advance by working families, and it is key to mastering the politics of globalization. Developing a coherent story about the economics of neoliberal globalization around which working families can coalesce is a key ingredient for solidarity. So, too, is understanding how globalization divides labor. These narratives and analyses can help counter deep cultural proclivities to individualism, as well as other historic divides such as racism. However, as if this were not difficult enough, globalization creates additional challenges. National political solutions that worked in the past are not adequate to the task of controlling international competition. That means the solidarity bar is further raised, calling for international solidarity that supports new forms of international economic regulation. ❑

Article 6.2

CAMPUS STRUGGLES AGAINST SWEATSHOPS CONTINUE
Indonesian workers and U.S. students fight back against Adidas.

BY SARAH BLASKEY AND PHIL GASPER
September/October 2012

Abandoning his financially ailing factory in the Tangerang region of Indonesia, owner Jin Woo Kim fled the country for his home, South Korea, in January 2011 without leaving money to pay his workers. The factory, PT Kizone, stayed open for several months and then closed in financial ruin in April, leaving 2,700 workers with no jobs and owed $3.4 million of legally mandated severance pay.

In countries like Indonesia, with no unemployment insurance, severance pay is what keeps workers and their families from literal starvation. "The important thing is to be able to have rice. Maybe we add some chili pepper, some salt, if we can," explained an ex-Kizone worker, Marlina, in a report released by the Worker Rights Consortium (WRC), a U.S.-based labor-rights monitoring group, in May 2012. Marlina, widowed mother of two, worked at PT Kizone for eleven years before the factory closed. She needs the severance payment in order to pay her son's high school registration fee and monthly tuition, and to make important repairs to her house.

When the owner fled, the responsibility for severance payments to PT Kizone workers fell on the companies that sourced from the factory—Adidas, Nike, and the Dallas Cowboys. Within a year, both Nike and the Dallas Cowboys made severance payments that they claim are proportional to the size of their orders from the factory, around $1.5 million total. But Adidas has refused to pay any of the $1.8 million still owed to workers.

Workers in PT Kizone factory mainly produced athletic clothing sold to hundreds of universities throughout the United States. All collegiate licensees like Adidas and Nike sign contracts with the universities that buy their apparel. At least 180 universities around the nation are affiliated with the WRC and have licensing contracts mandating that brands pay "all applicable back wages found due to workers who manufactured the licensed articles." If wages or severance pay are not paid to workers that produce university goods, then the school has the right to terminate the contract.

Using the language in these contracts, activists on these campuses coordinate nationwide divestment campaigns to pressure brands like Adidas to uphold previously unenforceable labor codes of conduct.

Unpaid back wages and benefits are a major problem in the garment industry. Apparel brands rarely own factories. Rather, they contract with independent manufacturers all over the world to produce their wares. When a factory closes for any reason, a brand can simply take its business somewhere else and wash its hands of any responsibilities to the fired workers.

Brands like Nike and Russell have lost millions of dollars when, pressed by United Students Against Sweatshops (USAS), universities haver terminated their contracts.

According to the USAS website, campus activism has forced Nike to pay severance and Russell to rehire over 1,000 workers it had laid off, in order to avoid losing more collegiate contracts. Now many college activists have their sights set on Adidas.

At the University of Wisconsin (UW) in Madison, the USAS-affiliated Student Labor Action Coalition (SLAC) and sympathetic faculty are in the middle of a more than year-long campaign to pressure the school to terminate its contract with Adidas in solidarity with the PT Kizone workers.

The chair of UW's Labor Licensing Policy Committee (LLPC) says that Adidas is in violation of the code of conduct for the school's licensees. Even the university's senior counsel, Brian Vaughn, stated publicly at a June LLPC meeting that Adidas is "in breach of the contract based on its failure to adhere to the standards of the labor code." But despite the fact that Vaughn claimed at the time that the University's "two overriding goals are to get money back in the hands of the workers and to maintain the integrity of the labor code," the administration has dragged its feet in responding to Adidas.

Instead of putting the company on notice for potential contract termination and giving it a deadline to meet its obligations as recommended by the LLPC, UW entered into months of fruitless negotiations with Adidas in spring 2012. In July, when these negotiations had led nowhere, UW's interim chancellor David Ward asked a state court to decide whether or not Adidas had violated the contract (despite the senior counsel's earlier public admission that it had). This process will delay a decision for many more months--perhaps years if there are appeals.

Since the Adidas campaign's inception in the fall of 2011, SLAC members have actively opposed the school's cautious approach, calling both the mediation process and the current court action a "stalling tactic" by the UW administration and Adidas to avoid responsibility to the PT Kizone workers. In response, student organizers planned everything from frequent letter deliveries to campus administrators, to petition drives, teach-ins, and even a banner drop from the administration building that over 300 people attended, all in hopes of pressuring the chancellor (who ultimately has the final say in the matter) to cut the contract with Adidas.

While the administration claims that it is moving slowly to avoid being sued by Adidas, it is also getting considerable pressure from its powerful athletics director, Barry Alvarez, to continue its contract with Adidas. As part of the deal, UW's sports programs receive royalties and sports gear worth about $2.5 million every year.

"Just look at the money—what we lose and what it would cost us," Alvarez told the *Wisconsin State Journal*, even though other major brands would certainly jump at the opportunity to replace Adidas. "We have four building projects going on. It could hurt recruiting. There's a trickle-down effect that would be devastating to our whole athletic program." But Tina Treviño-Murphy, a student activist with SLAC, rejects this logic. "A strong athletics department shouldn't have to be built on a foundation of stolen labor," she told *Dollars & Sense*. "Our department and our students deserve better."

Adidas is now facing pressure from both campus activists in the United States and the workers in Indonesia--including sit-ins by the latter at the German and British embassies in Jakarta. (Adidas' world headquarters are in Germany, and the company sponsored the recent London Olympics.) This led to a meeting between their union and an Adidas representative, who refused to admit responsibility but instead offered food vouchers to some of the workers. The offer amounted to a tiny fraction of the owed severance and was rejected as insulting by former Kizone workers.

In the face of intransigence from university administrations and multinational companies prepared to shift production quickly from one location to another to stay one step ahead of labor-rights monitors, campus activism to fight sweatshops can seem like a labor of Sisyphus. After more than a decade of organizing, a recent fundraising appeal from USAS noted that "today sweatshop conditions are worse than ever."

Brands threaten to pull out of particular factories if labor costs rise, encouraging a work environment characterized by "forced overtime, physical and sexual harassment, and extreme anti-union intimidation, even death threats," says Natalie Yoon, a USAS member who recently participated in a delegation to factories in Honduras and El Salvador.

According to Snehal Shingavi, a professor at the University of Texas, Austin who was a USAS activist at Berkeley for many years, finding ways to build links with the struggles of the affected workers is key. "What I think would help the campaign the most is if there were actually more sustained and engaged connections between students here and workers who are in factories who are facing these conditions," Shingavi told *Dollars & Sense*. Ultimately, he said, only workers' self-activity can "make the kind of changes that I think we all want, which is an end to exploitative working conditions."

But in the meantime, even small victories are important. Anti-sweatshop activists around the country received a boost in September, when Cornell University President David Skorton announced that his school was ending its licensing contract with Adidas effective October 1, because of the company's failure to pay severance to PT Kizone workers. The announcement followed a sustained campaign by the Sweatfree Cornell Coalition, leading up to a "study in" at the president's office. While the contract itself was small, USAS described the decision as the "first domino," which may lead other campuses to follow suit. Shortly afterwards, Oberlin College in Ohio told Adidas that it would not renew its current four-year contract with the company if the workers in Indonesia are not paid severance.

Perhaps just as significant are the lessons that some activists are drawing from these campaigns. "The people who have a lot of power are going to want to keep that power and the only way to make people give some of that up is if we make them," Treviño-Murphy said. "So it's really pressure from below, grassroots organizing, that makes the difference. We see that every day in SLAC and I think it teaches us to be not just better students but better citizens who will stand up to fight injustice every time." ❑

Sources: Worker Rights Consortium, "Status Update Re: PT Kizone (Indonesia)," May 15, 2012 (workersrights.org); Andy Baggot, "Alvarez Anxiously Awaits Adidas Decision," *Wisconsin State Journal*, July 13, 2012 (host.madison.com); United Students Against Sweatshops (usas.org), PT Kizone update, June 15, 2012 (cleanclothes.org/urgent-actions/kizoneupdate).

Article 6.3

AFTER HORROR, CHANGE?
Taking Stock of Conditions in Bangladesh's Garment Factories

BY JOHN MILLER
September/October 2014

"I believe Bangladesh is making history as it creates new standards for the apparel industry globally."
——Dan Mozena, U.S. Ambassador to Bangladesh
"After the collapse of Rana Plaza, there has been an unprecedented level of cooperation, good will, and practical action toward better and safer places to work in Bangladesh."
——Srinivas B. Reddy, Country Director, International Labor Organization (ILO) Bangladesh
"It is fair to say that neither the government, nor the brands, is dealing adequately with the rising crescendo of employer-sponsored violence."
——U.S. Rep. George Miller (D-Calif.)
Statements made at the International Conference on Globalization and Sustainability of the Bangladesh Garment Sector, Harvard University, June 14, 2014

On April 24, 2013, the Rana Plaza factory building, just outside of Bangladesh's capital city of Dhaka, collapsed—killing 1,138 workers and inflicting serious long-term injuries on at least 1,000 others.

While the collapse of Rana Plaza was in one sense an accident, the policies that led to it surely were not. Bangladesh's garment industry grew to be the world's second largest exporter, behind only China's, by endangering and exploiting workers. Bangladesh's 5,000 garment factories paid rock-bottom wages, much lower than those in China, and just half of those in Vietnam. One foreign buyer told *The Economist* magazine, "There are no rules whatsoever that can not be bent." Cost-saving measures included the widespread use of retail buildings as factories—including at Rana Plaza—adding weight that sometimes exceeded the load-bearing capacity of the structures.

As Scott Nova, executive director of the Worker Rights Consortium, testified before Congress, "the danger to workers in Bangladesh has been apparent for many years." The first documented mass-fatality incident in the country's export garment sector occurred in December 1990. In addition to those killed at Rana Plaza, more than 600 garment workers have died in factory fires in Bangladesh since 2005. After Rana Plaza, however, Bangladesh finally reached a crossroads. The policies that had led to the stunning growth of its garment industry had so tarnished the "Made in Bangladesh" label that they were no longer sustainable.

But just how much change has taken place since Rana Plaza? That was the focus of an International Conference at Harvard this June, bringing together government officials from Bangladesh and the United States, representatives of the Bangladesh garment industry, the international brands, women's groups, trade unions, the International Labor Organization (ILO), and monitoring groups working in Bangladesh.

How Much Change on the Ground?

Srinivas B. Reddy of the ILO spoke favorably of an "unprecedented level of ... practical action" toward workplace safety in Bangladesh.

The "practical action" on the ground, however, has been much more of a mixed bag than Reddy suggests. In the wake of massive protests and mounting international pressure, Bangladesh amended its labor laws to remove some obstacles to workers forming unions. Most importantly, the new law bars the country's labor ministry from giving factory owners lists of workers who want to organize.

But formidable obstacles to unionization still remain. At least 30% of the workers at an entire company are required to join a union before the government will grant recognition. This is a higher hurdle than workers face even in the not-so-union-friendly United States, where recognition is based at the level of the workplace, not the company. Workers in special export-processing zones (the source of about 16% of Bangladesh's exports), moreover, remain ineligible to form unions.

The Bangladesh government did register 160 new garment unions in 2013 and the first half of this year, compared to just two between 2010 and 2012. Nonetheless, collective bargaining happens in only 3% of garment plants. And employers have responded with firings and violence to workers registering for union recognition or making bargaining demands. Union organizers have been kidnapped, brutally beaten, and killed.

After protests that shut down over 400 factories last fall, the Bangladesh government raised the minimum wage for garment workers from the equivalent of $38 a month to $68. The higher minimum wage, however, fell short of the $103 demanded by workers.

The government and the garment brands have also set up the Rana Plaza Donor Trust Fund to compensate victims and their families for their losses and injuries. But according to the fund's website, it stood at just $17.9 million at the beginning of August, well below its $40 million target. Only about half of the 29 international brands that had their clothes sewn at Rana Plaza have made contributions. Ineke Zeldenrust of the Amsterdam-based labor-rights group Clean Clothes Campaign estimates that those 29 brands are being asked to contribute less than 0.2% of their $22 billion in total profits for 2013.

The Accord and the Alliance

Following Rana Plaza, a group of mostly European retail chains turned away from the business-as-usual approach of company codes that had failed to ensure safe working conditions in the factories that made their clothes. Some 151 apparel brands and retailers doing business in Bangladesh, including 16 U.S.-based retailers, signed the Accord on Fire and Building Safety in Bangladesh. Together the signatories of this five-year agreement contracted with 1,639 of the 3,498 Bangladesh factories making garments for export.

The Accord broke important new ground. Unlike earlier efforts:

- It was negotiated with two global unions, UndustriALL and UNI (Global).
- It sets up a governing board with equal numbers of labor and retail representatives, and a chair chosen by the ILO.
- Independent inspectors will conduct audits of factory hazards and make their results public on the Accord website, including the name of the factory, detailed information about the hazard, and recommended repairs.
- The retailers will provide direct funding for repairs (up to a maximum of $2.5 million per company) and assume responsibility for ensuring that all needed renovations and repairs are paid for.
- Most importantly, the Accord is legally binding. Disputes between retailers and union representatives are subject to arbitration, with decisions enforceable by a court of law in the retailer's home country.

But most U.S. retailers doing business in Bangladesh—including giants like Wal-Mart, JCPenney, The Gap, and Sears—refused to sign. They objected to the Accord's open-ended financial commitment and to its legally binding provisions.

Those companies, along with 21 other North American retailers and brands, developed an alternative five-year agreement, called the Alliance For Bangladesh Worker Safety. Some 770 factories in Bangladesh produce garments for these 26 companies.

Unlike the Accord, the Alliance is not legally binding and lacks labor-organization representatives. Moreover, retailers contribute a maximum of $1 million per retailer (less than half the $2.5 million under the Accord) to implement their safety plan and needed repairs, and face no binding commitment to pay for needed improvements beyond that. The responsibility to comply with safety standards falls to factory owners, although the Alliance does offer up to $100 million in loans for these expenses.

Kalpona Akter, executive director of the Bangladesh Center for Worker Solidarity, told the U.S. Senate Foreign Relations Committee, "There is no meaningful difference between the Alliance and the corporate-controlled 'corporate social responsibility' programs that have failed Bangladeshi garment workers in the past, and have left behind thousands of dead and injured workers."

Historic and Unprecedented?

Dan Mozena, U.S. Ambassador to Bangladesh, believes that, despite facing significant obstacles, "Bangladesh is making history as it creates new standards for the apparel industry globally."

While the Accord may be without contemporary precedent, joint liability agreements that make retailers responsible for the safety conditions of their subcontractor's factories do have historical antecedents. As political scientist Mark Anner has documented, beginning in the 1920s the International Ladies Garment Workers Union (ILGWU) began negotiating "jobber agreements" in the United States that held the buyer (or "jobber") for an apparel brand "jointly liable" for wages and working conditions in the contractor's factories. Jobber agreements played a central role in the near-eradication of sweatshops in the United States by the late 1950s. In today's global economy, however, international buyers are once again able to escape responsibility for conditions in the far-flung factories of their subcontractors.

Like jobber agreements, the Accord holds apparel manufacturers and retailers legally accountable for the safety conditions in the factories that make their clothes through agreements negotiated between workers or unions and buyers or brands. The next steps for the Accord model, as Anner has argued, are to address working conditions other than building safety (as jobber agreements had), to get more brands to sign on to the Accord, and to negotiate similar agreements in other countries.

That will be no easy task. But, according to Arnold Zack, who helped to negotiate the Better Factories program that brought ILO monitoring of Cambodian garment factories, "Bangladesh is the lynch pin that can bring an end to the bottom feeding shopping the brands practice." ❑

Sources: Arnold M. Zack, "In an Era of Accelerating Attention to Workplace Equity: What Place for Bangladesh," Boston Global Forum, July 8, 2014; Testimony of Kalpona Akter, Testimony of Scott Nova, Senate Committee on Foreign Relations, Feb. 11, 2014; Mark Anner, Jennifer Bair, and Jeremy Blasi, "Toward Joint Liability in Global Supply Chains," *Comparative Labor Law & Policy Journal*, Vol. 35:1, Fall 2013; Prepared Remarks for Rep. George Miller (D-Calif.), Keynote Remarks by U.S. Ambassador to Bangladesh Dan Mozena, Remarks by Country Director ILO Bangladesh Srinivas B. Reddy, International Conference on Globalization and Sustainability of the Bangladesh Garment Sector, June 14, 2014; "Rags in the ruins," *The Economist*, May 4, 2013; "Bangladesh: Amended Labor Law Falls Short," Human Rights Watch, July 18, 2013; Rana Plaza Donor Trust Fund (ranaplaza-arrangement.org/fund).

Article 6.4

THE GLOBAL INDUSTRIAL WORKING CLASS

AN INTERVIEW WITH IMMANUEL NESS
November 2016

Dollars & Sense: You've written that there are more industrial workers in the world today than ever before. Can you explain how that growth has occurred and how it has reshaped the world's industrial working class in recent decades?

Immanuel Ness: Yes, there are two major factors. The first is the deindustrialization of the traditional industries in North America and Western Europe, the garment manufacturing, electronics, automobiles, and other heavy industry, and the relocation of those industries in the global south—Africa, South Asia, and South East Asia in particular, as well as to some extent Latin America. As a consequence, these countries have become major centers of production and export. And as part of that, the number of manufacturing workers has grown dramatically.

The second factor is that within industrial countries like India, China, Bangladesh, and Indonesia, there has been a dramatic urbanization—forced by the end of productive farming in rural areas for many of the working peasants, and moving into urban centers where there have been concentrations of industry. In major cities of South Asia as well as Africa, and Latin America, this is taking place, and the populations have dramatically grown.

So while many in North America, Western Europe, and beyond would say "the industrial working classes is virtually dead," I would make the case that there are in fact more industrial workers on the planet today than anytime in human history—under capitalism, obviously—and roughly speaking, the industrial working class has grown over the last 50 years from somewhere around 200 million to nearly a billion population. Of course, that doesn't include other workers outside of manufacturing and so forth. The process has been unrelenting and one in which a number of the Marxist arguments about capitalist globalization are now really coming to fruition, where workers are engaged in very significant industrial struggles in places like New Delhi, Shenzhen, Cairo, and beyond.

D&S: Can you take us through some of the ways that you see labor struggles playing out in the global South in this context, especially in the countries that you focus some of your research on—China, India, South Africa?

Ness: I think one general theme across the countries in the global south—China, India, South Africa, Indonesia, Egypt, Brazil, Mexico, and beyond—is the fact that there is an absolute level of contingency on a global level.

We don't have in the global South the traditional Fordist factory. Of course, you have large installations, but workers are cycled in and out of these industries so that the tinker, tailor, and candlestick maker is more like the industrial working class today than ever before—where workers are typically not guaranteed jobs for a very long time. Their value as workers is largely over a five- or ten-year period and then they become expendable. And they come in and out of industry on a regular basis, so they may actually one day work in a steel mill and then the next day work as a peddler on the streets. And this is something that takes place especially in the poorest regions in the global South, such as India, Africa, and elsewhere where people are cycled in and out of industries.

Also, you have to focus on the labor struggles themselves as industrialization grows and becomes formalized. There has been a widespread growth in strike activity. So, for instance, the major strikes of the world—Beverly Silver documents these strikes as taking place in the 1990s and she's continuing to do that in her work *Forces of Labor*. This level of industrial militancy is taking place within factories in China, for instance, where workers have gone on mass strikes. In fact, China is the center of thousands of strikes that take place every year. It has more strikes without question than anywhere else in the world, even with a single union—a state dominated union, the All-China Federation of Trade Unions (FTU).

For instance, the largest strike in the private sector in China took place in the city of Dongguan not too far from Hong Kong in the Pearl River Delta of China, the manufacturing hub of China outside of Hong Kong. You had 40,000 workers who were making athletic shoes for Adidas and other companies who went on a strike that lasted about a month between May and June 2014. And of course, that was a very important transformation because many people who are not in China would say, "Well you know the Chinese workers are completely oppressed and so forth and they don't really engage in activity—militancy and so forth—because of the single state union, the FTU."

In fact, there is a lot of grassroots organizing that's going on which tangibly improve conditions, because in China wages are negotiated on a municipal level, especially minimum wages. And so, major changes are taking place in China, which is leading to higher wages, improved working conditions, improved healthcare. A lot of people don't want to admit it, but this is a very important development even within a single-party union.

Of course, in South Africa, we had the epic experience, also in early 2014, the entire period of January to June 2014, where mine workers in the platinum sector went on a five- or six-month strike demanding dramatic increases in wages. Of course, workers lost a lot going on strike in such an extended period in terms of non-payment of wages. But, as a consequence, wages did go up appreciably, over a period that I would say started around 2009 and is continuing to this day. So that in the platinum sector, this has actually contributed to the formation of a major union—an expansion of the union, called AMCU, the Association of Mineworkers and Construction Union—which went from literally no workers to 1,000 workers and now probably representing well over 100,000 workers in the mining sector. And in fact, probably growing dramatically in the years to come.

One aspect of this is, of course, economism [labor struggles focused on economic demands like higher wages] but there are also demands for political change. In South Africa, there is a challenge to the Tripartite Alliance government—composed of the African National Congress, South African Communist Party, and Congress of South African Trade Unions—which came into existence in 1994. It did allow democratic freedoms, but did not at all allow for any kind of redistribution of wealth, so whites continued to maintain the vast majority. And perhaps this will lead to a major movement in the years to come.

In India, this situation is taking place a lot more slowly, but there are extremely interesting formations of unions across different types of industries and different models of unionization that are extremely interesting—even though many would argue that the situation and conditions of Indian workers are actually worsening in the contemporary era. But, no question, workers are going on strike and are also protesting. There's just a need for a political vehicle for that to take place.

D&S: In your book, you argue that observers the world over have to understand this shift of manufacturing and industrial employment to the global South. Of course, people in the global North are acutely aware of the changes of the composition of employment away from manufacturing, away from industry into services and so forth. Do you see a possibility of revitalization of labor movements, presumably now centered outside of manufacturing, in the global North? And are there lessons to be learned by workers and the labor movements in the global North from workers, often struggling under often highly unfavorable conditions, in the global South today?

Ness: Well I'd like to process this by saying that I actually think that the major movements of the future will take place in the global South, where 85% of the working class is situated. In the global North, in some ways, we are beneficiaries of the exploitation of global South workers. But there is no question that these new industries that are formed in services, new technology, and so on are creating high levels of exploitation: For instance, in the restaurant and retail sectors; in telecommunications, where you have call-center workers in the global North that are highly exploited; certainly in the "for-hire" transportation sector, where you have the growth of companies like Uber, which are turning workers theoretically into owners, when in fact they force workers to expend even more in working for these companies.

I think the lesson is that in the global South, struggle is rooted in spontaneity. For instance, throughout a number of unions—in China, India, South Africa, Indonesia, and so on—you have a lot of strike activity going on. You have a lot of militancy taking place. That is the real lesson that we can learn. Uber drivers can go on a strike by not picking up passengers for a period of time. And these are very important developments that obviously were found in the North as well as the South.

And so the point is, most importantly, that these are spontaneous movements and as a consequence, it's really important to recognize there's a need to build institutional power. These spontaneous movements in places like South Africa and India are taking place inside and outside unions—even in China to some degree, but especially for India and South Africa because we don't know what can happen with respect to the internal functions of the ACFU in China—that workers are willing to form new unions, or switch from one union to another. In South Africa and in India you have a lot of unions that are vying for leadership over the auto sector. The same thing is true in South Africa where you have workers who have switched from the National Union of Mine Workers to the AMCU, the Association of Mineworkers and Construction Union, in the mining belt. So you need to take this spontaneous power and turn it into some kind of mobilization. There are lessons that still need to made in the global South and certainly in the North because we have—well, while unions are good and so forth—many of them are ossified and frequently represent, in most cases, older struggles that took place across these generations.

D&S: Finally, you alluded to some of the struggles that are taking place today as basically economistic in their demands, by which we mean centered on questions like wages, benefits, hours, and so forth. You posed the question of the possibilities of broader politicization of labor struggles. What do you see as the potential for labor movements to develop a broader political agenda up to and including questions of challenging, on a systemic level imperialism, financialization, and capitalism itself?

Ness: I would go back to the point that unions are forming. There's no shortage of worker militancy. You have that happening everyday. Workers will always rebel, workers will always form their own workers' assemblies, engage in struggles even without unions—that's something that's always a given. And in fact that's growing as we are having a larger industrial workforce on a global level. There is a great need for the trade unions that are interested in organizing to actually stand for something other than these kinds of economistic objectives, to believe in reform in political systems to make them more equitable, and to actually have a plan in the organizational perspective on what that will look like in the years to come.

I think that with the number of failures over the last century or so, many argue that socialism is no longer valid. In fact, I think it is probably more necessary today than any time in history. And many unions, for instance the National Union of Medical Workers in South Africa, are engaging in political education. They're educating their workers in Marxism, they're educating their workers in political struggles, in this case outside of the electoral domain. They're educating their workers and workers are demanding equality with respect to housing, with respect to education, with respect to healthcare. These are all very important struggles that workers are engaged in. There is a growing level of opposition to policies of free trade, neo-liberalism, and so forth, and a rejection of them.

We haven't really seen the fruits in any specific place, except for minor examples over the last decade or two. But in fact, I think we're now seeing—there's no question about it—the beginnings of trade unions and political movements forming around socialism, maybe in a region or maybe in a country. It would have to be a very large country—I think that's the only way to have that happen. For instance, in South Africa there will be regional struggles of workers throughout the mining belt, throughout industry, throughout agriculture, and in urban areas as well. So that there are a lot of movements that are building formations that have not necessarily consolidated as yet, but there's no question that they will.

I think that this is something that we need in the global North as well—unions that are in fact anti-capitalist. While there are very few—most unions are rooted in economistic policies—I think that we should certainly should learn to fight against the system. I think that the Battle of Seattle [protest against the World Trade Organization (WTO)] that took place in 1999 was a good start, but again in some ways spontaneous. Traditional trade unions, existing ones, are opposed to any kind of comprehensive policy. We have to recognize that, given the globalization of the entire capitalist world, we need to fight in solidarity on an internationalist level, global North-global South, South-South, and so forth. ❑

Article 6.5

ON STRIKE IN CHINA
A Chinese New Deal in the Making?

BY CHRIS TILLY AND MARIE KENNEDY
September/October 2010

> "[There will] never be a strike [at the Hyundai plant in Beijing]. Strikes in China would jeopardize the company's reputation."
> —*Zhang Zhixiong, deputy chairman of the union at that plant, 2003*

> "About 1,000 workers at Hyundai's auto parts factory [in Beijing] staged a two-day strike and demanded wage increases."
> —*China Daily/Asia News Network, June 4, 2010*

Workers in China are on the move. The media initially fixed on the downward trajectory of desperate workers jumping from the roofs of Foxconn, the enormous electronics manufacturer that assembles the iPhone and numerous other familiar gadgets, but soon shifted to the upward arc of strike activity concentrated in the supply chains of Honda and Toyota.

But the auto-sector strikes in China's industrialized Southeast, as well as in the northeastern city of Tianjin, are just the tip of the iceberg. June strikes also pulled out thousands of workers at Brother sewing machine factories and a Carlsberg brewery in the central part of the country; machinery, LCD, and rubber parts plants in the east-central Shanghai area; a shoe manufacturer further inland in Jiujiang; and apparel and electronics workers outside the auto sector in the Southeast and Tianjin. "There are fifteen factories launching strikes now," Qiao Jian of the Chinese Institute of Industrial Relations (CIIR) told us in mid-June. Since that time, still more strikes have been reported, and many others are likely going unreported by Chinese media, which despite their growing independence remain sensitive to government pressure. None of the strikes had approval by the All China Federation of Trade Unions (ACFTU), the only labor movement authorized by Chinese law.

This explosion of wildcat walkouts prompts several questions. Why did it happen? What do the strikes mean for China's low-wage, low-cost manufacturing model? Equally important, what do they imply for China's party- and state-dominated labor relations? China's labor relations scholars—an outspoken bunch—are animatedly discussing that last question in public and in private.

What Happened and Why

The spark for the recent strike wave was the May 17th walkout of hundreds of workers from a Honda transmission plant in Nanhai, near Guangzhou in the Southeast.

According to research by Wang Kan of CIIR, the strike was an accident: two employees embroiled in a dispute with Honda consulted a lawyer who advised them to threaten a strike as a bluff and even drew up a set of demands for them. They apparently were as shocked as anyone when workers spontaneously walked out. Accident or not, the workers demanded a 67% raise. Two weeks later, they agreed to return to work with a 42% wage increase. By that time, copycat strikes had erupted at other Honda suppliers in the Southeast and at Hyundai; workers at Toyota suppliers soon followed suit, as did employees from other sectors and regions. Most of these actions won wage settlements in the 20% range.

Why did this strike wave happen now? The first thing to understand is that strikes in China did not begin in 2010. As Berkeley doctoral student Eli Friedman points out, "the number of strikes and officially mediated labor disputes in China [has] been increasing rapidly for at least fifteen years." So-called "mass incidents," of which experts estimate about a third to be strikes, numbered 87,000 in 2005, and were unofficially pegged at 120,000 in 2008. Mediated labor disputes, many of which only involve an individual, have grown even faster, rising in round figures from 19,000 in 1994 to 135,000 in 2000, 350,000 in 2007, and 700,000 in 2008. The huge increase in 2008 is due at least in part to new laws on labor contracts and labor mediation passed that year that bolster workers' ability to bring complaints.

Still, "the Honda strike marks a turning point," in the words of law professor Liu Cheng of Shanghai Normal University. "Previous strikes were mainly about enforcing labor law. This is the first successful strike about collective bargaining." Anita Chan, a labor researcher at the University of Technology in Sydney, agrees, saying the current strikers "are negotiating for their interests and not for their rights—it's a very different set of stakes." The Nanhai Honda action was also a breakthrough in that for the first time strikers demanded the right to elect their own union representatives—a demand to which the provincial union federation has agreed, though the election has not yet taken place. Many subsequent strikes reiterated this demand, although they have focused more on economic issues. Even the economic demands extend beyond wages: at Honda Lock, strikers demanded noise reduction measures to improve the work environment.

The long-term growth in strike activity owes much to demographic changes. Predominantly women, China's industrial workers hail overwhelmingly from the ranks of rural migrants, 140 million of whom live and work in the cities but lack long-term permission to stay there or receive social benefits there. When Deng Xiaoping's market liberalization first spurred rapid industrial growth in the 1980s, migrants were willing to "eat bitterness," enduring hardships and low wages to send remittances home to families who were worse off than they. This stoic attitude and decades of policies aimed at growth at almost any cost are reflected in the decline of labor's share of total national income from 57% in 1983 to 37% in 2005. Unpaid or underpaid overtime and only one or two days off a month—violations of Chinese law—became common in China's manufacturing sector.

But the new generation of migrants, reared in a time of relative prosperity and comparing themselves to their peers in the cities, expect more. "Our demands are higher because we have higher material and spiritual needs," a young Honda striker who identified himself only as Chen told Agence France-Presse. "Our strike demands are based on our need to maintain our living standards." With urban housing costs soaring, this has become a pressing issue. "I dream of one day buying a car or apartment," said Zhang, a 22-year-old man working at the same plant, "but with the salary I'm making now, I will never succeed."

Another long-run factor is the government's new willingness to tolerate strikes as long as they stay within bounds, in contrast to the harsh repression meted out in the 1980s and early 1990s.

Still the "Workshop of the World"?

The current wave of strikes owes its energy, too, to the lopsided policies China's government adopted in response to the global economic crunch. "With the global financial crisis, the income gap and social disparities worsened," commented Qiao of the CIIR. Panicking at the fall-off in demand for Chinese exports, authorities froze the minimum wage in 2009 even as the cost of living continued its upward march. They also put hundreds of billions of dollars into loans to help exporters and allowed employers to defer their tax payments and social insurance contributions.

Perhaps most important for workers' quality of life, provincial and local governments relaxed their enforcement of labor regulations—at a time when examples of hard-pressed businesses closing down and cheating workers out of months of back pay were becoming increasingly common. In Foshan, a government official declared in 2009 that employers violating the Labor Contract Law protecting basic worker rights would "not be fined, and will not have their operating licenses revoked." A year later, Honda workers in the city walked off the job.

But the business-friendly, worker-unfriendly government response to the crisis does not explain why autoworkers went out. "I don't know why the Honda workers went on strike, because their salaries and conditions are better than ours," Chen Jian, a 24-year-old worker at Yontai Plastics, not far from the Nanhai Honda plant, said to the Guardian newspaper. "We are not satisfied, but we will not go on strike. Some workers tried that last year and they were all fired. That is normal."

Despite Chen's puzzlement, his comments touch on the reason autoworkers led the way: power rooted in the specifics of the auto production process. Autoworkers wield a degree of skill that makes them more difficult to replace. Assembly line technology within the plant, and a division of labor that often locates fabrication of a particular part in a single plant, make it possible for a small number of strategically located workers to shut down the whole production process, a fact exploited by autoworkers around the world going back to the Flint sit-down strike in 1937. And Japanese-initiated just-in-time techniques have cut down inventories, speeding up the impact of strikes. Friedman reports that by the fourth day of the Nanhai strike, work at all four Honda assembly plants in China had ground to a halt due to lack of transmissions.

Pundits have speculated on whether the Chinese workforce's new demands will upend China's export machine. Andy Xie, a Hong Kong-based economist and business analyst formerly with Morgan Stanley, remarks, "To put it bluntly, the key competence of a successful [manufacturer] in China is to squeeze labor to the maximum extent possible." But in fact, Chinese manufacturing wages had already begun rising significantly in the years before the crisis—in part because of earlier strikes and protests. Some companies had already begun relocating work to Vietnam or Bangladesh. Most observers, including Xie, expect incremental adjustment by businesses, not a stampede. Limited worker demands could even play into the Chinese government's goal of increasing productivity and shifting into higher value-added manufacturing, as well as expanding the buying power of Chinese consumers. But as James Pomfret and Kelvin Soh of Reuters write, China's Communist Party "has faced a policy tightrope. It must also ensure that strikes don't proliferate and scare investors or ignite broader confrontation that erodes Party rule."

"Taking the Same Boat Together to Protect Growth"

Where was the All China Federation of Trade Unions as the working class rose up? Friedman points out that though ACFTU leaders were concerned about defending worker interests in the crisis, they were equally concerned with defending employers' interests. The result was what the ACFTU called "mutually agreed upon actions," which combined promises to desist from job actions with what Friedman describes as "weakly worded requests for employers." "Taking the same boat together to protect growth," a joint March 2009 release by government, unions, and the employer association in Guangdong, was typical, imploring businesses to "work hard" to avoid layoffs and wage cuts—an appeal that seems to have had little real impact on employers.

This ACFTU stance grows directly out of the federation's longstanding focus on "harmonious enterprises," which is rooted in the unions' historic role in state enterprises. "Each trade union is under the control of the local Party branch," Lin Yanling of the CIIR told us. "So, Party, company, and union leadership are often the same." Indeed, the ACFTU typically invites companies to name their union officials; as a result, middle managers often hold those posts. Along the same lines, Shanghai Normal's Liu Cheng stated, "These company unions don't work. They have nothing to do but entertainment. In the summer, they buy watermelon for the workers to celebrate the festivals." Lin Yanling concluded, "Now is the time to change trade unions in China!"

Recommendations for change circulating within China vary widely. "Some local trade union leaders say to reform the trade union, you must sever the relation between the trade union and the local Party branch," said Lin. "If the local union would only listen to upper trade union officials, the problem could be solved." Local state and Party representatives are particularly closely tied to the local businesses, whereas the national officialdom has more often advocated for workers' interests, for example through the new 2008 labor laws. He Zengke, executive director of the Center for Comparative Politics and Economics, expressed support for shifting control to the national level: "Local government has historically supported business, but the [Party Secretary] Hu government is now asking them to pursue a balanced policy—also pro-people, pro-poor."

But Lin is skeptical of this limited fix, arguing that "if you want the unions to change, you need the workers to elect the trade union chairperson." Liu Cheng agrees, but also advocates for unions to have the right to litigate on behalf of workers. Liu argues it is premature to push for the right to strike, whereas Zheng Qiao of CIIR holds that this is a good opportunity to define that right. Qiao Jian of CIIR advocates democratizing unions within a revitalized tripartite (union federation/employer association/government) system, but his colleague Lin insists, "That system will not function," because the unions don't yet have enough independence within the triad to adequately represent workers. The disagreements are passionate, if good-humored, since these scholars see the future of their country at stake.

Western observers, and some Hong Kong-based worker-rights groups, have gone farther to call for the right for workers to form their own independent unions— what the International Labor Organization calls "freedom of association." But labor relations experts within mainland China, and the strikers themselves, have so far steered clear of such radical proposals. Liu Cheng commented, "Without reform of the unions, I think freedom of association would result in disorder, and destroy the process of evolution. I don't like revolution—with most revolutions, there is no real progress, just a change of emperors." However, he did express the view that as the Chinese labor movement matures, it will reach a point when freedom of association will be possible and desirable.

"If People Are Oppressed, They Must Rebel"

But will the unions change—and will the Party and state let them? The question is complicated by the conflicting currents within the union federation itself and within China's official ideology. The same Party that promotes "harmonious enterprises" also enshrines Mao Zedong's dictum, "It's right to rebel." So perhaps it's not surprising that Li, a young striker at Honda's exhaust plant, told Agence France-Presse, "Safeguarding your own rights is always legitimate … . If people are oppressed they must rebel. This is only natural."

ACFTU responses to date, reported by Friedman and labor activist and blogger Paul Garver, reflect this mixed consciousness. At the Nanhai Honda strike that inaugurated the current wave, the local ACFTU leadership sent a group of 100 people with union hats and armbands to persuade the strikers to stand down. Whether by design or not, the conversation degenerated into a physical confrontation in which some strikers were injured, none severely. On the other hand, provincial-level union leaders then agreed to the strikers' demands to elect their own representatives. The top two Guangdong ACFTU officials, Deng Weilong and Kong Xianghong, subsequently spoke out in favor of the right to strike and pledged to replace current management-appointed officials with worker-elected ones.

When workers at the Denso (Nansha) car-parts factory in Guangzhou (also in Guangdong province) later went on strike, the local union response was different from that in Nanhai. The municipal union federation publicly supported the strikers, refusing to mediate between labor and management. There have even been signs of life from unions in other sectors: about a month after the Nanhai strike, the municipal union federation in Shenyang, in the far northeast of the country, hammered out the nation's first collective bargaining contract with KFC (whose fast-food restaurants blanket China), including a wage increase of nearly 30%.

On the government side, authorities in many provinces have responded to the strike wave with a wave of minimum-wage hikes. Premier Wen Jiabao declared in a June address to migrant workers, "Your work is a glorious thing, and it should be respected by society," and in August told the Japanese government that its companies operating in China should raise wages. Acknowledging that "a wide range of social conflicts have occurred recently," Zhou Yongkang, another top Party official, stated, "Improving people's livelihoods should be the starting and end point of all our work." In August, BusinessWeek reported that Guangdong's state legislature was discussing a law formalizing collective bargaining, empowering workers to elect local representatives, and even recognizing the right to strike—particularly noteworthy since Guangdong is China's industrial heartland. Still, pro-worker rhetoric is nothing new, the Guangdong provincial union federation is more progressive and powerful than most, and right around the time of Wen's June speech the Chinese government shut down a website calling for ACFTU democratization.

Amidst these cross-currents, China's labor relations scholars, aware that their own role is "marginal," as one of them put it, remain cautiously optimistic. "I think the situation will lead to union reform," said the CIIR's Zheng Qiao. When asked how activists in the United States can support the Chinese workers, her colleague Lin suggested, "Ask the big American brands to give a larger percentage back to the workers at their suppliers!" At Shanghai Normal, Liu Cheng reasoned through the prospects for change. "If the ACFTU does not do more, there will be more and more independent strikes, and in the end some kind of independent union. So the ACFTU will be scared, and the party will be angry with the ACFTU."

"So," Liu Cheng concluded, "the strike wave is a very good thing." ❑

Sources: Eli Friedman, "Getting through hard times together? Worker insurgency and Chinese unions' response to the economic crisis," paper presented at the International Sociological Association annual conference, Gothenburg, Sweden, July 2010; LabourStart page on China labor news, www.labourstart.org; James Pomfret and Kelvin Soh, "Special Report: China's new migrant workers pushing the line," Reuters, July 5, 2010; "The right to strike may be coming to China," *Bloomberg Businessweek*, August 5, 2010; ITUC/GUF Hong Kong Liaison Office, "A political economic analysis of the strike in Honda and the auto parts industry in China," July 2010.

Article 6.6

INEQUALITY: THE SILLY TALES ECONOMISTS LIKE TO TELL

BY DEAN BAKER

October 2012; Al Jazeera English

There is no serious dispute that the United States has seen a massive increase in inequality over the last three decades. However there is a major dispute over the causes of this rise in inequality.

The explanation most popular in elite and policy circles is that the rise in inequality was simply the natural working of the economy. Their story is that the explosion of information technology and globalization have increased demand for highly-skilled workers while sharply reducing the demand for less-educated workers.

While the first part of this story is at best questionable, the second part should invite ridicule and derision. It doesn't pass the laugh test.

As far as the technology story, yes, information technologies have displaced large amounts of less-skilled labor. So did the technologies that preceded them. There are hundreds of books and articles from the 1950s and 1960s that expressed grave concerns that automation would leave much of the workforce unemployed. Is there evidence that the displacement is taking place more rapidly today than in that era? If so, it is not showing up on our productivity data.

More germane to the issue at hand, unlike the earlier wave of technology, computerization offers the potential for displacing vast amounts of highly skilled labor. Legal research that might have previously required a highly skilled lawyer can now be done by an intelligent college grad and a good search engine. Medical diagnosis and the interpretation of test results that may have previously required a physician, and quite possibly a highly paid specialist, can now be done by technical specialists who may not even have a college education.

There is no reason to believe that current technologies are replacing comparatively more less-educated workers than highly educated workers. The fact that lawyers and doctors largely control how their professions are practiced almost certainly has much more to do with the demand for their services.

If the technology explanation for inequality is weak, the globalization part of the story is positively pernicious. The basic story is that globalization has integrated a huge labor force of billions of workers in developing countries into the world economy. These workers are able to fill many of the jobs that used to provide middle class living standards to workers in the United States and will accept a fraction of the wage. This makes many formerly middle class jobs uncompetitive in the world economy given current wages and currency values.

This part of the story is true. The part that our elite leave out is that there are tens of millions of bright and highly educated workers in the developing world who could fill most of the top paying jobs in the US economy: doctors, lawyers, accountants, etc. These workers are also willing to work for a small fraction of the wages of their US counterparts since they come from poor countries with much lower standards of living.

The reason why the manufacturing workers, construction workers, and restaurant workers lose their jobs to low-paid workers from the developing world, and doctors and lawyers don't, is that doctors and lawyers use their political power to limit the extent to which they are exposed to competition from their low-paid counterparts in the developing world. Our trade policy has been explicitly designed to remove barriers that prevent General Electric and other companies from moving their manufacturing operations to Mexico, China or other developing countries. By contrast, many of the barriers that make it difficult for foreign professionals to work in the United States have actually been strengthened in the last two decades.

If economics was an honest profession, economists would focus their efforts on documenting the waste associated with protectionist barriers for professionals. They devoted endless research studies to estimating the cost to consumers of tariffs on products like shoes and tires. It speaks to the incredible corruption of the economics profession that there are not hundreds of studies showing the loss to consumers from the barriers to trade in physicians' services. If trade could bring down the wages of physicians in the United States just to European levels, it would save consumers close to $100 billion a year.

But economists are not rewarded for studying the economy. That is why almost everyone in the profession missed the $8 trillion housing bubble, the collapse of which stands to cost the country more than $7 trillion in lost output according to the Congressional Budget Office (that comes to around $60,000 per household).

Few if any economists lost their 6-figure paychecks for this disastrous mistake. But most economists are not paid for knowing about the economy. They are paid for telling stories that justify giving more money to rich people. Hence we can look forward to many more people telling us that all the money going to the rich was just the natural workings of the economy. When it comes to all the government rules and regulations that shifted income upward, they just don't know what you're talking about. ❑

Chapter 7

MIGRATION

Article 7.1

WALLED OFF FROM REALITY

Trump's claims about immigration economics are without merit.

BY JOHN MILLER
November/December 2015

> Mexico's leaders have been taking advantage of the United States by using illegal immigration to export the crime and poverty in their own country. The costs for the United – States have been extraordinary: U.S. taxpayers have been asked to pick up hundreds of billions in healthcare costs, housing costs, education costs, welfare costs, etc. ... The influx of foreign workers holds down salaries, keeps unemployment high, and makes it difficult for poor and working class Americans—including immigrants themselves and their children—to earn a middle class wage.
> — "Immigration Reform That Will Make America Great Again," Donald Trump campaign website

Donald Trump's immigration plan has accomplished something many thought was impossible. He has gotten mainstream and progressive economists to agree about something: his claims about the economics of immigration have "no basis in social science research," as economist Benjamin Powell of Texas Tech's Free Market Institute put it. That describes most every economic claim Trump's website makes about immigration: that it has destroyed the middle class, held down wages, and drained hundreds of billions from government coffers. Such claims are hardly unique to Trump, among presidential candidates. Even Bernie Sanders has said that immigration drives down wages (though he does not support repressive nativist policies like those proposed by Trump and other GOP candidates).

Beyond that, even attempting to implement Trump's nativist proposals, from building a permanent border wall to the mass deportation of undocumented immigrants, would cost hundreds of billions of dollars directly, and forfeit the possibility of adding trillions of dollars to the U.S. and global economies by liberalizing current immigration policies. That's not counting the human suffering that Trump's proposals would inflict.

No Drag on the Economy

Even the most prominent economist among immigration critics, Harvard's George Borjas, recognizes that immigration has had a large positive effect on the U.S. economy. By his calculations, immigrant workers (documented and undocumented) add $1.6 trillion to the U.S. economy each year, or 11% of Gross Domestic Product (GDP). The great bulk of that additional income (97.8% according to Borjas) goes to immigrant workers. But that still leaves what he calls an "immigrant surplus" of $35 billion a year, which goes to non-immigrants, including workers, employers, and other users of services provided by immigrants.

Others have emphasized the disproportionate impact that immigrants have had on innovation in the U.S. economy. A study for the Kauffman Foundation found that, in 2006, foreign nationals residing in the United States were named as inventors or co-inventors in over 25% of all U.S. patent applications. Around the same time, another study found that immigrants were the founders of over half of all Silicon Valley startups and almost one-third of Boston startups.

Immigrants Didn't Do It

U.S. workers have undoubtedly fallen on hard times. The reasons are manifold: slow economic growth; pro-rich, anti-worker, anti-poor policies; the decline of unions; "free-trade" globalization; and so on. But immigration isn't one of those reasons, especially when it comes to "the middle class." Not only has immigration benefitted the U.S. economy, but economists find no evidence that immigration causes a widespread decrease in the wages of U.S.-born workers.

Estimates vary, but the best economic studies point to the same conclusion: over the long run, immigration has not caused the wages of the average U.S. born worker to fall. Immigration critic Borjas calculated that, from 1990 to 2010, immigrant labor pushed down the wages of (pre-existing) U.S. workers by 3.2% in the short run. But even he conceded that over the long run, wages of native-born and earlier immigrant workers recovered to their previous level. Other economists find immigration to have a positive long-run effect on wages. Gianmarco Ottaviano and Giovanni Peri found that, from 1990 to 2006, immigration reduced wages of native-born workers in the short run (one to two years) by 0.7%, while over the long run (ten years) immigration into the United States boosted wages 0.6%.

Neither Ottaviano and Peri's nor even Borjas's estimates of the wage effects of immigration are consistent with Trump's claim that immigration is destroying the middle class. But what happens when we look at the wages of native-born workers by level of education? The Ottaviano-Peri study shows, in the long run, immigration is associated with an increase in wages across all education levels. Borjas's study reports that immigration has negative effects on the wages of native-born college graduates and especially on workers with less than a high-school education (those at the "bottom" of the labor market, mostly in low-wage jobs), even in the long run. But again concedes a positive effect for the 60% of U.S. workers with either a high school degree or some college (but no degree).

These results are probably a headscratcher for anyone who has taken introductory economics. After all doesn't increasing the supply of labor, through immigration, drive down its price (the going wage)? Well, no.

Immigrant workers do add to the supply of labor. But the economic effects of immigration do not stop there. Immigrants largely spend their wages within the U.S. economy. Businesses produce more—and hire more workers—to meet the increased demand. The cost savings from hiring cheaper immigrant labor also frees up businesses to expand production and hire more workers overall. Both those effects increase the demand for labor, offsetting the effects of added labor supply.

Economist David Card concludes that, taking into account these demand-side effects, "the overall impacts on native wages are small—far smaller than the effects of other factors like new technology, institutional changes, and recessionary macro conditions that have cumulatively led to several decades of slow wage growth for most U.S. workers."

Complements or Substitutes?

The effect of immigration on native-born workers with less than a high-school education remains a matter of dispute. Borjas insists that the costs of immigration are visited disproportionately upon those with the least education (and, to a lesser extent, those with the most education). He estimates, in a couple of different studies, that over the long run the wages of native-born high school dropouts fell 3-5% due to immigration.

But these estimates rely on the assumption that immigrant and native-born workers are substitutes for each other, and therefore compete for the same jobs. But, in fact, their skills differ in important ways. The first is their command of English. The Immigrant Policy Institute found that approximately one-half of the 41 million immigrants ages five and older speak English less than "very well." In addition, immigrant workers often have culture-specific skills— from cooking to opera singing to soccer playing, to cite examples given by Ottaviano and Peri—that differ from those of native-born workers.

When Ottaviano and Peri accounted for the imperfect substitutability between immigrants and natives, the negative of effect of immigration on native high school dropouts disappeared, and their wages were shown to rise by 0.3% over the long run.

Giving More Than They Get

Nor is there a credible case that undocumented immigrants are draining the public coffers by consuming more public services than they pay for. Immigrants migrate to jobs, not to welfare, and are disproportionately of working age. They are not major beneficiaries of the most generous U.S. welfare-state programs—Social Security and Medicare, which serve the elderly, not the young or the poor. And undocumented immigrants are already ineligible for most government benefits. (Even documented immigrants are ineligible for many federal programs, at least for some years after their arrival.)

On top of that, immigrants, both documented and undocumented, do pay taxes. They pay sales taxes, payroll taxes, and often income taxes. And they pay far more in taxes than they receive in benefits. That puts Trump's outrage over $4.2 billion in "free tax credits ... paid to illegal immigrants" in a different light. In 2009, the federal government did in fact pay $4.2 billion in child tax credits to low-income tax filers using an Individual Taxpayer Identification Number (ITIN), the vast majority of them undocumented immigrants. But that same year, those ITIN filers paid an estimated $12 billion into a Social Security system from which they are not eligible to collect any benefits.

Trillions Left on the Sidewalk

Before the 1882 Chinese Exclusion Act, the United States allowed completely free immigration into our country. Immigration from elsewhere remained unrestricted until the eve of World War I. And immigrants flooded into the country and contributed mightily to its economic development.

Liberalizing immigration policies, unlike Trump's proposed border wall or mass deportations, could once again benefit the U.S. economy. Economists Angel Aguiar and Terrie Walmsley found that deporting all undocumented Mexican immigrants from the United States would reduce U.S. GDP by about $150 billion, while granting legal status to unskilled, undocumented Mexican workers (without additional effective border enforcement) would raise it by nearly that amount. And the potential gain for the global economy from liberalizing immigration policies is far greater. In fact so large that economist Michael Clemens likens liberalizing immigration to picking up "trillion-dollar bills on the sidewalk."

Such policies would also specifically improve conditions for workers, immigrant and native, in the United States. Immigrant workers, especially the estimated eleven million undocumented immigrants, tend to have less bargaining power than native-born workers. A policy granting undocumented immigrants legal status would make it easier for them to insist on their rights at work, and to organize and form unions. That's why the AFL-CIO and unions like UNITE HERE and SEIU now favor it.

For those who remain concerned about the effects of immigration on U.S. born low-wage workers, there are obvious policies that would improve the lot of all low-wage workers: Boosting the minimum wage, making it easier for workers to organize unions, and making the welfare state more generous and inclusive, so people don't have to accept whatever lousy job they can find. These are the policies that are called for, not keeping immigrants out. ❏

Sources: George Borjas, "Immigration and the American Worker: A Review of the Academic Literature," Center for Immigration Studies, April 2013; Vivek Wadhwa, Foreign-Born Entrepreneurs: An Underestimated American Resource," Kauffman Foundation, Nov. 24, 2008; Michael A. Clemens, "Economics and Emigration: Trillion-Dollars Bills on the Sidewalk?" *Journal of Economic Perspectives*, Summer 2011; Gianmarco Ottaviano and Giovanni Peri, "Rethinking the Effects of Immigration on Wages," National Bureau of Economic Research, August 2006; Gianmarco Ottaviano and Giovanni Peri, "Immigration and National Wages: Clarifying the Theory and Empirics," National Bureau of Economic Research, August 2008; Gianmarco Ottaviano and Giovanni Peri, "Rethinking the Effect of Immigration on Wages," *Journal of the European Economic Association*, February 2012; George Borjas and Lawrence Katz, "The Evolution of the Mexican-Born Workforce n the United States," in George Borjas, ed., *Mexican Immigration to the United States*, 2007; Benjamin Powell, "Why Trump's Wrong on Immigration," Independent Institute, Sept. 15, 2015; Angel Aguiar and Terrie Walmsley, "The Importance of Timing in the U.S. Response to Illegal Immigrants: A Recursive Dynamic Approach," Global Trade Analysis Project, Working Paper No. 75, 2013; David Card, "Comment: The Elusive Search For Negative Wage Impacts of Immigration," *Journal of the European and Economic Association*, February 2012; Glenn Kessler, "Trump's Immigration plan include many claims that lack context," *Washington Post*, Aug. 20, 2015; Linda Qiu, "Trump's says illegal immigrants get $4.2B in tax credits but doesn't count their taxes paid," PolitiFact, Aug. 18, 2015; Michael Greenstone and Adam Looney, "What Immigration Means for U.S. Employment and Wages," Brookings on Job Numbers, May 4, 2012; Jie Zong and Jeanne Batalova, "Frequently Requested Statistics on Immigrants and Immigration in the United States," Migration Policy Institute, Feb. 26, 2015.

Article 7.2

EUROPE'S REFUGEE "CRISIS"

BY JAYATI GHOSH
September 2015; Frontline

If you read or watched or listened only to the mainstream media in the North, you could be forgiven for believing that the current influx of refugees into countries of Europe is not just an important concern, but actually even the single biggest crisis in that continent. You might also think that the flow of desperate refugees escaping from terrible conditions is mainly confined to that region, and that their numbers are so large that the societies will be simply unable to cope, because of the hugely increased burden on basic infrastructure and facilities in those countries.

Every day, television screens show images of people pouring into towns and cities, crowding up border crossings or landing at sea (if they are lucky) and filling up transport hubs in certain European countries. International and national newspapers carry stories of some compassion, along with greater instances of more xenophobic responses of local populations. Government leaders (particularly in eastern and central Europe) are shown declaring that their country cannot possibly take in so many people, many of whom may not even be "real" refugees but simply economic migrants. Borders are being reinforced and aggressively policed; walls and barbed wire fences are being put up; desperate groups of travellers are even being shot at in the attempt to prevent further influx.

Yet this tragic phenomenon that is receiving so much global publicity is but a small trickle in the huge flow of people displaced globally by wars and conflicts in the areas where they live. According to UNHCR [the United Nations Refugee Agency], in 2014 alone, nearly 14 million people were forcibly displaced due to civil war or other violence. Most of these moved within their own country—11 million people, who are internal refugees losing everything, and often retaining only the most uncertain of citizenship rights precisely because of the internal conflicts.

The three million who were cross-border refugees added to the estimated global total of 60 million displaced people, 19.5 million cross-border refugees and 1.95 million asylum seekers in 2014. Obviously in 2015 the numbers have gone up further, and the conflicts in many countries of origin have only intensified. But most of these displaced people—86 percent of them, in fact—are hosted by developing countries. The Least Developed Countries, with some of the lowest per capita incomes in the world and very poor conditions of infrastructure available to their own previously resident populations, were home to a quarter of the world's refugees in 2014.

Last year, Turkey became the country with the largest number of refugees, at 1.59 million. It was followed by Pakistan (1.51 million), Lebanon (1.15 million), Iran (982,000), Ethiopia (659,500), and Jordan (654,100). In terms of population, Jordan was the most affected, with one refugee for every three local residents, followed by Lebanon with one refugee to every four Lebanese. Some of the poorest countries in the world, like Chad and South Sudan, provide refuge to large numbers of displaced people who are significant in number in relation to the local population.

Put these huge numbers in the context of the much smaller number of people trying to enter Europe (still in their thousands), and there is really no comparison in terms of burden on the host society. This is especially so as all the countries of Europe (including those that see themselves as poorer and economically struggling at present) are far better off not only in terms of per capita income but also in terms of provision of basic amenities and services for the people.

Coping with large numbers of refugees is obviously much more difficult for poor countries. In areas that are already drought-prone, water-starved, and with large hungry populations, consider the burden of ensuring water and food access to many newly displaced people. Where medical facilities are already very inadequate, imagine trying to provide even minimal medical services to refugees who are probably in even greater dire need. In societies where even all the local children are not in school, think of what adding large numbers of refugee children who probably do not share the language and also are likely to be traumatised and so may require therapy, will entail in terms of public costs.

The material implications of having larger numbers of refugees are clearly being felt in many of these countries, whether in terms of increased rationing of electricity and water, a greater burden on health services, or pressure on other infrastructure. Yet we do not hear of these countries closing their borders on people who are desperately fleeing to save their lives, nor is it the case that right-wing tendencies in these societies have gained huge public support by attacking these helpless migrants. It is also significant that somehow the huge and growing numbers of refugees across the developing world are never treated as crisis situations by the global media.

So it is worth asking why the European response (and the U.S. attempt to look away from the issues as having no direct relevance to themselves) has been, in the main, so very churlish and self-obsessed. The most relevant question, of course, is of how the establishment in both the United States and Europe has been able to deny any responsibility for the current movement of displaced persons across borders— and how complicit the mainstream media has been in this process.

At the end of 2014, according to the UNHCR, more than half (53 percent) of all refugees worldwide came from just three countries: the Syrian Arab Republic (3.88 million), Afghanistan (2.59 million), and Somalia (1.11 million). Since the start of the current year, the number from Syria has increased greatly, and just the number of asylum seekers from Syria in the developed countries has more than doubled in the first six months of 2015 compared to the same period last year. Large numbers of refugees have also come from Iraq and Libya, all countries now devastated by internal conflicts arising from the clumsy western imperialist attempts to force political change in these countries through the use of external force.

Not for nothing have many observers like James Paul and Vijay Prashad described these unhappy people as "regime change refugees," fleeing countries that are now in the throes of dreadful civil wars driven by very extremist forces, including those that are particularly oppressive to women. Yet the overt accountability of the governments of countries that went to war and thereby created these huge instabilities is certainly acknowledged by themselves, and rarely alluded to in the media coverage of all this. It is true that this is somewhere in the back of many minds: in recent weeks an official of one of the least welcoming East European countries is reported to have asked "Why should we provide homes for these refugees when we didn't invade their countries?" Yet the essential culpability and therefore responsibility of those who did invade those countries is not pointed to when the issue of dealing with the refugees comes up. And so the leaders in the United States and the UK, for example, can simply look the other way since the migrants are not washing up against their own shores.

The petty selfishness of western leaders—and, unfortunately, far too many in their societies—has thus been most thoroughly exposed. The horrific conditions and direct threats to life and security in the countries that people are fleeing; the extremely dangerous and life-threatening journeys that must be made (almost daily confirmed by the appalling accounts of deaths in transit); the knowledge of the highly precarious existence in largely unwelcoming countries of destination—all of these suggest that such migrants are truly desperate and deserve the greatest compassion. Yet this most basic human empathy has been sadly lacking for the most part.

Indeed, Germany has been praised for its relatively generous response. Yet this too has been more churlish in recent weeks, and it pales into insignificance compared to the much greater generosity of countries that are far less materially equipped to handle such inflows, such as Jordan, Lebanon, and Pakistan. Asylum seekers do not have an easy time anywhere, but the richer countries have without question been meaner, more oppressive, and more restrictive in their dealings with them.

So then the question must be: why such a difference in social and public response? It is hard to think that this is largely because of racial or cultural differences alone, because the refugees do not come from homogenous societies, nor do they necessarily enter similar ones in other developing countries. One possible explanation could still be a cultural one, though: the deep penetration of the ideology of neoliberalism, which celebrates individualism and generates a Darwinian sense of competition and struggle for survival, in which one's own success ultimately depends on someone else's failure. It is worth noting that even in Europe, the formerly socialist countries that have become the most eager adherents to "free market" principles have also turned to becoming the most aggressively right-wing, even fascist, in their approach to less fortunate outsiders.

It is as if all principles of social solidarity were thrown out along with any vestiges of economic socialism. Countries that have in addition been exposed to a long period of public austerity that has undermined living standards of the masses seem to be even more prone to such resentful swings. Sadly, the celebration of the market seems to have done more than generate patterns of unequal growth and reduced respect for human rights: it also seems to have undermined the basic principles of solidarity and ethical behaviour without which human societies will find it hard to function. ❏

Article 7.3

MADE IN ARGENTINA

Bolivian Migrant Workers Fight Neoliberal Fashion

BY MARIE TRIGONA
January/February 2007

Dubbed "the Paris of the South," Buenos Aires is known for its European architecture, tango clubs, and *haute couture*. But few people are aware that Argentina's top fashion brands employ tens of thousands of undocumented Bolivian workers in slave-labor conditions. In residential neighborhoods across Buenos Aires, top clothing companies have turned small warehouses or gutted buildings into clandestine sweatshops. Locked in, workers are forced to live and work in cramped quarters with little ventilation and, often, limited access to water and gas. The *Unión de Trabajadores Costureros* (Union of Seamstress Workers—UTC), an assembly of undocumented textile workers, has reported more than 8,000 cases of labor abuses inside the city's nearly 400 clandestine shops in the past year. Around 100,000 undocumented immigrants work in these unsafe plants with an average wage—if they are paid at all—of $100 per month.

According to Olga Cruz, a 29-year-old textile worker, slave-labor conditions in textile factories are systematic. "During a normal workday in a shop you work from 7 a.m. until midnight or 1 a.m. Many times they don't pay the women and they owe them two or three years' pay. For not having our legal documents or not knowing what our rights are in Argentina, we've had to remain silent. You don't have rights to rent a room or to work legally."

Another Bolivian textile worker, Naomi Hernández, traveled to Argentina three years ago in hopes of a well-paying job. "I ended up working in a clandestine sweatshop without knowing the conditions I would have to endure. For two years I worked and slept in a three-square-meter room along with my two children and three sewing machines my boss provided. They would bring us two meals a day. For breakfast a cup of tea with a piece of bread and lunch consisting of a portion of rice, a potato, and an egg. We had to share our two meals with our children because according to my boss, my children didn't have the right to food rations because they aren't workers and don't yield production." She reported the subhuman conditions in her workplace and was subsequently fired.

Diseases like tuberculosis and lung complications are common due to the subhuman working conditions and constant exposure to dust and fibers. Many workers suffer from back injuries and tendonitis from sitting at a sewing machine 12 to 16 hours a day. And there are other hazards. A blaze that killed six people last year brought to light abusive working conditions inside a network of clandestine textile plants in Buenos Aires. The two women and four children who were killed had been locked inside the factory.

The situation of these workers shows that exploitation of migrant labor is not just a first-world/third-world phenomenon. The system of exploitative subcontracting of migrant workers that has arisen in U.S. cities as a result of neoliberal globalization also occurs in the countries of the global south—as does organized resistance to such exploitation.

Survival for Bolivian Workers

Buenos Aires is the number one destination for migrants from Bolivia, Paraguay, and Peru, whose numbers have grown in the past decade because of the declining economic conditions in those countries. More than one million Bolivians have migrated to Argentina since 1999; approximately one-third are undocumented.

Even when Argentina's economy took a nosedive in the 1990s, Bolivians were still driven to migrate there given their homeland's far more bleak economic conditions. Over two-thirds of Bolivians live in poverty, and nearly half subsist on less than a dollar a day. For decades, migration of rural workers (44% of the population) to urban areas kept many families afloat. Now, facing limited employment opportunities and low salaries in Bolivia's cities, many workers have opted to migrate to Argentina or Brazil.

Buenos Aires' clandestine network of sweatshops emerged in the late 1990s, following the influx of inexpensive Asian textile imports. Most of the textile factory owners are Argentine, Korean, or Bolivian. The workers manufacture garments for high-end brands like Lacár, Kosiuko, Adidas, and Montage in what has become a $700 million a year industry.

In many cases workers are lured by radio or newspaper ads in Bolivia promising transportation to Buenos Aires and decent wages plus room and board once they arrive. Truck drivers working for the trafficking rings transport workers in the back of trucks to cross into Argentina illegally.

For undocumented immigrants in Argentina, survival itself is a vicious cycle. The undocumented are especially susceptible to threats of losing their jobs. Workers can't afford to rent a room; even if they could, many residential hotel managers are unwilling to rent rooms to immigrants, especially when they have children.

Finding legal work is almost impossible without a national identity card. For years, Bolivian citizens had reported that Alvaro Gonzalez Quint, the head of Bolivia's consulate in Buenos Aires, would charge immigrants up to $100—equivalent to a textile worker's average monthly pay—to complete paperwork necessary for their documentation. The Argentine League for Human Rights has also brought charges against Gonzalez Quint in federal court, alleging he is tied to the network of smugglers who profit from bringing immigrants into Argentina to work in the sweatshops.

A New Chapter in Argentina's Labor Struggles

Argentina has a notable tradition of labor organizing among immigrants. Since the 19th century, working-class immigrants have fought for basic rights, including

Sundays off, eight-hour workdays, and a minimum wage. The eight-hour workday became law in 1933, but employers have not always complied. Beginning with the 1976-1983 military dictatorship, and continuing through the neoliberal 1990s, many labor laws have been altered to allow flexible labor standards. University of Buenos Aires economist Eduardo Lucita, a member of UDI (Economists from the Left), says that although the law for an eight-hour workday stands, the average workday in Argentina is 10 to 12 hours. "Only half of workers have formal labor contracts; the rest are laboring as subcontracted workers in the unregulated, informal sector. For such workers there are no regulations for production rates and lengths of a workday—much less criteria for salaries." The average salary for Argentines is only around $200 a month, in contrast to the minimum of $600 required to meet the basic needs of a family of four.

Today, the extreme abuses in the new sweatshops have prompted a new generation of immigrant workers to organize.

"We have had to remain silent and accept abuse. I'm tired of taking the blows. We are starting to fight, *compañeros*; thank you for attending the assembly." These are the words of Ana Salazar at an assembly of textile workers that met in Buenos Aires on a Sunday evening last April. The UTC formed out of a neighborhood assembly in the working class neighborhood of Parque Avalleneda. Initially, the assembly was a weekly social event for families on Sundays, the only day textile workers can leave the shop. Families began to gather at the assembly location, situated at the corner of a park. Later, because Argentina's traditional unions refuse to accept undocumented affiliates, the workers expanded their informal assembly into a full-fledged union.

Since the factory fire that killed six on March 30, 2006, the UTC has stepped up actions against the brand-name clothing companies that subcontract with clandestine sweatshops. The group has held a number of *escraches*, or exposure protests, outside fashion makers' offices in Buenos Aires to push the city government to hold inspections inside the companies' textile workshops. Workers from the UTC also presented legal complaints against the top jean manufacturer Kosiuko.

At a recent surprise protest, young women held placards: "I kill myself for your jeans," signed, "a Bolivian textile worker." During the protest, outside Kosiuko's offices in the exclusive Barrio Norte neighborhood, UTC presented an in-depth research report into the brand's labor violations. "The Kosiuko company is concealing slave shops," said Gustavo Vera, member of the La Alemeda popular assembly. "They disclosed false addresses to inspectors and they have other workshops which they are not reporting to the city government." The UTC released a detailed list of the locations of alleged sweatshops. Most of the addresses that the Kosiuko company had provided turned out to be private residences or stores.

To further spotlight large brand names that exploit susceptible undocumented workers, the UTC held a unique fashion show in front of the Buenos Aires city legislature last September. "Welcome to the neoliberal fashion show—Spring Season 2006," announced the host, as spectators cheered—or jeered—the top brands that use slave labor. Models from a local theatre group paraded down a red carpet in brands like Kosiuko, Montagne, Porte Said, and Lacar, while the host shouted out the addresses of the brands' sweatshops and details of subhuman conditions inside shops.

"I repressed all of my rage about my working conditions and violations of my rights. Inside a clandestine workshop you don't have any rights. You don't have dignity," said Naomi Hernández, pedaling away at a sewing machine during the "fashion show."

After the show, Hernández stood up in front of the spectators and choked down tears while giving testimony of her experience as a slave laborer in a sweatshop: "I found out what it is to fight as a human being." She says her life has changed since joining the UTC.

Inspection-Free Garment Shops

To date, the union's campaign has had some successes. In April of 2006, the Buenos Aires city government initiated inspections of sweatshops employing Bolivians and Paraguayans; inspectors shut down at least 100. (Perhaps not surprisingly, Bolivian consul Gonzalez Quint has protested the city government's moves to regulate sweatshops, arguing that the measures discriminate against Bolivian employers who run some of the largest textile shops.) But since then, inspections have been suspended and many clothes manufacturers have simply moved their sweatshops to the suburban industrial belt or to new locations in the city. The UTC has reported that other manufacturers force workers to labor during the night to avoid daytime inspections.

Nestor Escudero, an Argentine who participates in the UTC, says that police, inspectors, and the courts are also responsible for the documented slave-labor conditions inside textile factories. "They bring in illegal immigrants to brutally exploit them. The textile worker is paid 75 cents for a garment that is later sold for $50. This profit is enough to pay bribes and keep this system going."

Since 2003, thousands of reports of slave-labor conditions have piled up in the courts without any resolution. In many cases when workers have presented reports to police of poor treatment, including threats, physical abuse, and forced labor, the police say they can't act because the victims do not have national identity cards.

Seeing their complaints go unheeded is sometimes the least of it. Escudero has confirmed that over a dozen textile workers have received death threats for reporting to media outlets on slave-labor conditions inside the textile plants. Shortly after the UTC went public last spring with hundreds of reports of abuses, over a dozen of the union's representatives were threatened. And in a particularly shocking episode, two men kidnapped the 9-year-old son of José Orellano and Monica Frías, textile workers who had reported slave-labor conditions in their shop. The attackers held the boy at knifepoint and told him to "tell your parents that they should stop messing around with the reports against the sweatshops." The UTC filed criminal charges of abandonment and abuse of power against Argentina's Interior Minister Aníbal Fernández in November for not providing the couple with witness protection.

The Road Ahead

Although the Buenos Aires city government has yet to make much headway in regulating the city's sweatshops, the UTC continues to press for an end to sweatshop slavery, along with mass legalization of immigrants and housing for immigrants living in poverty. Organizing efforts have not been in vain. In an important victory, the city government has opened a number of offices to process immigration documents free of charge for Bolivian and Paraguayan citizens, circumventing the Bolivian Consulate.

The UTC has also proposed that clandestine textile shops be shut down and handed over to the workers to manage them as co-ops and, ultimately, build a cooperative network that can bypass the middlemen and the entire piece-work system. Already, the Alameda assembly has joined with the UTC to form the Alameda Workers' Cooperative as an alternative to sweatshops. Nearly 30 former sweatshop workers work at the cooperative in the same space where the weekly assemblies are held.

Olga Cruz now works with the cooperative sewing garments. She says that although it's a struggle, she now has dignity that she didn't have when she worked in one of the piece-work shops. "We are working as a cooperative, we all make the same wage. In the clandestine shops you are paid per garment: they give you the fabric and you have to hand over the garment fully manufactured. Here we have a line system, which is more advanced and everyone works the same amount."

Fired for reporting on abusive conditions at her sweatshop, Naomi Hernández has also found work at the cooperative. "We are freeing ourselves, that's what I feel. Before I wasn't a free person and didn't have any rights," said Hernández to a crowd of spectators in front of the city legislature. She sent a special message and invitation: "Now we are fighting together with the Alameda cooperative and the UTC. I invite all workers who know their rights are being violated to join the movement against slave labor." ❑

Resources: To contact UTC activists at La Alameda assembly in Parque Avellaneda, email: asambleaparqueavellaneda@hotmail.com. To see videos of recent UTC actions, go to: www.revolutionvideo.org/agoratv/secciones/luchas_obreras/costureros_utc.html; www.revolutionvideo.org/agoratv/secciones/luchas_obreras/escrache_costureros.html.

Article 7.4

THE RIGHT TO STAY HOME

Transnational communities are creating new ways of looking at citizenship and residence that correspond to the realities of migration.

BY DAVID BACON
September/October 2008

For almost half a century, migration has been the main fact of social life in hundreds of indigenous towns spread through the hills of Oaxaca, one of Mexico's poorest states. That's made migrants' rights, and the conditions they face, central concerns for communities like Santiago de Juxtlahuaca. Today the right to travel to seek work is a matter of survival. But this June in Juxtlahuaca, in the heart of Oaxaca's Mixteca region, dozens of farmers left their fields, and weavers their looms, to talk about another right—the right to stay home.

In the town's community center, 200 Mixtec, Zapotec, and Triqui farmers, and a handful of their relatives working in the United States, made impassioned speeches asserting this right at the triannual assembly of the Indigenous Front of Binational Organizations (FIOB). Hot debates ended in numerous votes. The voices of mothers and fathers arguing over the future of their children echoed from the cinderblock walls of the cavernous hall. In Spanish, Mixteco, and Triqui, people repeated one phrase over and over: *el derecho de no migrar*—the right to *not* migrate. Asserting this right challenges not just inequality and exploitation facing migrants, but the very reasons why people have to migrate to begin with. Indigenous communities are pointing to the need for social change.

About 500,000 indigenous people from Oaxaca live in the United States, including 300,000 in California alone, according to Rufino Dominguez, one of FIOB's founders. These men and women come from communities whose economies are totally dependent on migration. The ability to send a son or daughter across the border to the north, to work and send back money, makes the difference between eating chicken or eating salt and tortillas. Migration means not having to manhandle a wooden plough behind an ox, cutting furrows in dry soil for a corn crop that can't be sold for what it cost to plant it. It means that dollars arrive in the mail when kids need shoes to go to school, or when a grandparent needs a doctor.

Seventy-five percent of Oaxaca's 3.4 million residents live in extreme poverty, according to EDUCA, an education and development organization. For more than two decades, under pressure from international lenders, the Mexican government has cut spending intended to raise rural incomes. Prices have risen dramatically since price controls and subsidies were eliminated for necessities like gasoline, electricity, bus fares, tortillas, and milk.

Raquel Cruz Manzano, principal of the Formal Primary School in San Pablo Macuiltianguis, a town in the indigenous Zapotec region, says only 900,000 Oaxacans receive organized health care, and the illiteracy rate is 21.8%. "The educational level in Oaxaca is 5.8 years," Cruz notes, "against a national average of 7.3 years. The average monthly wage for non-governmental employees is less than 2,000 pesos [about $200] per family," the lowest in the nation. "Around 75,000 children have to work in order to survive or to help their families," says Jaime Medina, a reporter for Oaxaca's daily *Noticias*. "A typical teacher earns about 2200 pesos every two weeks [about $220]. From that they have to purchase chalk, pencils and other school supplies for the children." Towns like Juxtlahuaca don't even have waste water treatment. Rural communities rely on the same rivers for drinking water that are also used to carry away sewage.

"There are no jobs here, and NAFTA [the North American Free Trade Agreement] made the price of corn so low that it's not economically possible to plant a crop anymore," Dominguez asserts. "We come to the U.S. to work because we can't get a price for our product at home. There is no alternative." Without large-scale political change, most communities won't have the resources for productive projects and economic development that could provide a decent living.

Because of its indigenous membership, FIOB campaigns for the rights of migrants in the United States who come from those communities. It calls for immigration amnesty and legalization for undocumented migrants. FIOB has also condemned the proposals for guestworker programs. Migrants need the right to work, but "these workers don't have labor rights or benefits," Dominguez charges. "It's like slavery."

At the same time, "we need development that makes migration a choice rather than a necessity—the right to not migrate," explains Gaspar Rivera Salgado, a professor at UCLA. "Both rights are part of the same solution. We have to change the debate from one in which immigration is presented as a problem to a debate over rights. The real problem is exploitation." But the right to stay home, to not migrate, has to mean more than the right to be poor, the right to go hungry and be homeless. Choosing whether to stay home or leave only has meaning if each choice can provide a meaningful future.

In Juxtlahuaca, Rivera Salgado was elected as FIOB's new binational coordinator. His father and mother still live on a ranch half an hour up a dirt road from the main highway, in the tiny town of Santa Cruz Rancho Viejo. There his father Sidronio planted three hundred avocado trees a few years ago, in the hope that someday their fruit would take the place of the corn and beans that were once his staple crops. He's fortunate—his relatives have water, and a pipe from their spring has kept most of his trees, and those hopes, alive. Fernando, Gaspar's brother, has started growing mushrooms in a FIOB-sponsored project, and even put up a greenhouse for tomatoes. Those projects, they hope, will produce enough money that Fernando won't have to go back to Seattle, where he worked for seven years.

This family perhaps has come close to achieving the *derecho de no migrar*. For the millions of farmers throughout the indigenous countryside, not migrating means doing something like what Gaspar's family has done. But finding the necessary resources, even for a small number of families and communities, presents FIOB with its biggest challenge. Rivera Salgado says, "we will find the answer to migration in our communities of origin. To make the right to not migrate concrete, we need to organize the forces in our communities, and combine them with the resources and experiences we've accumulated in 16 years of cross-border organizing." Over the years FIOB has organized women weavers in Juxtlahuaca, helping them sell their textiles and garments through its chapters in California. It set up a union for rural taxis, both to help farming families get from Juxtlahuaca to the tiny towns in the surrounding hills, and to provide jobs for drivers. Artisan co-ops make traditional products, helped by a cooperative loan fund.

The government does have some money for loans to start similar projects, but it usually goes to officials who often just pocket it. They are supporters of the ruling PRI, which has ruled Oaxaca since it was formed in the 1940s. "Part of our political culture is the use of *regalos*, or government favors, to buy votes," Rivera Salgado explains. "People want *regalos*, and think an organization is strong because of what it can give. It's critical that our members see organization as the answer to problems, not a gift from the government or a political party. FIOB members need political education."

But for the 16 years of its existence, FIOB has been a crucial part of the political opposition to Oaxaca's PRI government. Juan Romualdo Gutierrez Cortéz, a school teacher in Tecomaxtlahuaca, was FIOB's Oaxaca coordinator until he stepped down at the Juxtlahuaca assembly. He is also a leader of Oaxaca's teachers union, Section 22 of the National Education Workers Union, and of the Popular Association of the People of Oaxaca (APPO).

A June 2006 strike by Section 22 sparked a months-long uprising, led by APPO, which sought to remove the state's governor, Ulises Ruíz, and make a basic change in development and economic policy. The uprising was crushed by Federal armed intervention, and dozens of activists were arrested. According to Leoncio Vásquez, an FIOB activist in Fresno, "the lack of human rights itself is a factor contributing to migration from Oaxaca and Mexico, since it closes off our ability to call for any change." This spring teachers again occupied the central plaza, or *zócalo*, of the state capital, protesting the same conditions that sparked the uprising two years ago.

In the late 1990s Gutierrez was elected to the Oaxaca Chamber of Deputies, in an alliance between FIOB and Mexico's left-wing Democratic Revolutionary Party (PRD). Following his term in office, he was imprisoned by Ruíz' predecessor, José Murat, until a binational campaign won his release. His crime, and that of many others filling Oaxaca's jails, was insisting on a new path of economic development that would raise rural living standards and make migration just an option, rather than an indispensable means of survival.

Despite the fact that APPO wasn't successful in getting rid of Ruíz and the PRI, Rivera Salgado believes that "in Mexico we're very close to getting power in our communities on a local and state level." FIOB delegates agreed that the organization would continue its alliance with the PRD. "We know the PRD is caught up in an internal crisis, and there's no real alternative vision on the left," Rivera Salgado says. "But there are no other choices if we want to participate in electoral politics. Migration is part of globalization," he emphasizes, "an aspect of state policies that expel people. Creating an alternative to that requires political power. There's no way to avoid that." ❑

Article 7.5

THE RISE OF MIGRANT WORKER MILITANCY

IMMANUEL NESS
September/October 2006

Testifying before the Senate immigration hearings in early July, Mayor Michael Bloomberg affirmed that undocumented immigrants have become indispensable to the economy of New York City: "Although they broke the law by illegally crossing our borders or overstaying their visas, and our businesses broke the law by employing them, our city's economy would be a shell of itself had they not, and it would collapse if they were deported. The same holds true for the nation." Bloomberg's comment outraged right-wing pundits, but how much more outraged would they be if they knew that immigrant workers, beyond being economically indispensable, are beginning to transform the U.S. labor movement with a bold new militancy?

After years of working in obscurity in the unregulated economy, migrant workers in New York City catapulted themselves to the forefront of labor activism beginning in late 1999 through three separate organizing drives among low-wage workers. Immigrants initiated all three drives: Mexican immigrants organized and struck for improved wages and working conditions at greengroceries; Francophone African delivery workers struck for unpaid wages and respect from labor contractors for leading supermarket chains; and South Asians organized for improved conditions and a union in the for-hire car service industry. (In New York, "car services" are taxis that cannot be hailed on the street, only arranged by phone.) These organizing efforts have persisted, and are part of a growing militancy among migrant workers in New York City and across the United States.

Why would seemingly invisible workers rise up to contest power in their workplaces? Why are vulnerable migrant workers currently more likely to organize than are U.S.-born workers? To answer these questions, we have to look at immigrants' distinct position in the political economy of a globalized New York City and at their specific economic and social niches, ones in which exploitation and isolation nurture class consciousness and militancy.

Labor Migration and Industrial Restructuring

New immigrant workers in the United States, many here illegally, stand at the crossroads of two overwhelming trends. On one hand, industrial restructuring and capital mobility have eroded traditional industries and remade the U.S. political economy in the last 30 years in ways that have led many companies to create millions of low-wage jobs and to seek vulnerable workers to fill them. On the other hand, at the behest of international financial institutions like the International Monetary Fund, and to meet the requirements of free-trade agreements such as NAFTA, governments throughout the global South have adopted neoliberal policies that have restructured their economies, resulting in the displacement of urban workers and rural farmers alike. Many have no choice but to migrate north.

A century ago the United States likewise experienced a large influx of immigrants, many of whom worked in factories for their entire lives. There they formed social networks across ethnic lines and developed a class consciousness that spurred the organizing of unions; they made up the generation of workers whose efforts began with the fight for the eight-hour day around the turn of the last century and culminated in the great organizing victories of the 1930s and 1940s across the entire spectrum of mining and manufacturing industries.

Today's immigrants face an entirely different political-economic landscape. Unlike most of their European counterparts a century ago, immigration restrictions mean that many newcomers to the United States are now here illegally. Workers from Latin America frequently migrate illegally without proper documentation; those from Africa, Asia, and Europe commonly arrive with business, worker, student, or tourist visas, then overstay them.

The urban areas where many immigrants arrive have undergone a 30-year decline in manufacturing jobs. The growing pool of service jobs which have come in their stead tend to be dispersed in small firms throughout the city. The proliferation of geographically dispersed subcontractors who compete on the basis of low wages encourages a process of informalization—a term referring to a redistribution of work from regulated sectors of the economy to new unregulated sectors of the underground or informal economy. As a result, wages and working conditions have fallen, often below government-established norms.

Although informal work is typically associated with the developing world—or Global South—observers are increasingly recognizing the link between the regulated and unregulated sectors in advanced industrial regions. More and more the regulated sector depends on unregulated economic activity through subcontracting and outsourcing of work to firms employing low-wage immigrant labor. Major corporations employ or subcontract to businesses employing migrant workers in what were once established sectors of the economy with decent wages and working conditions.

Informalization requires government regulatory agencies to look the other way. For decades federal and state regulatory bodies have ignored violations of laws governing wages, hours, and workplace safety, leading to illegally low wages and declining workplace health and safety practices. The process of informalization is furthered by the reduction or elimination of protections such as disability insurance, Social Security, health care coverage, unemployment insurance, and workers compensation.

By the 1990s, substandard jobs employing almost exclusively migrant workers had become crucial to key sectors of the national economy. Today, immigrants have gained a major presence as bricklayers, demolition workers, and hazardous waste workers on construction and building rehab sites; as cooks, dishwashers, and busboys in restaurants; and as taxi drivers, domestic workers, and delivery people.

Employers frequently treat these workers as self-employed. They typically have no union protection and little or no job security. With government enforcement shrinking, they lack the protection of minimum-wage laws and they have been excluded from Social Security and unemployment insurance.

These workers are increasingly victimized by employers who force them to accept 19th-century working conditions and sub-minimum wages. Today, New York City, Los Angeles, Miami, Houston, and Boston form a nexus of international labor migration, with constantly churning labor markets. As long as there is a demand for cheap labor, immigrants will continue to enter the United States in large numbers. Like water, capital always flows to the lowest level, a state of symmetry where wages are cheapest.

In turn, the availability of a reserve army of immigrant labor provides an enormous incentive for larger corporations to create and use subcontracting firms. Without this workforce, employers in the regulated economy would have more incentive to invest in labor-saving technology, increase the capital-labor ratio, and seek accommodation with unions.

New unauthorized immigrants residing and working in the United States are ideal workers in the new informalized sectors: Their undocumented legal status makes them more tractable since they constantly fear deportation. Undocumented immigrants are less likely to know about, or demand adherence to, established labor standards, and even low U.S. wages represent an improvement over earnings in their home countries.

Forging Migrant Labor Solidarity

The perception that new immigrants undermine U.S.-born workers by undercutting prevailing wage and work standards cannot be entirely dismissed. The entry of a large number of immigrants into the underground economy unquestionably reduces the labor market leverage of U.S.-born workers. But the story is more complicated. In spite of their vulnerability, migrant workers have demonstrated a willingness and a capacity to organize for improvements in their wages and working conditions; they arguably are responding to tough conditions on the job with greater militancy than U.S.-born workers.

New York City has been the site of a number of instances of immigrant worker organizing. In 1998, Mexicans working in greengroceries embarked on a citywide organizing campaign to improve their conditions of work. Most of the 20,000 greengrocery workers were paid below $3.00 an hour, working on average 72 hours a week. Some did not make enough to pay their living expenses, no less send remittances back home to Mexico. Following a relentless and coordinated four-year organizing campaign among the workers, employers agreed to raise wages above the minimum and improve working conditions. Moreover, the campaign led state Attorney General Eliot Spitzer to establish a Greengrocer Code of Conduct and to strengthen enforcement of labor regulations.

In another display of immigrant worker militancy, beginning in 1999 Francophone African supermarket delivery workers in New York City fought for and won equality with other workers in the same stores. The workers were responsible for bagging groceries and delivering them to affluent customers in Manhattan and throughout the city. As contractors, the delivery workers were paid no wage, instead relying on the goodwill of customers in affluent neighborhoods to pay tips for each delivery.

The workers were employed in supermarkets and drug stores where some others had a union. Without union support themselves, delivery workers staged a significant strike and insurrection that made consumers aware of their appalling conditions of work. In late October, workers went on strike and marched from supermarket to supermarket, demanding living wages and dignity on the job. At the start of their campaign, wages averaged less than $70 a week. In the months following the strike the workers all won recognition from the stores through the United Food and Commercial Workers that had earlier neglected to include them in negotiations with management. The National Employee Law Project, a national worker advocacy organization, filed landmark lawsuits against the supermarkets and delivery companies and won backwage settlements as the courts deemed them to be workers—not independent contractors in business for themselves.

Immigrant workers have organized countless other campaigns, in New York and across the country. How do new immigrants, with weak ties to organized labor and the state, manage to assert their interests? The explanation lies in the character of immigrant work and social life; the constraints immigrant workers face paradoxically encourage them to draw on shared experiences to create solidarity at work and in their communities.

The typical migrant worker can expect to work twelve-hour days, seven days a week. When arriving home, immigrant workers frequently share the same apartments, buildings, and neighborhoods. These employment ghettos typify immigrant communities across the nation. Workers cook for one another, share stories about their oppressively long and hard days, commiserate about their ill treatment at work, and then go to sleep only to start anew the next day.

Migrant women, surrounded by a world of exploitation, typically suffer even more abuse than their male counterparts, suffering from low wages, long hours, and dangerous conditions. Patterns of gender stratification found in the general labor market are even more apparent among migrant women workers. Most jobs in the nonunion economy, such as construction and driving, are stereotypically considered "men's work." Women predominate in the garment industry, as domestic and child care workers, in laundries, hotels, restaurants, and ever more in sex work. A striking example of migrant women's perilous work environment is the massive recruitment of migrant women to clean up the hazardous materials in the rubble left by the collapse of the World Trade Center without proper safety training.

Isolated in their jobs and communities, immigrant workers have few social ties to unions, community groups, and public officials, and few resources to call upon to assist them in transforming their workplaces. Because new immigrants have few social networks outside the workplace, the ties they develop on the job are especially solid and meaningful—and are nurtured every day. The workers' very isolation and status as outsiders, and their concentration into industrial niches by employers who hire on the basis of ethnicity, tend to strengthen old social ties, build new ones, and deepen class solidarity.

Immigrant social networks contribute to workplace militancy. Conversely, activism at work can stimulate new social networks that can expand workers' power. It is through relationships developed on the job and in the community that shared social identities and mutual resentment of the boss evolves into class consciousness and class solidarity: migrant workers begin to form informal organizations, meet with coworkers to respond to poor working conditions, and take action on the shop floor in defiance of employer abuse.

Typically, few workplace hierarchies exist among immigrants, since few reach supervisory positions. As a result, immigrant workers suffer poor treatment equally at the hands of employers. A gathering sense of collective exploitation usually transforms individualistic activities into shared ones. In rare cases where there are immigrant foremen and crew leaders, they may recognize this solidarity and side with the workers rather than with management. One former manager employed for a fast-food sandwich chain in New York City said: "We are hired only to divide the workers but I was really trying to help the workers get better pay and shorter hours."

Migrant workers bring social identities from their home countries, and those identities are shaped through socialization and work in this country. In cities and towns across the United States, segmentation of migrant workers from specific countries reinforces ethnic, national, and religious identities and helps to form other identities that may stimulate solidarity. Before arriving in the United States, Mexican immigrant workers often see themselves as peasants but not initially as "people of color," while Francophone Africans see themselves as Malian or Senegalese ethnics but not necessarily "black." Life and work in New York can encourage them to adopt new identifications, including a new class consciousness that can spur organizing and militancy.

Once triggered, organizing can go from workplace to workplace like wildfire. When workers realize that they can fight and prevail, this creates a sense of invincibility that stimulates militant action that would otherwise be avoided at all costs. This demonstration effect is vitally important, as was the case in the strikes among garment workers and coal miners in the history of the U.S. labor movement.

"Solidarity Forever" vs. "Take This Job and Shove It"

The militancy of many migrant workers contrasts sharply with the passivity of many U.S.-born workers facing the same low wages and poor working conditions. Why do most workers at chain stores and restaurants like Walmart and McDonalds—most of whom were born in the United States—appear so complacent, while new immigrants are often so militant?

Migrants are not inherently more militant or less passive. Instead, the real workplace conditions of migrant workers seem to produce greater militancy on the job. First, collective social isolation engenders strong ties among migrants in low-wage jobs where organizing is frequently the only way to improve conditions. Because migrants work in jobs that are more amenable to organizing, they are highly represented among newly unionized workers. Strong social ties in the workplace drive migrants to form their own embryonic organizations at work and in their communities that are ripe for union representation. Organizing among migrant workers gains the attention of labor unions, which then see a chance to recruit new members and may provide resources to help immigrant workers mobilize at work and join the union.

Employers also play a major role. Firms employing U.S. workers tend to be larger and are often much harder to organize than the small businesses where immigrants work. In 2003, the Merriam-Webster dictionary added the new word McJob, defined as "a low-paying job that requires little skill and provides little opportunity for advancement." The widely accepted coinage reflects the relentless 30-year economic restructuring creating low-end jobs in the retail sector.

Organizing against Home Depot, McDonalds, Taco Bell, or Walmart is completely different from organizing against smaller employers. Walmart uses many of the same tactics against workers that immigrants contend with: failure to pay overtime, stealing time (intentionally paying workers for fewer hours than actually worked), no health care, part-time work, high turnover, and gender division of labor. The difference is that Walmart has far more resources to oppose unionization than do the smaller employers who are frequently subcontractors to larger firms. But Walmart's opposition to labor unions is so forceful that workers choose to leave rather than stay and fight it out. Relentless labor turnover mitigates against the formation of working class consciousness and militancy.

The expanding non-immigrant low-end service sector tends to produce unskilled part-time jobs that do not train workers in skills that keep them in the same sector of the labor market. Because jobs at the low end of the economy require little training, workers frequently move from one industry to the next. One day a U.S.-born worker may work as a sales clerk for Target, the next day as a waiter at Olive Garden. Because they are not stuck in identity-defined niches, U.S. workers change their world by quitting and finding a job elsewhere, giving them less reason to organize and unionize.

The fact that U.S.-born workers have an exit strategy and migrant workers do not is a significant and important difference. Immigrant workers are more prone to take action to change their working conditions because they have far fewer options than U.S.-born workers. Workers employed by companies like Walmart are unable to change their conditions, since they have little power and will be summarily fired for any form of dissent. If workers violate the terms of Walmart's or McDonalds' employee manual by, say, arriving late, and then are summarily fired, no one is likely to fend for them, as is usually the case among many migrant workers. While migrant workers engage in direct action against their employers to obtain higher wages and respect on the job, U.S. workers do not develop the same dense connections in labor market niches that forge solidarity. Employers firing new immigrants may risk demonstrations, picket lines, or even strikes.

Immigrant workers are pushed into low-wage labor market niches as day laborers, food handlers, delivery workers, and nannies; these niches are difficult if not impossible to escape. Yet immigrant workers relegated to dead-end jobs in the lowest echelons of the labor market in food, delivery, and car service work show a greater eagerness to fight it out to improve their wages and conditions than do U.S. workers who can move on to another dead-end job.

The Role of Unions

Today's labor movement is in serious trouble; membership is spiraling downward as employers demand union-free workplaces. Unionized manufacturing and service workers are losing their jobs to low-wage operations abroad. Unions and, more importantly, the U.S. working class, are in dire straits and must find a means to triumph over the neoliberal dogma that dominates the capitalist system.

As organizing campaigns in New York City show, migrant workers are indispensable to the revitalization of the labor movement. As employers turn to migrant labor to fill low-wage jobs, unions must encourage and support organizing drives that emerge from the oppressive conditions of work. As the 1930s workers' movement demonstrates, if conditions improve for immigrants, all workers will prosper. To gain traction, unions must recognize that capital is pitting migrant workers against native-born laborers to lower wages and improve profitability. Although unions have had some success organizing immigrants, most are circling the wagons, disinterested in building a more inclusive mass labor movement. The first step is for unions to go beyond rhetoric and form a broad and inclusive coalition embracing migrant workers. ❑

Article 7.6

NATIVISM: AS AMERICAN AS (ROTTEN) APPLE PIE

BY GERALD FRIEDMAN
November/December 2016

> [W]hy should the Palatine Boors be suffered to swarm into our settle-
> ments, and by herding together establish their languages and manners
> to the exclusion of ours? Why should Pennsylvania, founded by the
> English, become a colony of Aliens, who will shortly be so numerous as
> to Germanize us instead of our Anglifying them, and will never adopt our
> language or customs, any more than they can acquire our complexion?
> —Benjamin Franklin, "Observations Concerning the Increase of
> Mankind" (1751)

While he was one of the first American nativists, Benjamin Franklin was far from
the last. Instead, he inaugurated a tradition that has persisted in American
society and politics, occasionally rearing its ugly head to threaten our society. From
Franklin, to the Protestant nativists who warned against Irish and German immigrants in the 1850s, to the anti-Chinese crusaders of the 1880s, it was a short step to
the Ku Klux Klan movement of the 1920s, which was anti-Catholic and anti-Jewish
in addition to being anti-Black. And, of course, to Donald Trump today.

Since the United States is largely populated by people who came here from
Africa, Asia, and Europe—of course, most who came from Africa were kidnapped and brought involuntarily—it should seem odd for Americans to disparage
"aliens." The founding documents of the United States welcomed immigrants. The
Declaration of Independence proclaims the equality of all, the Constitution provides that immigrants are to be accorded equal rights with those born here with
only minor restrictions, and the first naturalization laws provided for a short and
easy path to citizenship open to all without restriction. Unlike other countries, the
United States has no official language or religion, and all citizens, regardless of place
of birth, are guaranteed all the "privileges or immunities of citizens of the United
States" and cannot be deprived of "life, liberty, or property" or "equal protection of
the laws" without due process.

Indeed, Americans have often maintained an open and welcoming attitude
towards immigrants. Through the 19th century, many states allowed all residents to vote without regard for citizenship, and schools and public services were
offered in languages other than English. Native English speakers learned German,
Spanish, Yiddish, and other languages so that they could do business with their
non-English-speaking neighbors. Even now, in the midst of a new nativist surge,
public-opinion polls report that a majority of Americans (in contrast with residents

of most European countries) believe ethnic and cultural diversity makes the country better. This view attracts significant support across the political spectrum (ranging from nearly half of self-described "conservatives" to over three-fourths of "liberals").

Against such welcoming attitudes has been a stubborn and resilient nativism which has periodically found political expression.

Waves of Immigration and Waves of Nativism

Sometimes, nativism has been linked with national security scares. Fear of a French invasion in 1798, for example, prompted Congress to pass the so-called Alien and Sedition Acts—including the Naturalization Act, which increased the period of residence required for immigrants to become full citizens from just five years to 14. Another law authorized the president to expel without hearing or judicial recourse any noncitizen deemed "dangerous to the peace and safety" of the United States. And the Alien Enemies Act authorized the president to arrest, imprison, or banish any resident alien hailing from a country against which the United States has declared war.

These anti-immigrant measures were defended by Federalist politicians who warned against inviting "hordes of Wild Irishmen, nor the turbulent and disorderly of all the world, to come here with a basic view to distract our tranquility." The passing of the war scare and the defeat of the Federalists in the elections of 1800 led to repeal of two of the Alien Acts in 1801. After the repeal, political nativism was weakened for the next few decades—possibly as a result of embarrassment at this experience. Widespread nativist politics only returned in the 1850s, after famine and civil war led to a dramatic increase in European immigration. Compared to previous decades, annual immigration to the United States increased four-fold in the 1840s , including an annual influx of over 150,000 fleeing the Irish famine. While each year's immigration equaled barely 1% of the population of the United States, and the Irish were less than half of that, the concentration of Irish immigrants in a few localities had large economic and political effects.

Fears of labor-market competition have also stoked nativist movements. In cities like Boston and New York, Irish immigrants quickly came to dominate the market for common laborers, including construction workers and domestic servants. Often desperate for money and food, the Irish took any work they could find: cleaning stables, unloading ships, digging trenches.

While avoiding the southern states with slave labor and agricultural economies, the new immigrants spread throughout the Northern states. In New England, the Irish would settle in Lynn to work in the shoe factories, or in Lowell and Lawrence to operate looms in the textile mills and build the dams that powered the factories. Around Boston, as throughout the United States, Irish immigrants built the roads and laid the track for the network of railroads that came to tie together the United States after 1850.

Not that their work was appreciated by all of their neighbors.

The Native American Party (renamed the "American Party" in 1855 but better known as the "Know Nothings") ran candidates on an anti-Catholic and anti-immigrant platform. At its peak, in the mid-1850s, the Know Nothings dominated the Massachusetts legislature and elected mayors in Philadelphia, Chicago, and other cities. The Know Nothings were more than an electoral vehicle. In 1854, election-related violence led to the deaths of 22 people in Louisville, Ky., and the burning of a Catholic church in Bath, Me., among other incidents.

After 1854, the Know Nothings faded quickly when "Bleeding Kansas" and slavery replaced immigration as the major political issues. For decades after the Civil War, the prominent role that many Irish- and German-born soldiers played in the Union cause may have contributed to the sharp decline of nativism. When nativism returned in the 1880s, its center had moved west to the Pacific coast, and it had a new focus with attacks on Asian immigrants, especially the Chinese.

Like the Irish before them, Chinese immigrants took many of the hardest and dirtiest jobs, working in laundries, in construction gangs building railroads, and in mines. Chinese workers dug much of the gold during the California Gold Rush, and many died building the First Transcontinental Railroad. Competition for work and the use of Chinese workers as strike-breakers certainly contributed to the anti-Chinese campaign. Formed in 1876 to "rid the country of Chinese cheap labor," the Workingmen's Party of California was led by an Irish immigrant, Denis Kearney, who liked to end his speeches with the phrase: "Whatever happens, the Chinese must go!"

Nativist movements have been opposed by advocates of equal rights (though not always successfully). While some Republicans and most Democrats joined Kearney in his racism, most Republicans, especially radicals and former abolitionists, defended the Chinese and other immigrants. The great abolitionist Sen. Charles Sumner (R-Mass.) insisted on equal rights for the Chinese: it is, he said, "the question of the Declaration of Independence and whether we will be true to it. 'All men are created equal' without distinction of color." Sen. Samuel Pomeroy, a Kansas Republican, agreed and pragmatically warned that denying equal rights to the Chinese would threaten the rights of all: "If you deny citizenship to a large class, you have a dangerous element; you have an element that you can enslave; you have an element in the community that you can proscribe."

Such warnings fell on deaf ears after the end of Reconstruction. The return of Democrats to power in the South brought to Congress a large racist block just when anxious northern Republicans feared to push an aggressive equal-rights agenda. A united Democratic Party was joined by enough Republicans to enact racist laws against the Chinese. In 1875, Congress, with a newly elected Democratic majority, enacted the Page Act preventing Chinese women from entering the United States on the assumption that they were prostitutes. And, in 1878, Congress passed a Chinese Exclusion Act. Vetoed by Republican President Rutherford B. Hayes, it was eventually signed into law by Chester A. Arthur in 1882.

As memories of the Civil War and emancipation struggles faded, and migration from southern and eastern Europe surged, nativism spread. In 1894, three Harvard graduates, Charles Warren, Robert DeCourcy Ward, and Prescott Farnsworth Hall, met in Boston to form the Immigration Restriction League (IRL). Arguing that these recently arrived "undesirables" were inherently unable to participate in self-government or to adopt American values, the IRL sought to "arouse public opinion to the necessity of a further exclusion of elements undesirable for citizenship or injurious to our national character."

The IRL quickly attracted a large membership, including many prominent scholars and philanthropists. On its behalf, Sen. Henry Cabot Lodge (R-Mass.) sponsored a literacy bill to prohibit the entry of immigrants unable to read at least 40 words in any language. In 1896, Congress enacted the Lodge proposal only to have it vetoed by Pres. Grover Cleveland as contrary to traditional American policy and values. The failure of immigration restriction left the golden door open to new waves of immigrants from southern and eastern Europe: Jews to work in New York's apparel industry, Slavs for the Pennsylvania coal fields and steel mills, and Italians, Greeks, Poles, and others to build and to operate America's growing industries. Re-introduced repeatedly, the proposed literacy test became law only in 1917, during World War I, when Congress overrode President Woodrow Wilson's third veto.

And once again, fears of foreign "subversives" fueled nativism. The war inaugurated a new period of American nativism, one fed less by fear of economic displacement than by fear of subversion and anger at foreign ideas and involvements. The fear was fed by terrorist incidents. On June 2, 1919, for example, followers of the Italian-born anarchist Luigi Galleani exploded bombs in seven cities, including at the homes of John D. Rockefeller and of U.S. Attorney General A. Mitchell Palmer. A progressive Democrat with a pro-labor record in Congress, Palmer met the bombing campaign with a wave of arrests of radicals and by deporting immigrants and others. Called the "Red Scare," Palmer's attacks targeted immigrants as much as anarchists and communists. The Palmer raids resulted in the arrest of over 10,000 labor activists, radicals, and liberals and the deportations of 556 resident aliens. The warrantless arrests and deportations were widely denounced as "utterly illegal" and led to the establishment of the American Civil Liberties Union. Nearly all the resulting arrests were ultimately voided.

The involvement of immigrant radicals and of immigrant workers in the great strike wave of 1919-20 fed nativist fears. Eastern and Southern Europeans were condemned as incapable of assimilation and incapable of responsible self-government because they were genetically inferior. A broad coalition formed around a program of immigration restriction focused on limiting the admission of immigrants from the "lower races" seen as threats to the nation's gene pool, its democratic institutions, and the American "way of life." Immigration laws enacted in 1921 and 1924 created a national-origins quota system, restricting the absolute number of immigrants and the number from southern and eastern Europe.

Legislation restricting immigration did not end the culture war. Nativists flocked to a revived Ku Klux Klan seeking to limit the rights of African-Americans and of immigrants, especially Catholics and Jews. The rise of the Klan in the 1920s was inspired by one of Hollywood's first full-length epics, D.W. Griffith's 1915 "Birth of a Nation." With its story of how the Klan saved white Americans from African-American rapists and corrupt politicians, the firm brought renewed attention to the Klan. Reborn at a rally at Stone Mountain, Ga., shortly after the film's release, the "second era" Klan soon grew beyond its southern base. By 1924, the KKK had four million members, and professed to control over 24 of the nation's 48 state legislatures. The KKK claimed that it prevented Al Smith, the progressive governor of New York State, from winning the Democratic presidential nomination. While this may be an exaggeration, the Klan may have contributed to the wave of lynchings in the early 1920s.

Beset by corruption and internal dissension, the KKK soon lost most of its new membership. The nativist cause was taken up by others. The industrialist Henry Ford financed the dissemination of the notorious anti-Semitic forgery, *The Protocols of the Elders of Zion*, and for ninety-one consecutive issues beginning May 22, 1920, his weekly newspaper, the *Dearborn Independent*, published articles describing an international Jewish conspiracy. Broadcasting from his Detroit parish, the Catholic priest Charles Coughlin added economic populism to Ford's anti-Semitism. Coughlin reached a radio audience estimated in the tens of millions with a message that blamed the economic crisis on financiers and communists, especially Jews, who have "murdered more than 20 million Christians" and have stolen "40 billion [dollars] ... of Christian property." Inspired by the success of the German Nazis, he founded a Christian Front to defend the country from communists and Jews and he urged his listeners to "buy Christian."

Coughlin's support for Nazi Germany was his undoing. The association of nativism and racial supremacism with Nazi genocide discredited such ideas. By the 1960s, the United States abandoned the system of national preferences in immigration, opening the country to new waves of immigrants from China, Asia, Africa, and Latin America, as well as the southern and eastern Europeans who had been targeted by the 1921 and 1924 laws.

The (Not So) New Nativism

The repeal of the system of national preferences opened the door to renewed immigration with the number of documented immigrants tripling between the 1960s and 1990s. While the number of immigrants is comparable to past waves, as a share of the much larger population of the 21st century United States, the new immigration wave is much smaller than those of the past. As in the past, however, the new immigration wave has brought migrants from countries previously little represented in the United States. American cities are now filled with immigrants from Africa, Asia, and Latin America, and this is true not only of traditional immigration centers on the East and West Coasts like Boston, New York, and San Francisco, but also big cities in the South and West, like Atlanta and Houston, and small towns throughout the country with motels managed by Indian-Americans, and restaurants and other small businesses run by migrants from throughout the world.

Like the Irish and Germans of the 1840s or the Jews, Italians, and Slavs of 1900, the new immigrants of today are helping to build a new American economy while changing and enriching our culture. And like their predecessors, the new immigrants face racists and nativists. In 1994, California Republicans rode to state-wide victory on their support of Proposition 187, touted as a way to stop undocumented immigration by requiring local police and social services agents to report suspected immigrants. While passed with nearly 60% of the vote, Proposition 187 was never enforced because of challenges in the courts.

Political nativism has found renewed strength after the terrorist attacks of September 11, 2001, and, even more, with the economic crisis beginning in 2007. Again, we are seeing the familiar political and economic fears underlying the surge in nativism. While most Americans continue to support allowing immigrants into the United States and allowing those here to become citizens, a very boisterous minority has emerged calling for a restrictive, even punitive, policy like that in Proposition 187. Particularly active in Republican Party politics, nativists have won some signal victories, including the primary defeat of Republican House Majority Leader Eric Cantor. (Cantor, the only Jewish Republican in Congress, supported reforms that would have provided for a path toward citizenship for undocumented migrants.) Cantor's defeat killed immigration reform in the Republican-led Congress, and pointed the way for Donald Trump's successful campaign for the Republican presidential nomination on a nativist program—including a wall on the Mexico border, mass deportation of undocumented immigrants, and "extreme vetting" of immigrants from Islamic countries—not too different from that of the Know Nothings of the 1840s, or the KKK of the 1920s. ❑

Sources: Benjamin Franklin, "Observations Concerning the Increase of Mankind" (1751) (archive.org); John Higham, *Strangers in the Land: Patterns of American Nativism*, 1860-1925 (Rutgers University Press, 1988); Alexander Saxton, *The Indispensable Enemy: Labor and the Anti-Chinese Movement in California* (University of California Press, 1995); Gwendolyn Mink, *Old Labor and New Immigrants in American Political Development: Union, Party, and State, 1875-1920* (Cornell University Press, 1986); Jennifer Ludden, "In Rural Wisconsin, German Reigned For Decades" (NPR.org); Bruce Drake, "In Views of Diversity, Many Europeans Are Less Positive than Americans," Pew Research Center, July 12, 2016 (pewresearch.org); Philip Chin, "The Path to the Chinese Exclusion Act: 1868 to 1882," Chinese American Heroes (chineseamericanheroes.org); "Constitution of the Immigration Restriction League" (1894) (ocp.hul.harvard.edu); "Charles E. Coughlin," United States Holocaust Memorial Museum (ushmm.org); Alan Brinkley, *Voices of Protest: Huey Long, Father Coughlin, & the Great Depression* (Vintage, 1983); Steven Camarota, "Immigrants in the United States, 2010: A Profile of America's Foreign-Born Population," Center for Immigration Studies (cis.org); Frank Newport, "Americans Widely Support Immigration Reform Proposals" (gallup.com); Sara Goo, "What Americans Want to Do about Illegal Immigration," Pew Research Center, August 24, 2015 (pewresearch.org); Samantha Smith, "Trump Supporters Differ from Other GOP Voters on Foreign Policy, Immigration Issues," Pew Research Center, May 11, 2016 (pewresearch.org).

Article 7.7

GLOBALIZATION, NATIVISM, AND THE BREXIT VOTE

BY ALEJANDRO REUSS
July/August 2016

The June referendum vote in the United Kingdom, narrowly in favor of departure from the European Union (or "Brexit," a combination of "Britain" and "exit"), has thrown the future of the U.K. and its constituent nations into turmoil. The votes in England and Wales favored Brexit by modest margins. In contrast, the votes in Scotland and Northern Ireland favored remaining in the EU; in Scotland, overwhelmingly so. Already, the leaders of the Scottish government have called for a new referendum on independence from the U.K. (which, if victorious, would likely result in the country seeking to remain in the EU). It remains to be seen, meanwhile, whether Brexit is just the first in a domino tumble of exits from the union.

There has been a great deal of analysis, in the days since the vote, on the motives animating pro-Brexit voters. Many commentators have looked to underlying economic discontents, from the economic crisis of the 1970s and the death spiral of British industry and mining, to the age of neoliberal economic policy since the advent of Thatcher, to the global Great Recession and searing austerity under the current government. It is unmistakable, though, that the politics of Brexit, and the campaign led by the right-wing U.K. Independence Party (UKIP), are heavily laden with anti-immigrant sentiment. (In polls, over half of "leave" voters identified immigration into Britain as a "very important" issue, compared to just 14% of "remain" voters.) Right-wing, anti-immigrant leaders elsewhere in Europe, like Geert Wilders in the Netherlands and Marine Le Pen in France, have hailed Brexit as an example and called for referendums, in the near future, on their own countries' EU membership. Commentators are reading the rise of nationalism in Europe as a frightening echo of the events—leading up to the world wars—that shattered the last great age of capitalist globalization.

Just over a century ago, leaders and theorists of European Marxian socialism engaged in a pitched debate about the international integration of capital and the possibility that this would attenuate the conflicts between rival imperialist powers. The German Marxist theorist Karl Kautsky was a leading exponent of this theory of "ultra-imperialism." The Russian Marxists and Bolshevik leaders Lenin and Bukharin argued, against Kautsky, that the contradictions between rival imperialisms were too great to be reconciled anytime soon, whatever the far-off future might hold. They had a point, since the debate was taking place as the First World War raged. Ultimately, of course, the 20th century would see two World Wars erupt in the heart of Europe.

Kautsky saw ultra-imperialism as a possible result of capitalism's tendency toward international economic integration, along with the ruling classes' conscious desire to avoid future ruinous conflicts. He did not, however, openly advocate this as a system—in fact, he wrote "of course we must struggle against [ultra-imperialism] as energetically as we do against imperialism." The politics of post-World War II social democracy were a different story. Leading figures in Western Europe's mainstream social democratic parties embraced European political and economic integration as a way to avert a replay of the disasters of the first half of the 20th century. (Some were, surely, also motivated by the aim of strengthening Western Europe vis-a-vis the United States. And some had dreams for a united Europe that were genuinely social democratic—though not anti-capitalist.) In the most recent period, the "Third Way" figures who came to dominate the mainstream social democratic parties (like "New Labour" in the U.K.) signed on to the neoliberal project and to the selling of it as a triumph of globalism and cosmopolitanism over nationalism and parochialism. Now that this corporate-dominated and finance-dominated globalization has fallen into a disastrous crisis, a nationalist revanchism—embodied in nativist and "economic nationalist" movements—is capturing the backlash.

It is now a central challenge for the left, in Europe and around the world, to rescue internationalist politics from the disaster of capitalist globalization. The answer to surging nationalism is not to be found in the dream of a peaceful internationally integrated capitalism. There needs to be a radical left alternative that rejects nationalism and racism, that rejects the false equation of capitalist globalization with internationalism, and that fights for a new internationalism founded in workers' solidarity. ❑

Sources: Melissa Etehad, "This map shows Britain's striking geographical divide over Brexit, *Washington Post*, June 24, 2016; Elisabeth O'Leary, "New Scotland independence referendum 'highly likely': Sturgeon," June 24, 2016; Zack Beauchamp, "Brexit is terrifying—and no, not because of the economics," Vox World, June 24, 2016; Mary Pascaline, "Brexit Sparks Calls For More EU Exits, World Leaders React To EU Referendum Result," *International Business Times*, June 24, 2016; Amanda Taub, "Making Sense of 'Brexit' in 4 Charts," The Interpreter blog, *New York Times*, June 23, 2016; Luke Reader, "Why Brexit Won," History News Network, June 26, 2016 (historynewsnetwork.org); Karl Kautsky, "Ultra-Imperialism," September 2014 (marxists.org); Nikolai Bukharin, *Imperialism and World Economy* (1917) (marxists.org).

Chapter 8

DEVELOPMENT AND "UNDERDEVELOPMENT"

Article 8.1

THE "EMERGING ECONOMIES" TODAY

AN INTERVIEW WITH JAYATI GHOSH
May/June 2016

The terms "emerging markets" and "emerging economies" have come into fashion, especially to refer to countries supposedly poised to make the leap from "developing" to "developed" economies. There's no definitive list, but Brazil, India, Indonesia, Mexico, Russia, South Africa, Turkey, and China are among the large countries that often headline articles on "emerging economies." Economic growth rates—as well as the drop-off in growth during the global Great Recession and the recovery since—vary widely between countries typically placed in this group.

China is by far the most prominent of the emerging economies—the most populous country in the world, with an extraordinary period of industrial growth since the 1980s, and with an enormous impact (not only as an exporter of manufactured goods but also as an importer of raw-material and intermediate inputs to manufacturing) on the world economy. The "secular stagnation" of the high-income capitalist economies and resulting growth slowdown in China, therefore, has much wider implications for the developing world. In this interview, economist Jayati Ghosh addresses the current challenges for China and other countries—and possible paths toward inclusive and sustainable development. – Eds.

Dollars & Sense: You've written about the "retreat" of emerging-market economies, which until recently had been held up as examples of robust growth, in contrast to the stagnant economies of the so-called capitalist "core." What's driving the slowdown of economic growth in the emerging economies today?

Jayati Ghosh: The emerging economies are really those that have integrated much more into the global financial system, not just the global trade system. And I think what happened during the period of the economic boom is that many people forgot that their growth was still ultimately driven by what was happening in the North. That is, the engine of demand was still the northern economies. So whether you're talking about China in particular or the range of emerging economies that was seen as more prominent in the first half of the 2000s, all of them depended on exports to the North and particularly to the United States.

It was the U.S. boom that drew in more and more of the exports from developing countries. When it came to an end—as it inevitably had to—these economies had to look for other sources of demand. There are two ways of doing this. One is to try and do a domestic demand-driven expansion based on higher domestic incomes because of wage and employment growth. And the other is the model which unfortunately seems to be the more popular one, which is to have a debt-driven kind of growth, based on both consumption and accumulation that is essentially led by taking on more and more debt. This is, of course, also what the U.S. did in the 2000s, which unraveled in 2007 and 2008. But it's also what a number of European economies did, and they're paying the price now.

Remarkably, developing countries that don't need to take this path, and can see all the problems associated with it, also took this path in the wake of the global financial crisis. In China there was a doubling of the debt-to-GDP ratio between 2007 and 2014. This reflected increases in debt to every single sector, but it was dominantly for investment. In a range of other important developing countries, from Mexico to Indonesia, Malaysia, South Korea, etc., there was a dramatic expansion of household debt, particularly real estate and housing debt. We all know that these real-estate and housing bubbles that are led by taking on more debt, these end in tears. And that's really what has been happening.

In these "emerging" economies, financial integration allowed them to break the link between productive investment and growth. It fueled a debt-driven pattern of expansion, which inevitably has to end. It's ending now. The problem is that it's ending at a time when demand from the North is slowing dramatically. So there is a double whammy for these emerging economies. The slowdown in northern markets means that China—which had become the major driver of expansion—can no longer continue to export at the same rate. That means its imports have also come down. In the past year, China's exports fell by 5%, but its imports fell by 20%. That has affected all the other developing countries. And that's in combination with this end of the debt-driven expansion model.

D&S: A number of economists have argued for quite some time that China's export-oriented growth model would inevitably reach its limits. Are we seeing it finally reach an impasse now, and if so, is there a prospect for China to make a transition from a low-wage export-oriented model to a domestic demand-driven model that would necessarily require higher wages?

JG: I think it's indisputable that the export-driven model is over for the time being, for sure, certainly for the next five years, probably the next decade. That's not a bad thing, because one of the problems with that export-driven model is that it persists in seeing wages as costs rather than as a source of internal demand that you can use to your benefit. It encourages massive degradation of nature and taking on environmental costs that are now recognized to be completely unsustainable and socially undesirable. And, overall, we know that these can't last—these export-driven models can't last.

So, yes, it has ended. It does mean that the Chinese government and authorities have to look for an alternative. Many of us have been arguing that the alternative necessarily requires much more emphasis on increasing consumption, not through debt, but by increasing real incomes. And that means encouraging more employment of a desirable type—"decent work" as it's been called—and increasing wages. Now, this doesn't mean that the rates of growth will continue as high as they have been, but that doesn't matter.

In fact, the obsession with GDP growth is becoming a real negative now in the search for alternatives. The Chinese authorities, like all the financial analysts across the world who are constantly looking at China, are obsessed with GDP: Is it going to be 6.5% annual growth? Is it going to be 6.1%? Is it going to fall below 6%? As if that's all that matters. What they should really be looking at is the incomes of, let us say, the bottom 50 or 60%. Are these growing? If these are growing at about 4 or 5%, that's fantastic. That's wonderful. And that's really what the economy needs in a sustainable way. If these are growing in combination with patterns of production and consumption that are more sustainable, that are environmentally friendly, that are less carbon-emitting, then that is of course even more desirable.

But that means the focus has to shift away from GDP growth, and away from just pushing up GDP by any means whatsoever—to one which looks at how to improve the real incomes and the quality of life of the majority of the citizens. Unfortunately, the Chinese government doesn't seem to be choosing that path just yet. There have been some moves—in terms of increasing health spending, in terms of some attempts to increase wages and social protection for some workers—but overall the focus is still once again on more accumulation, on more investment, usually driven by more debt.

D&S: When you say the export-oriented model is "over," does that mean you think sticking to this approach will no longer deliver what policymakers and elites are aiming for, in terms of growth and accumulation? (And perhaps that this will lead to an elite-driven restructuring in the near term?) Or is it that this approach just cannot plausibly deliver in terms of inclusive development—the improvement in the quality of life for the majority?

JG: Both, really. The conditions of the global economy at present are such that an economy as large as that of China (and many other smaller economies as well) cannot expect much stimulus from external demand Significant increases in exports would only be possible by increasing markets share; that is, eating into some other country's exports. So the past pattern of accumulation based on external demand is unlikely to work in the near future.

But in addition, this approach has not delivered in terms of inclusive growth over the past decade except to some extent in China, which has been able to use it to generate a "Lewisian" process (theorized by economist Arthur Lewis in the 1950s) of shifting labor out of lower productivity activities. Even in China it was successful because wages increased much less than productivity and so export prices could fall or remain low. In many other countries, export-led expansion has actually been associated stagnant or lower wages and greater fragility of incomes, along with very substantial environmental costs that are typically not factored in.

D&S: Is it possible that that kind of transition is not going to happen in China until we see the development of a robust labor movement that's capable of winning a higher share of the national income in the form of wages, and pushing up mass consumption in that way?

JG: There is probably much greater public concern about all this in China than is often depicted in the media, certainly in the Chinese media, but even abroad. We know that there are thousands, literally, tens of thousands of protests in China—often about land grabs and so on in the peasantry, but also many, many workers' protests, and many other protests by citizens about environmental conditions. They have mostly been suppressed, but I don't think you can keep on suppressing these.

I do believe the Chinese elite has recognized that there are a couple of things that are becoming very important for them to maintain their political legitimacy. One is, of course, inequality and, associated with that, corruption. That is why the anti-corruption drive of President Xi Jinping retains a lot of popularity. Then there is the fact of the environmental unsustainability. Both India and China have created monstrosities in urban areas, in terms of the pollution, congestion, degradation, which are really making many of our cities and towns unlivable. There is widespread protest about that, and about the pollution of water sources, of the atmosphere, of land quality. And there is real concern that ordinary Chinese citizens are not continuously experiencing the better life that they have grown accustomed to expect.

So I think, even without a very large-scale social mobilization, there is growing awareness in China—among officialdom, as well—that they can't carry on as before. It is likely that there's a tussle at the very higher echelons of the leadership and in the Communist Party, between those who are arguing for the slower but more sustainable and more wage-led path, and those who just want to keep propping up growth by more financial liberalization, by encouraging investors to jump in and invest even in projects that are unlikely to continue, and somehow keep that GDP growth going. It's a political tussle but of course that will determine the direction of the economy as well.

D&S: In the midst of this period of stagnation of the very high-income capitalist economies, and a resulting slowdown of growth in the so-called emerging economies, we also have an effect on countries that had primarily remained raw-material (or "primary-product") exporters. Is that boom in commodities exports now also over for the foreseeable future, and do you see those countries as now reinventing their economic development models?

JG: I think that the period of the boom was really a bit of an aberration. Since the early 20th century, these periods of relatively high commodity prices have always been outliers, and they don't last very long. They last for about five, six, maybe eight years at most, and then they you come back to this more depressed situation relative to other prices. I have a feeling this is now going to continue, and that boom is, for the time being, over. It definitely means that the manna from heaven that many countries experienced has reduced, and therefore you have to think of other ways of diversifying your economies.

Many countries actually tried to do this but, you know, when you're getting so much income from the primary product exports it's very hard to diversify. It's actually easier to diversify when primary product prices are lower. So, once again, I think it's important for these countries to stop thinking of this as a huge loss, and start thinking of it as an opportunity—as an opportunity to use cheap primary commodities as a means of industrializing for domestic and regional markets. So it means a different strategy. The export-led obsession has to end. Without that, we're not going to get viable and sustainable strategies.

I'd like to make one other point, though, about the slowdown in China and the impact on developing countries, which is that it's also going to affect manufacturing exporters. China had become the center of a global production chain that was heavily exporting to the North but was drawing in more and more raw material and intermediate products from other developing countries. So almost every country had China become their main trade partner in both imports and exports. Many of these manufacturing economies are now going to face, once again, a double whammy. They will face a reduction, from China, in terms of lower Chinese imports of raw materials and intermediate goods for final export, and they're going to face greater competition from China in terms of their own export markets and their own domestic markets. Because China is now devaluing its currency, even though thus far it has been minor. It is looking to cheapen its exports even further, and this will definitely impact on both export markets and internal markets in developing countries.

So I think both primary exporters and manufacturing exporters are in for a bit of a bad time. They need to think of creative ways of dealing with the situation. It is not helped by believing that integration into global value chains is the only option, because these global value chains basically reduce the incomes of the actual producers. If you look at it, the emergence of global value chains and the associated trade treaties—not just the World Trade Organization (WTO) but the proliferation of regional trading agreements and things like the Trans-Pacific Partnership (TPP)—increase competition and reduce the value of the actual production stage of all commodities and goods. And they simultaneously increase the pre-production and post-production value. That is, all of the aspects that are driven by intellectual property monopolies—their values increase. So whether it is design elements or it is the marketing and branding and all of that—the intellectual property rights over which are retained by companies in the North—all of those are getting more and more value. And the actual production is getting less value because of the greater competitive pressure unleashed by these various trade agreements.

Developing countries that are seeking to get out of this really have to think of alternative arrangements—possibly regional arrangements, more reliance on domestic demand and South-South trade, which is more possible today than it has ever been—and moving away from a system that allows global and northern-led multinationals to capture all the rents and most of the profits of production everywhere.

D&S: So, in the course of this discussion, I think two major questions emerge about the way forward in so-called developing economies. One is how to square economic development—in terms of raising the quality of life for the majority—with environmental sustainability. The other is how to ensure the economic development of some countries isn't at odds with development in others. Are there ways of mutually fostering development—and in particular sustainable development—across the developing economies?

JG: Yes, I think we need to really move away from the traditional way of looking at growth and development, which is ultimately still based on GDP. As long as we keep doing that, we're going to be caught in this trap. We have to be focusing much more on quality of life and ensuring what we would call the basic needs or minimum requirements for a civilized life among all the citizenry. If we do that, then we're less in competition with one another and we're less obsessed with having to be the cheapest show in town. We then see wages and employment growth as a means of expansion of economic activity. We will see social policies as delivering not just better welfare for the people but also more employment, and therefore a better quality of life.

If we look for regional trading arrangements that recognize this, if we look to increase the value of domestic economic activity by encouraging the things that matter for ordinary people (especially, let's say, the bottom half of the population), if we focus on new technologies that are adapted to specific local requirements—in terms of being more green, more environmentally sustainable, as well as recognizing the specific availability of labor in these economies—I think we can do a lot more. It may be slower in terms of GDP growth, but really that doesn't mean anything. So we have to move away from GDP growth as the basic indicator of what is desirable. I think that's the ultimate and most essential issue. ❏

Article 8.2

FAMINE MYTHS

Five Misunderstandings Related to the 2011 Hunger Crisis in the Horn of Africa

BY WILLIAM G. MOSELEY
March/April 2012

T he 2011 famine in the horn of Africa was one of the worst in recent decades in terms of loss of life and human suffering. While the UN has yet to release an official death toll, the British government estimates that between 50,000 and 100,000 people died, most of them children, between April and September of 2011. While Kenya, Ethiopia, and Djibouti were all badly affected, the famine hit hardest in certain (mainly southern) areas of Somalia. This was the worst humanitarian disaster to strike the country since 1991-1992, with roughly a third of the Somali population displaced for some period of time.

Despite the scholarly and policy community's tremendous advances in understanding famine over the past 40 years, and increasingly sophisticated famine early-warning systems, much of this knowledge and information was seemingly ignored or forgotten in 2011. While the famine had been forecasted nearly nine months in advance, the global community failed to prepare for, and react in a timely manner to, this event. The famine was officially declared in early July of 2011 by the United Nations and recently (February 3, 2012) stated to be officially over. Despite the official end of the famine, 31% of the population (or 2.3 million people) in southern Somalia remains in crisis. Across the region, 9.5 million people continue to need assistance. Millions of Somalis remain in refugee camps in Ethiopia and Kenya.

The famine reached its height in the period from July to September, 2011, with approximately 13 million people at risk of starvation. While this was a regional problem, it was was most acute in southern Somalia because aid to this region was much delayed. Figure 1 provides a picture of food insecurity in the region in the November-December 2011 period (a few months after the peak of the crisis).

The 2011 famine received relatively little attention in the U.S. media and much of the coverage that did occur was biased, ahistorical, or perpetuated long-held misunderstandings about the nature and causes of famine. This article addresses "famine myths"—five key misunderstandings related to the famine in the Horn of Africa.

Myth #1: Drought was the cause of the famine.

While drought certainly contributed to the crisis in the Horn of Africa, there were more fundamental causes at play. Drought is not a new environmental condition for much of Africa, but a recurring one. The Horn of Africa has long experienced erratic rainfall. While climate change may be exacerbating rainfall variability, traditional livelihoods in the region are adapted to deal with situations where rainfall is not dependable.

The dominant livelihood in the Horn of Africa has long been herding, which is well adapted to the semi-arid conditions of the region. Herders traditionally ranged widely across the landscape in search of better pasture, focusing on different areas depending on meteorological conditions.

The approach worked because, unlike fenced in pastures in America, it was incredibly flexible and well adapted to variable rainfall conditions. As farming expanded, including large-scale commercial farms in some instances, the routes of herders became more concentrated, more vulnerable to drought, and more detrimental to the landscape.

Agricultural livelihoods also evolved in problematic ways. In anticipation of poor rainfall years, farming households and communities historically stored surplus crop production in granaries. Sadly this traditional strategy for mitigating the risk of drought was undermined from the colonial period moving forward as

FIGURE 1: FOOD INSECURITY IN THE HORN OF AFRICA REGION, NOVEMBER-DECEMBER 2011.

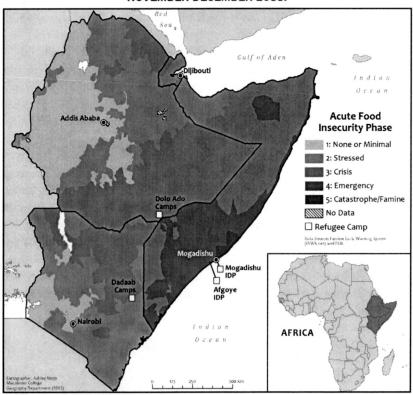

Based on data and assessment by FEWS-Net (a USAID-sponsored program).

Cartography by Ashley Nepp, Macalester College.

households were encouraged (if not coerced by taxation) to grow cash crops for the market and store less excess grain for bad years. This increasing market orientation was also encouraged by development banks, such as the World Bank, International Monetary Fund, and African Development Bank.

The moral of the story is that famine is not a natural consequence of drought (just as death from exposure is not the inherent result of a cold winter), but it is the structure of human society which often determines who is affected and to what degree.

Myth #2: Overpopulation was the cause of the famine.

With nearly 13 million people at risk of starvation last fall in a region whose population doubled in the previous 24 years, one might assume that these two factors were causally related in the Horn of Africa. Ever since the British political economist Thomas Malthus wrote "An Essay on the Principle of Population" in 1798, we have been concerned that human population growth will outstrip available food supply. While the crisis in Somalia, Ethiopia and Kenya appeared to be perfect proof of the Malthusian scenario, we must be careful not to make overly simplistic assumptions.

For starters, the semi-arid zones in the Horn of Africa are relatively lightly populated compared to other regions of the world. For example, the population

---

Land Grabs in Africa

Long term leases of African land for export-oriented food production, or "land grabs," have been on the rise in the past decade. Rather than simply buying food and commodity crops from African farmers, foreign entities increasingly take control of ownership and management of farms on African soil. This trend stems from at least two factors. First, increasingly high global food prices are a problem for many Asian and Middle Eastern countries that depend on food imports. As such, foreign governments and sovereign wealth funds may engage in long-term leases of African land in order to supply their own populations with affordable food. Secondly, high global food prices are also seen as an opportunity for some Western investors who lease African land to produce crops and commodities for profitable global markets.

In the Horn of Africa, Ethiopia (which has historically been one of the world's largest recipients of humanitarian food aid) has made a series of long-term land leases to foreign entities. The World Bank estimates that at least 35 million hectares of land have been leased to 36 different countries, including China, Pakistan, India and Saudi Arabia. Supporters of these leases argue that they provide employment to local people and disseminate modern agricultural approaches. Critics counter that these leases undermine food sovereignty, or people's ability to feed themselves via environmentally sustainable technologies that they control.

density of Somalia is about 13 persons per sq. kilometer, whereas that of the U.S. state of Oklahoma is 21.1. The western half of Oklahoma is also semi-arid, suffered from a serious drought in 2011, and was the poster child for the 1930s Dust Bowl. Furthermore, if we take into account differing levels of consumption, with the average American consuming at least 28 times as much as the average Somali in a normal year, then Oklahoma's population density of 21.1 persons per sq. kilometer equates to that of 591 Somalis.

Despite the fact that Oklahoma's per capita impact on the landscape is over 45 times that of Somalia (when accounting for population density and consumption levels), we don't talk about overpopulation in Oklahoma. This is because, in spite of the drought and the collapse of agriculture, there was no famine in Oklahoma. In contrast, the presence of famine in the Horn of Africa led many to assume that too many people was a key part of the problem.

Why is it that many assume that population growth is the driver of famine? For starters, perhaps we assume that reducing the birthrate, and thereby reducing the number of mouths to feed, is one of the easiest ways to prevent hunger. This is actually a difficult calculation for most families in rural Africa. It's true that many families desire access to modern contraceptives, and filling this unmet need is important. However, for many others, children are crucial sources of farm labor or important wage earners who help sustain the family. Children also act as the old-age social security system for their parents. For these families, having fewer children is not an easy decision. Families in this region will have fewer children when it makes economic sense to do so. As we have seen over time and throughout the world, the average family size shrinks when economies develop and expectations for offspring change.

Second, many tend to focus on the additional resources required to nourish each new person, and often forget the productive capacity of these individuals. Throughout Africa, some of the most productive farmland is in those regions with the highest population densities. In Machakos, Kenya, for example, agricultural production and environmental conservation improved as population densities increased. Furthermore, we have seen agricultural production collapse in some areas where population declined (often due to outmigration) because there was insufficient labor to maintain intensive agricultural production.

Third, we must not forget that much of the region's agricultural production is not consumed locally. From the colonial era moving forward, farmers and herders have been encouraged to become more commercially oriented, producing crops and livestock for the market rather than home consumption. This might have been a reasonable strategy if the prices for exports from the Horn of Africa were high (which they rarely have been) and the cost of food imports low. Also, large land leases (or "land grabs") to foreign governments and corporations in Ethiopia (and to a lesser extent in Kenya and Somalia) have further exacerbated this problem. These farms, designed solely for export production, effectively subsidize the food security of other regions of the world (most notably the Middle East and Asia) at the expense of populations in the Horn of Africa.

Myth #3: Increasing food production through advanced techniques will resolve food insecurity over the long run.

As Sub-Saharan Africa has grappled with high food prices in some regions and famine in others, many experts argue that increasing food production through a program of hybrid seeds and chemical inputs (a so-called "New Green Revolution") is the way to go.

While outsiders benefit from this New Green Revolution strategy (by selling inputs or purchasing surplus crops), it is not clear if the same is true for small farmers and poor households in Sub-Saharan Africa. For most food insecure households on the continent, there are at least two problems with this strategy. First, such an approach to farming is energy intensive because most fertilizers and pesticides are petroleum based. Inducing poor farmers to adopt energy-intensive farming methods is short sighted, if not unethical, if experts know that global energy prices are likely to rise. Second, irrespective of energy prices, the New Green Revolution approach requires farmers to purchase seeds and inputs, which means that it will be inaccessible to the poorest of the poor, i.e., those who are the most likely to suffer from periods of hunger.

If not the New Green Revolution approach, then what? Many forms of bio-intensive agriculture are, in fact, highly productive and much more efficient than those of industrial agriculture. For example, crops grown in intelligent combinations allow one plant to fix nitrogen for another rather than relying solely on increasingly expensive, fossil fuel-based inorganic fertilizers for these plant nutrients. Mixed cropping strategies are also less vulnerable to insect damage and require little to no pesticide use for a reasonable harvest. These techniques have existed for centuries in the African context and could be greatly enhanced by supporting collaboration among local people, African research institutes, and foreign scientists.

Myth #4: U.S. foreign policy in the Horn of Africa was unrelated to the crisis.

Many Americans assume that U.S. foreign policy bears no blame for the food crisis in the Horn and, more specifically, Somalia. This is simply untrue. The weakness of the Somali state was and is related to U.S. policy, which interfered in Somali affairs based on Cold War politics (the case in the 1970s and 80s) or the War on Terror (the case in the 2000s).

During the Cold War, Somalia was a pawn in a U.S.-Soviet chess match in the geopolitically significant Horn of Africa region. In 1974, the U.S. ally Emperor Haile Selassie of Ethiopia was deposed in a revolution. He was eventually replaced by Mengistu Haile Mariam, a socialist. In response, the leader of Ethiopia's bitter rival Somalia, Siad Barre, switched from being pro-Soviet to pro-Western. Somalia was the only country in Africa to switch Cold War allegiances under the same government. The U.S. supported Siad Barre until 1989 (shortly before his demise in

1991). By doing this, the United States played a key role in supporting a long-running dictator and undermined democratic governance.

More recently, the Union of Islamic Courts (UIC) came to power in 2006. The UIC defeated the warlords, restored peace to Mogadishu for the first time in 15 years, and brought most of southern Somalia under its orbit. The United States and its Ethiopian ally claimed that these Islamists were terrorists and a threat to the region. In contrast, the vast majority of Somalis supported the UIC and pleaded with the international community to engage them peacefully. Unfortunately, this peace did not last. The U.S.-supported Ethiopian invasion of Somalia begun in December 2006 and displaced more than a million people and killed close to 15,000 civilians. Those displaced then became a part of last summer and fall's famine victims.

The power vacuum created by the displacement of the more moderate UIC also led to the rise of its more radical military wing, al-Shabaab. Al-Shabaab emerged to engage the Transitional Federal Government (TFG), which was put in place by the international community and composed of the most moderate elements of the UIC (which were more favorable to the United States). The TFG was weak, corrupt, and ineffective, controlling little more than the capital Mogadishu, if that. A low-grade civil war emerged between these two groups in southern Somalia. Indeed, as we repeatedly heard in the media last year, it was al-Shabaab that restricted access to southern Somalia for several months leading up to the crisis and greatly exacerbated the situation in this sub-region. Unfortunately, the history of factors which gave rise to al-Shabaab was never adequately explained to the U.S. public. Until July 2011, the U.S. government forbade American charities from operating in areas controlled by al-Shabaab—which delayed relief efforts in these areas.

Myth #5: An austere response may be best in the long run.

Efforts to raise funds to address the famine in the Horn of Africa were well below those for previous (and recent) humanitarian crises. Why was this? Part of it likely had to do with the economic malaise in the U.S. and Europe. Many Americans suggested that we could not afford to help in this crisis because we had to pay off our own debt. This stinginess may, in part, be related to a general misunderstanding about how much of the U.S. budget goes to foreign assistance. Many Americans assume we spend over 25% of our budget on such assistance when it is actually less than 1%.

Furthermore, contemporary public discourse in America has become more inward-looking and isolationist than in the past. As a result, many Americans have difficulty relating to people beyond their borders. Sadly, it is now much easier to separate ourselves from them, to discount our common humanity, and to essentially suppose that it's okay if they starve. This last point brings us back to Thomas Malthus, who was writing against the poor laws in England in the late 18th century. The poor laws were somewhat analogous to contemporary welfare programs and Malthus argued (rather problematically) that they encouraged the poor to have more children. His essential argument was that starvation is acceptable because it is a natural check to over-population. In other words, support for the poor will only exacerbate the situation. We see this in the way that some conservative commentators reacted to last year's famine.

The reality was that a delayed response to the famine only made the situation worse. Of course, the worst-case scenario is death, but short of death, many households were forced to sell off all of their assets (cattle, farming implements, etc.) in order to survive. This sets up a very difficult recovery scenario because livelihoods are so severely compromised. We know from best practices among famine researchers and relief agencies in that you not only to detect a potential famine early, but to intervene before livelihoods are devastated. This means that households will recover more quickly and be more resilient in the face of future perturbations.

Preventing Famines

While the official famine in the horn of Africa region is over, 9.5 million people continue to need assistance and millions of Somalis remain in refugee camps in Ethiopia and Kenya. While this region of the world will always be drought prone, it needn't be famine prone. The solution lies in rebuilding the Somali state and fostering more robust rural livelihoods in Somalia, western Ethiopia and northern Kenya. The former will likely mean giving the Somali people the space they need to rebuild their own democratic institutions (and not making them needless pawns in the War on Terror). The latter will entail a new approach to agriculture that emphasizes food sovereignty, or locally appropriate food production technologies that are accessible to the poorest of the poor, as well as systems of grain storage at the local level that anticipate bad rainfall years. Finally, the international community should discourage wealthy, yet food-insufficient, countries from preying on poorer countries in Sub Saharan African countries through the practice of land grabs. ❏

Sources: Alex de Waal, *Famine That Kills: Darfur, Sudan*, Oxford University Press, 2005; William G. Moseley, "Why They're Starving: The man-made roots of famine in the Horn of Africa," *The Washington Post*. July 29, 2011; William G. Moseley and B. Ikubolajeh Logan, "Food Security," in B. Wisner, C. Toulmin and R. Chitiga (eds)., *Toward a New Map of Africa*, Earthscan Publications, 2005; Abdi I. Samatar, "Genocidal Politics and the Somali Famine," Aljazeera English, July 30, 2011; Amartya Sen, *Poverty and Famines*, Oxford/Clarendon, 1981; Michael Watts and Hans Bohle, "The space of vulnerability: the causal structure of hunger and famine," *Progress in Human Geography*, 1993.

Article 8.3

ARGENTINA: WELCOME TO 21ST CENTURY NEOLIBERALISM

BY ALAN CIBILS
November 2016; Triple Crisis Blog

A s the United States and the world grapple with the potential implications of a Trump presidency, Argentina is evaluating the results of Mauricio Macri's first year in office. Macri's electoral victory on November 22, 2015, marked the end of twelve years of populist, expansionary economic policies and the return to neoliberalism. While government officials and supporters deny this, a close look at the Macri administration's discourse on economic issues and policies implemented force the conclusion that this is neoliberalism—again.

From Campaign Rhetoric to Economic Policy

Macri campaigned as an outsider to politics (despite two consecutive four-year terms as mayor of the City of Buenos Aires), whose main goal was to solve ordinary people's problems. His message was that he would keep those policies of *kirchnerismo* (the previous two presidents were Néstor Kirchner and Cristina Fernández de Kirchner) that had worked and improve or change those that hadn't.

However, when Macri took office it became clear that his program was a major rollback of the populist legacy and a return to neoliberalism. Macri stacked key ministries with corporate CEOs, leading some to state that Argentina was now a CEO-cracy, rather than a democracy. Bloomberg heralded Macri's arrival to office with an eloquent "Wall Street Is in Charge in Argentina (Again)." Argentine Treasury Minister Alfonso Prat Gay stated the Macri government's intentions clearly at a G7 minister meeting: "The world is threatened by protectionism and populism, and Macri was elected to emancipate Argentina from these evils." In other words, Macri would do away with the populist legacy and open the economy to the world.

So, what have been Macri's main economic policies in his first year in office?

First, exchange controls, a Kirchner-era policy strongly opposed by the middle class, were lifted. Doing so involved a 40% currency devaluation, despite campaign promises to the contrary.

Second, export taxes were eliminated on most agriculture and mining products (Argentina's main exports). These taxes served not only as a source of fiscal revenue, but also to delink domestic market prices from world market prices.

Third, monetary policy changed radically to an "inflation targeting" regime. The Central Bank's nominal interest rate was initially set to 38% and gradually lowered to its current 26.25%. Inflation control has become the dominant goal of macroeconomic policy.

Fourth, subsidies to utilities and public transport were slashed, dramatically increasing prices. These increases impacted greatly on households, small and medium businesses, commerce, and, of course, inflation.

What have been the results of Macri's chosen policy set?

First, the combination of devaluation, export tax elimination, and higher utility and interest rates (a cost to businesses) have resulted in a sharp increase in inflation, almost doubling the already high rates inherited from the Kirchner years. It is expected that the inflation rate for 2016 will be about 40%.

High inflation has resulted in a considerable reduction of real wages and consumption, resulting in a recession. Economic activity indicators turned negative in March, and have yet to show a sign of recovery.

The recession resulted in a substantial increase in unemployment, averaging 9.3% nationally and more than 10% in urban areas. As a result, poverty and indigence (severe poverty) have risen substantially. The official poverty rate now stands at 32.3% of the population, and 6.3% are indigent. According to a report produced by a research institute of the Argentine Catholic University, in the first five months of the Macri government, 1.4 million people newly fell below the poverty line.

Export tax reduction and high nominal interest rates have resulted in windfall profits for exporters and the financial sector, resulting in a substantial upward income redistribution. It seems that "trickle-down economics" is back in town.

Neoliberalism Recharged

The radical policy change has come with a significant change in official discourse on economic issues:

Wages are now a cost to be reduced in order to be "more competitive" internationally. The labor market needs to be deregulated, as unions and labor legislation make labor uncompetitive. In other words, wages are no longer a source of demand, development, and welfare.

Monetarism and outdated views of money and banks are back: money is a commodity, saving (not credit) finances investment, fiscal deficits are bad and, should they exist, must be "financed" with debt.

Strong and unilateral alignment with the United States, reminiscent of the "carnal relations" during the presidency of Carlos Menem (1989-1999). Regional integration initiatives like the Union of South American Nations (UNASUR), Banco del Sur, etc., have been all but abandoned.

The official approach to public debt has also changed dramatically from the Kirchners' debt reduction strategy. The "vulture funds" were paid off according to a New York court's outrageous ruling. The stock of both dollar- and peso-denominated debt is rapidly growing again as a percent of GDP, causing worries about its future sustainability.

Finally, the International Monetary Fund (IMF) was invited back. An Article IV consultation, the first since Argentina cancelled its debt with the institution in

2006, was recently concluded. The Fund's conclusions hold no surprises, with recommendations for more austerity, less subsidies, and a fiscal surplus. The IMF's satisfaction with the Macri government is clear in recent documents, praising Macri's "social sensitivity" and blaming past governments for all current problems.

Whither Argentina?

Like the IMF, the Macri administration blames the significant current problems on the "heavy inheritance" received from twelve years of *kirchnerismo*. It is true that Macri received an economy with imbalances which needed to be addressed: outdated utility subsidies, foreign-exchange constraint, moderate inflation, etc. However, the explicitly neoliberal policy set was an choice of the Macri administration: it was not inevitable or the only choice, and certainly not the best. Macri has clearly chosen to benefit the corporate and financial sectors and foreign capital over Argentine workers. With a technocratic discourse, Macri is leading the country down a road that has already proven to be disastrous. One can only hope that this time the ending won't be as catastrophic as it was in 2001. ❏

Article 8.4

MEASURING ECONOMIC DEVELOPMENT
The "Human Development" Approach

BY ALEJANDRO REUSS
April 2012

Some development economists have proposed abandoning per capita GDP, the dominant single-number measure of economic development, in favor of the "human development" approach—which focuses less on changes in average income and more on widespread access to basic goods.

Advocates of this approach to the measurement of development, notably Nobel Prize-winning economist Amartya Sen, aim to focus attention directly on the *ends* (goals) of economic development. Higher incomes, Sen notes, are *means* people use to get the things that they want. The human development approach shifts the focus away from the means and toward ends like a long life, good health, freedom from hunger, the opportunity to get an education, and the ability to take part in community and civic life. Sen has argued that these basic "capabilities" or "freedoms"—the kinds of things almost everyone wants no matter what their goals in life may be—are the highest development priorities and should, therefore, be the primary focus of our development measures.

If a rising average income guaranteed that everyone, or almost everyone, in a society would be better able to reach these goals, we might as well use average income (GDP per capita) to measure development. Increases in GDP per capita, however, do not always deliver longer life, better health, more education, or other basic capabilities to most people In particular, if these income increases go primarily to those who are already better-off (and already enjoy a long life-expectancy, good health, access to education, and so on), they probably will not have much effect on people's access to basic capabilities.

Sen and others have shown that, in "developing" countries, increased average income by itself is not associated with higher life expectancy or better health. In countries where average income was increasing, but public spending on food security, health care, education, and similar programs did not increase along with it, they have found, the increase in average income did not appear to improve access to basic capabilities. If spending on these "public supports" increased, on the other hand, access to basic capabilities tended to improve, whether average income was increasing or not. Sen emphasizes two main lessons based on these observations: 1) A country cannot count on economic growth alone to improve access to basic capabilities. Increased average income appears to deliver "human development" largely by *increasing the wealth a society has available for public supports*, and not in other ways. 2) A country does not have to prioritize economic growth—*does not have to "wait" until it grows richer*—to make basic capabilities like long life, good health, and a decent education available to all.

The Human Development Index (HDI)

The "human development" approach has led to a series of annual reports from the United Nations Development Programme (UNDP) ranking countries according to a "human development index" (HDI). The HDI includes measures of three things: 1) health, measured by average life expectancy, 2) education, measured by average years of schooling and expected years of schooling, and 3) income, measured by GDP per capita. The three categories are then combined, each counting equally, into a single index. The HDI has become the most influential alternative to GDP per capita as a single-number development measure.

Looking at the HDI rankings, many of the results are not surprising. The HDI top 20 is dominated by very high-income countries, including thirteen Western European countries, four "offshoots" of Great Britain (Australia, Canada, New Zealand, and the United States), and two high-income East Asian countries (Japan and South Korea). Most of the next 20 or so are Western or Eastern European, plus a few small oil-rich states in the Middle East. The next 50 or so include most of Latin America and the Caribbean, much of the Middle East, and a good deal of Eastern Europe (including Russia and several former Soviet republics). The next 50 or so are a mix of Latin American, Middle Eastern, South and Southeast Asian, and African countries. The world's poorest continent, Africa, accounts for almost all of the last 30, including the bottom 24.

TABLE 1: HDI RANKS COMPARED TO INCOME-PER-CAPITA RANKS (2010)

Highest HDI ranks compared to income per capita ranks (difference in parenteses)*	Lowest HDI ranks compared to income per capita ranks (difference in parenteses)
New Zealand (+30)	Equatorial Guinea (-78)
Georgia (+26)	Angola (-47)
Tonga (+23)	Kuwait (-42)
Tajikistan (+22)	Botswana (-38)
Madagascar (+22_	South Africa (-37)
Togo (+22)	Qatar (-36)
Fiji (+22)	Brunei (-30)
Ireland (+20	Gabon (-29)
Iceland (+20)	United Arab Emirates (-28)
Ukraine (+20)	Turkey (-26)

* The numbers in parentheses represent a country's GDP-per-capita rank minus its HDI rank. Remember that in a ranking system, a "higher" (better) rank is indicated by a lower number. If a country is ranked, say, 50th in GDP per capita and 20th in HDI, its number would be 50 – 20 = +30. The positive number indicates that the country had a "higher" HDI rank than GDP per capita rank. If a country is ranked, say, 10th in GDP per capita and 35th in HDI, its number would be 10 – 35 = -25. The negative number indicates that the country had a "lower" HDI rank than GDP per capita rank.

Source: United Nations Development Programme, Indices, Getting and using data, 2010 Report—Table 1: Human Development Index and its components (hdr.undp.org/en/statistics/data/).

It is not surprising that higher GDP per capita is associated with a higher HDI score. After all, GDP per capita counts for one third of the HDI score itself. The relationship between the two, however, is not perfect. Some countries have a higher HDI rank than GDP per capita rank. These countries are "over-performing," getting more human development from their incomes, compared to other countries. Meanwhile, some countries have a lower HDI rank than GDP per capita rank. These countries are "under-performing," not getting as much human development from their incomes, compared to other countries. The list of top "over-performing" countries includes three very high-income countries that had still higher HDI ranks (Iceland, Ireland, and New Zealand), three former Soviet republics (Georgia, Tajikistan, and Ukraine), two small South Pacific island nations (Fiji, Togo), and two African countries (Madagascar, Tonga). The list of top "under-performing" countries includes four small oil-rich countries (Brunei, Kuwait, Qatar, and United Arab Emirates) and five African countries (Angola, Botswana, Equatorial Guinea, Gabon, and South Africa).

The UNDP also calculates an inequality-adjusted HDI. Note that, for all the measures included in the HDI, there is inequality within countries. The inequality-adjusted HDI is calculated so that, the greater the inequality for any measure included in the HDI (for health, education, or income), the lower the country's score. Since all countries have some inequality, the inequality-adjusted HDI for any country is always lower than the regular HDI. However, the scores for countries with greater inequality drop more than for those with less inequality. That pushes some countries up in the rankings, when inequality is penalized, and others down. Among the thirteen countries moving up the

TABLE 1: INEQUALITY-ADJUSTED HDI RANKS
COMPARED TO UNDADJUSTED HDI RANKS (2010)

Highest inequality-adjusted HDI ranks compared to undadjusted HDI ranks (difference in parenteses)	Lowest inequality-adjusted HDI ranks compared to undadjusted HDI ranks (difference in parenteses)
Uzbekistan (+17)	Peru (-26)
Mongolia (+21)	Panama (-20)
Moldova (+16)	Colomcia (-18)
Kyrgistan (+15)	South Korea (-18)
Maldives (+14)	Bolivia (-17)
Ukraine (+14)	Belize (-16)
Philippines (+11)	Brazil (-15)
Sri Lanka (+11)	Namibia (-15)
Tanzania, Viet Nam, Indonesia, Jamaica, Belarus (+9)	El Salvador (-14)
	Turkmenistan (-12)

Source: United Nations Development Programme, 2010 Report, Table 3: Inequality-adjusted Human Development Index (hdr.undp.org/en/media/HDR_2010_EN_Table3_reprint.pdf).

most, five are former Soviet republics. Among the ten moving down the most, seven are Latin American countries. The United States narrowly misses the list of those moving down the most, with its rank dropping by nine places when inequality is taken into account.

GDP Per Capita and HDI

The relationship between income per capita and the HDI is shown in the "scatterplot" graph below. (Instead of GDP per capita, the graph uses a closely related measure called Gross National Income (GNI) per capita.) Each point represents a country, with its income per capita represented on the horizontal scale and its HDI score represented on the vertical scale. The further to the right a point is, the higher the country's per capita income. The higher up a point is, the higher the country's HDI score. As we can see, the cloud of points forms a curve, rising up as income per capita increases from a very low level, and then flattening out. This means that a change in GDP per capita from a very low level to a moderate level of around $8000 per year is associated with large gains in human development. Above that, we see, the curve flattens out dramatically. A change in income per capita from this moderate level to a high level of around $25,000 is associated with smaller gains in human development. Further increases in income per capita are associated with little or no gain in human development.

This relationship suggests two major conclusions, both related to greater economic equality.

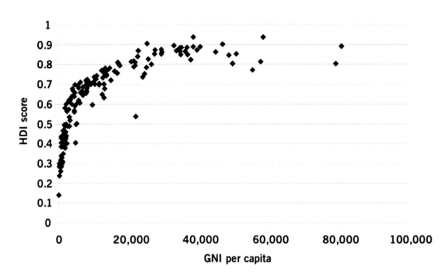

RELATIONSHIP BETWEEN HDI AND INCOME PER CAPITA (2010)

Source: United Nations Development Programme, Indices, 2010 Report - Table 1 Human Development Index and its components (hdr.undp.org/en/statistics/data/).

First, achieving greater equality in incomes between countries, including by redistributing income from high-income countries to low-income countries, could result in increased human development. Over the highest per capita income range, from about $25,000 on up, increases in income are not associated with higher human development. Decreases in income above this threshold, by the same token, need not mean lower human development. On the other hand, over the lowest income range, below $8000, increases in income are associated with dramatic gains in HDI (largely due to increased public supports). Therefore, the redistribution of incomes from high-income countries to low-income countries could increase human development in the latter a great deal, while not diminishing human development in the former by very much (if at all)—resulting in a net gain in human development.

Second, high-income countries might make greater gains in HDI, as their incomes continued to increase, if a larger share of income went to low-income people or to public supports. Part of the reason that the relationship between per capita income and HDI flattens out at high income levels may be that there are inherent limits to variables like life expectancy (perhaps 90-100 years) or educational attainment (perhaps 20 years). These "saturation" levels, however, have clearly not been reached by all individuals, even in very high-income countries. In the United States, as of 2008, the infant mortality rate for African-Americans was more than double that for whites. The life expectancy at birth for white females was more than three years greater than that of African-American females; for white males, more than five years greater than for African-American males. As of 2010, over 40% of individuals over 25 years old have no education above high school. Over 60% have no degree from a two- or four-year college. It is little wonder that higher income would not bring about greatly increased human development, considering that, over the last 30 years, many public supports have faced sustained attack and most income growth has gone to people already at the top. ❏

Sources: Amartya Sen, *Development as Freedom* (New York: Oxford University Press, 1999); United Nations Development Programme, Indices, Getting and using data, *2010 Human Development Report*, Table 1 Human Development Index and its components (hdr.undp.org/en/statistics/data/); United Nations Development Programme, *2010 Human Development Report*, Table 3: Inequality-adjusted Human Development Index (hdr.undp.org/en/media/HDR_2010_EN_Table3_reprint.pdf); U.S. Census Bureau, *The 2012 Statistical Abstract*, Births, Deaths, Marriages, & Divorces: Life Expectancy, Table 107. Expectation of Life and Expected Deaths by Race, Sex, and Age: 2008; Educational Attainment, Population 25 Years and Over, U.S. Census Bureau, Selected Social Characteristics in the United States, *2010 American Community Survey*, 1-Year Estimates.

Article 8.5

LAND REFORM
A Precondition for Sustainable Economic Development

BY JAWIED NAWABI
May/June 2015

> *It is in the agricultural sector that the battle for long-term economic development will be won or lost.* —*Gunnar Myrdal, economist and Nobel laureate*

The phrase "land reform" often conjures up memories, for those leaning right, of frightening extreme-left ideologies. On the progressive left, meanwhile, land reform is often treated as a passé topic.

With the advent of rising inequality, climate change, weak government institutions, failed states, terrorism, corruption, and a whole slew of other socio-economic problems—sown or exacerbated by three decades of neoliberal policies in the "developing world" (Global South)—it is high time we revisit the issue of land reform. We need to bring it back to the center of the discussion on sustainable economic development. Land reform is not political extremism; rather, it is a critical policy mechanism for the world to address issues of poverty, hunger, urban slums, and good governance.

What is "land reform"? It is usually defined as the redistribution of large landholdings to smaller ones. Land is transferred from large landlords to those who have been working the land as tenants (such as sharecroppers) or paid agricultural workers, as well as dispossessed underemployed or unemployed urban workers who migrated from rural areas looking for employment and wound up living in urban slums. That is one model of land reform. Another model is redistribution in the form of rural communes or cooperative or collective farms. A combination of the two models is also possible.

Reemergence of Land Reform Movements

Despite the attempts by international institutions (like the IMF and World Bank) and oligarchic political elites in the global South to suppress land reform policies, there have been growing social movements pushing for land reform in the last two decades. Neoliberal "free trade" policies have exposed small farmers to devastating global competition (especially from giant mechanized industrial farms in the global North), leaving hundreds of millions of them dispossessed, and have forced them into the reserve army of impoverished unemployed or underemployed living in urban slums. From Brazil and Mexico to the Philippines and Zimbabwe, social movements for a more just and fair distribution of wealth—particularly land—are confronting these devastating consequences of neoliberalism.

Social protest has led even elite institutions such as the World Bank to acknowledge the issue. The Bank's World Development Report 2008: Agriculture for

Development, at least rhetorically put agriculture and the productivity of small farmers "at the heart of a global agenda to reduce poverty."

Agriculture as a Technical Problem?

The central tendency of mainstream economic development theory since the 1940s and 1950s has been to view agriculture as a mere stepping stone towards industrialization. Economist Arthur W. Lewis' "dualist" model was particularly influential in casting agricultural labor in developing countries as redundant—with a "surplus" of workers adding little or nothing to agricultural production. This surplus labor force, Lewis argued, should be moved out of the agricultural sector—this would supposedly not reduce output—and into the industrial, which he viewed as the key sector of the economy.

Besides moving inefficient peasants out of the rural sector, mainstream development economists proposed to boost agricultural yields by consolidating small farms into large ones—supposedly to take advantages of economies of scale. Thus, instead of reducing land concentration, this would increase it, essentially accomplishing a reverse land reform. Such an industrial model of agriculture would use expensive capital equipment (imported from the global North), petroleum-based fertilizers, herbicides, and pesticides. Today's version of the model increasingly pushes the adoption of genetically modified seeds controlled by corporations like Monsanto.

During the 1960s and 1970s, this frame of thought led many international institutions (such as the World Bank, Asian Development Bank, etc.) and governments in the global South to embrace the "Green Revolution." The Green Revolution was essentially a plan to use "science and technology" to increase crop production in developing countries. The use of fertilizers, pesticides, and high-yield crop varieties was supposed to boost agricultural productivity, reduce rural poverty, solve problems of hunger and malnutrition, and thus avoid peasant movements and rural political instability. This was, as economists James M. Cypher and James L. Dietz put it, a "strategy wherein it was hoped that seed technologies could be substituted for missing land reform and for more radical 'red revolutions' of the socialist variety threatening to sweep across the globe at the time."

Viewing agricultural productivity as a purely technical problem, advocates of the Green Revolution did not aim to transform the structure of land inequality and landlord power. To take the case of India, the Green Revolution boosted agricultural yields, making the country

Land Reform and Colonization

If we broaden the concept of land reform, the whole process of colonial settlement in North America, Central and South America, Australia, and New Zealand was one big land reform, appropriating the lands of indigenous peoples and distributing it to the European settlers. So land reform can be understood as a much more common experience of the "developed" world than it is usually thought of in the economic literature.

technically self-sufficient in food production. However, the changes primarily benefited medium and large-sized landowners who used capital-intensive technologies, high-yielding mono-crop seeds, and large inputs of fertilizers and pesticides. "Rural inequity worsened because of the growing prosperity of the large and medium farmers and the unchanged position of the landless and small farmers," concludes Indian scholar Siddharth Dube. "And because large farms use more capital and less labour per unit of produce than small farms, rural employment grew much less than it would have if land reform had taken place and the increase in production come from smaller farms."

The Economic and Socio-Political Cases for Land Reform

There are two broad arguments for the importance of land reform. The first is based on the widely observed inverse relationship between farm size and output per unit of land area: smaller farms produce more per acre of land than larger farms. Smaller land holdings are more productive and ecologically sustainable for a number of reasons:

1) Higher labor intensity. Small farmers use more labor per unit of land, which helps generate more output and more employment per unit.

2) Higher multiple cropping. They grow more crops per year on a given piece of land.

3) Higher intensity of cultivation. Small farmers leave a lower proportion of land fallow or uncultivated. In addition, they cultivate crops that are higher value-added per unit of land.

4) Lower negative environmental impacts. Small farms use fertilizers, pesticides, and other agrochemicals more sparingly than large farms. This reduces negative impacts of harmful chemicals on workers and neighbors. Small farmers, overall, have a greater incentive to employ environmentally sustainable techniques than large industrial ones.

While the economic case for land reform can be construed as a narrow technical argument on how best to boost agricultural productivity—which land-reform opponents could argue is unnecessary due to the advent of the Green Revolution—the socio-political argument is aimed against this kind of narrow

---

Good Governance

The "good-governance functions" of the state are policies beneficial to the large majority of the population. Good-governance states exercise control over a certain territory, depend on a broad part of their population for revenue, and in turn provide the population with a wide range of public goods: the rule of law, transportation infrastructure (paved roads, extensive and affordable public transportation, etc.), public utilities (electricity, clean water, sewage systems), human services (health, education systems), and job security or at least temporary unemployment insurance.

technical thinking. The importance of a land reform is in changing the hierarchical structure of agrarian class relations while increasing productivity. The idea is to break the power of landlords, who keep peasants as a captive labor force in rural areas and act as a conservative political force at the local and national levels of the state.

The central mechanism by which landlords wield their power is through patron-client networks that give them control over local and regional government institutions. Landlords keep the poor majority dependent on them for jobs and access to land, while also using them as a captive power base for local elections (in countries where there are elections, such as India and Brazil). This way, they can block the development of state programs providing public goods—like public roads, clinics, schools, water systems, etc.—for everyone. Instead, they perpetuate a more narrowly targeted development relying on private goods—fertilizer, pesticides, expensive high-yield seeds, privately controlled water wells, loans that put peasants in ever-deeper debt, etc. They provide, also, a form of private insurance system for those clients who exhibit proper loyalty, in contrast to social support systems available to all—which would reduce the peasants' vulnerability and the landlord's power. The consequence is that the state's good-governance capacities are distorted and corrupted, favoring the narrow interests of the landlords and the political elite that is connected to them (often by kinship).

Transformative socio-political land reform for developing countries is aimed at diminishing wealth inequalities in the initial stages of development and breaking the grip on power of the upper-class elite (including not only landlords but also big industrial, financial, and commercial capitalists generally allied with them). This democratization of society would make it possible to orient the state towards long-term national development policies which can create more conducive socioeconomic and sociopolitical conditions serving the population as a whole, and not just the elite.

The socioeconomic conditions would include a more egalitarian class structure in the rural sector, greater incentives for farmers to increase their productivity due to owning the land they work, greater farmer incomes allowing the farmers to send their children to school, better nutrition due to higher caloric intake, and greater small-farmer purchasing power leading to greater demand for the products of labor-intensive manufacturing. The sociopolitical democratization would mean the breaking of landlord power, political stabilization resulting from the inclusion of the peasant masses in the political system, and democratization of decision making now liberated from landlord capture of local and national state bureaucracies.

Land Reform Is Not Enough

There have been many more failed land reforms than successful ones. Reforms have failed mainly because they have not been thorough enough in breaking the power of the landed elite, and in extending the role of the government in an inclusive development process. Across Latin America—in Mexico, Bolivia, Brazil, Chile, and Peru—land reforms have had partial success, but for the most part have not dislodged rural elites and their industrial counterparts from political dominance. This has contributed to an image of land reform, even among the progressive left, as a tried and failed policy. There are also examples of half-successful land reforms in South and East Asia—in India, the Philippines, Indonesia, and Thailand—where peasants did reap some benefits like reliable ownership titles, which allowed them to borrow on better terms, boosted crop yields, and reduced malnutrition, though without fundamentally altering the class structure.

On the other hand, successful land reforms were thorough, extensive, and swift. Key examples in the twentieth century include Japan, Taiwan, South Korea, and China. Land in the first three countries was distributed as family-sized farms. (China initially had a collectivized land reform.) Looking at the Japanese and South Korean cases: In Japan in 1945, 45% of the peasants were landless tenants. By 1955, only 9% were tenants and even they benefited from much-strengthened protective laws. In pre-reform South Korea in 1944, the top 3% of landholders owned about 64% of the land, with an average holding of 26 hectares. By 1956, the top 6% owned just 18% of the land, with an average of about 2.6 hectares. Meanwhile, 51% of family farmers owned about 65% of the land, with an average holding of 1.1 hectares.

Nowhere in Latin America or Africa, nor elsewhere in Asia (except Kerala, India), did land reforms come so close to such equalization and radical reshaping of traditional social structures. The East Asian land reforms succeeded in bringing about the long-term national development policies by creating more conducive socioeconomic and sociopolitical conditions—breaking the existing power structure, allowing for the emergence of developmentally oriented states (as opposed to neoliberal models that saw state promotion of economic development as anachronistic and "inefficient"). Successful land reforms require follow up—supportive policies investing in rural infrastructure development (irrigation, electricity, roads, health clinics, schools), plus providing services such as clear and legitimate land records, micro-credit at reasonable rates of interest, and training for farmers in the newest skills for sustainable farming. Japan, Taiwan, South Korea, and arguably even China's development paths serve as examples of transformative land reforms in the last fifty years. What these countries achieved was remarkable growth with equity. ❑

Sources: Irma Adelman, "Income Distribution, Economic Development and Land Reform," *American Behavioral Scientist*, Vol. 23, No. 3 (pgs. 437-456), Jan/Feb 1980; Miguel A. Altieri, "No: Poor Farmers Won't Reap The Benefits," *Foreign Policy*, Summer 2000; James K. Boyce, Peter Rosset, Elizabeth A. Stanton, "Land Reform and Sustainable Development," Working Paper Series No. 98, Political Economy Research Institute, University of Massachusetts-Amherst, 2005; Sarah Blaskey and Jessee Chapman, "Palm Oil Oppression," *Dollars & Sense*, May/June 2013; Celia A. Dugger, "World Bank Report Puts Agriculture at Core of Antipoverty Effort," *New York Times*, Oct. 20, 2007; H. Ronald Chilcote, *Power and The Ruling Classes in Northeast Brazil: Juazeiro and Petrolina in Transition*, Cambridge University Press, 1990; Michael Courville and Raj Patel, "The Resurgence of Agrarian Reform in the Twenty-First Century," In Peter Rosset, Raj Patel, and Michael Courville, eds., *Promised Land: Competing Visions Agrarian Reform*, Food

First Book, 2006; James M. Cypher and James L. Dietz, *The Process of Economic Development* (3rd ed., Routledge, 2009; Siddarth Dube, *In the Land of Poverty: Memoirs of an Indian Family: 1947-1997*, Zed Books, 1998; Mike Davis, P*lanet of Slums*, Verso, 2007; Peter Dorner, *Land Reforms and Economic Development*, Penguin Books, 1972; Peter Evans, *Embedded Autonomy: States and Industrial Transformation*, Princeton University Press, 1995; Penelope Francks, with Johanna Boestel and Choo Hyop Kim, *Agriculture and Economic Development in East Asia: From Growth to Protectionism in Japan, Korea and Taiwan*, Routledge, 1999; Jayati Ghosh, "Equality, Sustainability, Solidarity," *Dollars & Sense*, Jan/Feb 2015; Keith Griffin, Azizur Rahman Khan, and Amy Ickowitz (GKI), "Poverty and Distribution of Land," *Journal of Agrarian Change*, July 2002; Jonathan M. Harris, *Environmental and Natural Resource Economics: A Contemporary Approach*, Houghton Mifflin Company, 2002; Frances Hagopian, "Traditional Politics Against State Transformation in Brazil," In Joel S. Migdal, Atul Kohli and Vivienne Shue, eds., *State Power and Social Forces: Domination and Transformation in the Third World*, Cambridge University Press, 1994; Yoong-Deok Jeon and Young-Yong Kim, "Land Reform, Income Redistribution, and Agricultural Production in Korea," *Economic Development and Cultural Change*, Vol. 48, No. 2, January 2000; Cristobal Kay, "Why East Asia Overtook Latin America: Agrarian Reform, Industrialization and Development," *Third World Quarterly*, Vol. 23, No. 6, December 2002; John Lie, *Han Unbound: The Political Economy of South Korea*, Stanford University Press, 1998; Moyo Sam and Paris Yeros, eds., *Reclaiming the Land: The Resurgence of Rural Movements in Africa, Asia and Latin America*, Zed Books, 2005; Raj Patel, *Stuffed and Starved: The Hidden Battle for World's Food System*, 2nd ed, Melville House, 2012; James Putzel, "Land Reforms in Asia: Lessons From the Past for the 21st Century," Working Paper Series No. 00-04, London School of Economics Development Studies Institute, 2000; Debraj Ray, *Development Economics*, Princeton University Press, 1998; Peter M. Rosset, "Fixing Our Global Food System: Food Sovereignty and Redistributive Land Reform," In *Agriculture and Food in Crisis: Conflict, Resistance, and Renewal*, Monthly Review Press, 2010; Peter M. Rosset, "The Multiple Functions and Benefits of Small Farm Agriculture," Policy Brief No. 4, The Institute For Food and Development Policy, Oakland, California, 1999; Vandana Shiva, *Soil Not Oil: Environmental Justice in an Age of Climate Crisis*, South End Press, 2008; Rehman Sobhan, *Agrarian Reform and Social Transformation: Preconditions for Development*, Zed Books, 1993; Lance Taylor, Santosh Mehrotra, and Enrique Delamonica, "The Links between Economic Growth, Poverty Reduction, and Social Development: Theory and Policy," In Santosh Mehrotra and Richard Jolly, *Development with a Human Face: Experiences in Social Achievement and Economic Growth*, Oxford University Press, 2000; Michael P. Todaro, *Economic Development*, 7th ed., Addison-Wesley, 2000; Jong-Sung You, "Inequality and Corruption: The Role of Land Reform in Korea, Taiwan, and the Philippines," Presented at the Annual Conference of the Association for Asian Studies, Atlanta, April 2008; Jong-Sung You, "Embedded Autonomy or Crony Capitalism? Explaining Corruption in South Korea, Relative to Taiwan and the Philippines, Focusing on the Role of Land Reform and Industrial Policy," Annual Meeting of the American Political Science Association, Washington, D.C., Sept. 1-4, 2005; Tim Wegenast, "The Legacy of Landlords: Educational Distribution and Development in a Comparative Perspective," *Zeitschrift für Vergleichende Politikwissenschaft*, Volume 3, Issue 1, April 2009; Maurice Zeitlin and Richard Earl Ratcliff, *Landlords and Capitalists: The Dominant Class of Chile*, Princeton University Press, 1988.

Article 8.6

DEBT AND DEVELOPMENT: FREQUENTLY ASKED QUESTIONS

BY ALEJANDRO REUSS
November 2015

W*e used to hear all the time about the "Third World" debt crisis—and how it was keeping Latin America and Africa poor. But now I hear that those economies have actually been growing pretty fast. Was all that talk about debt overblown?*

For both regions, the return to economic growth was far removed from the severe debt crises in the 1980s and 1990s. In Latin America, the entire 1980s came to be known as the "lost decade." Per capita gross domestic product (GDP) for the region as a whole was actually lower in 1990 than it was in 1980. For sub-Saharan Africa, the story was even worse. In 1974, the region's per capita GDP was just over $950, according to World Bank data. Over the next two decades, it would plunge by more than 20%, and would not regain its 1974 level until 2008.

Per capita GDP has indeed grown again in Latin America since the 1990s (and more rapidly since the early 2000s). In sub-Saharan Africa, per capita GDP bottomed out in the early 1990s, and growth through the rest of the decade was so modest as to be practically nonexistent. GDP growth for the region, as for Latin America, has been faster in the 2000s. Economies in both regions have grown, in part, due to the boom in agricultural and mineral commodities prices. In Latin America, center-left governments in several countries have adopted policies to reduce income inequality, which has also boosted economic growth. In both regions, too, burdens of external debt have declined in recent years—in Africa, partially due to debt-cancellation campaigns—and this has also played a role.

None of this is to say that external debt—that is, debt owed to foreign financial institutions or governments—was the sole cause for economic crisis and stagnation in either region. However, debt has certainly played a large negative role, in the recent history of much of the "developing world," by thwarting economic development.

If debt is so harmful, shouldn't developing countries avoid getting into debt in the first place?

Well, debt isn't always bad from the standpoint of economic growth or development. A developing country may borrow to finance an infrastructural or industrial project—for example, to pay for imports of machinery, materials, energy, or other needed inputs that are not produced domestically—expecting that the project will more than pay for itself. That is, the resulting revenues will be large enough that the loan can be paid back with interest, plus leave some revenue left over.

We don't usually think of the United States as a "developing country," but in the mid-to-late 19th century, it was going through a period of rapid industrialization, financed in large measure by external debt. As economist Jayati Ghosh put it in a recent interview: "If you think about it, the United States would not be a developed economy if throughout the 19th century it had not been able to borrow vast sums, mostly from England. ... So in fact the United States ran current account deficits between 5-7% of GDP for nearly 70 years. And this is what really enabled it to become the industrial power that we saw before the First World War."

Note that the experience of the United States was unusual, especially in that it enjoyed such large and steady flows of credit for so long. Other countries were not so fortunate. Ghosh has pointed out that other countries in Britain's informal commercial empire during the mid-to-late 19th century—like Argentina—also received very large credit flows, but these were subject to sudden interruptions. A sudden interruption of credit can be very damaging—forcing the borrower to suddenly come up with payment for the full principal, causing the discontinuation of long-term projects for want of further credit, and so on. In the 1890s, for example, a major British bank went bankrupt after many of its loans in Argentina went bad, triggering a much broader shut-off of credit to Argentina and playing a major role in the "reversal" of the country's economic development.

In a way, that suggests a loss of access to credit can be a big problem. Are there ways that debt itself can impede economic development?

One way is that the burden of debt repayment (or "debt service") is so great that it leaves little left over for high-priority domestic spending, including basics like nutrition, health, housing, and education, as well as investments on infrasctructure or industy to promote economic growth.

Economists James K. Boyce and Léonce Ndikumana estimated, in their recent book *Africa's Odious Debts*, that each dollar in external debt service is associated with a decrease of about $0.29 in public health spending. Just one consequence of this reduction, in turn, is increased infant mortality—seven more infant deaths per year for every $290,000 reduction in health spending. In other words, every additional $1 million in debt service results in seven more infant deaths. Boyce and Ndikumana estimate that there are 77,000 more infant deaths per year, for Africa as a whole, from just the portion of debt service (about 60% of the total) that has fueled capital flight.

High debt service on past loans can also impede domestic "capital formation"— new investment in assets like machinery, factories, infrastructure, etc.—and therefore economic growth. Slow growth, in turn, can make it difficult to repay even the principal on past debts, so the country could go on making interest payments indefinitely. There are many cases where countries have, in effect, repaid international debts many times over for exactly this reason.

Sub-Saharan Africa in the 1980s and 1990s illustrates this vicious circle. In 1981, the region's debt service (payments of principal and interest) was less than 4% of GDP. It would drop again below that threshold in 2010. In the 28 years between, it would average over 7% of GDP, twice hitting a full 10% of GDP. Another common way to look at the debt service burden is as a percent of the region's exports. (Exports mean a flow of goods out of the country, and a flow of payments back in. These payments can be used to pay back principal and interest on previous debt, so this ratio is sometimes used as a measure of a country's ability to pay its debt. Here, we're more interested in it as showing the diversion to debt repayment of resources that could otherwise have been used for domestic development.) Again, we find much the same story. For sub-Saharan Africa, debt service goes from about 15% of exports in the early 1980s to an average of over 30% for the 20 years between 1982 and 2001. In other words, the region's debt crisis meant that it was paying up to one-tenth of its total income, or nearly one-third of its revenue from exports, just to service its debts. Domestic capital formation, meanwhile, was substantially lower than it had been since the late 1960s.

So how do countries actually get into debt trouble? It seems that what we usually hear about is a country having big trade deficits—or "living beyond their means"—and having to borrow heavily to finance them.

That's misleading for several reasons. First, the phrase "living beyond their means" suggests that the borrowing is being done to finance consumption beyond the country's own capacity for production. Developing countries, however, often run trade deficits (or the slightly broader concept of current account deficits) because they import large quantities of production goods, rather than consumption goods. The "import substitution industrialization" policies adopted by many Latin America countries in the 1950s and 1960s, for example, were designed to reduce reliance on imports of manufactured consumer goods. Tariffs and other "barriers" were put in place to protect budding domestic industries from import competition. Yet trade deficits increased, largely due to rising imports of machinery and other production goods needed for domestic industrialization.

Second, there are other factors in trade balances besides the physical quantities of imports and exports. Changes in the relative prices of a country's imports and exports may have a big effect on its trade balance. This is especially true for countries that are exporters of "primary" goods—raw materials like agricultural products and minerals—whose prices tend to be highly volatile. A petroleum-exporting country, for example, might run large trade surpluses when oil prices are high, but trade deficits when oil prices are low. (By the same token, the reverse might be true for a petroleum importing country.) A country might not start running trade deficits because it is importing larger quantities of goods—or because its people are enjoying higher consumption—but because its exports are suddenly worth less, or its imports suddenly cost more.

Third, the actual cause-effect relationship often runs not from trade deficits to debt, but the other way around. The story can start with large capital flows into a country—when individuals, companies, or governments of other countries buy tangible assets, buy stocks or other securities, or make loans in that country. This can cause the currency of the country experiencing the financial inflows to increase in value relative to other currencies. A "stronger" (higher valued) currency makes the country's imports cheaper and its exports more expensive. Rising imports and declining exports, in turn, push the trade balance in a negative direction (from surplus towards deficit).

Finally, a country's debt burden depends not just on the amount borrowed, but also on the interest rates the country faces. Those rates depend on the risk that lenders assign to different borrowers. As a country becomes heavily indebted, lenders may begin to see it as a bigger credit risk, and it may have to pay higher interest rates to get further loans—if it can get them at all. The yield on long-term Greek government bonds (the IOUs that a government or other borrower issues for the money it borrows), for example, went from less than 6% as late as 2009 to as high as 36% in 2012. Lenders' calculations of how risky it is to lend to a particular country, however, may not be based solely on economic conditions within that country. During the Latin American debt crisis of the 1980s, for example, some countries' default on debt led to a tightening of credit throughout the region. (In effect, lenders were treating the entire region as a single unit, for the purpose of evaluating risk.)

The interest rates that one borrower faces, meanwhile, also depend on the interest rates that lenders can get elsewhere. This, too, was a big factor in the 1980s debt crisis. In the late 1970s, the United States government adopted policies to deliberately drive up interest rates, mainly to rein in domestic demand and reduce upward pressure on wages. Lenders prefer to make loans to borrowers who will pay higher interest rates, keeping in mind differences in risk. With interest rates on the rise in the United States, the country became a more attractive place for lenders to make loans. Borrowers in developing countries, therefore, suddenly had to pay higher rates to keep attracting credit.

Are countries better off, if they start getting into debt trouble, tightening their belts to repay it as soon as they can, rather than getting deeper and deeper into the hole?

A country's external debt may be public (owed by the government) or private (owed by private individuals and companies), but for now let's think about a large public debt. The pro-austerity reasoning is that the best way to bring down the debt fast is to cut spending and/or raise taxes. The resulting "primary surplus" (current revenues minus current expenditures, excluding payments on past debts) will then make it possible to pay down debt and bring down the country's debt-to-GDP ratio.

This argument for austerity seems to make sense if we're thinking about a single household—if it gets too deep in debt, it can cut back on its spending and maybe find more paid work or other income opportunities, and over time whittle down what it owes. Reasoning by analogy with an individual household, however, is not a good way to approach public policy. When we think about a household "tightening its belt" and cutting back on spending, we usually don't think of this as getting in the way of its income opportunities. The austerity policies described above, however, may have the effect of reducing demand, output, and incomes for the society as a whole.

Think about it this way: Governments often adopt fiscal "stimulus" programs when the economy goes into a downturn. By increasing spending and reducing taxes, they increase demand for goods and services. That causes businesses to increase their planned output, to increase their orders for inputs, and to hire more workers. The workers and suppliers, in turn, spend their new incomes, further boosting demand.

Austerity programs, however, do just the opposite—reducing demand in the economy. If the idea is to bring down debt relative to GDP, this kind of policy can backfire—since it may bring down GDP. (It may also fail to bring about the sought-after primary surpluses, since recession conditions will usually reduce tax revenue and may actually increase some kinds of spending, such as unemployment insurance and other government social-welfare payments.) A big reason that Latin America's debt crisis turned into a "lost decade" was not the loss of access to credit itself, but that austerity policies—pushed, in many countries, by the International Monetary Fund—depressed these economies.

Fiscal austerity policies can also be aimed at pushing a country's trade balance in a positive direction (from deficit toward surplus). The reduction of demand reduces output and employment. The resulting unemployment, in turn, puts downward pressure on wages. Lower wages tend to make the country's goods cheaper relative to those of other countries, and therefore reduce its imports and increase its exports. Of all ways to accomplish this change in relative prices, however, austerity is just about the worst—coming at a high cost in lost output of goods and services and an even higher human cost, especially in the form of mass unemployment. An alternative way to accomplish this is through "devaluation"—making the country's currency weaker, and so its exports cheaper and imports more expensive. There may be impediments to such a policy for countries, however, that are in a fixed exchange-rate system or that share a currency with other countries.

Finally, no matter what policy is used to pay back debt—including devaluation or other policies that reduce imports and boost exports—we have to ask whose belts it is that are getting tightened. The burdens of debt are never borne equally by all—and are not necessarily even borne by those who took out the debt in the first place, or who benefited from taking it out. In many developing countries, external debt has not been used to develop infrastructure, promote industrialization, or reduce poverty—but to enrich the already rich and powerful. Economists Boyce and Ndikumana have shown that external debt is strongly associated with "capital flight." In some cases, autocratic rulers have stolen billions of dollars in loans, transferring the money to their own bank accounts overseas, yet it is ordinary people who are on the hook to pay back the loans. (More on this later.)

More generally, austerity policies tend to fall hardest on workers and poor people. This was certainly the case, for example, in the Latin American debt crisis of the 1980s. Austerity policies included cuts to public subsidies on basic goods like food and fuel, reductions in social welfare spending, reductions or elimination of minimum wages, cutbacks in public employment, and so on—all of which quite transparently targeted lower-income people. These policies transferred income not from the debtor countries to the creditor countries in general, but specifically from workers and the poor in the debtor countries to the wealthy bondholders in the creditor countries.

OK, so if austerity policies aren't the solution, how are poor countries that get into debt trouble supposed to get out?

If one is determined to make sure highly indebted low-income countries be able to repay their debts, then austerity is surely not the solution, because it is a recipe for "lost decades." An alternative would be policies that 1) include debt restructuring—that is, reduction or postponement of debt repayment—and 2) promote growth—so that debt can be repaid out of growing income. Many of today's high-income countries have benefited from debt restructuring in the past, or from "growing their way out of debt" over time, without demands for immediate payment when they could ill-afford it.

If one is not determined that debtor countries repay their debts—put another way, if one is not determined that, above all else, the banks should be repaid—then debt repudiation is an option. Many countries have repudiated (refused to pay) past debts. One argument in favor of repudiation is that of "odious debt"—sovereign debt that did not benefit the people of a country. This idea has been frequently invoked, in recent years, in regard to debt incurred by dictators—and largely used to enrich the dictators, their families, and their cronies. Advocates of repudiation argue that the people have no moral obligation to pay such debts.

With the possible move of debt repudiation up their sleeve, indebted countries need not knuckle under to creditors' demands for payment in full (whatever suffering this may mean for their people). Rather, they can negotiate more favorable terms. One recent example is Argentina, which defaulted on its external debt in 2001, and then managed to negotiate a restructuring of its debts with the vast majority of its creditors. Getting some relief from debt repayments and avoiding austerity policies that would have undermined growth, Argentina enjoyed a surprising economic rebound. (Since then, the debt-restructuring deal has been endangered by the so-called "vulture funds." These are speculators who bought Argentinean bonds after the default, for a fraction of their face value. Now they're fighting in the courts to be paid the full value of the bonds, and standing in the way of the restructuring deal that most creditors had already accepted.)

One reason people believe a country shouldn't default on its debts—that the country will cut itself off from future credit—turns out not to be generally true. This raises the question of why heavily indebted countries do not default more often. There's no one simple answer, but the example of the Latin American debt crisis of the 1980s is instructive. As multiple Latin American countries had become heavily indebted, serious discussion emerged about forming a "debtors' cartel." If they all threatened to default, many argued, they would be able to get better terms from the banks. In the end, however, the proposed debtors' cartel did not materialize, and the various countries ended up accepting quite onerous debt-repayment conditions. One reason was that there were significant divisions between more-indebted and less-indebted countries, with policymakers in the latter thinking that they could negotiate better terms going it alone than if they threw in their lot with the worse-off. More importantly, elites in debtor countries faced a choice—either confront a creditors' alliance including the giant international banks, the U.S. government, and international institutions or push the burdens of repayment onto the workers and poor of their own societies. Not surprisingly, they chose not to confront the high and mighty, but the poor and downtrodden.

Is there no way for lower-income countries to increase standards of living for their people without recourse to external debt?

Raising future standards of living requires that some current resources not be used to produce goods for consumption today, but rather goods that will make it possible to produce and consume more tomorrow. For example, rather than consumer goods like food, clothing, televisions, and houses, some resources are used instead to produce industrial machinery, factory buildings, and so on. If the alternative is to ferociously restrict consumption now, in order to finance such investments domestically, external debt may seem like the lesser evil.

There are ways, however, that countries that countries can promote economic development without having to "bite the bullet" and choose one of these two options. First, many developing countries could greatly reduce their need for credit or other inflows of capital, in order to finance investments in future production, if they did not suffer from enormous financial outflows. As economists Boyce and Ndikumana have documented, as of 2010, capital flight from the 33 countries of sub-Saharan Africa had resulted in total ownership, by citizens of those countries, of over $1 trillion in assets abroad. Basically, this is what the region is lending to the rest of the world. At the same time, the region's total external liabilities—basically, what it owes to the rest of the world—added up to less than $200 billion. In effect, Boyce and Ndikumana conclude, "making the region a net creditor to the rest of the world." Think about that. Heavily indebted sub-Saharan Africa is not actually borrowing from the rest of the world, on balance, but lending! Capital flight is draining many countries of resources that could be used for domestic development. International credit is not only failing to fill the resulting void, but as Boyce and Ndikumana argue, is actually fueling much of this capital flight (as the wealthy and powerful divert loans, including public loans, for their own enrichment). Leading global banks have been culpable in this, both as originators of the loans and as receipients of the diverted funds. (See Boyce, pp. 98-102, and Petras, p. 100.)

Second, economic development and economic growth are not the same thing. If we define economic development, following economist and philosopher Amartya Sen, as the expansion of substantive human freedoms (or "capabilities"), then we can ask whether economic growth is either necessary or sufficient to achieve development. Sen emphasizes universal access to basic capabilities, like long life, good health, education, and the ability to participate in community life. Many countries have achieved substantial economic growth without achieving economic development in this sense. If the fruits of growth are mainly appropriated by the already well-off (and well-housed, well-fed, well-clothed, and well-educated), it's not surprising that growth would not bring about much improvement in the general level of these "capabilities." So economic growth is not *sufficient* for economic development. Neither, however, is substantial economic growth (raising per capita incomes) *necessary* for dramatic progress in "human development." High levels of human development can be (and have been) achieved, even at very low per capita incomes, in countries or sub-national regions where income is distributed quite equally and there is a strong public commitment to universal provision of basic goods (e.g., adequate nutrition, public health, elementary education, etc.).

On some level, we can imagine "unilateral" changes in the political and economic institutions of a lower-income country dramatically altering these two factors. More democratic and egalitarian societies are likely to be more successful both in avoiding the theft of resources by elites and in deploying the available resources to meet fundamental human needs. However, individual countries are also embedded in the capitalist world economy. The basic way capitalist economies operate is no different on the world scale than it is at the level of the individual enterprise—those who own resources only make them available to those who don't if the owners expect to profit by doing so. That is why so much discussion of development policy is about how lower-income countries can make themselves attractive for foreign investment. The only apparent way to get access to needed resources—by means of credit, foreign direct investment, etc.—is to convince the global banks or other global corporations that they will profit from it.

An alternative would be a world system in which there were large transfers from high- to low-income countries, without expectation of repayment or profit. These resources could be deployed, given sufficiently democratic and egalitarian institutions in the recipient countries, to spur development—including investments to increase future productive capacity and standards of living, but especially focusing on universal achievement of the basic capabilities that define "human development."

Global mechanisms for wealth redistribution may seem like an unrealizable and utopian fantasy. In fact, though, they have existed in recent history—only operating in the reverse direction. Colonialism, among other things, was a giant engine for transferring wealth from the "periphery" of the capitalist world economy (Africa, Asia, and Latin America) to the "core" (Western Europe and North America). Indeed, that system helped to create the division of the capitalist world into its "developed" and "underdeveloped" regions, producing development at one pole along with underdevelopment (subordinate, dependent development) at the other. In short, it created the world we know—not only one in which there are rich and poor countries, but in which the peripheral-subordinate-poor are used for the further enrichment of the core-dominant-rich.

A system that did the opposite is not unimaginable, but it does require that we imagine a very different world. ❏

Sources: Jayati Ghosh, "Who Benefits from Sovereign Debt Crises?" The Real News Network, Oct. 26, 2015; World Bank, Data, GDP per capita (constant 2005 US$) (data.worldbank.org); International Monetary Fund, Data and Statistics, External debt, total debt service (imf.org); James K. Boyce and Léonce Ndikumana, "Capital Flight from Sub-Saharan African Countries: Updated Estimates, 1970-2010," Political Economy Research Institute, University of Massachusetts-Amherst (October 2012); Léonce Ndikumana and James K. Boyce, *Africa's Odious Debts* (Zed Books, 2011); Amartya Sen, Development as Freedom (Oxford University Press, 1999).

Chapter 9

THE POLITICAL ECONOMY
OF EMPIRE

Article 9.1

COLONIALISM, "UNDERDEVELOPMENT," AND
THE INTERNATIONAL DIVISION OF LABOR
BY ALEJANDRO REUSS
November 2012

The creation of large modern empires, in the last 500 years or so, linked together, for the first time, the economies of different continents into a "world economy." Colonial powers like Spain, Portugal, France, and Britain (also Belgium and the Netherlands) conquered territories and peoples in Africa, Asia, and the Americas, creating far-flung global empires. The horrors of colonialism included plunder, slavery, and genocide on an epic scale. The conquest of the Americas resulted in the greatest "demographic catastrophe" (sudden fall in population) in human history. Many indigenous people were killed by violence or the strains of forced labor, many more by the exotic diseases brought in by European colonists (against which the peoples of the Americas had no natural immunity). Europeans kidnapped and enslaved millions of Africans, many of whom died from the horrors of the "middle passage." Those who survived arrived in the Americas in chains, to be exploited on plantations and in mines.

People often think of colonialism as "ancient history." Unlike the United States and much of the rest of the Americas, however, most of the countries of Africa and Asia have gained independence only in recent decades. The Indian subcontinent was a British colony until the late 1940s, ultimately dividing into three independent countries (India, Pakistan, and Bangladesh) in two subsequent partitions. Much of southeast Asia, likewise, did not gain independence until the 1940s or 1950s. For most current African states, meanwhile, independence dates from the 1950s, 1960s, or 1970s.

Colonialism and the International Division of Labor

When we speak of the division of labor within a society, we mean that different people specialize in different kinds of work. The international division of labor, in turn, involves different countries producing different kinds of goods. One country, for example, may be mostly agricultural; another, mostly industrial. Even among agricultural producers, one may produce mostly grains and another mostly fruits and vegetables. Among industrial countries, one may be a major producer of cars or planes, while another may produce clothing.

While the breakdown of total production, among different industries, is often pretty similar for different "developed" economies, it is likely to differ quite a bit between "developed" and "developing" economies. Sometimes, international trade in goods links together countries that produce similar types of goods. A great deal of world trade goes between different "developed" economies, many of which export the same kinds of goods to each other. However, international trade also links together economies that produce different kinds of goods. It is this second kind of linkage that we have in mind when we talk about the "international division of labor."

Colonialism created patterns in the international division of labor that have proved very difficult to escape. Colonial powers were not, by and large, interested in the development of conquered areas for its own sake. Often, the were interested simply in stripping a colony of all the wealth they could as fast as they could. The original Spanish conquerors of the Americas, for example, were interested first and foremost in gold and silver. First they took all the gold and silver ornaments they could lay their hands on. Then they enslaved the indigenous people and forced them

---

Changing Labels: "Underdeveloped" or "Developing"?

What are now termed "less-developed" or "developing" countries were, until recently, often described as "underdeveloped." The use of this term declined for a couple of reasons:

First, it came to be viewed as having pejorative connotations. That is, it took on very negative unspoken meanings, in particular the view that the people of "underdeveloped" countries were to blame for their own plight. It is now widely viewed as offensive to call a country "underdeveloped."

Second, political movements in many of these countries between the 1960s and 1980s took over and transformed the meaning of the word. Their countries, they argued, had not been born "underdeveloped," they had been "underdeveloped" by the colonial powers (or former colonial powers) that dominated the world economy. The shift away from the use of this term was, in part, a way for political and economic elites (both in "developed" and "developing" countries) to silence this argument.

to labor in the mines, shipping vast quantities of gold and silver back to Europe. European empires also began to develop agricultural colonies. Colonies in tropical regions, especially, made it possible to produce goods—like sugar, coffee, and tobacco—which were highly prized and not widely available in Europe. In many places, slaves (in the Americas, mainly Africans) did the back-breaking plantation work. Sometimes, colonists simply took the lands of local people, leaving them with little choice but to work for meager wages on the plantations.

As some colonial powers began to industrialize, their colonies took on new significance. First, colonies became sources of materials for industry. Britain's textile industry, for example, began with woolen cloth, but gradually shifted toward cotton. Partly, the cotton came from its former colony, the United States, where it was grown primarily on slave plantations in the South. Increasingly, however, it came from colonies like Egypt and India. Second, colonies became "captive" markets for manufactured exports. Colonial powers restricted their colonies' trade with other countries, so one country's colony could not trade with another colonial power. (In effect, the imperial powers were practicing their own form of "protectionism," with barriers to trade surrounding the entire empire.) They sometimes even required that trade *between* their colonies go through the "mother" country, where customs duties (taxes) were collected for the imperial coffers.

Partly, colonial powers got the most out of their colonies by restricting the kinds of goods that could be produced there. Some economic historians argue that colonial restrictions, designed to keep India a captive market for the British textile industry, destroyed India's own textile industry. Others emphasize the cheapness of British-made cloth, made using modern water- or coal-powered machinery. Even if the latter is true, however, this does not mean colonialism was blameless. If India had been an independent country, it could have imposed tariffs, in order to protect its "infant" textile manufacturing. But economic policy for India was made in London, and those policies were designed to keep India open to British manufactures. In the end, instead of producing textiles itself, India became a producer of raw material for the British textile industry. This was a pattern that repeated itself across the colonial world, with industrial development stifled and the colonies pushed into "primary goods" production.

Political Independence and Economic "Dependency"

Even after becoming politically independent, many former colonial countries seemed to remain trapped in the colonial-era international division of labor. They had not been able to develop manufacturing industries as colonies, and so they continued to import manufactured goods. To pay for these goods, they continued to export primary products. In many countries, the specialization in a single export good was so extreme that these became known as "monoculture" economies ("mono" = one). In some former colonies, important resources like land and mines remained under the control of foreign companies. In many cases, these were from the former colonial "mother" country. Sometimes, however, a rising new power replaced the old colonial power. After independence from Spain, for example, much of South America became part of Britain's "informal empire." Meanwhile, the United States supplanted Spain and other European colonial countries as the dominant power in Central America and the Caribbean, plus parts of South America.

Critics argued that this situation kept the former colonies poor and "dependent" on the rich industrial countries. (The subordination of the former colonies was so reminiscent of the old patterns of colonialism, that this was often labeled "neo-colonialism" or "imperialism.") The United States' relationship to smaller, poorer, and less powerful countries—especially in its "sphere of influence" of Latin America—exemplified many of the key patterns of post-independence neo-colonialism: Foreign companies extracted vast amounts of wealth, in the form of agricultural goods and minerals, while paying paltry wages to local workers. They employed skilled personnel from their home countries and used imported machinery, so their operations formed economic "enclaves" unconnected to the rest of the country's economy. Finally, they sent the profits back to their home countries, rather than reinvesting them locally, and so did little to spur broader economic development. Critics argued that this system was designed, in the words of Uruguayan author Eduardo Galeano, to bleed wealth out of these countries' "open veins."

Some economists pointed out some major economic disadvantages to specialization in "primary products," which are worth discussing in more detail.

First, economists associated with the United Nations Economic Commission for Latin America (known by its Spanish acronym, CEPAL) observed that the prices of primary products had tended to decline, over time, in relation to the prices of manufactured goods. The lower-income countries, therefore, had to sell larger and larger amounts of the goods they exported (more tons of sugar, coffee, copper, aluminum, or whatever) to afford the same amounts of the goods they imported (cars, televisions, or whatever).

Second, specialization in primary-product exports exposed low-income countries to wild fluctuations of world-market prices for these goods. The world-market price of a cash crop could be very high one year and very low the next. An especially bad year, or a few bad years in a row, might wipe out any savings farmers or farm workers might have from previous good years, and leave them destitute. Ironically, farmers might go hungry, even if the land was fertile and the weather had been good. For most cash crops, including fiber crops (like cotton) and specialized food crops (like coffee and sugar), the farmers could not survive by eating the harvest if world prices were too low. So a move towards cash crops could exacerbate poverty and food insecurity.

The governments of these countries might have found it difficult to challenge this state of affairs, even had they wanted to. Their economies, after all, were heavily dependent on exports to the dominant country (whose government could cut off access to its markets, should it be provoked). In many cases, however, local political elites have enjoyed close political and economic ties to the multinational companies, and little interest in changing anything. As long as they maintained "order," kept workers from organizing unions or demanding higher wages, and protected the multinational companies' investments, they could be sure to keep the favor of the dominant country's government and the multinational companies. In the cases where opposition movements did arise, calling for changes like the redistribution of land ownership or the nationalization of important resources, the dominant power could intervene militarily, if local elites were not up to the task of putting the rebels down.

Changes in the International Division of Labor

For much of the twentieth century, a key dividing line among capitalist economies was between the "industrial" economies of the United States and Western Europe and the "non-industrial" economies of most of Latin America, Africa, and Asia. These two kinds of economies were linked: The high-income industrial economies imported agricultural products and minerals (or "primary products") from the low-income non-industrial economies, and exported manufactured goods (or "secondary products") in return.

In more recent decades, the international division of labor has changed in important ways. First, many formerly "non-industrial" economies have developed substantial manufacturing sectors, often by deliberately promoting manufacturing development through government policies like protective trade barriers, low-interest loans, etc. In some cases, what had been "less developed" economies, such as Japan and South Korea, have become major global industrial producers. Second, foreign investment has created a growing "export platform" manufacturing sector in some countries. Large corporations have increasingly engaged in "offshoring"—locating production facilities outside the countries where they are headquartered and have their traditional base of operations, and exporting the output back to the "home" market or to other countries.

In high-income countries, even as manufacturing employment has declined as a percentage of total employment, other sectors have grown. Over the last few decades, employment in "services" has accounted for an increasing proportion of total employment in high-income countries. When people think of services, they often think of low-wage employment in fast-food restaurants or big-box stores. Services, however, also include education, health care, finance, and other industries which can involve high-skill, and sometimes highly paid, work. All of these services can be "exported"— performed for people who reside in and earn their incomes in other countries—either because they can be done remotely (like most financial services, and some health care and education) or because the recipients travel to the place where providers are located (like students from abroad studying at U.S. universities).

Often, people think the relative decline in manufacturing employment in high-income countries is due only to offshoring—to companies "moving" manufacturing jobs from one country to another. To a great extent, however, the increasing mechanization of production (the substitution of machines for labor) was already driving this process decades before offshoring became a significant factor. As assembly-line employment has declined in high-income countries, fields like product engineering and design have accounted for an increasing proportion of the jobs in the manufacturing sector.

The End of "Underdevelopment"?

Advocates of "globalization" have pointed to the growth of export-oriented manufacturing in some less developed countries as a positive sign. The countries experiencing the least development, they argue, are those that have remained marginal to the new global economy—especially because official corruption, political instability, or government hostility toward foreign investment have made them unattractive locations for offshore production. These countries, the globalization advocates argue, need *more* globalization, not less—and therefore should adopt "neoliberal" policies eliminating barriers to international trade and investment.

Critics of the current form of globalization, and of the "offshoring" approach to economic development, on the other hand, point to several less-than-shining realities.

First, it is not always true that the least-developed economies have been relatively untouched by the global economy. In many cases, multinational companies, usually with the connivance of local elites, have seized and extracted valuable resources such as minerals or petroleum, with near-total disregard for the effects on the local population. This process has led to the most extreme patterns of "enclave" development, where the only things developed are the means to get the wealth out of the ground and bound for world markets.

Second, countries aggressively embracing neoliberal economic policies have not always seen a dramatic increase in manufacturing employment. "Free trade agreements" have typically eliminated both barriers to trade and barriers to international investment. The elimination of trade barriers has opened up profitable new markets for multinational companies, while also being an essential ingredient of the offshore-production model. The imports that have flooded in to lower-income countries due to the elimination of tariffs and other barriers, however, have battered domestic industries. As a result, many countries have seen the increase in "offshore" or "export-platform" employment in manufacturing offset by the decimation of domestic manufacturing for the domestic market.

Third, when multinational companies "offshore" manufacturing to lower-income countries, they do not relocate all phases of the manufacturing process. Export-platform production typically involves relatively "low-skill" assembly and finishing work. Meanwhile, functions like engineering, design and styling, marketing, and management largely remain in the company's "home" country. (If you look on the back of an iPhone, for example, you will see that it says, "Designed by Apple in California. Assembled in China.") Countries whose governments simply throw their doors open to multinational corporations—without imposing, for example, "technology transfer" requirements that can help spur domestic technological development—may remain stuck in the assembly-and-finishing phase, much as "less-developed" countries in an earlier era were stuck as primary-product producers.

In the 1950s and 1960s, radical theorists of economic dependency emphasized that "underdevelopment" was not simply an *absence* of development. Indeed, even in that era, there was visible economic development in so-called underdeveloped countries, as there is today in what are now termed "developing" countries. Rather, they argued that we should think of underdevelopment as a *form* of development— of dependent, subordinated, exploited development. Capitalist development, they argued, produced both development (for countries in the wealthy "core") and underdevelopment (in the poorer "periphery"). While offshore production may bring a certain form of industrial development, and may be changing the international division of labor in some ways, it is also reproducing old patterns of subordination. ❑

Article 9.2

HAITI'S FAULT LINES: MADE IN THE U.S.A.

BY MARIE KENNEDY AND CHRIS TILLY

March/April 2010

The mainstream media got half the story right about Haiti. Reporters observed that Haiti's stark poverty intensified the devastation caused by the recent earthquake. True: hillside shantytowns, widespread concrete construction without rebar reinforcement, a grossly inadequate road network, and a healthcare system mainly designed to cater to the small elite all contributed mightily to death and destruction.

But what caused that poverty? U.S. readers and viewers might be forgiven for concluding that some inexplicable curse has handed Haiti corrupt and unstable governments, unproductive agriculture, and widespread illiteracy. Televangelist Pat Robertson simply took this line of "explanation" to its nutty, racist conclusion when he opined that Haitians were paying for a pact with the devil.

But the devil had little to do with Haiti's underdevelopment. Instead, the fingerprints of more mundane actors—France and later the United States—are all over the crime scene. After the slave rebellion of 1791, France wrought massive destruction in attempting to recapture its former colony, then extracted 150 million francs of reparations, only fully paid off in 1947. France's most poisonous legacy may have been the skin-color hierarchy that sparked fratricidal violence and still divides Haiti.

While France accepted Haiti once the government started paying up, the United States, alarmed by the example of a slave republic, refused to recognize Haiti until 1862. That late-arriving recognition kicked off a continuing series of military and political interventions. The U.S. Marines occupied Haiti outright from 1915 to 1934, modernizing the infrastructure but also revising laws to allow foreign ownership, turning over the country's treasury to a New York bank, saddling Haiti with a $40 million debt to the United States, and reinforcing the status gap between mulattos and blacks. American governments backed the brutal, kleptocratic, two-generation Duvalier dictatorship from 1957-86. When populist priest Jean-Bertrand Aristide was elected president in 1990, the Bush I administration winked at the coup that ousted him a year later. Bill Clinton reversed course, ordering an invasion to restore Aristide, but used that intervention to impose the same free-trade "structural adjustment" Bush had sought. Bush II closed the circle by backing rebels who re-overthrew the re-elected Aristide in 2004. No wonder many Haitians are suspicious of the U.S. troops who poured in after the earthquake.

Though coups and invasions grab headlines, U.S. economic interventions have had equally far-reaching effects. U.S. goals for the last 30 years have been to open Haiti to American products, push Haiti's self-sufficient peasants off the land, and redirect the Haitian economy to plantation-grown luxury crops and export assembly, both underpinned by cheap labor. Though Haiti has yet to boost its export capacity, the first two goals have succeeded, shattering Haiti's former productive capacity. In the early 1980s, the U.S. Agency for International Development exterminated Haiti's hardy Creole pigs in the name of preventing a swine flu epidemic, then helpfully offered U.S. pigs that require expensive U.S.-produced feeds and medicines. Cheap American rice imports crippled the country's breadbasket, the Artibonite, so that Haiti, a rice exporter in the 1980s, now imports massive amounts. Former peasants flooded into Port-au-Prince, doubling the population over the last quarter century, building makeshift housing, and setting the stage for the current catastrophe.

In the wake of the disaster, U.S. aid continues to have two-edged effects. Each aid shipment that flies in U.S. rice and flour instead of buying and distributing local rice or cassava continues to undermine agriculture and deepen dependency. Precious trucks and airstrips are used to marshal U.S. troops against overblown "security threats," crowding out humanitarian assistance. The United States and other international donors show signs of once more using aid to leverage a free-trade agenda. If we seek to end Haiti's curse, the first step is to realize that one of the curse's main sources is...us. ❑

Article 9.3

PUERTO RICO'S COLONIAL DEBT

BY JOSÉ A. LAGUARTA RAMÍREZ
July/August 2016

At least 23 of the 49 people killed in the mass shooting that took place at Pulse nightclub in Orlando on June 12 were born in Puerto Rico. While the horrendous hate crime targeted LGBT people of all ethnicities, the large proportion of island-born casualties is not surprising, as the central Florida city has become a preferred destination of Puerto Rican migrants over the past two decades. Steadily growing since the onset of the island's current "fiscal" crisis in 2006, yearly out-migration from Puerto Rico now surpasses that of the 1950s. The island's total population has begun to decline for the first time in its history.

Nearly a third of the island-born victims of the Orlando massacre were 25 or younger, most of them students employed in services or retail. This is the population group that will be hit hardest when the ironically named Puerto Rico Oversight, Management, and Economic Stability Act (PROMESA) comes into effect. Among its other "promises" for working-class Puerto Ricans, PROMESA will cut the minimum wage in Puerto Rico for those under 25, from the current federally mandated $7.25 to $4.25 per hour, and scale back the federal nutritional assistance program on the island. Purportedly aimed at "job-creation," these measures will likely intensify the outflow of able-bodied "low-skilled" workers. Ongoing out-migration has already decimated the number of available healthcare and other professionals on the island. Puerto Rico's 2013 median household income of $19,183 was barely half that of Mississippi, the poorest U.S. state (at $37,479), despite a cost of living that rivals that of most major cities in the United States. Inequality on the island is also greater than in any of the states.

The U.S. House of Representatives approved PROMESA on the evening of June 9, following a strong endorsement by President Barack Obama. The bill, which would also impose an unelected and unaccountable federal oversight board and allow court-supervised restructuring of part of the island's $73 billion debt, now awaits consideration by the Senate. Its advocates hope the president can sign PROMESA into law before July 1, when $1.9 billion's worth of Puerto Rico general obligation bonds will come due. Unlike those issued by public utility corporations and certain autonomous agencies, general obligation bonds, under Puerto Rico's colonial constitution, must be repaid before any further public spending for the following fiscal year is authorized. Puerto Rico's government has partially defaulted three times within the past year, but not on general obligation bonds. Puerto Rico is not the only place, under the global regime of austerity capitalism, to face predatory creditors and the imposition of unelected rulers—as illustrated by cases like Argentina, Greece, and post-industrial U.S. cities such as

Flint, Mich.—but its century-old colonial status has made it particularly vulnerable and defenseless.

The House vote followed a concerted, carefully timed media push by the Democratic establishment, on the premise that "despite its flaws" PROMESA represents a bipartisan compromise that is, in Obama's words, "far superior to the status quo." Among similar statements, a *New York Times* editorial on May 31 claimed that PROMESA "offers the island its best chance of survival." However, following the bill's approval, Republican House Speaker Paul Ryan tweeted in almost identical terms that PROMESA is "the best chance," but for something quite different—"for American taxpayers to be protected from a bailout of Puerto Rico." The threat of a taxpayer-funded "bailout" (which has never been on the table) has been deployed in anonymous scare ads, probably financed by high-risk/yield-seeking "vulture funds" that hold Puerto Rican bonds and so oppose PROMESA's mild restructuring provisions.

PROMESA's oversight board, which will be staffed by San Juan and Washington insiders with the bondholders' best interests at heart, is sure to continue to impose draconian austerity measures that have already slashed much-needed social services. (Former Puerto Rico governor Luis Fortuño, a Republican who enacted legislation laying off up to 30,000 public employees in order to appease credit rating agencies, has been mentioned as a likely appointee.) Democratic support for the bill was forthcoming despite the fact that neither the oversight provisions nor those reducing the minimum wage were removed.

Most U.S. observers reduce Puerto Rico's debt crisis to a result of "mismanagement" by its local administrators. (A Google search of the terms "Puerto Rico," "debt," and "mismanagement" yields pieces articulating this narrative from Bloomberg, CNN, *USA Today*, the *National Review*, and the Huffington Post, among others, within the top 10 hits.) This view conveniently erases the historical and structural roots of the crisis.

U.S. troops occupied Puerto Rico in 1898 and the Supreme Court quickly declared it an "unincorporated territory" subject to the authority of the U.S. Congress and federal courts system, without voting representation in Congress. Although U.S. citizenship was extended to individuals in 1917, and a local constitution was authorized and adopted in 1952 (not without significant amendments by Congress), the juridical fact of colonialism has remained unaltered, as reiterated by the Court on the very day of the House vote on PROMESA. (See *Puerto Rico v. Sánchez Valle*, a criminal case on double jeopardy, in which the Court reminds Puerto Rico's local government that unlike states, it is not legally considered a "sovereign" separate from Congress.) In the mid-1970s, Puerto Rico's comparative advantage as the only low-wage tax haven with direct access to the U.S. market waned. Washington's solution to the colony's economic stagnation was Section 936 of the Internal Revenue Code, which granted federal tax exemptions to U.S. corporations on products made in Puerto Rico, in addition to local tax breaks in place since the 1940s. The local government, in turn, pursued massive debt-fueled investment in infrastructure, whose use by these corporations it heavily subsidized. The resulting debt addiction spiraled out of control in the 1990s, fed by easy credit, and exacerbated after Congress began a ten-year phase out of Section 936 in 1996. Meanwhile, profits continue to leave the island to the tune of $30 billion annually.

In international law, the term for debt incurred by colonial, corrupt, or authoritarian regimes is "odious debt." A prominent example of its application was the cancellation of Cuba's colonial debt when that country achieved its independence from Spain, following the so-called Spanish-American War of 1898. The U.S. government's argument at the time, which Spain never formally accepted but most of Cuba's creditors eventually did, was that the debt was incurred neitherwith the consent of the Cuban people nor to their benefit. Although odious debt is a grey area of international law, with sufficient political resolve Puerto Rico's leadership could use it to bolster a claim to refuse payment. In 2008, Ecuador invoked the doctrine as part of a largely successful audit and partial default. Such a course would necessarily put Puerto Rico on a collision course with colonialism, as it would need to refuse to recognize any resulting lawsuits in U.S. courts.

This is precisely the type of outcome that PROMESA is designed to prevent. It is one which Puerto Rico's current administrators have proven entirely unwilling to pursue. Yet it is a path that is not alien to U.S. political history: one of the grievances that led to the thirteen colonies' Declaration of Independence was the imposition of new taxes—largely to pay debts incurred by Britain in the Seven Years' War. An independent Puerto Rico, released of an illegitimate debt burden incurred to profit U.S. corporations, could better focus on serving the needs of its poor and working-class majority. A movement capable of leading such a process has yet to materialize, but with U.S. statehood farther away than ever and housing and labor markets in migrant destinations becoming increasingly saturated, the matter is far from decided.

As living conditions on the island continue to deteriorate under PROMESA (and they surely will), young Puerto Rican students and workers will continue to flood those places where family connections, climate, the price of airfare, and job opportunities pull them. Not all will be targeted for physical violence because of their multiple identities, as the Orlando victims were. Their fate, however, will continue to be a haunting reminder of the ways in which invisible forces pattern seemingly random events in the lives of individuals and communities. ❑

Article 9.4

"TIED" FOREIGN AID

BY ARTHUR MacEWAN
January/February 2012

Dear Dr. Dollar:

People complaining about the ungrateful world often talk about the "huge" U.S. foreign aid budget.In fact, isn't U.S. foreign aid relatively small compared to other countries?What's worse, I understand that a lot of economic aid comes with strings attached, requiring that goods and services purchased with the aid be purchased from firms in the aid-giving country.This channels much of the money back out of the recipient country.That sounds nuts!What's going on? —*Katharine Rylaarsdam, Baltimore, Md.*

The U.S. government does provide a "huge" amount of development aid, far more than any of the other rich countries.In 2009, the United States provided $29.6 billion, in development aid—Japan was number two, at $16.4 billion.

But wait a minute.What appears huge may not be so huge. The graph below shows the amount of foreign development aid provided by ten high-income countries *and* that amount as a share of the countries' gross domestic products (GDP).Yes, the graph shows that the United States gives far more than any of these other countries.But the graph also shows the United States gives a small amount relative to its GDP.In 2009, U.S. foreign development aid was two-tenths of 1% of the country's GDP.Only Italy gave a lesser amount relative to its GDP.

DEVELOPMENT AID, AMOUNT AND PERCENT OF GDP, 2009

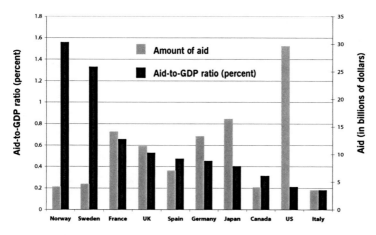

Source: OECD, Official Development Assistance by Donor (stats.oecd.org).

The world's rich countries have long committed to providing 0.7% of GDP to foreign development aid.In 2009, only Norway and Sweden met this goal. The U.S. government did not come close.

Moreover, a large share of U.S. foreign aid is "tied aid"; governments that receive the aid must spend the funds by buying goods and services from U.S. firms. Generally the recipient countries could get more goods and services if they could spend the money without this restriction.So the economic development impact of the aid is less than it appears. Also, whatever the "foreign aid" does for the recipient country, it is a way of channeling money to U.S. firms.

Not only must the recipient country pay more for the goods and services, but the "multiplier impact" is much less.That is, since the money goes to U.S. companies rather than local suppliers, fewer local jobs and salary payments are created; so less is re-spent in the local economy.A 2009 report on aid to Afghanistan by the Peace Dividend Trust notes: "By using Afghan goods and services to carry out development projects in Afghanistan, the international community has the opportunity to spend a development dollar twice. How? Local procurement creates jobs, increases incomes, generates revenue and develops the Afghan marketplace —all of which support economic recovery and stability."Yet most of the aid "for Afghanistan" went to foreign "experts," foreign construction firms, and foreign suppliers of goods.

The U.S. government ties much more of its aid than do most other donor countries.A report by the Organization for Economic Cooperation and Development (OECD) estimated that in the mid-2000s, 54.5% of U.S. aid was tied.Of the 22 donor countries listed in the report (including the United States), the average share of tied aid was only 28.4%.The report notes a "widespread movement to untying [aid], with the exception of the United States."

It is important to recognize that U.S. foreign aid is an instrument of U.S. foreign policy, and is thus highly concentrated in countries where the U.S. government has what it views as "strategic interests." For example, in 2008 almost 16% of U.S. development assistance went to Afghanistan and Iraq, while the top 20 recipient countries received over 50%.

So, yes, the U.S. government provides a "huge" amount of foreign development aid—or not so much.It depends on how you look at things. ❑

Article 9.5

IS IT OIL?

BY ARTHUR MacEWAN
May/June 2003

Foreword, October 2013

The long U.S. military engagement in Iraq is over. There were no weapons of mass destruction, so the U.S. government shifted its rationale for the invasion to "regime change" and the establishment of a democratic Iraq. While regime change was accomplished, virtually no one would claim that a meaningful democracy was left in place as U.S. troops departed. Untold numbers of Iraqis died—estimates range from 100,000 upwards to one-million—and over 4,000 U.S. deaths were recorded.

From the perspective of U.S. and other internationally operating major oil companies, however, the U.S. invasion was a success—at least a partial success. ExxonMobil, Shell, BP, Haliburton and others are back in Iraq. Having secured contracts to extract the county's low-cost oil, they are expanding their operations in the country—and expanding their profits from those operations. Iraq's oil production in 2011 stood at 2,798 thousand barrels a day (bpd), surpassing output in all previous years except for the 2,832 bpd in 1989.

However, the western firms—the "majors" that have dominated the international oil industry for decades—have not obtained all they had hoped for when the invasion began a decade ago. Some U.S. firms—Chevron and ConocoPhillips—have failed to get contacts that they sought.

Most important, the major oil companies have had to share the lucrative Iraqi contacts with newer players in the global industry. Firms from China especially, but also from Russia, Norway, and elsewhere are getting in on the action. In 2013 China is the largest customer for Iraqi oil, buying nearly half of the country's production. Also, Chinese companies are increasingly making inroads into production by accepting less favorable terms—both lower profit rates and more restrictions—than U.S. firms. Apparently, Chinese firms, largely under the control of the Chinese government, are more concerned with securing sources of supply than with profits.

Substantial opposition to the foreign oil companies has developed in Iraq, including actions by unions and popular demonstrations. This opposition has had an impact in spite of its repression by the Iraqi government.

The Iraqi parliament has never enacted the Iraq Oil Law, a law which would secure the full opening of the country's oil reserves to the major firms and which the U.S. government continues to push.

Iraq events of the decade since this article was originally written have verified the importance of the interests of U.S.-based firms—and especially of the oil companies— in affecting the course of the U.S. government's global policies. At the same time, those

events have demonstrated the limits of U.S. power. Neither the government, with all its
military might, nor the firms can shape the world's economy exactly as they wish. There
are, it turns out, people involved, and they don't always cooperate.
—Arthur MacEwan

Before U.S. forces invaded Iraq, the United Nations inspection team that had been
searching the country for weapons of mass destruction was unable to find either
such weapons or a capacity to produce them in the near future. As of mid-April,
while the U.S. military is apparently wrapping up its invasion, it too has not found
the alleged weapons. The U.S. government continues to claim that weapons of mass
destruction exist in Iraq but provides scant evidence to substantiate its claim.

While weapons of mass destruction are hard to find in Iraq, there is one thing
that is relatively easy to find: oil. Lots of oil. With 112.5 billion barrels of proven
reserves, Iraq has greater stores of oil than any country except Saudi Arabia. This
combination—lots of oil and no weapons of mass destruction—begs the question:
Is it oil and not weapons of mass destruction that motivates the U.S. government's
aggressive policy towards Iraq?

The U.S. "Need" for Oil?

Much of the discussion of the United States, oil, and Iraq focuses on the U.S. economy's overall dependence on oil. We are a country highly dependent on oil, consuming far more than we produce. We have a small share, about 3%, of the world's total
proven oil reserves. By depleting our reserves at a much higher rate than most other
countries, the United States accounts for about 10% of world production. But, by
importing from the rest of the world, we can consume oil at a still higher rate: U.S. oil
consumption is over 25% of the world's total. (See the accompanying figures for these
and related data.) Thus, the United States relies on the rest of the world's oil in order
to keep its economy running—or at least running in its present oil-dependent form.
Moreover, for the United States to operate as it does and maintain current standards
of living, we need access to oil at low prices. Otherwise we would have to turn over a
large share of U.S. GDP as payment to those who supply us with oil.

Iraq could present the United States with supply problems. With a hostile government in Baghdad, the likelihood that the United States would be subject to some
sort of boycott as in the early 1970s is greater than otherwise. Likewise, a government in Baghdad that does not cooperate with Washington could be a catalyst to a
reinvigoration of the Organization of Petroleum Exporting Countries (OPEC) and
the result could be higher oil prices.

Such threats, however, while real, are not as great as they might first appear.
Boycotts are hard to maintain. The sellers of oil need to sell as much as the buyers
need to buy; oil exporters depend on the U.S. market, just as U.S. consumers depend
on those exporters. (An illustration of this mutual dependence is provided by the continuing oil trade between Iraq and the United States in recent years. During 2001,

FIGURE 1: YEARS OF RESERVES AT CURRENT ANNUAL PRODUCTION RATES*

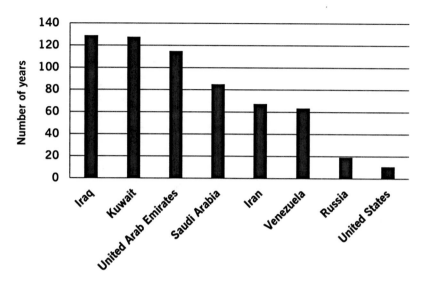

*The number of years it would take to use up existing reserves at current production rate. Past experience, however, suggests that more reserves will be found. In the 1980s, the world's proven reserves expanded by 47%, even as the consumption continued apace. With a more rapid rate of economic growth in the 1990s, and thus with the more rapid rate of oil consumption, the world's reserves rose by almost 5%.

Source: BP Statistical Review of World Energy 2002 <www.bp.com/centres/energy2002>

while the two countries were in a virtual state of war, the United States bought 284 million barrels of oil from Iraq, about 7% of U.S. imports and almost a third of Iraq's exports.) Also, U.S. oil imports come from diverse sources, with less than half from OPEC countries and less than one-quarter from Persian Gulf nations.

Most important, ever since the initial surge of OPEC in the 1970s, the organization has followed a policy of price restraint. While price restraint may in part be a strategy of political cooperation, resulting from the close U.S.-Saudi relationship in particular, it is also a policy adopted because high prices are counter-productive for OPEC itself; high prices lead consumers to switch sources of supply and conserve energy, undercutting the longer term profits for the oil suppliers. Furthermore, a sudden rise in prices can lead to general economic disruption, which is no more desirable for the oil exporters than for the oil importers. To be sure, the United States would prefer to have cooperative governments in oil producing countries, but the specter of another boycott as in the 1970s or somewhat higher prices for oil hardly provides a rationale, let alone a justification, for war.

The Profits Problem

There is, however, also the importance of oil in the profits of large U.S. firms: the oil companies themselves (with ExxonMobil at the head of the list) but also the numerous drilling, shipping, refining, and marketing firms that make up the rest of the oil industry. Perhaps the most famous of this latter group, because former CEO Dick Cheney is now vice president, is the Halliburton Company, which supplies a wide range of equipment and engineering services to the industry. Even while many governments—Saudi Arabia, Kuwait, and Venezuela, for example—have taken ownership of their countries' oil reserves, these companies have been able to maintain their profits because of their decisive roles at each stage in the long sequence from exploration through drilling to refining and marketing. Ultimately, however, as with any resource-based industry, the monopolistic position—and thus the large profits—of the firms that dominate the oil industry depends on their access to the supply of the resource. Their access, in turn, depends on the relations they are able to establish with the governments of oil-producing countries.

From the perspective of the major U.S. oil companies, a hostile Iraqi government presents a clear set of problems. To begin with, there is the obvious: because Iraq has a lot of oil, access to that oil would represent an important profit-making opportunity. What's more, Iraqi oil can be easily extracted and thus produced at very low cost. With all oil selling at the same price on the world market, Iraqi oil thus presents opportunities for especially large profits per unit of production. According to the *Guardian* newspaper (London), Iraqi oil could cost as little as 97 cents a barrel to produce, compared to the UK's North Sea oil produced at $3 to $4 per barrel. As one oil executive told the *Guardian* last November, "Ninety cents a barrel for oil that sells for $30—that's the kind of business anyone would want to be in. A 97% profit margin—you can live with that." The *Guardian* continues: "The stakes are high. Iraq could be producing 8 million barrels a day within the decade. The math is

FIGURE 2: OIL CONSUMPTION 2001

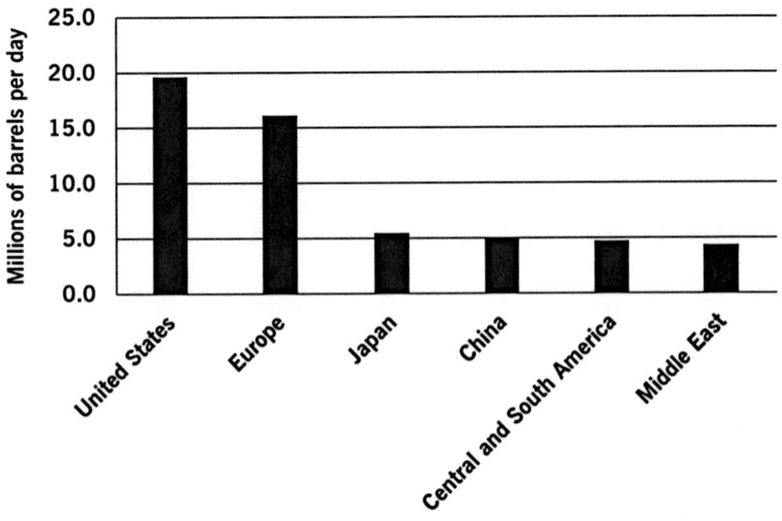

Source: BP Statistical Review of World Energy 2002 (www.bp.com/centres/energy2002

impressive—8 million times 365 at $30 per barrel or $87.5 billion a year. Any share would be worth fighting for." The question for the oil companies is: what share will they be able to claim and what share will be claimed by the Iraqi government? The split would undoubtedly be more favorable for the oil companies with a compliant U.S.-installed government in Baghdad.

Furthermore, the conflict is not simply one between the private oil companies and the government of Iraq. The U.S.-based firms and their British (and British-Dutch) allies are vying with French, Russian, and Chinese firms for access to Iraqi oil. During recent years, firms from these other nations signed oil exploration and development contracts with the Hussein government in Iraq, and, if there were no "regime change," they would preempt the operations of the U.S. and British firms in that country. If, however, the U.S. government succeeds in replacing the government of Saddam Hussein with its preferred allies in the Iraqi opposition, the outlook will change dramatically. According to Ahmed Chalabi, head of the Iraqi National Congress and a figure in the Iraqi opposition who seems to be currently favored by Washington, "The future democratic government in Iraq will be grateful to the United States for helping the Iraqi people liberate themselves and getting rid of Saddam.... American companies, we expect, will play an important and leading role in the future oil situation." (In recent years, U.S. firms have not been fully frozen out of the oil business in Iraq. For example, according to a June 2001 report in the *Washington Post*, while Vice President Cheney was CEO at Halliburton Company during the late 1990s, the firm operated through subsidiaries to sell some $73 million of oil production equipment and spare parts to Iraq.)

The rivalry with French, Russian and Chinese oil companies is in part driven by the direct prize of the profits to be obtained from Iraqi operations. In addition,

FIGURE 3: PROVEN OIL RESERVES 2001

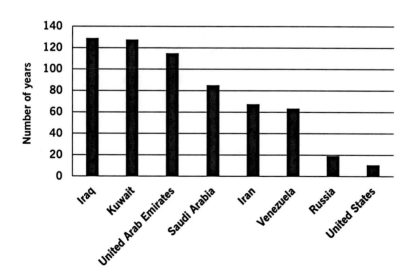

Source: BP Statistical Review of World Energy 2002 (www.bp.com/centres/energy2002

in order to maintain their dominant positions in the world oil industry, it is important for the U.S. and British-based firms to deprive their rivals of the growth potential that access to Iraq would afford. In any monopolistic industry, leading firms need to deny their potential competitors market position and control of new sources of supply; otherwise, those competitors will be in a better position to challenge the leaders. The British *Guardian* reports that the Hussein government is "believed to have offered the French company TotalFinaElf exclusive rights to the largest of Iraq's oil fields, the Majoon, which would more than double the company's entire output at a single stroke." Such a development would catapult TotalFinaElf from the second ranks into the first ranks of the major oil firms. The basic structure of the world oil industry would not change, but the sharing of power and profits among the leaders would be altered. Thus for ExxonMobil, Chevron, Shell and the other traditional "majors" in the industry, access to Iraq is a defensive as well as an offensive goal. ("Regime change" in Iraq will not necessarily provide the legal basis for cancellation of contracts signed between the Hussein regime and various oil companies. International law would not allow a new regime simply to turn things over to the U.S. oil companies. "Should 'regime change' happen, one thing is guaranteed," according to the *Guardian*, "shortly afterwards there will be the mother of all legal battles.")

Oil companies are big and powerful. The biggest, ExxonMobil, had 2002 profits of $15 billion, more than any other corporation, in the United States or in the world. Chevron-Texaco came in with $3.3 billion in 2002 profits, and Phillips-Tosco garnered $1.7 billion. British Petroleum-Amoco-Arco pulled in $8 billion, while Royal Dutch/Shell Group registered almost $11 billion. Firms of this magnitude have a large role affecting the policies of their governments, and, for that matter, the governments of many other countries.

With the ascendancy of the Bush-Cheney team to the White House in 2000, perhaps the relationship between oil and the government became more personal, but it was not new. Big oil has been important in shaping U.S. foreign policy since the end of the 19th century (to say nothing of its role in shaping other policy realms, particularly environmental regulation). From 1914, when the Marines landed at Mexico's Tampico Bay to protect U.S. oil interests, to the CIA-engineered overthrow of the Mosadegh government in Iran in 1953, to the close relationship with the oppressive Saudi monarchy through the past 70 years, oil and the interests of the oil companies have been central factors in U.S. foreign policy. Iraq today is one more chapter in a long story.

The Larger Issue

Yet in Iraq today, as in many other instances of the U.S. government's international actions, oil is not the whole story. The international policies of the U.S. government are certainly shaped in significant part by the interests of U.S.-based firms, but not only the oil companies. ExxonMobil may have had the largest 2002 profits, but there are many additional large U.S. firms with international interests: Citbank and the other huge financial firms; IBM, Microsoft, and other information technology companies; General Motors and Ford; Merck, Pfizer and the other pharmaceutical corporations; large retailers like MacDonald's and Walmart (and many more) depend on access to foreign markets and foreign sources of supply for large shares of their sales and profits.

The U.S. government (like other governments) has long defined its role in international affairs as protecting the interests of its nationals, and by far the largest interests of U.S. nationals abroad are the interests of these large U.S. companies. The day-to-day activities of U.S. embassies and consular offices around the world are dominated by efforts to further the interests of particular U.S. firms—for example, helping the firms establish local markets, negotiate a country's regulations, or develop relations with local businesses. When the issue is large, such as when governments in low-income countries have attempted to assure the availability of HIV-AIDS drugs in spite of patents held by U.S. firms, Washington steps directly into the fray. On the broadest level, the U.S. government tries to shape the rules and institutions of the world economy in ways that work well for U.S. firms. These rules are summed up under the heading of "free trade," which in practice means free access of U.S. firms to the markets and resources of the rest of the world.

In normal times, Washington uses diplomacy and institutions like the International Monetary Fund, the World Bank, and the World Trade Organization to shape the rules of the world economy. But times are not always "normal." When governments have attempted to remove their economies from the open system and break with the "rules of the game," the U.S. government has responded with overt or covert military interventions. Latin America has had a long history of such interventions, where Guatemala (1954), Cuba (1961), Chile (1973) and Nicaragua (1980s) provide fairly recent examples. The Middle East also provides several illustrations of this approach to foreign affairs, with U.S. interventions in Iran (1953), Lebanon (1958), Libya (1981), and now Iraq. These interventions are generally presented as efforts to preserve freedom and democracy, but, if freedom and democracy were actually the goals of U.S. interventions the record would be very different; both the Saudi monarchy and the Shah of Iran, in an earlier era, would then have been high on the U.S. hit list. (Also, as with maintaining the source of supply of oil, the U.S. government did not intervene in Guatemala in 1954 to maintain our supply of bananas; the profits of the United Fruit Company, however, did provide a powerful causal factor.)

The rhetorical rationale of U.S. foreign policy has seen many alterations and adjustments over the last century: at the end of the 19th century, U.S. officials spoke of the need to spread Christianity; Woodrow Wilson defined the mission as keeping the world safe for democracy; for most of the latter half of the 20th century, the fight against Communism was the paramount rationale; for a fleeting moment during the Carter administration, the protection of human rights entered the government's vocabulary; in recent years we have seen the war against drugs; and now we have the current administration's war against terrorism.

What distinguishes the current administration in Washington is neither its approach toward foreign affairs and U.S. business interests in general nor its policy in the Middle East and oil interests in particular. Even its rhetoric builds on well established traditions, albeit with new twists. What does distinguish the Bush administration is the clarity and aggressiveness with which it has put forth its goal of maintaining U.S. domination internationally. The "Bush Doctrine" that the administration has articulated claims legitimacy for pre-emptive action against those who might threaten U.S. interests, and it is clear from the statement of that doctrine in last September's issuance of *The National Security Strategy of the United States of America* that "U.S. interests" includes economic interests.

The economic story is never the whole story, and oil is never the whole economic story. In the particular application of U.S. power, numerous strategic and political considerations come into play. With the application of the Bush Doctrine in the case of Iraq, the especially heinous character of the Hussein regime is certainly a factor, as is the regime's history of conflict with other nations of the region (at times with U.S. support) and its apparent efforts at developing nuclear, chemical, and biological weapons; certainly the weakness of the Iraqi military also affects the U.S. government's willingness to go to war. Yet, as September's *Security Strategy* document makes clear, the U.S. government is concerned with domination and a major factor driving that goal of domination is economic. In the Middle East, Iraq and elsewhere, oil—or, more precisely, the profit from oil—looms large in the picture. ❏

An earlier version of this article was prepared for the newsletter of the Joiner Center for War and Social Consequences at the University of Massachusetts-Boston. This article was originally prepared largely before the start of the war on Iraq.

Chapter 10

NATURAL RESOURCES AND THE ENVIRONMENT

Article 10.1

THE BATTLE OVER THE FOOD SYSTEM

BY ELIZABETH FRASER AND ANURADHA MITTAL
March/April 2015

For most of history, farmers have had control over their seeds: saving, sharing, and replanting them with freedom. Developments in the course of the 20th century, however, have greatly eroded this autonomy. Legal changes, ranging from the Plant Variety Protection Act (1970) in the United States to the World Trade Organization's Agreement on Trade-Related Aspects of Intellectual Property Rights (TRIPS), have systematically eroded farmers' rights to save seeds for future use. By the end of 2012, Monsanto had sued 410 farmers and 56 small farm businesses in the United States for patent infringement, winning over $23 million in settlements. Here, we describe some of the key developments further intensifying corporate control over the food system. It is not, however, all bleak news. Civil society groups are using everything from grassroots protest to open-source licensing to ensure that the enclosure and privatization of seeds comes to an end.

Corporations Have Consolidated Their Control

In 2011, just four transnational agri-businesses—Monsanto, Dupont Pioneer, Syngenta, and Vilmorin (Groupe Limagrain)—controlled 58% of the commercial seed market. Four—Syngenta, Bayer CropScience, BASF, and Dow AgroSciences—controlled 62% of agrochemicals worldwide. The top six companies controlled 75% of all private plant breeding research, 60% of commercial seed sales, and 76% of the global agrochemical market. This consolidation of power has been aided by a large string of mergers and acquisitions, leading the Canada-based Action Group on Erosion, Technology and Concentration (ETC Group) to conclude that "there just aren't many seed companies left to buy."

The World Bank, too, has played a role in this increased consolidation. In 2014, a report from the Oakland Institute provided details on the World Bank's efforts to open African markets to private seed companies. (Full disclosure: The authors of this article both work at the Oakland Institute.) The report, titled "The World Bank's Bad Business with Seed and Fertilizer in African Agriculture," paints a stark picture of the possible consequences of these actions: removing farmers' rights to save seeds and implementing intellectual property claims over seeds does not improve food security, but rather undermines farmers' autonomy and further increases profits for the existing seed oligopoly.

Supposed Benefits of Genetically Modified Seeds Have Not Materialized

Two arguments often put forward in favor of genetically modified (GM) seeds are the need to feed the world's burgeoning population and the potential for these new seeds to reduce overall pesticide use. Neither of these claims promulgated by industry have proved true. Globally, we are currently producing more than enough food to adequately feed our population. However, that food isn't being distributed fairly, and malnutrition remains staggering—805 million people worldwide. As the Canadian Biodiversity Action Network reminds us in its report "Will GM Crops Feed the World?" hunger is not usually a result of low food production, but rather a result of poverty. This points to a greater need to address issues of inequality, distribution, and access.

Arguments that genetically modified crops could reduce overall agrochemical use also remain unfounded, with the rise of herbicide-resistant weeds requiring more and more chemical cocktails for the GM crops to remain productive. A report from Food and Water Watch, "Superweeds: How Biotech Crops Bolster the Pesticide Industry," notes that herbicide use on GM crops in the United States did initially fall in the late 1990s; however, once resistance in GM crops to the herbicide glyphosate (marketed by Monsanto under the trade name "RoundUp") developed, total herbicide use skyrocketed, leading to greater net herbicide use over time.

Large Agribusinesses Fight Labelling Ballot Measures

In the past few years, large agribusinesses have worked to defeat numerous U.S. state ballot measures intended to enforce the labelling of GM foods. Of the $46 million spent to defeat an anti-GM labelling campaign in the state of California in 2013, over $8 million came from Monsanto alone. Ballot measures in Washington State (2012), Colorado (2014), and Oregon (2014) met similar fates, with large agribusinesses outspending pro-labelling campaigns by a wide margin. In Vermont, state legislation to enforce GM labelling was approved in mid-2014 and is scheduled to come into force in early 2016. However, the Grocery Manufacturers Association (supported by corporations including Monsanto, Coca-Cola, and Starbucks) is now suing the state, alleging that the law would violate the U.S. Constitution in various ways. This further demonstrates the power wielded by large agribusinesses, even in the face of widespread consumer (and legislative) pressure.

Activists Develop New "Open Source" Options for Seeds

One positive development is the April 2014 launch of the Open Source Seed Initiative (OSSI), a group "dedicated to maintaining fair and open access to plant genetic resources worldwide." Jack Kloppenburg, a member of OSSI's board of directors, has written extensively about the potential modification of open-source licensing (which is used widely in software development, and led to the development of Linux, the vastly popular operating system) to seeds and other plant materials. Kloppenburg advocates a new type of plant licensing that makes plant materials a) widely available, b) modifiable by any actor, and c) distributable provided the same terms of the original license carry forward. These principles mirror those developed by the open-source technology movement, and it is anticipated that these licenses will lead to the creation of a "protected commons"—preventing the patenting of this material in the future. While the group is far from challenging the agribusiness seed cartel, initiatives like this are beginning to provide a way to legally protect plant genetic material from corporate capture.

Resistance to GM Crops Has Increased

The mobilization against the use of GM crops has gained momentum in recent years. In 2013, the global "March Against Monsanto" was estimated to have brought over two million citizens to the streets, across six continents, 52 nations, and 48 states of the United States. After an extended period of protests, anti-GM protesters celebrated a victory in 2014, when the Chilean government withdrew a bill that would have allowed large agribusinesses like Monsanto to patent seeds in the country. (With falling demand for GM seeds in South America, Monsanto's profits fell 34%, according to the company's most recent quarterly report. Whether the falling demand was a result of global resistance, falling corn prices, or both is unclear.)

Mexico imposed a ban on genetically modified corn in 2013, days after worldwide protests against Monsanto and the whole genetically modified organism (GMO) industry. This made Mexico a key front in the global battle against corporate giants that bring in GMOs and "genetic pollution"—the transfer of GMO genetic codes into other plants (as by cross-pollination). Last year, a Mexican judge revoked Monsanto's planting permit, which had allowed the company to sow more than 253,000 hectares of land across seven states. The ruling followed complaints from beekeepers in the state of Yucatán that Monsanto's planned planting of GM soybeans, made to withstand RoundUp, would decimate the bee population and demolish the honey industry.

China has maintained a strong stance against GM products, leading to lawsuits against seed companies like Syngenta, which released a GM seed variety to farmers before it had been approved in the country. While China has recently begun approving more GM seed and crop varieties, mandatory labelling laws also look likely to pass.

What Do These Developments Demonstrate?

On one hand, our global food system continues to be dominated by agribusiness giants, who use their power to quash legislation designed to protect consumer and farmer interests, with little demonstration of the benefits of their genetically modified products. At the same time, despite the power wielded by corporations, resistance is growing. In many cases, agribusiness has met this resistance with outspending and overwhelming legal challenges. But in countries like Chile and Mexico, victories have been won, and promising new alternatives like the Open Source Seed Initiative are creating new ways of protecting plant material going forward. The growing awareness of and mobilization against the corporatization of food cannot be denied. Movements around organic standards, Fair Trade, farmers' markets, and community supported agriculture have made huge gains over the last ten years. The next ten years have to build on these successes to reclaim seed sovereignty, to challenge the power of agribusinesses over our land and food system, and to increase popular engagement, advocating for the health of our planet and our food. ❑

Sources: Center for Food Safety and Save Our Seeds, "Seed Giants vs. U.S. Farmers," 2013 (centerforfoodsafety.org); ETC Group, "Putting the Cartel before the Horse ...and Farm, Seeds, Soil, Peasants, etc.: Who Will Control Agricultural Inputs, 2013?" September 2013 (etcgroup. org); Anuradha Mittal and Haley F. Kaplan, with Alice Martin-Prével and Frédéric Mousseau, "The World Bank's Bad Business with Seed and Fertilizer in African Agriculture," The Oakland Institute, 2014 (oaklandinstitute.org); Canadian Biotechnology Action Network (CBAN), "Will GM Crops Feed the World?" October 2014 (cban.ca); Global Food Politics, "Agricultural Biotechnology and the Use of Herbicides in US Agriculture," Dec. 1, 2013 (globalfoodpolitics.wordpress.com); Evan Fraser, "10 Things You Need to Know About the Global Food System," *The Guardian* (theguardian. com); Food and Water Watch, "Superweeds: How Biotech Crops Bolster the Pesticide Industry," July 2013 (foodandwaterwatch.org); Andrew Pollack, "After Loss, the Fight to Label Modified Food Continues," *New York Times*, Nov. 7, 2012 (nytimes.com); Luke Runyon, "Colorado, Oregon Reject GMO Labeling," NPR, Nov. 5, 2014 (npr.org); Peter Moskowitz, "In GMO labeling fight, all eyes on Vermont," Aljazeera America, Dec. 1, 2014 (america.aljazeera.com); Open Source Seed Initiative (opensourceseedinitiative.org); "Challenging Monsanto: Over two million march the streets of 436 cities, 52 countries," RT, May 24, 2013 (rt.com); Andrea Germanos, "'Monsanto Law' Brings Uproar to Chile," Common Dreams, Aug. 19, 2013 (commondreams.org); Belinda Torres-Leclercq, "Government Withdraws Controversial 'Monsanto Law' from Congress," *Santiago Times*, March 18, 2014 (santiagotimes.cl); "Monsanto Earnings Fall 34% After a Year of Global Protests," *The Guardian*, Jan. 7, 2014 (theguardian.com); *The Global Diary*, "China's Hard Line on Biotech Burns US Hay," Dec. 15, 2014 (theglobaldiary.com); "Syngenta Facing Dozens of Lawsuits Over GMO Seed," Nov. 18, 2014 (thonline.com); Zhang Yi and Zhong Nan, "Mandatory GM Food Labeling a Step Closer," *China Daily*, Dec. 23, 2014 (chinadaily.com).

Article 10.2

IS THE UNITED STATES A POLLUTION HAVEN?

BY FRANK ACKERMAN
March/April 2003

When this article was originally written, the North American Free Trade Agreement (NAFTA) was nearly a decade old, and many of its main effects were already apparent. One of these was the devastating impact of U.S. corn exports on Mexican small-farmer agriculture. As productive as Mexico's small farmers are, they have been not been able to compete with low-priced corn produced on the United States' gigantic, "super-mechanized" farms using the most petroleum- and chemical-intensive methods. Although some numbers and details have changed since this article was written, more recent findings bear out the continuing heavy toll on Mexican farmers. Researcher Timothy A. Wise points to U.S. agricultural subsidies, permitted under NAFTA, as a cause of U.S. producers' export "dumping" (sales a less than cost of production) in Mexico. This has not only cost Mexican farmers about a billion dollars a year (with the largest impact on corn farmers), but also helped turn Mexico into a large importer of corn. Recent spikes in corn prices, due to the promotion of corn-based ethanol as an alternative motor fuel, have inflicted a heavy blow on low-income Mexicans for whom corn is a staple food. Meanwhile, the environmental impacts of chemical-intensive agriculture in the United States remain serious—with agricultural runoff as a top source of water pollution. —Eds.

Sources: Timothy A. Wise, "Agricultural Dumping Under NAFTA," Woodrow Wilson International Center for Scholars, 2010; Timothy A. Wise, "The Cost to Mexico of U.S. Corn Ethanol Expansion," GDAE Working Paper 12-0, May 2012; Environmental Protection Agency (EPA), Water Quality Assessment and Total Maximum Daily Loads Information (epa.gov/waters/ir/).

Free trade, according to its critics, runs the risk of creating pollution havens—countries where lax environmental standards allow dirty industries to expand. Poor countries are the usual suspects; perhaps poverty drives them to desperate strategies, such as specializing in the most polluting industries.

But could the United States be a pollution haven? A look at agriculture under NAFTA, particularly the trade in corn, suggests that at least one polluting industry is thriving in the United States as a result of free trade.

In narrow economic terms, the United States is winning the corn market. U.S. corn exports to Mexico have doubled since 1994, NAFTA's first year, to more than five million tons annually. Cheap U.S. corn is undermining traditional production in Mexico; prices there have dropped 27% in just a few years, and a quarter of the corn consumed in Mexico is now grown in the United States. But in environmental terms, the U.S. victory comes at a great cost.

While the United States may not have more lax environmental *standards* than Mexico, when it comes to corn U.S. agriculture certainly uses more polluting *methods.* As it is grown in the United States, corn requires significantly more chemicals per acre than wheat or soybeans, the other two leading field crops. Runoff of excess nitrogen fertilizer causes water pollution, and has created a huge "dead zone" in the Gulf of Mexico around the mouth of the Mississippi River. Intensive application of toxic herbicides and insecticides threatens the health of farm workers, farming communities, and consumers. Genetically modified corn, which now accounts for about one-fifth of U.S. production, poses unknown long-term risks to consumers and to ecosystems.

Growing corn in very dry areas, where irrigation is required, causes more environmental problems. The United States also has a higher percentage of irrigated acreage than Mexico. While the traditional Corn Belt enjoys ample rainfall and does not need irrigation, 15% of U.S. corn acreage—almost all of it in Nebraska, Kansas, the Texas panhandle, and eastern Colorado—is now irrigated. These areas draw water from the Ogallala aquifer, a gigantic underground reservoir, much faster than the aquifer naturally refills. If present rates of overuse continue, the Ogallala, which now contains as much fresh water as Lake Huron, will be drained down to unusable levels within a few decades, causing a crisis for the huge areas of the plains states that depend on it for water supplies. Government subsidies, in years past, helped farmers buy the equipment needed to pump water out of the Ogallala, contributing to the impending crisis.

Moreover, the corn borer, a leading insect pest that likes to eat corn plants, flourishes best in dry climates. Thus the "irrigation states," particularly Texas and Colorado, are the hardest hit by corn borers. Corn growers in dry states have the greatest need for insecticides; they also have the greatest motivation to use genetically modified corn, which is designed to repel corn borers.

Sales to Mexico are particularly important to the United States because many countries are refusing to accept genetically modified corn. Europe no longer imports U.S. corn for this reason, and Japan and several East Asian countries may follow suit. Mexico prohibits growing genetically modified corn, but still allows it to be imported; it is one of the largest remaining markets where U.S. exports are not challenged on this issue.

Despite Mexico's ban, genetically modified corn was recently found growing in a remote rural area in the southern state of Oaxaca. As the ancestral home of corn, Mexico possesses a unique and irreplaceable genetic diversity. Although the extent of the problem is still uncertain, the unplanned and uncontrolled spread of artificially engineered plants from the United States could potentially contaminate Mexico's numerous naturally occurring corn varieties.

An even greater threat is the economic impact of cheap U.S. imports on peasant farmers and rural communities. Traditional farming practices, evolved over thousands of years, use combinations of different natural varieties of corn carefully matched to local conditions. Lose these traditions, and we will lose a living reservoir of biodiversity in the country of origin of one of the world's most important food grains.

The United States has won the North American corn market. But the cost looks increasingly unbearable when viewed through the lens of the U.S. environment, or of Mexico's biodiversity. ❑

Article 10.3

DO LOCAVORES HAVE A DILEMMA?
Economists debate the local food movement.

BY ANITA DANCS AND HELEN SCHARBER
July/August 2015

Food produced on small farms close to where it is consumed—or "local food" for short—accounts for only about 2% of all the food produced in the United States today, but demand for it is growing rapidly. According to the U.S. Department of Agriculture, sales of food going directly from farmers' fields to consumer's kitchens have more than tripled in the past twenty years. During the same period, the number of farmers' markets in the United States has quintupled, and it's increasingly easy to talk about "CSAs"—community-supported agriculture operations where consumers pay up front for a share in the season's output—without explaining the acronym. The National Restaurant Association's "What's Hot" Chef Survey found that locally sourced meats and locally grown produce were the top two trends reported by chefs in 2014, followed by environmental sustainability.

But as local food has grown, so have the number of critics who claim that locavores have a dilemma. The dilemma, prominently argued by Pierre Desrochers and Hiroko Shimizu in their 2012 book *The Locavore's Dilemma: In Praise of the 10,000-mile Diet*, is that local food conflicts with the goal of feeding more people better food in an ecologically sustainable way. In other words, well-meaning locavores are inadvertently promoting a future characterized by less food security and greater environmental destruction. The critics are typically academics, and while not all of them are economists, they rely on economic arguments to support their claims that the globalized food chain has improved our lives.

Why are critics pessimistic about the trend toward local food? Their arguments hinge on what we call the CASTE paradigm—the idea that Comparative Advantage and economies of Scale justify global Trade and lead to greater Efficiency (see sidebar).

Does Local Spinach Create Jobs?

Advocates of local food provide a host of reasons for its superiority, including its economic benefits. The mechanism for creating these benefits is what economists call the "multiplier effect": A dollar spent on local food results in a local farmer spending part of that dollar on other goods and services in the local economy, creating a virtuous circle of wealth and jobs. Despite clear evidence of the multiplier effect, critics argue that more wealth could be created overall through specialization and trade, because food can be grown with fewer resources, which frees up resources for creating wealth elsewhere.

In his 2008 article "Should We Buy Only Locally Grown Produce?" for the Ludwig von Mises Institute, economist Art Carden tries to illustrate the potential

The CASTE Paradigm

Efficiency, or maximizing benefits relative to costs, is the guiding principle in most economic analysis. For the critics, local food simply cannot be efficient because it does not take advantage of what we are calling "CASTE"—the idea that Comparative Advantage and economies of Scale justify global Trade and lead to greater Efficiency.

The theory of **comparative advantage**, developed by economist David Ricardo in the 19th century, says that because regions have different relative advantages in production, they should produce the goods and services that can be produced at the lowest opportunity cost. Even the best use of a resource—land, capital, time, labor—has an opportunity cost, which is the benefit that would have been gained from the next best use. Land devoted to growing food, for example, has a lower opportunity cost in Iowa than in New York City, since land in New York City is highly valued for office space or housing. So Iowa grows corn, this line of argument goes, because the alternatives are simply not as profitable to the owners of the land. As a rule, CASTE critics assert that food should be grown where it has the lowest opportunity cost, in places that tend *not* to be close to most potential consumers.

The concept of **economies of scale** suggests that larger farms can make more efficient use of modern-day farming methods than smaller ones. Someone cultivating an acre or two of rooftop garden in New York City, for example, cannot take advantage of the large tractors, harvesters and irrigation systems that can quickly plow, sow, fertilize and harvest a thousand acres of crops. Economies of scale help explain why the price of a bushel of corn is currently around $4, a price that might not be achievable by small farms producing diversified crops.

Taken together, the assumptions of comparative advantage and economies of scale lead to the conclusion that regions should specialize and **trade**. If Iowa's comparative advantage in corn production along with economies of scale in farm size allow it to produce corn more cheaply than other regions, economists say, it should specialize in corn and trade for other goods and services. New York City residents benefit from the inexpensively produced corn, and resources are freed up to use their land, labor, and capital to produce other goods. The idea that comparative advantage, economies of scale, and trade leads to the greatest **efficiency**—which we call the "CASTE" paradigm—is the foundation upon which modern economic thought has been built, and the critique of local food is just one recent example of how it has been applied.

consequences of producing spinach locally in an area lacking comparative advantage in spinach production: "[T]he cultivation of spinach in Memphis will require more fertilizer, more rakes, more tillers, and more hoes than the cultivation of spinach in California." Failing to exploit comparative advantage in food production, he concludes, "is, at its logical limit, a prescription for poverty and starvation."

In a 2010 blog post cheekily titled "Loco-vores," economist Steve Landsberg asks, "How can we possibly gather enough information to ... reach a conclusion about which tomato imposes the fewest costs on our neighbors?" His response to the question is simple: the price. For Landsberg and other critics, the higher-priced local tomato signals higher opportunity costs from not exploiting regional advantages in land, labor, and other resources and not taking advantage of economies of scale offered by large global farms. In effect, goes the argument, we are all poorer by paying the higher prices of local spinach and tomatoes, since those higher prices eat into our ability to buy other goods and services.

Are Local Tomatoes Environmentally Destructive?

Local food does not only undermine economic efficiency, according to critics. The same CASTE concepts (see sidebar) are used to argue against its supposed benefits in terms of environmental protection. Locavores have argued that transporting food long distances is bad environmental behavior and that reducing "food miles" is an important reason for buying local food. Critics point out that since food transport accounts for less than 5% of the carbon emissions embodied in food in the United States, it is better to exploit comparative advantage in growing conditions—reducing the use of land, water, chemicals, and energy—and engage in long-distance trade. For example, growing tomatoes in the UK reportedly produces three times the greenhouse gas emissions associated with importing them from Spain, since the extra energy and fertilizer required for greenhouse-grown tomatoes overwhelms the emissions savings from reduced transport. Further, individual car trips to farmers markets may cause more pollution than shipping large quantities of food via trucks or ships, which take advantage of economies of scale in transport.

The critics' environmental arguments go beyond debates over the importance of food miles. Economist Edward Glaeser, in a critique of the trend toward urban farming, estimates that urban population densities would need to be cut in half if just 7% of existing agricultural land were relocated to metro areas. Since lower population densities would lead to longer commutes, he argues that urban farming will increase rather than cut carbon emissions. In his book *Just Food*, agricultural historian James E. McWilliams argues that local food systems in water-scarce cities like Las Vegas and Santa Fe could only be created "through costly and environmentally damaging irrigation projects." Tyler Cowen, author of *An Economist Gets Lunch*, points to the failed Saudi wheat growing experiment in the 1980s that wasted hundreds of billions of cubic meters of water. According to Cowen, the international price of wheat at the time was $120 per ton while Saudi wheat, reflecting these high resource requirements, cost $500 per ton to produce. In sum, food grown in accordance with the principles of comparative advantage and economies of scale should save resources and reduce carbon emissions, all with the added upside of lower consumer prices.

Does That Local Squash Taste Better?

Surely, though, the critics would have a hard time using the CASTE paradigm to argue that global food tastes better than fresh, local food, right? Indeed, journalist

Stephen Budiansky, whose main argument in his *New York Times* editorial "Math Lessons for Locavores" is that local food is inefficient, concedes the "pleasures and advantages to the palate and the spirit of eating what's local, fresh and in season." Yet, he notes, shorter food-supply chains do not deliver fresh fruits and vegetables in the middle of winter to most people. According to agricultural economist Jaysen Lusk in his 2013 book *The Food Police*, if the choice is fresh peaches from afar or nothing but squash all winter, his preference is clear: it's peaches. Other critics believe it is clear that relying more heavily on local food would lead to a less nutritious diet. Steven Sexton, an agricultural economist and author of several articles critiquing local food, argues that because there is a correlation between income, on one hand, and the consumption of fresh fruits and vegetables, on the other, the higher prices of local food would make consumers poorer and more reliant on unhealthy food.

In the view of locavores, shorter food supply chains and agricultural diversification also promise increased food security in the face of environmental change, political instability, and speculation in global markets. Not surprisingly, critics question these propositions as well. Economists suggest that exploiting a region's comparative advantage in food production through specialization, and taking advantage of economies of scale, is the only way to efficiently feed the nine to ten billion people we can expect to inhabit the planet by 2050. In addition, specialization and trade is billed as a way to reduce geographic-specific risks, in the face of environmental and political change. Desrochers and Shimizu remind us that "subsistence farmers periodically starve" and when "they escape famine, it is typically because relief efforts were able to deliver the products of large-scale monocultures grown in distant lands."

Do We Need More CASTE?

While critics argue that a sustainable and food-secure future requires a more thorough application of the CASTE paradigm, actual evidence that a sustainable food system requires increasing reliance on comparative advantage and economies of scale seems to be lacking. Economies of scale undeniably exist with respect to various inputs to agricultural production, but the concept is not synonymous with "bigger is better." A 2013 U.S. Department of Agriculture report praising the trend toward industrial farming and long-distance trade nonetheless noted that "most economists are skeptical that scale economies usefully explain increased farm sizes" partly because "crop production still covers a wide range of viable farm sizes."

Comparative advantage based on climatic and soil conditions also exists, but the anti-locavore literature presents little evidence that cost reductions are mainly brought about through natural sources of comparative advantage. Carden's claim that spinach is better grown in California than in Memphis should come with a footnote, since California's supposed comparative advantage in spinach production is made possible by federally subsidized, imported irrigation water. As we witness the unfolding

The Marginal Benefit of Marginal Thinking

The extent of problems in the food system would certainly seem to require a big shift, but economic analysis tends to focus on "marginal" changes—small, incremental changes at the margins, like whether or not to cultivate one more acre of land, or whether or not to employ one more worker—to the exclusion of more systemic ones. This tendency is rooted in the desire of 19th-century economists to mathematically formalize economics principles. It may seem logical for a farmer to only decide to farm an acre of marginal land if the additional revenue gained is greater than the additional costs. But this logic has had substantive effects on the questions economists ask, the problems they identify, and the solutions they propose.

To show how "marginal thinking" affects the local food debate, we can point to a study by agricultural economist Steven Sexton. He constructs what might be a useful low-tech study to estimate the land and inputs needed to grow more food locally, but he underpins his research with "marginalist" assumptions. Specifically, he calculates the resources that would be needed to produce corn, soy, and dairy in the *same* amounts and using the *same* methods that the United States currently does, with only a shift toward more local production. He finds that the shift would require more land and other resources. This hypothetical example assumes that the only change is where production happens and does not alter any other component of either the production methods or the products which are grown.

Most advocates for agricultural alternatives, however, are not seeking to reproduce the existing food system, just closer to where they live; they believe systemic changes are needed. Yet, the dominance of marginal thinking among economists prevents them from even considering systemic changes .

drought crisis in California, it is hard to maintain that society benefits from growing so much spinach (or other water-intensive crops, like almonds) in the state.

Other important reasons for lower costs of food production may appear to be the result of comparative advantage, but instead highlight inequities in the food system. Florida's access to low-wage tomato pickers, for example, results in lower prices at American supermarkets—but these sources of comparative advantage are conspicuously absent from the critics' examples.

Locavores may also fault the CASTE paradigm for excessive "tradeoff thinking," which assumes any cost can be offset by any benefit. The assumption that all benefits (food, good soil, happiness) and all costs (inputs, pollution, psychological distress) might be measured and weighed against one another to make efficient decisions betrays the utilitarian philosophical basis of economics. It may seem like a reasonable way to make many decisions, but it is only one approach to making value judgments. Many ecological economists, for example, believe that ecosystem limits cannot be ignored and are not simply costs that can be traded off against monetary benefits. For instance, we may decide that four degrees of warming would lead to an unacceptable amount of climate disruption, whether or not economists believed that the benefits of the associated fossil fuel use outweigh its costs.

Even for those who agree that weighing benefits against costs is a reasonable way to make decisions, in practice, and in the local food critiques in particular, benefits and costs that do not have market values are often ignored. In particular, the critics fail to take many external costs—those that producers and consumers impose on third parties, and are therefore not reflected in market prices—into account. These authors observe that the bulk of the environmental impacts from agriculture come from the production phase but only use this observation in discussing the merits of comparative advantage. They do not critically examine production practices that routinely poison farmworkers, deplete soil nutrients, destroy rural communities, breed herbicide-resistant weeds, impoverish farmers, and contaminate waterways destroying marine life and biodiversity.

Finally, the role of power in the food system is conspicuously absent from the CASTE analysis. Its absence is not surprising; power is a concept that does not fit easily into a framework focusing on the freedom of autonomous and equal individuals to make utility-maximizing decisions. In that framework, the market is simply an institution that coordinates production and distribution decisions through its near-magical capacity to gather information about consumers' preferences and producers' costs. Yet, looking through the conceptual lens of power relations—between agribusiness and contract farmers, farm owners and farmworkers, food corporations and low-income consumers, the government and immigrant workers—gives us a clearer picture of who determines what costs and benefits are created in the food system and how these costs and benefits are distributed. Paying attention to power allows for the possibility that the falling food prices attributed to comparative advantage and economies of scale may be related, instead, to the ability of the powerful to offload social and environmental costs onto the relatively powerless.

Buy Local? Why Local?

As the near absence of power in the CASTE analysis indicates, much of the disagreement between local food supporters and these critics can be chalked up to differences in the values underlying them. Most economists value efficiency above all else and believe that uncertain social and environmental costs can be traded off against other benefits. Meanwhile, locavores have different end goals—providing enough food for all and creating more resilient local economies while staying within ecological limits. So these groups, of course, tend to talk past each other. Yet both the CASTE analysis and its shortcomings suggest some items for a locavore's "to do" list, including acknowledging the real benefits the existing food system provides, understanding how power affects who receives these benefits, and realizing the political changes needed to make sure the food system benefits everyone.

Local Food or a Just and Sustainable Food System?

For most locavores, the impulse to "buy local" is rooted in the desire to reject the ailing industrial food system and to feel a greater connection to how food is grown. With its emphasis on location and scale, however, the locavore movement can unintentionally confuse its means—local and small-scale—with the end goal of building a better food system. But what would a better food system look like? Though different communities will have different priorities, some goals common to local food movement might include

- Healthy people: The food system should provide safe, healthy food that nurtures people's bodies and minds.
- Accessibility: A wide variety of healthy food must be available to rich and poor alike.
- Decent work: The food system should ensure safe jobs and living wages for everyone working in it, including people working on farms, in food processing plants, and in stores and restaurants.
- Healthy ecosystems: Food should be grown and processed using less fossil fuel and fewer petrochemical fertilizers and pesticides, to prevent excess air and water pollution. A regenerative food system can help improve the quality of soil, water, and air.

Importantly, each of these goals must be placed ahead of profits. Keeping in mind such values and goals, which are at the root of "buy local"" campaigns, is important both so that we can monitor progress toward them and remain open-minded about how to achieve them.

Overlooking pressing social justice and ecological problems in the food system when making efficiency judgments, as economists have done, is not a balanced approach. The argument that local food activists have downplayed the benefits of the existing food system, however, is worth addressing. Many people do enjoy the diversity of foods that are now available year-round. Consumers in the northern United States are reluctant to give up citrus fruits and juices produced in the south, and many consumers desire fresh over preserved foods. Nutrition and lifespans have improved, thanks in part to increased food access. Likewise, because of inequalities—perpetuated, to be sure, by the system that allows agribusiness giants to profit year after year—higher-priced food would make food even more inaccessible to the nearly one in six Americans that is already food insecure.

It's possible to acknowledge the benefits of the existing industrialized food system without concluding, as the authors we have reviewed often do, that this is the best we can hope for. It's also possible to acknowledge these benefits while understanding that, in many cases, they are possible only because of costs imposed on already vulnerable groups of people. Only by having a clear view of who wins and who loses can we make informed, collective decisions that do not alienate or ignore important segments of the community.

These decisions to improve our food system will not likely come about purely through the market. Ironically, many locavores voice their preferences for a fair and sustainable food system mainly by exercising the consumer sovereignty that mainstream economists claim is the most important benefit of markets. Yet, simply "voting with our dollars" will not be enough to transform the current food system into a sustainable one. Even if the next twenty years brings another tripling of direct farm-to-consumer sales, local food will still be a sapling in the forest of big food. Knowing the farmers that grow your food may be worthwhile, but it's not enough.

Some changes that might not seem to have much to do with food at all can, in fact, contribute to building a just and sustainable food system. Environmental policies such as carbon and pollution taxes can help the prices of products come closer to reflecting their true social costs and provide incentives for more sustainable practices. Meanwhile, subsidies for renewable energy can help reduce the carbon footprint of food production and distribution. Such policies must be paired with others that address inequality, so that no one is forced to decide between buying healthy food and paying other bills. Expanding the SNAP program (formerly known as food stamps), raising the minimum wage, and increasing the earned income tax credit can all help increase food access, as can loftier goals like increasing top tax rates, guaranteeing jobs for all, and providing basic income guarantees. Shorter workweeks paired with good wages and benefits can also help move us toward a healthier food system, since many people simply do not have time to engage in food preparation or even learn what is in their food. These goals may not be easy to achieve, but because they can help improve the lives of so many people, they have the power to unite locavores with other social movements. By moving beyond the notion of shopping our way to a better world and embracing the wider set of changes necessary to increase social justice, locavores can help resolve dilemmas in the food system and beyond. ❑

Sources: Stephan Budiansky, Math lessons for locavores, *New York Times*, Aug. 19, 2010 (nytimes. com); Art Carden, "Should we buy only locally grown produce?", Ludwig von Mises Institute, July 15, 2008 (mises.org); Tyler Cowen, *An Economist Gets Lunch: New Rules for Everyday Foodies* (Dutton Adult, 2012); Pierre Desrochers and Hiroko Shimizu, *The Locavore's Dilemma: In Praise of the 10,000-Mile Diet* (Public Affairs, 2012); Edward Glaeser, "The Locavore's Dilemma: Urban Farms Do More Harm Than Good to the Environment," *Boston Globe*, June 16, 2011 (boston. com); Steve Landsburg, "Loco-vores," The Big Questions, August 23, 2010 (thebigquestions. com); Jaysen Lusk, *The Food Police: A Well-Fed Manifesto About the Politics of Your Plate* (Crown Publishing Group, 2013); James MacDonald, Penni Korb, and Robert Hoppe, "Farm Size and the Organization of U.S. Crop Farming," Economic Research Report No. 152, USDA Economic Research Service, 2013; James E. McWilliams, *Just Food: Where Locavores Get It Wrong and How We Can Truly Eat Responsibly* (Little, Brown and Company, 2009); National Restaurant Association, "What's Hot: 2015 Culinary Forecast, Dec. 3, 2014 (restaurant.org); David Ricardo, *The Principles of Political Economy and Taxation* (J. M. Dent & Sons, Ltd., 1973 [1817]); Steven Sexton, "Does local production improve environment and health outcomes?", ARE Updates 13: 5–8, 2009;Paul Watkiss, et al., *The Validity of Food Miles as an Indicator of Sustainable Development*, REPORT ED50254. London, UK: Department of Environment, Food and Rural Affairs, 2005.

Article 10.4

WHY SOME LEADERS IN POORER COUNTIRES ARE CHAMPIONING THE ENVIRONMENT

BY ROBIN BROAD AND JOHN CAVANAGH
July 2015; Triple Crisis Blog

We have heard surprise expressed that two religious leaders from poorer countries, Pope Francis from Argentina and Cardinal Turskon from Ghana, have emerged as leading voices for action on the environment with their compelling June 2015 encyclical. The surprise comes from the assumption that poorer countries invariably prioritize economic growth and financial revenues—not the environment—and that only when beyond a certain threshold of per capita income do they shift priorities and take action in favor of the environment. As many readers know, this theory that only richer people in richer countries care about the environment is what some call the Environmental Kuznets Curve or the post-materialist hypothesis.

Our research on decisive action to protect the environment in El Salvador and Costa Rica suggests that this stereotype is outdated and the theory wrong. We zeroed in on El Salvador and Costa Rica because both have halted potentially lucrative metallic mining within the last decade due to its negative environmental impact.

In our new article in the journal *World Development*, we ask "why did these two governments do this?" Our goal now is to share our answers to that question. We posit three conditions under which governments of poorer countries take action to protect the environment, at times sacrificing large-scale financial gain:

(1) The first condition is related to civil society: Poorer people, whose natural resource base is threatened by mining, can move from individual awareness to concern, to become organized, and then to engage with other sectors of civil society in pressuring their government to implement policy changes. This involves a combination of poorer people who have lived in the area long enough to grasp the environmental damage, with other segments of domestic civil society providing additional support and voice. Organizing begins locally in the mining areas but moves to a national level, putting pressure on governments.

(2) The second condition is related to domestic business elites: In our case studies, we find that segments of the domestic economic elite who have interests based in protecting natural resources are more powerful than the elite and corporate interests that benefit from exploiting minerals. The power of global corporations is not strong enough, or is not connected enough to local economic elites, to change this calculus. Thus, foreign mining firms that want to mine often move from the national level (where they have not been successful) into the global arena, where they sue the governments under investment agreements and investor-state dispute structures.

(3) The third condition is related to governments: We find that individuals and agencies within democratic governments who are willing and able not only to respond to civil society, but also to understand the ecological realities of natural-resource exploitation, can play a central role. We also find that far-sighted political leaders or bureaucrats, regardless of their party's politics, who come into office with either an understanding of environmental issues or a willingness to listen to non-governmental experts, can also become catalysts.

In both Salvadoran and Costa Rican mining policy, all three of these conditions came into play and reinforced one another, leading to decisive government action to halt environmentally destructive mining. In both countries, there was strong local citizen opposition to mining that combined with other civil society actors to form powerful national movements against mining. In El Salvador, rural farmers and communities provided the initial spark, with the church playing a significant integral role. In Costa Rica, rural communities were crucial, but urban environmentalists played an important role, as did academics and the media.

In terms of the business sector: in both countries, local and national business interests collectively had more to lose than gain from industrial mining and its ensuing environmental damage. In El Salvador, the farming and tourism sectors need water that mining seemed likely to further contaminate. The economic elites connected to these sectors were more numerous and powerful than local businesses that would benefit from foreign mining companies gaining mining concessions. In Costa Rica, the many sectors that benefit from eco-tourism (and agriculture) are similarly more numerous and powerful than the relatively small mining sector.

As for government, in both countries, at different times, there were key individuals and sometimes whole agencies within government who spoke out or took action against mining.

Comparing the influence of the three conditions: The first two conditions, strong civil society and weak pro-mining domestic business elites, seem particularly important since the recent histories of both El Salvador and Costa Rica reveal much more variation within key government agencies during the period in question. In El Salvador, even a relatively corrupt and pro-foreign business administration such as Antonio Saca's (2004-2009) could take action against gold mining given the country's strong civil society and weak pro-mining national business elites in the context of the country's extreme environmental degradation. In this case, individuals in the Saca government did indeed make a difference. And, in Costa Rica, there is the two-year period of 2008-2010 when, even with strong civil society, weak pro-mining national business elites, and a democratic government, the administration of Óscar Arias (who one might have assumed to be more pro-environment than the Saca administration) gave permission for Canadian firm Infinito Gold to mine at a very controversial site. Yet, even in this instance, a strong civil society and an independent Supreme Court eventually overturned Arias's pro-mining policies and stopped Infinito's mining.

The key point is that these two governments halted environmentally destructive gold mining even though both are relatively poor, small countries which would, according to conventional theory, choose short-term economic gains over longer-term environmental concerns.

Based on this work, we were not at all surprised that it was two religious leaders from poorer countries who have emerged as among the most vocal voices for action on environment (including climate). ❏

Sources: Robin Broad, "The Poor and the Environment: Friends or foes?" *World Development*, 22(6), June 1994; Robin Broad, "Corporate Bias in the World Bank Group's International Centre for Settlement of Investment Disputes: A Case Study of a Global Mining Corporation Suing El Salvador," *University of Pennsylvania Journal of International Law* 36 (2015); Robin Broad and John Cavanagh, "El Salvador Gold: Toward a Mining Ban," in Thomas Princen, Jack P. Martin, and Pamela L. Manno, eds., *Ending the Fossil Fuel Era* (MIT Press, 2015).

Article 10.5

CLIMATE POLICY AS WEALTH CREATION

The right policy would embody the principle that
we all own the earth's resources in equal and common measure.

BY JAMES K. BOYCE
July/August 2014

As the United Nations Climate Conference began in Paris on November 30, economist James K. Boyce joined D&S co-editor Alejandro Reuss for an interview on the future of climate policy. Boyce, professor of economics at UMass-Amherst and director of the Program on Development, Peacebuilding, and the Environment at the Political Economy Research Institute (PERI), has written extensively on a wide variety of environmental issues. (See, for example, "Mapping Environmental Injustice," co-authored by Klara Zwickl, Michael Ash, and Boyce, Dollars & Sense, November/December 2015.) In this interview, he emphasized how the dominant narrative about climate policy—the current generation's pain for future generations' gain—is both incorrect and politically damaging. —Eds.

Dollars & Sense: With the Paris Climate Change Conference now underway, climate policy is undoubtedly at the forefront of many people's minds. We often hear climate policy debates framed by the question of whether the current generation will be willing to sacrifice our standards of living, by reducing energy use and achieving emissions reductions, for the benefit of future generations. You've criticized that sort of framing of climate issues.

James K. Boyce: That's right. I mean that framing is almost ubiquitous. One of the reasons why these international negotiations have proven so difficult is that if everybody believes that this is going to be a painful thing to cut our carbon emissions, then they all want somebody else to go first. It's like a global free-rider problem—no one wants to be the one who cuts emissions more than someone else because they'll bear the pain and everybody else shares in the gain.

I think that framing of the problem has been a huge obstacle to progress, and it's not true. In fact, it is, on the contrary, true that we can design climate policies that benefit the majority of people here and now, in the present generation. So instead of always wanting somebody else to go first, if we designed the policies right, everyone will want to go first and I think that's a critical piece of the conversation that needs to be lifted up.

D&S: One of those benefits that you've talked about and written about is called "air quality co-benefits of climate policy." So what are air quality co- benefits, and why are those important?

JB: When we burn coal, oil, and natural gas—the fossil fuels—we not only release carbon dioxide into the atmosphere, which is the most important of the greenhouse gases propelling climate change, but we also release a lot of other really nasty stuff: particulate matter, sulfur dioxide, nitrogen oxide, a host of air toxics—things that are hazardous to people here and now when we breathe them. By cutting down on our use of fossil fuels, we will not only help to protect the climate for future genera-tions by reducing CO2 emissions, but we'll also help to improve air quality for the present generation. Those improvements can be really substantial. In fact, people who've tried to calculate how much, in terms of dollars, the public-health benefits of cutting carbon emissions would be find magnitudes of benefits that are as big, or even in some cases bigger, than the dollar values that have been put on reducing greenhouse gas emissions. So we're talking about big benefits here, even in a country like the United States which has relatively good air-quality regulation.

My grad student Brandon Taylor and I, for example, recently did some cal-culations on the clean-air benefits, the public-health benefits that would come from implementing one of the climate bills that's been introduced in the current session of Congress, the Healthy Climate and Family Security Act, introduced by Congressman Chris Van Hollen from Maryland. Van Hollen's bill would put a cap on carbon emissions, auction off the permits, give the money back to the people, and reduce the use of fossil fuels by 80% by the year 2050. We estimated that over that period, implementation of that bill would save about 700,000 lives in the United States. That is to say it would avert 700,000 premature deaths; that's about—what?—250 times the number of people who died in 9/11? We're talking

---

Is Climate Change a "Tragedy of the Commons"?

Ecologist Garret Hardin coined the now-familiar phrase "the tragedy of the commons" in a 1968 article in the journal Science. Hardin argued that people inevitably deplete com-monly held resources because they do not pay the full cost of using them. For example, livestock herders have an incentive to overgraze their own animals on common pasture—maximizing the benefits to themselves, while inflicting the costs of the overgrazing on oth-ers. Similar arguments have been made about the depletion of fisheries and many other environmental problems, among them climate change: each person enjoys the private benefits of fossil-fuel use, depleting the finite capacity of the atmosphere to absorb and recycle greenhouse gases, and inflicting damages on others. Mainstream economists have often seized upon this reasoning to argue that the solution to environmental problems is the division and enclosure of commons into private property, which would mean that each owner would bear the full cost of using his or her own property.

What economists are describing as "the tragedy of the commons," Boyce argues, would be better described as the "the tragedy of open access." Open access allows in-dividuals to appropriate resources at no cost, and when these resources are scarce, to inflict the costs of depletion on others. Understanding that a commons, however, can be "regulated through a system of common-property resource management," recasts the problem—and the solution. Protecting and preserving these resources does not require privatization: it can be achieved thought the development of public-property rights and regulations over their use. —Eds.

about a lot of preventable mortality that could be averted by moving forward in the clean-energy transition.

When you then look at countries like China or India, where the air-quality problems are even worse, the public health co-benefits of a clean-energy transition are that much greater. So I think this is something that really needs to be part of the conversation. When we're talking about cutting back on the use of fossil fuels, we're really talking about making cleaner air for everybody on the planet today, and improving public health, preventing premature deaths, preventing respiratory diseases, cancers, heart problems, asthma, and a host of other illnesses that are related to air pollution from fossil-fuel combustion.

D&S: Just to follow up on that point, probably a lot of our readers will have thought about the so-called "export of pollution"—the relocation of high-polluting industries from high-income countries like the United States to elsewhere in the world, and the insulation of people in high-income countries, especially affluent people, from the effects of that pollution. And yet, the argument that you make really says, well that may be true, but still there's a lot of benefit to be gained in countries like the United States from an air- quality and public-health standpoint.

JB: Yes, that's absolutely right. I mean, you can't export burning gasoline in your automobile. You can't export emissions from burning coal, oil, and natural gas to generate electricity. Those things are going to be in your own country, and we've still got a lot of that here in the United States. Despite having relatively strong air-quality legislation under the Clean Air Act, we've still got thousands of premature deaths every year that are attributable to burning fuels.

The only way to really drive down those public-health costs is to transition away from, what really, when you think about it, is an awfully primitive technology. It's digging up poisonous stuff that's been buried under the ground for millions of years and burning it to generate heat and power. Really, I think people are going to look back on that in a hundred years and say, "Boy, people were sure primitive back in the 19th and 20th, and early 21st century if that's the way they were generating their power," where we now know that in fact it's possible to generate energy very cleanly, at very low cost, by tapping the sun, the wind, geo-thermal sources of power, and so on. So I think we're not only talking here about trying to improve the environment for people yet to be born, we're talking about improving the environment for ourselves.

D&S: You've also written a lot about climate policies like a carbon tax, or auctioned carbon permit system, and argued that those could be designed in a way that would yield net income benefits to most people. Now, again, in the current discourse, the idea is that a carbon tax or some other price on carbon would hurt most people in the pocketbook, in particular lower-income people who tend to spend larger percentages of their incomes on fuel and the like. So how is it that most people would end up benefitting from such policies, properly designed?

JB: Well, this is another really important part of the conversation. The fact that a carbon price is one of the most important instruments to achieve reductions in emissions by making fossil fuels more expensive, is again part of the reason why people think, "Oh, it's going to be painful for us to reduce our use of fossil fuels because we're going to have to pay more for these things." It's true we are going to have to pay more, but the important thing to realize is that money doesn't disappear from our economy. When consumers pay more for oil, coal, natural gas, and everything that's produced and distributed using them, for electricity, for gasoline for their cars, etc.—that money doesn't get shipped to Saudi Arabia, it doesn't get buried in a tin can in your backyard, it doesn't get shot to the moon. It gets distributed somewhere, and the question is: Who gets the money?

In effect, by putting a limit on the amount of carbon we're burning, we're converting the atmosphere from something that was free, that you didn't have to pay to use, into something that's limited and that we have to pay to use—to park carbon in that limited atmospheric space. The question then is: Well if we're going to pay, who should get the money? Who does that space belong to? Who owns the parking lot, so to speak, the atmospheric parking lot for carbon emissions? I would submit that it's not owned by the corporations, it's not owned by the government, it's owned by all of us in common and equal measure. And consistent with that principle, then, the money that's collected by auctioning permits, or by charging a carbon tax, ought to go back to the people as the rightful owners of the resource we're paying to use.

If you did that, people who have smaller carbon footprints, who don't burn as much fossil fuel, will receive more in dividends than they pay in higher fuel bills. This includes mostt low-income people because they can't afford to burn as much fossil fuel—a lot of low income people in this country can't even afford to drive a car, they certainly don't have 4,000 or 8,000 foot houses that they're heating, they certainly don't fly off in airplanes to take vacations in sunny places in the middle of the winter, right? They don't burn as much carbon, and so their carbon footprints are relatively small compared to the more affluent people who have bigger houses, bigger cars, fly around in airplanes, etc. By putting a price on carbon, everybody pays in proportion to their use of the scarce resource—that limited ability of the atmosphere to absorb emissions—and by recycling that money to the people as equal per person dividends, everybody gets paid back the same amount regardless of the size of their carbon footprint. So what that means is that people who have smaller carbon footprints come out ahead, and people who have bigger ones come out behind.

When you do the math, what you learn is that the majority of the American people would actually benefit through a recycling of the money: Low-income households would come out ahead, middle-income households would be kept whole—so their real incomes wouldn't suffer by virtue of the rising prices of fossil fuels—and the wealthier households would end up paying more than they get back. But—you know what?—they can afford it.

D&S: I think that, when they hear a description of that policy, most people have a favorable reaction to the clarity and the simplicity of it: You pay in proportion to the carbon emissions that are embedded in what you consume, and then you get back an equal share of what everyone pays into that pool. Some people, however, may live in an area where the electrical utilities are all using coal-fired plants, and this is a kind of emissions that's very difficult for them to avoid individually. Is there an argument in favor of, say, adjusting the policy so that, if you're stuck in that kind of area paying for high-carbon-intensity electricity, you're not penalized for that?

JB: Well you're raising an important point, Alejandro, which is that there are some regional and interstate differences in carbon footprints based, above all, on the composition of the electricity supply. In states like Oregon or Vermont, that don't use much fossil fuel for electricity, people have lower carbon footprints at a given level of income than people in, say, Indiana or a number of other midwestern states that use more coal for their electricity supply. So that's an important issue. Now, on the other hand, there's a lot to be said for keeping the policy simple, and even in a state like Indiana, which has the most carbon-intensive electricity mix, when you calculate how carbon pricing would affect the households, the majority of households would come out ahead if the money's recycled as a dividend. But it would be a slimmer majority in Indiana than it would be in, say, Oregon.

For that reason, I think, it's desirable to think about other elements of the policy that could specifically try to channel resources to states like Indiana, to the most coal-intensive states—partly to assist those states in driving forward the clean energy transition and to cushion the impact on consumers in those states, and partly because in some of the coal-heavy states you've actually got jobs which are linked to the present energy infrastructure. We need to make sure that, as we transition to a clean-energy economy, we don't penalize the people who have been working in the old energy economy, but instead we make sure that they're able to take advantage of the expanded employment opportunities that come with the building-out of our clean-energy infrastructure.

One way to do that would be to channel 75%, let's say, of the carbon revenue back to the public as dividends, and to have 25% of it held as money for public investment—because overall in our economy, about 25% of the investment is by federal, state, and local governments. This is what Senators Maria Cantwell, Democrat of Washington state, and Susan Collins, Republican of Maine, actually proposed in an act they introduced back in 2009 called the CLEAR Act. If you do this—they proposed to channel 75% back to the public as dividends, 25% for public investment in clean and renewable energy—what you can do then is allocate that public investment in ways that takes these regional differences into account. And I think that's not a bad idea.

D&S: To bring this back around full circle to where you started: You talked at the beginning of this interview about this narrative of present-day sacrifice as something that has politically hamstrung serious action on climate change. What do you see as the potential for a real, significant impact of reframing the way that people think about this, away from present sacrifice and toward the potential for present benefits?

JB: I think we already see rising awareness around the world and within this country—really, across the nation and across the political spectrum—of the fact that climate change is real, that burning fossil fuels is a major contributor to the problem, and that we need to do something about it. So, the political will to do something about it has been building. What I think has been holding it in check has been in no small measure the idea that, "Ah gee, but even though we ought to do something, it's really going to hurt and should we really do it? Should we do it if the Chinese aren't doing it? Should we do it if we don't know for sure how much the planet's really going to warm up, etc.?" All these reservations about doing something have held progress back.

I think bringing out the ways in which we can design climate policy to achieve clean-air benefits—which means not just having carbon reductions happen regardless of where they're emitted, but also to target the reductions to the places, the industrial sectors, the most heavily impacted communities, to make sure that we get significant reductions in emissions in those places where the air quality and public health co-benefits are likely to be greatest—that's one way to try to break through that resistance. The other way is to design the policy so that the revenue generated by pricing carbon actually comes back to the people, so people end up, in most cases, financially better off in pocketbook terms than they would have been without the policy.

Once the public grasps that not only is this a good thing to do for future generations—for our children and grandchildren and those that will come after them—but it's actually a good thing for us too, I think at that point we have a foundation for really moving forward on a policy, and a policy that can command bipartisan support. Because it's not really a matter of red states vs. blue states or Republicans vs. Democrats. It's not a matter of bigger government vs. smaller government. It's a matter of getting the price on carbon to reflect the fact that burning this stuff comes at an environmental cost to the present and future generations, and making sure that that policy is implemented in a way that, far from hurting the public today, is going to benefit us. ❏

Article 10.6

HOW GROWTH CAN BE GREEN

AN INTERVIEW WITH ROBERT POLLIN

December 2014; Triple Crisis Blog

I n a Gallup poll earlier this year, almost two-thirds of those polled said that global warming worried them "a great deal" or "a fair amount." Yet many are also worried that
serious climate policy will require deep sacrifices—including big declines in production,
incomes, and employment. In August, Robert Pollin, professor of economics and co-director
of the Political Economy Research Institute (PERI) at UMass-Amherst, spoke with Dollars
& Sense co-editor Alejandro Reuss about these issues: Why "negative growth" is not a solution to climate change, why "green growth" is the best way to reduce greenhouse emissions,
and how it can work in both highincome and low-income countries. —Eds.

Dollars & Sense: You've argued in favor of "green growth" as a pathway for climate
stabilization. That cuts against a conventional wisdom—both among advocates of
serious action on climate policy and detractors of such action—that greenhouse gas
emissions reductions require a reduction in growth, no growth, or even negative
growth. What's the basic case you make for green growth?

Robert Pollin: The argument for green growth is premised on the notion that, while
an economy is growing, a given percentage of economic activity is devoted to the
transformation of the energy sector—from fossil-fuel based energy to clean energy.
According to my research, roughly speaking, if we look at about 1½% of GDP per
year—and I've done it for different countries, so it could be the United States, it could
be Spain, it could be Brazil, it could be South Africa, or it could be the world as
a whole—1½% of GDP invested in clean energy—that is, clean renewable energy
sources and energy efficiency—that I've costed this out and you could get to a global
reduction in absolute CO_2 emissions on the order of 40% within twenty years, which
is along the lines of the Intergovernmental Panel on Climate Change goals. That
means that what you're doing is, as the economy is growing, you're taking part of economic activity and moving it from dirty activities to clean energy activity. So growth
therefore becomes supportive of emissions and climate stabilization.

D&S: If the fruits of growth were heavily invested in projects to increase energy efficiency or develop sources of alternative "clean" energy (wind, water, solar), could a
green growth approach actually achieve greater GHG emissions reductions than a
hypothetical no-growth or de-growth alternative?

RP: If we're talking about no-growth or negative-growth scenario, unless you're
transforming the energy system you get no reduction in emissions. If you're at a flat

level of economic activity, you get exactly the same level of emissions. If we cut GDP by 10%, and you keep the energy system the same, then emissions will go down by 10%, period. And a 10% emissions reduction is nowhere near what's required. And on the other hand, reducing GDP by 10% would be the worst depression the world had ever experienced. GDP didn't go down by 10% during the 1930s. During the Great Recession of 2007-2008, global GDP went down by 2½%. So there's no way to get to a climate stabilization path just on the basis of cutting growth.

If we want to go to zero growth, or we want to go to negative growth, we still have to transform the energy system, and the best way to transform the energy system is in a framework in which the economy is growth, because then you have a lot of opportunities and a lot of investment. You're creating more jobs. If you're trying to transform the energy system in a phase of no growth, you're imposing a depression, and who's going to be for that? Nobody, except the most fanatical environmentalists. But working people are going to see massive job loss, on a scale much greater than 2007-2009, greater than the 1930s. That has no political support and doesn't solve the problem anyway.

D&S: Is "green growth" a viable course of action for the developing world today? The high income countries, including some that are now moving in the direction of greener energy, have mostly achieved high incomes through a carbon-intensive path. Can developing countries dramatically raise standards of living on the basis of a low-carbon-intensity path?

RP: Yeah, well the key is that the costs of delivering energy through clean renewable sources plus high efficiency are basically at parity now. In developing countries, under average conditions. "Under average conditions" means that there is wide dispersion. It doesn't mean that in every single site if you put up a wind farm or install solar panels that the costs are going to be at parity with, say, the rich countries. But on average, if we believe the research that's out there, they are. And this also depends a lot on investments in high efficiency, because in developing countries the energy systems are very wasteful, so it's easy to get high returns from investing in raising efficiency standards. So actually the green growth path is even more effective in developing countries. I myself have written about it for India, for Brazil, for South Africa, for Indonesia. In a country like Indonesia or India—they expect to be high-growth countries, growing at 6, 7, or 8%—they can actually do that if they keep putting 1½% of GDP so that their growth dividend moves into clean energy, and you start to see their emissions going down as a feature of economic growth itself.

D&S: What about the means of promoting investment in energy efficiency and alternative energy that you're talking about. You've written about the importance of a leading government role in promoting investment in those sectors. Are you skeptical that governments can just re-set the incentives to private actors—through a carbon tax or emissions permits system—and have that bring about the necessary investments?

RP: Well, we have to be skeptical, because it hasn't happened. And we have to be skeptical because there are obviously extremely powerful interests that are quite pleased with the profits that they're receiving from burning fossil fuels. That's a political question. On the other hand, as I said, on average the costs of renewable energy are close to parity or on parity with fossil fuel energy. Energy efficiency pays for itself, by definition. In fact, in the United States in 2007, under President George Bush, a law was passed that required the federal government to raise efficiency standards in all federal building by 30% as of the year 2015. Now, we didn't do it, but in the buildings that were retrofitted—there's a website and it shows it was saving the taxpayers hundreds of millions of dollars.

So why isn't it happening? One, there's inertia. You do have to do the up-front investment. Two, there's opposition from the fossil fuel industry. So we have to struggle around those things, at the same time recognizing that achieving these kinds of growth projections for clean energy are quite feasible economically and are good for jobs. That's the other big barrier, this notion that you're going to hurt jobs if you're going to protect the environment. Well, you know, the thing that I've been focusing on for several years is that it's actually beneficial for employment to pursue the green growth path as opposed to maintaining the fossil fuel infrastructure. ❑

Chapter 11

CRISIS, AUSTERITY, AND STAGNATION

Article 11.1

THE SPECTER OF SECULAR STAGNATION
Will economists face up to the crummy, unequal economy?

BY JOHN MILLER
May/June 2015

> The secular stagnation challenge then is not just to achieve reasonable growth, but to do so in a financially sustainable way.
> — Lawrence Summers, "What to Do about Secular Stagnation," World Economic Forum, Oct. 31, 2014.
> Does the U.S. economy face secular stagnation? I am skeptical, and the sources of my skepticism go beyond the fact that the U.S. economy looks to be well on the way to full employment today.
> — Ben Bernanke, "Why Are Interest Rates So Low, Part 2: Secular Stagnation," Ben Bernanke's Blog, Brookings Institution, March 31, 2015.

Hyman Minsky, one of the 20th century's leading theorists of financial fragility, used to say that there was nothing wrong with the discipline of macroeconomics that another Great Depression wouldn't cure. Today, almost six years since the official end of the Great Recession, such an effect might finally be taking hold.

Economist (and former treasury secretary and World Bank chief economist) Lawrence Summers is championing what he calls the "secular stagnation" hypothesis: the United States and other industrialized economies have been suffering for nearly two decades from a chronic lack of demand—a shortfall of both private and public spending not just inducing a temporary recession, but causing long-term (or "secular") economic growth to slow. Summers maintains that underlying economic growth has declined to the point that "it may be impossible to achieve full employment, satisfactory growth and financial stability simultaneously simply through the operation of conventional monetary policy [that lowers interest rates]."

It's certainly ironic that Larry Summers is today's chief proponent of the secular stagnation hypothesis, since he played a key role in enacting policies that contributed to stagnation. As treasury secretary under Clinton, he led the charge to deregulate derivatives trading, which would contribute mightily to the financial crisis. And as chief economic advisor in the Obama administration, Summers quashed proposals to enlarge the size of the fiscal stimulus, which would have gone a long way toward boosting growth.

Nonetheless, should the secular stagnation hypothesis take hold, it could help open up space for policies that could improve many people's lives.

The Secular Stagnation Debate

Nearly five years into the economic recovery, the U.S. economy expanded by just 2.4% in 2104, a far cry from the 4.1% average for all other economic recoveries since 1960. Even more importantly, secular stagnation is not just the "new mediocre" since the Great Recession. The U.S. economy has produced just two periods of rapid growth in the last twenty years—in the late 1990s and in the mid 2000s. Both were supported by low interest rates, massive debt, and speculative bubbles. Summers concludes that the U.S. economy has been unable to achieve adequate growth for a long time, but that this has been "masked by unsustainable finances."

The signs of stagnation are even clearer around the world. The IMF has repeatedly lowered its growth forecast for Japan, which is mired in decades of stagnation, and has done the same for the eurozone since 2007. It estimates growth in both Japan and the eurozone at little more than 1% a year through 2020.

The mediocre growth persists despite very low interest rates, embraced by governments to encourage borrowing and boost spending. As far back as the early 1990s, the Bank of Japan cut short-term interest rates by dramatically expanding the money supply. With the onset of the Great Recession in 2008, the European Central Bank and the U.S. Federal Reserve Board did the same, with the Fed also buying long-term corporate and government bonds (engaging in "quantitative easing") in an attempt to bring down long-term interest rates. "Interest rates have been, and remain, very low," Federal Reserve Chair Janet Yellen rightly cautions, "and if underlying conditions had truly returned to normal, the economy should be booming."

Today, short-term interest rates controlled by central banks remain barely above zero: 0.25% in the United States, 0.1% in Japan, and 0.05% in the eurozone. Such low interest rates leave central banks with practically no room to cut interest rates further to boost economic growth.

Real (inflation-adjusted) long-term interest rates are down as well. Real interest rates on ten-year government bonds in the Group of Seven (G7) industrialized countries (Canada, France, Germany, Italy, Japan, the UK, and the United States) have fallen from just under 5% in the early 1990s to 0.6% at the end of 2013.

What explains this decline in interest rates? Expansionary monetary policy, initiated by central banks to lower rates and counteract slowing economic growth, is part of the answer. For Summers, however, the chief explanation for the drop in the real interest rate (the price of savings), is the chronic excess of savings (the supply of savings) over investment (the demand for savings). He calls this the "essence of secular stagnation." Private savings (largely retained earnings held by corporations) have exceeded private investment in the eurozone since 2001, in Japan since well before 2000, and in the United States since 2008 (after the housing bubble burst).

Demand-Side or Supply-Side? Summers attributes the excess of savings to too little private investment. A shortfall of overall spending (or "aggregate demand") is holding investment below the levels necessary for full employment. In the middle of last year (second quarter 2014) business investment in the G-7 countries stood at 12.4% of GDP, well below the 13.3% level in 2008 and further behind the 13.8% peak in 2001.

That's not the way former Fed Chair Ben Bernanke sees it. Yes, economic growth is slow, interest rates are low, and private investment has fallen short of private savings. But Bernanke attributes that shortfall to a "savings glut," an oversupply of savings, rather than a paucity of investment. What held back economic growth (outside of the housing sector) from 2002 to 2006, he argues, was that China and other countries with large trade surpluses saved more than they invested and used their excess savings to buy U.S. securities. That helped to finance the housing boom, but also drove up the value of the dollar, making Chinese exports cheaper for U.S. buyers, and causing domestic production to suffer.

Does it really matter if the problem is a glut of savings or a dearth of investment opportunities? In fact, it does. The policy implications are quite different. If what's plaguing the global economy is Bernanke's savings glut, the appropriate policy is to get emerging economies " to reduce interventions in foreign exchange markets for the purpose of gaining trade advantage." But chalking up excess savings entirely to developingworld trade policies, as Bernanke does— not acknowledging the role of everrising domestic inequality and massive debt burdens—is literally one-sided. Moreover, changing exchange rates, as Summer points out, merely transfers spending from one country to another, instead of adding to it.

On the other hand, if Summers is right and the main problem is a persistent shortfall in private-sector demand (in particular, due to lack of investment demand), then the public sector needs to boost spending. For economist Paul Krugman, who has long maintained that today's economy suffers from a chronic lack of demand, that makes the secular stagnation hypothesis "a very radical manifesto."

Summers, for instance, favors a program of enlarged and sustained public investment, "a natural instrument to promote growth." Public investment is, indeed, much needed. Net public investment (subtracting out depreciation) in the United States fell from 1.5% of GDP in 2008 to just 0.5% of GDP in 2012, and had actually turned negative in the eurozone. And he has an answer for those concerned that increasing public spending would push government debt to unsustainable levels: In a world with near-zero real interest rates for government debt, public investment projects would generate enough revenue to service the associated debt as long as those projects yielded any positive return. For those in the United States still concerned about the buildup of public debt, Summers has proposed that the U.S. government enact a carbon and gas tax to pay for infrastructure investments.

There are yet more radical implications of the stagnation hypothesis that get us closer to the roots of the ongoing economic crisis. Among the factors that Summers lists as contributing to a shortfall of investment is income inequality. Stagnant wages and booming profits have reduced consumer spending and added to corporate retained earnings. Worsening inequality—which Summers says threaten to turn the United States into a "Downton Abbey economy"— does not only diminish demand. It also empowers moneyed interests to resist public spending that would bring about continuous full employment.

In the last analysis, the secular stagnation problem is a political problem rather than an economic one. With sufficient political will—and political might—we could enact a program of large-scale public investment that would put an end to secular stagnation. Investments in clean energy (retro-fitting homes, upgrading the electrical system, building mass-transit) and education (reducing class size, improving school building, and boosting financial aid for students) are both worthwhile for their own sake and have been shown to effectively create jobs.

Surely that would be far better than an economy that depends on financial bubbles and unsustainable household debt to keep it from stagnating—and that rewards the elites who stand in the way of needed reforms. ❑

Article 11.2

CAN "ABENOMICS" REVIVE JAPAN'S ECONOMY?

Why we need a progressive alternative embracing greater income equality and alternative energy investment.

BY JUNJI TOKUNAGA
May/June 2015

Japan's conservative Liberal Democratic Party (LDP)—led by Prime Minister Shinzo Abe (pronounced "AH-bay")—won a landslide victory in the December 2014 snap election for the House of Representatives, the lower house of the national parliament. The Liberal Democrats and their partner party in the ruling coalition, the Komeito, won 326 of 475 seats, giving them a two-thirds supermajority in the House of Representatives.

Why did Abe win so handily? Since the end of 2012, the Abe government has carried out an economic revitalization program called "Abenomics"—its response to Japan's ongoing economic stagnation, the "lost decades" of the 1990s and 2000s. Abenomics consists of three "arrows": aggressive monetary "quantitative easing," massive fiscal stimulus, and "structural reforms" to the economy. The main reason for Abe's resounding victory is that he succeeded in persuading the electorate to stay the course, with slogans like "Abenomics is progressing" and "There is no other way to economic recovery." Meanwhile, he shifted voters' attention away from more controversial matters, such as his plans to restart Japan's nuclear power plants (after the March 2011 Fukushima nuclear disaster) and to bolster the country's military forces.

Rather than leading to a rebound of domestic consumption and investment spending, which could lift the economy as a whole, however, Abe's neoliberal reforms would lead to rising inequality and continued stagnation. We certainly need significant public spending. The Abe government, however, has carried out pork-barrel public projects that will not revive the Japanese economy in the long term, while averting another recession. Rather, we must explore programs to facilitate the development of new industries, such as renewable energy (RE), instead of the defense and nuclear power industries that the Abe cabinet favors.

What is Abenomics?

Abenomics has been mainly about more aggressive monetary "quantitative easing"—central bank purchases of various kinds of bonds (other than short-term government bonds, purchases of which are considered "conventional" expansionary monetary policy) from banks and other private owners of financial assets. The Bank of Japan, the country's central bank, has been engaging in "Quantitative and Qualitative Monetary Easing" (QQE) since April 2013, with the goal of raising the inflation rate to 2% within two years.

According to advocates of Abenomics, inflationary expectations driven by aggressive monetary easing would reduce real interest rates (that is, interest rates adjusted for inflation, which are calculated by subtracting the inflation rate from the nominal interest rate). In turn, lower real interest rates will make corporations willing to borrow more, raising investment spending and generating domestic employment. The increase in investment would lead to strong corporate profits, eventually translating into higher wages, which would in turn increase consumption spending by households. This is basically a form of "trickle-down economics," in the sense that, according to its advocates, strong corporate profits would trickle down to everyone else in the economy.

Under the QQE program, the Bank of Japan (BOJ) pledged to double the size of the monetary base (currency in circulation plus banks' reserves on deposit at the central bank). By the end of October 2014, unsatisfied with the results of the program, it decided to accelerate this enlargement of the monetary base. With the BOJ being twice as aggressive as the U.S. Federal Reserve in its bond-buying, its balance sheet has gone above 50% of GDP.

Economist Paul Krugman has strongly supported Abenomics—"the sharp turn toward monetary and fiscal stimulus adopted by the government of Prime Minster Shinzo Abe"—and hailed it as a model for other countries to emulate. In a 2013 column in the New York Times, he stressed that Japan could be the first major country to climb out of the kind of recession and stagnation in which has also befallen Western countries since the global financial crisis in 2008.

What Have Been the Effects of Abenomics So Far?

The effects of aggressive monetary easing have, mainly, been limited to higher stock prices on the Tokyo Stock Exchange and the drastic depreciation of the Japanese yen in foreign exchange markets. The Nikkei 225, the index for the Tokyo stock market (analogous to the S&P 500 for the New York Stock Exchange and NASDAQ), has soared. The yen, meanwhile, has depreciated by more than 42% relative to the dollar in the last two years. Some have pointed to these developments as proof that Abenomics is working.

In fact, these effects will not contribute to the trickle-down economics which advocates of Abe's policy expect, for two reasons. First, aggressive monetary easing will not stimulate overall household consumption spending. The dramatic stock market rally has sparked a "wealth effect," which might lead those who own a lot of financial assets—feeling flush with their new riches—to spend more. Meanwhile, however, workers' wages have not kept pace with inflation. In addition, the Abe government introduced a sales tax hike, from 5% to 8%, in April 2014. Such conditions tend to make ordinary people reduce their consumption spending. The benefits of trickle-down Abenomics clearly have not reached everyone.

Second, corporations, particularly big multinationals, are hoarding their profits. Corporate profits have been rising significantly, underpinned by the drastic depreciation of the yen. This has boosted the competitiveness of Japanese industry in global markets. But corporations have held onto most of these profits as internal reserves, rather than engaging in investment spending that would lift the economy. According to Japan's Finance Ministry, the reserves of Japanese nonfinancial companies reached a record 304 trillion yen (nearly $3 trillion) by of the end of fiscal year 2013. As a consequence, Japan's GDP shrunk for two consecutive quarters, a common definition for recession, after the second quarter of 2014. (Figures for the first quarter of 2015 were not available at this writing.)

What Kinds of Policies Will Abe Push Now?

Abe's landslide victory in the snap election could not only enable him to stay in office until late 2018, making him longest-serving prime minister in Japan since World War II, but also give him abundant political capital for further pursuing his economic agenda.

On what kind of policies will Abe spend this political capital? First of all, he will likely purse the "third arrow" of Abenomics: structural reforms of the economy. The Abe cabinet announced a "Revision of Japan Revitalization Strategy: 10 Key Reforms" in June 2014. Parts of the strategy, such as enhancing women's labor-force participation and advancement could be epoch-making in Japan, if they worked well. But most of structural reform plans are based on a neoliberal approach of low corporate taxation, deregulation, reduction of fiscal deficits, and free trade.

Broadly, Abe would likely push four neoliberal policies:

First, lowering corporate taxes, while planning the second stage of the sales tax hike from 8% to 10% in April 2017. The Abe government has agreed on the basic outline of fiscal year 2015 tax reforms, including a 2.51 percentage-point reduction in the effective corporate tax rate. The tax cut could be a further boost for big corporations that have already received the windfall from the depreciation of the yen.

Second, accelerating the push for labor market "flexibility." Labor market deregulation would make it easier for big corporations to fire full-time employees, lowering incomes for wage earners even further.

Third, radically reducing social welfare spending in the fiscal year 2015 budget, in order to reduce the massive fiscal deficit.

Finally, completing the final stage of negotiations over a free-trade agreement, the Trans-Pacific Partnership (TPP), with the United States. The TPP would open the agricultural market in Japan to an unprecedented level of imports, which would inflict big damage on many Japanese farmers.

Do We Have a Progressive Alternative for Reviving the Economy?

Many voters understood the problems with Abenomics before the December snap election. An November opinion poll by Nikkei, Japan's leading economics and business news company, reported that 51% of the public opposed Abenomics, compared with 33% who favored it. Disappointingly, a lack of strongly progressive alternatives from the opposition parties helped Abe win his landslide victory.

What kind of policy should we implement to avert a return to recession? As economist Richard Koo argues in his recent book *The Escape from Balance Sheet Recession and the QE Trap*, we have to carry out not austerity policies but fiscal stimulus, which can stabilize the economy. Reasonably, the Abe government announced expenditures totaling 3.5 trillion yen (US$29 billion) in 2015. But fiscal stimulus and monetary easing can only buy time to sow the seeds of economic revival in Japan. Now is the time to explore an alternative program for long-term recovery.

First, we need to increase real wages, which could lead to a rise in consumption spending. Abe and Haruhiko Kuroda, governor of the Bank of Japan, are trying to encourage big companies to raise wages in 2015, which is part of their program to achieve 2% inflation. To spread the benefits of economic recovery through the economy as a whole, however, we have to extend higher wages not only to workers at big corporations, but also to those at small- and medium-sized enterprises (SMEs), which are the main engines of the Japanese economy.

Second, we need a new set of public investment projects that could foster basic industry for the next generation. Japan is a global leader in renewable energy technology. In fact, the country accounts for the majority of renewable-energy patent applications worldwide. (Japan's share is 55%; the United States', 20%; Europe's, 9%.) The Japanese government should drastically redirect the energy research and development (R&D) budget away from nuclear power generation—which reached 69% of total energy R&D spending in 2010—and toward renewables.

The financial system in Japan has the potential to serve as a bridge between lenders and financial investors who want to finance RE projects, and borrowers who plan to start renewable energy businesses. On the lending side, Japanese individual investors have been among those most interested, worldwide, in "World Bank Green Bonds," which are designed to raise funds for green economy projects in developing countries. On the borrowing side, many firms and entrepreneurs, some supported by local governments, have applied to start businesses including solar, wind, geothermal, and biomass power generation.

A "feed-in-tariff" (FIT) law, passed in July 2012, allows private providers to sell renewable energy to big electricity companies at prices to be fixed by the central government. This has fostered a boom in RE business, particularly in solar power generation. According to Japan's Agency for Natural Resources and Energy, renewable-energy generating capacity has increased from about 567,000 kilowatts in July 2012 to nearly 72 million kilowatts in October 2014. These developments imply that Japan has both extraordinary financial resources that could provide funds to RE businesses and numerous firms and entrepreneurs eager to make use of them, if given a chance.

As Koo explains, Japan's "lost decades" and its deflation are attributable to insufficient private investment demand. It could take a significant amount of time for these alternative programs to create new investment opportunities and lift the economy as a whole. But Japan has to learn the lessons of the Fukushima nuclear disaster and start to develop renewable energy. This could end deflation and move the country onto a path of sustainable economic growth. ❑

Sources: Paul Krugman, "Japan the model," *New York Times,* May 23, 2013; "Without reforms, Japan's leader remains vulnerable," *Wall Street Journal,* Dec. 15, 2014; "Acquisitions, financing worries behind Japan Inc.'s bulging reserves," *Nikkei Asian Review,* June 23, 2014; Richard Koo, *The Escape from Balance Sheet Recession and the QE Trap* (Wiley, 2015); "Japan cabinet approves Y3.5tn stimulus spending," Financial Times, Dec. 27, 2014; "Patent-based Technology Analysis Report-Alternative Energy Technology," World Intellectual Property Organization, 2009; "Japan and nuclear power," *Mainichi,* Jan. 22, 2012; Against the Tide: How Developing Countries Are Coping with the Global Crisis," Background Paper prepared by World Bank Staff for the G20 Finance Ministers and Central Bank Governors Meeting, Horsham, United Kingdom on March 13-14, 2009; Jayati Ghosh, "Current Global Financial Crisis: Curse or Blessing in Disguise for Developing Countries?" Presentation prepared for the IWG-GEM Workshop, Levy Economics Institute, New York, June 29-July 10, 2009.

Article 11.3

GERMAN WAGE REPRESSION
Getting to the Roots of the Eurozone Crisis

BY JOHN MILLER
September/October 2015

> Germany has been insistent that the so-called peripheral countries increase their competitiveness through slower wages rises or even wage cuts. Wage increases in Germany are an equally important, and symmetrical, part of this necessary adjustment process.
>
> The wage increases are steps in the right direction, but relatively small steps. More gains for German workers in the future would be both warranted and a win-win proposition for Germany and its trade partners.
>
> — Ben Bernanke, "German wages hikes: A small step in the right direction," Brookings Institution, April 13, 2015.

Ben Bernanke not only supports recent German wage increases, he also thinks further wage increases for German workers are "warranted and a win-win proposition for Germany and its trade partners"?

Now that's a jaw-dropper. Has the former head of the Federal Reserve Board—the guardian of "price stability" that makes policy designed to keep U.S. wages in check—switched sides in the class war, now that he is retired?

Hardly. Rather, it's that catering to the demands of German high finance and other elites has been so disastrous that even the former chair of the Fed cannot deny the undeniable: unless Germany changes course and boosts workers' wages, the euro crisis will only worsen.

Let's look more closely at just how German wage repression and currency manipulation pushed the eurozone into crisis, ignited a conflict between northern and southern eurozone countries (with Germany as the enforcer of austerity), and left Greece teetering on the edge of collapse.

From "Sick Man" to Export Bully

In the year 2000, Germany was widely considered "the sick man of Europe." Through much of the previous decade, the German economy grew more slowly than the European Union average, its manufacturing base shrunk, and its unemployment rate rose to near double-digits levels. Nor was Germany an export powerhouse, with its current account (the mostly widely used and most comprehensive measure of a nation's financial balance with the rest of the world) showing a modest deficit in 2000.

Adopting the euro as its sole currency, in January 2002, was no panacea. For the next two years, Germany's economy continued to stagnate. But converting to the euro—whose value was more or less an average of that of the stronger and weaker former currencies of the member countries—soon did improve Germany's competitive position internationally. German exports, no longer valued in strong deutschmarks, but in weaker euros, became cheaper to buyers in other countries. At the same time, the exports of countries that used to have weaker currencies, such as the Greek drachma and the Spanish peseta, became more expensive. That alone transformed Germany's current account deficit into a surplus.

China is widely accused of "currency manipulation," keeping the renminbi weak to boost its exports. But few see that the eurozone—the now 19-country bloc sharing the euro as its common currency—has functioned for Germany as a built-in currency manipulation system. And much like China, Germany used a lethal combination of wage repression and an undervalued currency to boost its exports and output at the expense of its trading partners.

Following the adoption of the euro, Germany instituted a set of "labor-market flexibility" policies intended to further improve its international competitiveness. Known as the Agenda 2010 Reforms, the new policies reduced pensions, cut medical benefits, and slashed the duration of unemployment benefits from nearly three years to just one. They also made it easier to fire workers, while encouraging the creation of part-time and short-term jobs. Employers increasingly divided formerly full-time jobs into state-subsidized, low-paying, insecure "mini-jobs." A decade later, one in five German jobs was a mini-job.

Germany's repressive labor policies kept a lid on wage growth. In every year from 2000 through the onset of the financial crisis in 2009, German compensation per employee increased more slowly than the eurozone average, and less even than in the United States.

During the 1990s, German workers' real (inflation-adjusted) wages rose along with productivity gains, meaning that employers could pay the higher wages without facing higher labor costs per unit of output. After 1999, wage gains no longer kept pace with productivity, and the gap between the two widened. As wages stagnated, inequality worsened, and poverty rates rose. Total labor compensation (wages and benefits) fell from 61% of GDP in 2001 to just 55% of GDP in 2007, its lowest level in five decades.

German wage repression went even further than necessary to meet the 2% inflation target mandated by the eurozone agreement, and insisted upon by German policymakers. Unit labor costs (workers' compensation per unit of output) is perhaps the most important determinant of prices and competitiveness. Unit labor costs rise with wage increases but fall with gains in productivity. From 1999 to 2013, German unit labor costs increased by just 0.4% a year. The reason was not German productivity growth, which was no greater than the eurozone average over the period; rather, it was that German labor market policies kept wage growth in check.

This combination of a built-in system of currency manipulation afforded by the euro and labor-market policies holding labor costs in check turned Germany into the world's preeminent trade-surplus country. As its competitive advantage grew, its exports soared. Germany's current account surplus became the largest in the world relative to the size of its economy, reaching 7.6% of the country's GDP, more than twice the size of China's surplus compared to its GDP.

Beggar Thy Neighborhood

Germany's transformation into an export powerhouse came at the expense of the southern eurozone economies. Despite posting productivity gains that were equal or almost equal to Germany's, Greece, Portugal, Spain, and Italy saw their labor costs per unit of output and prices rise considerably faster than Germany's. Wage growth in these countries exceeded productivity growth, and the resulting higher unit labor costs pushed prices up by more than the eurozone's low 2% annual inflation target (by a small margin).

The widening gap in unit labor costs gave Germany a tremendous competitive advantage and left the southern eurozone economies at a tremendous disadvantage. Germany amassed its ever-larger current account surplus, while the southern eurozone economies were saddled with worsening deficits. Later in the decade, the Greek, Portuguese, and Spanish current account deficits approached or even reached alarming double-digit levels, relative to the sizes of their economies.

In this way, German wage repression is an essential component of the euro crisis. Heiner Flassbeck, the German economist and longtime critic of wage repression, and Costas Lapavistas, the Greek economist best known for his work on financialization, put it best in their recent book *Against the Troika: Crisis and Austerity in the Eurozone*: "Germany has operated a policy of 'beggar-thy-neighbor' but only after 'beggaring its own people' by essentially freezing wages. This is the secret of German success during the last fifteen years."

While Germany's huge exports across Europe and elsewhere created German jobs and lowered the country's unemployment rate, the German economy never grew robustly. Wage repression subsidized exports, but it sapped domestic spending. And, held back by this chronic lack of domestic demand, Germany's economic growth was far-from-impressive, before or after the Great Recession. From 2002 to 2008, the German economy grew more slowly than the eurozone average, and over the last five years has failed to match even the sluggish growth rates posted by the U.S. economic recovery. With low wage growth, consumption stagnated. German corporations hoarded their profits and private investment relative to GDP fell almost continuously from 2000 on. The same was true for German public investment, held back by the eurozone budgetary constraints.

At the same time, Germany spread instability. Germany's reliance on foreign demand for its exports drained spending from elsewhere in the eurozone and slowed growth in those countries. That, in turn, made it less likely that German banks and elites would recover their loans and investments in southern Europe.

Wage Repression and the Crisis

No wonder Bernanke now describes higher German wages as an important step toward reducing Europe's trade imbalances. More spending by German workers on domestic goods and imports would help Germany and its trading partners grow, and improve the lot of working people throughout the eurozone.

Of course, much more needs to be done. Putting an end to the austerity measures imposed on Greece and the other struggling eurozone economies would boost their demand as well. In fact, it would also better serve the interests of Germany and the profitmaking class, by helping to stabilize a system from which they have benefited so greatly at the expense of much of the region's population.

Still, raising the wages of German workers to match productivity gains is, as Bernanke recognizes, surely a step in the right direction. Raising U.S. wages to match productivity gains would help defuse U.S. wage repression and boost economic growth here as well. If Bernanke throws his weight behind that proposition, we'll truly wonder which side is he on. ❑

Article 11.4

THE EUROZONE CRISIS: MONETARY UNION AND FISCAL DISUNION

BY ALEJANDRO REUSS
July/August 2016

In 2007–8, after the real estate bubble burst, the entire U.S. economy plunged into a deep recession, the worst since the 1930s. But the downturn hit some parts of the country harder than others. Overall, real gross domestic product shrank by just over 4% between the pre-recession peak and the trough. Meanwhile, Florida, for example, saw its state GDP decline by over 11%—so, more than 2½ times as much. The official unemployment rate for the United States as a whole more than doubled from a pre-recession low of 4.4% (May 2007) to a peak of 10.0% (October 2009). In Florida, it more than tripled, from 3.1% (March–April 2006) to 11.2% (November 2009–January 2010). Florida's state and local tax revenues declined from nearly $37.5 billion in fiscal year 2006 to about $28.8 billion in fiscal year 2010.

Do you remember, then, how officials from Florida had to engage in protracted negotiations with the federal government—the Department of the Treasury, the Federal Reserve, etc.—to get federal assistance in dealing with the crisis? Do you remember the recriminations from the governors and legislators of other, less severely affected states, decrying Floridians for their profligate spending and lazy work habits? Federal authorities' insistence on state tax hikes and deep spending cuts, as Florida's just penance for a crisis of its own making? The mass marches in the streets of Miami, Tampa, and Tallahassee as Floridians resisted this painful austerity?

Me neither.

The United States, like Europe, experienced what economists call an "asymmetric crisis"—affecting some regions more severely than others. We may only now be seeing some of the political repercussions of economic problems—both acute and chronic—in the United States. Yet the kind of turmoil that happened in Greece and other countries of the European "periphery"—the negotiations, recriminations, austerity measures, and massive street protests—did not happen in the especially hard-hit parts of the United States. One reason was that large-scale fiscal transfers between one part of the union and another happen quite automatically, and with relatively little contention, in the United States. Economist Paul Krugman, who has used Florida as an example of what was missing in Europe in response to the Great Recession, put it this way in a 2012 blog post: "Florida received what amounted to an annual transfer from Washington of $31 billion plus, or more than 4% of state GDP. That's a transfer, not a loan. ... Aid on this scale is inconceivable in Europe as currently constituted."

Krugman's analysis points to one of the structural problems with the eurozone—monetary union without fiscal union. *Monetary union*, the adoption of a single currency throughout the eurozone, deprived member countries of policy tools which they otherwise might have used in response to the sharp downturn. (Not all of those, mind you, would have been painless or desirable.) Meanwhile, the absence of *fiscal union*, that is, the lack of unification of taxation and spending at the federal level, ruled out large "automatic" transfers from less-affected to harder-hit countries.

Too United?

In one diagnosis, the severity of the European crisis—especially for the "peripheral" countries of Ireland, Italy, Portugal, Spain, and (most of all) Greece—can be thought of as a result of Europe taking economic unification too far. Key elements of Europe's economic unification—in terms of finance, trade, and monetary union—played some role in setting off the crisis. Financial liberalization helped enormous financial flows pour from Europe's higher-income "core" countries to its lower-income "periphery," helping to fuel large housing bubbles in countries like Ireland, Italy, and Spain. Trade liberalization exposed domestic industry in Europe's periphery to withering import competition from Europe's core. The bubble-fueled boom, in addition, drove up domestic prices relative to import prices, helping push up trade deficits in the peripheral countries. The adoption of a single currency, the euro, by 19 of the 28 EU member states, however, merits special attention. Monetary union deprived member countries of two important policy instruments that they might have deployed as the crisis developed.

First, a eurozone member could not devalue its currency against those of other members. Greece's current account deficit soared from the mid-1990s on, peaking at nearly 15% of GDP in 2008. (The current account balance is a standard international-accounts concept that includes the trade balance.) A country with its own currency might have "devalued" its currency; that is, Greece might have allowed the drachma (if there were still a drachma) to decline in value relative to, say, the deutschmark (if there were still a deutschmark). Here's the standard argument: Devaluation would have made imports of goods from Germany more expensive to Greeks, and so tended to reduce imports. Meanwhile, it would have made Greek exports less expensive to Germans, and so tended to increase exports. Together, these effects would have tended to reduce Greece's trade deficit. How fast or strong the effects would have been is debatable, considering how much Greek industries had been weakened over the years by punishing international competition. (To be clear, currency devaluation is not a rosy or painless option. Devaluations drive up the prices of imports and, by reducing import competition, the prices of domestically produced goods as well. The result is an erosion of real incomes, often hitting lower-income people especially hard. The country may be producing more goods and services, but because it is exporting more, its people—especially ordinary people—may be consuming less.)

In the absence of the policy option of a currency devaluation, Greek policymakers engaged in what economists call an "internal devaluation"—pushing down domestic wages in order to make Greek goods cheaper and more internationally competitive. One might say that, rather than devaluing its currency relative to other currencies, it devalued Greek workers relative to the workers of other eurozone countries. How can government economic policy bring about a reduction in wages across an entire national economy? Massive unemployment can do the trick—and it did so in Greece, to the tune of a 20% total decline in real wages between 2009 and 2013. Unemployment, of course, exacts an enormous cost in lost production and human suffering (see Evita Nolka, "The Human Toll of Greek Austerity," pp. 289-294).

Second, no eurozone country could unilaterally increase the money supply to pull down interest rates or increase the inflation rate. Both lower interest rates and higher inflation, arguably, could have been good for Greece. Lower interest rates would have made it cheaper for Greek households and businesses to borrow, stimulating spending and boosting output. This is why "expansionary" monetary policy—increasing the money supply and lowering interest rates—is a common central-bank response to an economic downturn. Higher inflation, meanwhile, would have reduced real debt burdens. Debts are usually specified, at some point in the past, as a specific quantity of money. Inflation means that a certain number of dollars or euros (or whatever monetary unit) becomes easier to come by for anyone getting paid in the new, higher prices. This makes debts easier to pay off. A hard-hit country, then, might have quite sensibly adopted a highly expansionary monetary policy.

Monetary policy in the eurozone, however, is made not by individual countries but by the European Central Bank (ECB). The ECB's mandate, as economist Gerald Epstein points out, is strictly about maintaining price stability (that is, low inflation). Contrast this to the U.S. Federal Reserve's so-called "dual mandate" to maintain both low inflation and low unemployment. One might think that, in the midst of depression conditions and massive unemployment, the singular focus on low inflation would go out the window. Under a different balance of political power, it might have. But for much of the crisis, the most powerful country in Europe, Germany, successfully opposed a more aggressively expansionary monetary policy.

Germany was not hit very hard by the crisis, thanks in no small measure to its large trade surpluses with the rest of the eurozone and the world. (These large surpluses have developed since the creation of the eurozone, which economist JohnMiller argues "has functioned for Germany as a built-in currency manipulation system" (see Miller, "German Wage Repression: Getting to the Roots of the Eurozone Crisis," pp. 278-281). Germany's unemployment rate, declining dramatically before the crisis, turned upward briefly (to about 8% in 2009) before continuing its decline. So the urgency of stimulating spending, for German policymakers, was relatively low. In addition, German policymakers are notoriously inflation-averse. Some point to the scarring historical experience of hyperinflation in the 1920s, but the main reasons are probably more prosaic. As *Frankfurter Allgemeine Zeitung* economic correspondent Winand von Petersdoff remarked in a 2011 article, the real issue is not a historical "trauma" but the simple fact that "inflation is a major redistribution," with debtors among the winners and creditors among the losers.

The structure of the European Union, it should be pointed out, also limited member countries' fiscal policy space in two major ways (both constraints, though, were closely related to the logic of monetary union).

First, the 1997 Treaty on European Union, better known as the Maastricht Treaty, placed limits on government deficits and debt. (The 1998 Stability and Growth Pact (SGP) added mechanisms for monitoring and enforcing these limits.) As the website of the European Commission puts it, "The [Maastricht] treaty limits government deficits to 3% of GDP and public debt levels to 60%, *so as to enable countries to share a single currency.*" The logic of monetary union—and the fear, especially on the part of German policymakers, that deficit spending could fuel inflation—explicitly drove the imposition of "fiscal discipline" on the member states. (As it turned out, Germany and France, mired in recession in the early 2000s, both repeatedly breached the deficit limits without punishment.) The European Commission states that, since the limits imposed by the Maastricht Treaty and SGP are based on the structural deficit (the portion of the overall deficit that is not driven by the business cycle), they "take into consideration business cycle swings." However, critics argue that the Maastricht/SGP limits have nonetheless been a major driver of austerity policies. As Sebastian Dulien, a researcher at the European Council on Foreign Relations, put it in 2012, "The severe [fiscal] adjustment programmes in Spain and Italy are all part of the normal working of these legislative acts."

Second, when a government borrows by selling bonds in a currency it controls, it has the option of paying back the creditors by creating more money (known as "monetizing the debt"). This means that such a country really never has to default on its debts, and the creditors who have loaned it money need not fear that they will not get paid back. (As former Federal Reserve chair Alan Greenspan put it in 2011, "The United States can pay any debt it has because we can always print money to do that. So there is zero probability of default.") Lenders charge higher interest to compensate for higher risk of not getting repaid. So if creditors do not fear default, they will lend at lower interest rates than they would otherwise. Even if a country's public debt becomes large, so long as it controls the currency in which it has borrowed, its creditors will have little reason to panic, cut off further credit, demand immediate repayment, and thereby trigger a crisis (the equivalent, at the national level, of a "run on the bank").

The European countries that got deep into debt, in contrast to the United States or the U.K. (which, for now at least, is a member of the EU, but has never been a member of the eurozone), owed their debts in a currency they did not control (the euro), and did not have the option of creating more money to pay it back. "When investors lost confidence in these countries, they ... [pushed] interest rates to unsustainably high levels," explains economist Paul De Grauwe of the London School of Economics, "making it impossible for the governments of these countries to fund the rollover of their debt at reasonable interest rate." What does this have to do with fiscal policy? Unable to borrow further, these countries "had to scramble for cash and were forced into instantaneous austerity programs."

Or Not United Enough?

If one could argue that the eurozone was "too united," in regard to monetary union, however, one could equally argue that it was not united enough, in terms of the lack of fiscal union. In a federal political structure, fiscal union means that households and firms in the member states pay their taxes (at least in part) into a common federal treasury, and expenditures are paid out from this treasury back to people across the member states. This is not an exotic idea: The United States is a fiscal union in precisely this sense.

During a business-cycle downturn, a standard "Keynesian" policy response is to increase government spending or reduce taxes (or both)—to boost demand, output, and employment. Governments may push through new spending and tax legislation (fiscal "stimulus" programs) for this purpose—as, indeed, the U.S. government did during the Great Recession. However, some existing government programs result in increased government spending and reduced tax collection during downturns without any need for deliberate policy changes. These are known as "automatic stabilizers." As an economy goes into a downturn, some people lose their jobs. Some see their hours cut. This reduces their incomes—but since many taxes are dependent on incomes, tax collections are reduced automatically. This helps to blunt the impact of the downturn. (As a thought experiment, to see how things would be if this were not the case, imagine that incomes were falling but each person or household still had to pay a fixed monthly tax bill.) There are automatic stabilizers on the revenue side as well. Government expenditures on unemployment insurance, for example, rise as people start losing their jobs. So, too, do public expenditures on pensions (like Social Security in the United States), as some employers downsize by enticing older workers to take "early retirement." These expenditures, too, slow the fall in demand, compared to what it would be otherwise.

In the case of a crisis that affects different states differently, automatic stabilizers have the biggest impact in the states that are hit hardest. Their tax payments to the federal government decline more dramatically than those of other states, while expenditures from the federal government increase more dramatically. Florida and other U.S. states that were especially hard hit by the crisis were—like Greece, Ireland, Italy, Portugal, and Spain—part of a large monetary union. The states do not have their own currencies or conduct their own monetary policy. U.S. states are also greatly constrained in their fiscal policy. For example, most states have balanced budget requirements, which tend to result in dramatic spending cuts during economic downturns. (As incomes fall, tax revenues drop and spending must be cut to maintain balanced budgets.) That is, U.S. states shared many of the policy constraints that hamstrung individual eurozone countries in responding to the crisis. One ingredient that could have reduced the magnitude of the eurozone crisis, present in the United States but missing in Europe, was a mechanism for large and automatic fiscal transfers between member states.

Bad Design or Bad Politics?

"The Eurozone looked like a wonderful construction at the time it was built," writes Paul De Grauwe. "Yet it appeared to be loaded with design failures. In 1999 I compared the Eurozone to a beautiful villa in which Europeans were ready to enter. Yet it was a villa that did not have a roof. As long as the weather was fine, we would like to have settled in the villa. We would regret it when the weather turned ugly."

In the wake of the crisis, criticism of the "design" flaws in the foundations of the eurozone has become widespread. If we take this to mean that the structure of the eurozone left the region vulnerable to a crisis, this is surely correct. The language of "design" flaws, however, is off in an important way. The problems of the eurozone were not merely the result of a technocratic design failure, but rather a political failure. There is plenty of blame to go around, and plenty of culpable parties should share in it—including industrial and financial capitalists, economists who spun appealing fairy tales about the benefits of "free markets," and mainstream politicians who bought into an agenda of economic "liberalization." Part of the blame, however, belongs at the feet of Europe's mainstream social democratic parties.

The political failings of these parties—whether they go by the name Social Democratic, Labour, Socialist, or whatever—should by now be plain to see. In hard-hit "peripheral" countries, like Spain and Greece, the mainstream socialist parties not only failed to lead a resistance against austerity policies, but actually administered these policies. Meanwhile, the German government—one of the main villains in pressing austerity policies—includes the Social Democrats (SPD) in a "grand coalition" with the parties of the Christian Democratic right.

The abdication of European social democracy, however, dates from much earlier than the current crisis or the imposition of painful austerity policies. Greece's former finance minister in the Syriza government, Yanis Varoufakis, traces it to social democrats' embrace of neoliberal and financialized capitalism in the 1990s. "Europe's 'official,' social democratic Left fell into the trap of believing that the welfare state need no longer be financed from a portion of profits exacted by political means from industry and commerce," Varoufakis argued in a June 2014 post on his blog. "Instead, they could finance the welfare state by tapping into the rivers of privately minted money that the financial sector was printing (while waged labour was being squeezed and real estate prices soared)." These parties, in other words, dreamed of a technocratic administration of the social welfare state, utterly divorced from class struggle. Even as political and economic institutions—a European parliament, a European central bank, the euro, etc.—were being constructed for the EU as a whole, the social democratic welfare state remained confined to the level of the individual country. At the national level, individuals make payments into a common pool according to the tax code (some pay more, others less), and receive payments from that common pool—or services funded from that pool—according to various program criteria (some receive more, others less). The welfare state, largely a product of the workers' movement and its political parties, is one institutional expression of the politics of social solidarity within those countries. The absence of fiscal union, at least in regard to social welfare, then, can be traced in part to the absence of a comparable politics of solidarity at the level of the EU as a whole.

What was constructed in Europe was, in short, not a social democracy writ large. Rather, as *Financial Times* columnist Wolfgang Münchau puts it, "when the eurozone was constructed, it was given neoliberal foundations." ❏

Sources: Bureau of Economic Analysis, National Income and Product Accounts (NIPA), Table 1.1.6. Real Gross Domestic Product, Chained Dollars; Bureau of Economic Analysis, Regional Data, Real GDP by state (millions of chained 2009 dollars), Florida; Bureau of Labor Statistics, Unemployment Rate, Seasonally Adjusted, 16 years and over, Series ID: LNS14000000; Bureau of Labor Statistics, Local Area Unemployment Statistics, Unemployment Rate, Florida, Series ID: LASST120000000000003; Florida Department of Revenue, Tax Collections from July 2003; Paul Krugman, "Greece as Victim," *New York Times*, June 17, 2012; Paul Krugman, "Florida Versus Spain," *New York Times*, June 2, 2012; Trading Economics, Greece Current Account to GDP, 1980-2016; Organisation for Economic Co-operation and Development (OECD), Average annual wages; Evita Nolka, "The Human Toll of Greek Austerity," *Dollars & Sense*, March/April 2016; John Miller, "German Wage Repression: Getting to the Roots of the Eurozone Crisis," *Dollars & Sense*, September/October 2015; Gerald Epstein, "Inflation Targeting and Neoliberalism," Parts 1 and 2, Triple Crisis blog; Trading Economics, Germany Unemployment Rate; Winand von Petersdoff, "German Angst," *Frankfurter Allgemeine Zeitung*, Dec. 12, 2011; European Commission, Economic and Financial Affairs, Stability and Growth Pact; Philip Arestis and Malcolm Sawyer, "Eurozone Balanced-Budget Disaster," *Dollars & Sense*, January/February 2014; Mattias Vermerein, "The limits of German power: How ECB decisions have put constraints on Berlin's management of the crisis," The London School of Economics and Political Science, Sept. 8, 2015; Sebastian Dulien, "Reinventing Europe: Explaining the Fiscal Compact, European Council on Foreign Relations," May 1, 2012; Patrick Allen, "No Chance of Default, US Can Print Money: Greenspan," CNBC, Aug. 7, 2011; Paul De Grauwe, "Design Failures in the Eurozone: Can they be fixed?, London School of Economics and Political Science," LSE 'Europe in Question' Discussion Paper Series, LEQS Paper No. 57/2013, February 2013; Yanis Varoufakis, "Europe's Crisis and the Rise of the Ultra-Right is the Left's Fault," Yanis Varoufakis: Thoughts for the Post-2008 World, June 9, 2014; Wolfgang Münchau, "Perplexing failure of Europe's centre-left," *Financial Times* Sept. 20, 2015; Leila E. Davis, Charalampos Konstantinidis, and Yorghos Tripodis, "A Proposal for a Federalized Unemployment Insurance Mechanism for Europe," Political Economy Research Institute (PERI), Working Paper Number 402, Sept. 21, 2015.

Article 11.5

THE HUMAN TOLL OF GREEK AUSTERITY

BY EVITA NOLKA
March/April 2016

Giannis and Lena, both in their early 30s and with MBA degrees, consider themselves lucky to be employed. Living in Thessaloniki, Greece's second largest city, located in the heart of Macedonia, Giannis is a merchandise buyer at a company that imports household items. Lena works in the export department of a pasta-producing enterprise.

"Every Greek family is experiencing the crisis their own way," Lena tells me. "Unemployment, wage and pension cuts, taxes, and increases in prices of basic goods have caused despair to millions of people."

Giannis shares a bit more. His family's income has taken a real hit. His father's wages have been reduced by one third and his mother got laid off three years ago. She used to work at a ready-made garments factory that went bankrupt soon after. For a year and a half, she hasn't been paid and she is still claiming the money she is owed.

Like so many others, Giannis had been unemployed for years. There was nothing he could do other than hope to get accepted at one of the five-month temporary work programs in the country funded by the European Union (EU). "You're being deprived of the opportunity to work during the most productive years of your life," Giannis tells me as he explains the psychological burden of unemployment. "There's a feeling that you're standing still even though the whole world keeps moving and after a while you feel numb. You accept that's how things are and you are unable to get out of the rut."

Sticking with Austerity

For six years now, Greece has lived under unprecedented austerity policies demanded by its lenders and accepted by a succession of governments. The social and political reality created by austerity was demonstrated sharply by two events on the same day in October 2015.

First, Eurostat, the European statistical service, released a report on poverty and social exclusion in Greece. The report showed that, in 2014, 22.1% of the Greek population lived in conditions of poverty, 21.5% were severely materially deprived, and 17.2% lived in families with very low work intensity. (Economists define "work intensity" as the total number of months that all working-age household members have worked as a percentage of the total number of months they theoretically could have worked. Households under 20% are considered to have "very low" work intensity.) Altogether, 36% of the population faced one or more of these terrible conditions. That figure was 7.9% percentage points higher than in 2008.

Second, the Greek parliament approved a new piece of legislation imposing further austerity measures as demanded by its creditors—primarily the EU and the International Monetary Fund (IMF)—to meet the terms of Greece's most recent (third) bailout agreement. The new package involves cutting public spending by 14.32 billion euros, while raising taxes by 14.09 billion euros, over the next five years. The measures will primarily affect privately owned businesses, homeowners, and employees close to retirement.

Austerity policies were first adopted in 2010 as a "solution" to the economic crisis that erupted in 2009–10. Severe cuts in public spending, deep reductions in wages and pensions, enormous tax increases, and a stripping back of labor protections were imposed—ostensibly—to stabilize the economy and gain the confidence of financial markets. In practice, the measures have plunged the Greek economy into a prolonged recession that has led to the disastrous results outlined by Eurostat. Unfortunately, the current Greek government, formed by the left-wing SYRIZA party, appears determined to keep the country on the same path.

The Crushing Burden of Unemployment

In the course of the recession, the Greek economy has shrunk by more than 25%. At present, more than one out of four workers is unemployed (one out of two among the nation's youth), and more than one million jobs have disappeared. The prospects for improvement, given the austerity policies imposed under the third bailout agreement, are dim at best. "No legislation can guarantee even the most basic labor rights," Lena says in describing the way employers have used the specter of unemployment to further reduce wages. "It's no wonder," she adds, "that so many well-educated young people choose to leave the country."

Since the unemployment rate for people with higher education is nearly 20%—the highest in the world—more than 200,000 young Greeks have left the country in search of better opportunities abroad. I discussed Greece's brain drain with Victoria, 18, a first-year electrical and computer engineering student at the University of Thessaly. "Don't be mistaken," she says, "all those young people that seek a better life abroad care deeply for Greece and won't hesitate to return once things have improved." Victoria herself is already considering leaving Greece once she finishes her studies. Who can blame her? She is highly unlikely to find a job in her field after graduation.

Collapse of Production

Austerity policies have also led the country's productive sector to near collapse, with industrial production in 2015 down by a staggering 35% compared to its level in 2008. Industrial production currently represents less than 10% of Greece's GDP, an exceptionally low level historically for the country, as well as for the eurozone today.

To be sure, the deindustrialization of the Greek economy started a lot earlier, in the early 1980s. The country's new development model, after its integration into the

European Community and the emerging Single Market, systematically favored the tertiary (services) sector and ignored the primary (agriculture, mining, etc.) and secondary (manufacturing) sectors. Greek industries, accustomed to the heavy protectionist measures of the post-war period and poorly prepared for the requirements of market integration and the liberalization of trade, failed to adapt. The massive influx of European funds to the tertiary sector (mainly tourism) shaped a services-centered economy (the services sector contributes over 80% to the country's GDP), while weakening the country's competitiveness and contributing decisively to the dismantling of its industrial base.

Things got immeasurably worse after 2009. During the recession, about 250,000 small and medium-sized enterprises closed down. Many more have been forced to the verge of closure due to reduced revenues and increased financial obligations to social security funds, tax offices, and banks. Thousands of small business owners have opted to relocate to neighboring Balkan countries, which offer lower labor costs and corporate tax breaks.

"Reality has shown that the austerity measures applied across Europe are not the most effective response to the crisis," says Costas, a civil engineer from Patra, Greece's third largest city, in the southern region of the Peloponnese. Costas is 45 years old and a former member of SYRIZA, the current governing party. "No other country in the eurozone has had to impose such far-reaching austerity programs," he says, "and I just don't see how Greek society can sustain the burden of yet another bailout."

The policy is simply not working, even on its own terms. After five years of austerity and three bailout agreements, Greece's national debt of 320 billion euros is right where it was in 2010. But its debt-to-GDP ratio has shot up to 175% (compared to 150% in 2010), and the European Commission projects that it will rise to 200% in 2016. The country's destroyed economy will never be able to repay this huge volume of debt.

SYRIZA U-Turn, Popular Disillusionment

Originally elected in January 2015 on a vehement anti-austerity platform, Greek Prime Minister Alexis Tsipras subsequently made a complete U-turn. Ignoring the popular outcry against austerity, loudly expressed in a referendum on July 5, he has given in to the creditors' demands. In August, SYRIZA and the creditors signed a new bailout agreement, including not only another round of austerity measures but also neocolonial restrictions on Greece's national sovereignty. No legislation related to the objectives of the bailout, however minor, can be taken by Greece's political institutions without the prior approval of its creditors. The creditors thus have the right to monitor the Greek government and to wield veto power over virtually all policy measures in Greece.

And yet, on September 20, Tsipras won a new election, again forming a government. The result seemed to vindicate his capitulation. It appears that Greek voters, confronted with a narrative presenting the new agreement as inescapable, opted to give the governing party a second chance. "This wasn't a vote of hope," says Costas, the civil engineer from Patra, "but a vote for the 'lesser evil' within the limits of a 'nothing can really change' mentality."

Costas is even convinced that if there were another general election soon, the governing party would still emerge victorious. Greek voters appear to think that there is no credible alternative to austerity. "Ever since the PM marginalized any voices in SYRIZA that tried to show a different way and declared there was no alternative," he says, "Greek society, having lost its morale, has come to accept its fate."

Defeat and Apathy

To fully understand the popular mood, one must look at the abstention rates in the recent election. Turnout plummeted, with a record-high abstention rate of 45%. In addition, blank ballots reached an extraordinary 2.5%. The message is quite clear: the Greek people's disappointment has led to a massive rejection of the political process altogether. Victoria tells me that most of her friends either cast a blank ballot or didn't bother to vote at all since "they didn't believe any of the existing political parties could actually make a difference."

The low turnout was not an isolated incident. During the past few years, social unrest and frustration over the austerity measures have given rise to widespread discontent and large-scale demonstrations. But the decline of the struggle as unemployment began to bite and, especially, SYRIZA's betrayal of popular hopes have led to a wholesale rejection of politics by broad layers of the population. The sense of defeat and indifference is pronounced among workers, and especially the young.

"Wishful thinking," says Costas about SYRIZA's hopes to overturn austerity by creating a domino effect in the countries of the European periphery. The balance of power has proven not that easy to change and now people feel that Greece is being punished for daring to question Europe's neoliberal policies.

European Union officials have categorically ruled out any possibility of a debt write-down. Restructuring in the form of a lengthening of maturity or perhaps a lowering of interest rates is still on the table, but it would have very debatable long-term results. Greece would probably be given more time to get back on its feet, but this would not eliminate short-term financing problems. Besides, even though Greek aid loans are very long-term (over thirty years) and interest rates have already been lowered several times (lower than 1%), the country's national debt is still considered unsustainable.

As for the SYRIZA government's current promise to implement a "parallel" social program that would ease the burden of harsh new austerity policies on poorer Greeks, it has already been forced to withdraw the intended bill following severe objections by the country's creditors. Many of the proposed measures lacked required budget-impact estimates. There were also concerns about the program's compatibility with the conditions of the third bailout agreement. "Parallel" programs running alongside austerity measures are not what the EU has in mind, nor would they be possible to implement within the strict framework of the latest bailout.

> ### ENKLO: Life, Death—and Rebirth?
>
> A case in point of Greece's manufacturing decline is provided by United Textiles (ENKLO), a 140-year-old company operating in Central Macedonia and Thrace with a strong presence in international markets, a skilled workforce, advanced technology, and excellent product quality. The company closed down in 2009, sinking under a debt burden of 350 million euros due mostly to poor management decisions and the expansion of its business activities beyond the textiles industry.
>
> Ever since its shutdown, the laid-off workers, unable to find other jobs and refusing to accept that the company would never operate again, have been maintaining the equipment and guarding the buildings in order to prevent theft. "We are here night and day to make sure that the machines remain unharmed," says Petros, who has worked as an electrician for 25 years.
>
> Instead of the scheduled liquidation of the company's property, the workers now propose its revival by converting its debts into stockholders' equity, taking advantage of the country's bankruptcy code. It is an ambitious business plan that aspires to utilize the existing equipment and the invaluable expertise of the workers.
>
> No public funds are needed to re-start production. All that's required is a government intervention that would settle any legal complications that may arise. With the government's support, Petros argues, the company could operate the very next day.

The Prospect of Change

The only real question for Greece at the moment is: Could there be an alternative path?

Not everyone has given in to despondency and apathy. In a school building in central Athens, I meet Georgia, a young teacher and mother of three, who offers extra classes to underprivileged students free of charge. "People would take to the streets because they hoped they could make an actual difference," she says. "Now it is clear that our hopes were false." Nonetheless, she tells me, the economic crisis has made her more politically aware. She now chooses to spend much of her time and energy in political and social movements and social solidarity structures, where she can actually feel useful.

Popular Unity, a new political front including SYRIZA's left wing, which split from the party by refusing to accept the new bailout, has so far offered the only coherent argument about how Greece could adopt an anti-bailout strategy. Its radical program includes the introduction of a new national currency, a deep national debt write-off, a lifting of austerity measures, and a restructuring of the productive sector and the welfare state. However, Popular Unity has so far failed to convince Greek voters, and did not gain parliamentary representation in the last elections.

Social injustice has spurred new modes of resistance far from political parties and trade unions. As the state becomes ever more hostile to the Greek people, many choose to self-organize by forming neighborhood assemblies and solidarity networks that support basic human rights, organizing micro-economies without middle-men, and setting up "solidarity clinics" providing free health care.

This is a period of reflection and finding alternative forms of resistance that could potentially be the basis for something new to emerge in the future. All hope is not yet lost that Greece may regain some economic stability and find a development policy in the interest of its people. "People feel exhausted, defeated and betrayed," says Georgia, "but many refuse to give up." ❑

Sources: Eurostat news release 181/2015 (ec.europa.eu/eurostat/documents); Eurostat dataset (ec. europa.eu/eurostat), "Youth unemployment rate," "Long-term unemployment rate," "Production in industry—manufacturing," "Production in industry—total (excluding construction)," "Production in industry—annual data, percentage change," "General government gross debt—annual data"; "Young, gifted and Greek: Generation G—the world's biggest brain drain," *The Guardian* (theguardian.com); C. Pitelis & N. Antonakis (2003), "Manufacturing and competitiveness: the case of Greece," *Journal of Economic Studies*, Vol. 30, Issue 5, pp. 535—547; H. Louri and I. Pepelasis Minoglou (2002), "A hesitant evolution: industrialisation and de-industrialisation in Greece over the long run", *Journal of European Economic Studies*, Vol. 31, No. 2, pp. 321-348; M. Nence, "Greek entrepreneurship after crisis—investment abroad, the easiest solution" (pecob.eu); Kathimerini, "Crisis wipes out a quarter of Greece's SMEs" (ekathimerini.com); September 2015 official election results (ekloges.ypes.gr)..

Article 11.6

GREECE AND THE CRISIS OF EUROPE: WHICH WAY OUT?

BY MARJOLEIN van der VEEN
May/June 2013

The Greek economy has crashed, and now lies broken on the ground. The causes of the crisis are pretty well understood, but there hasn't been enough attention to the different possible ways out. Our flight crew has shown us only one emergency exit—one that is broken and just making things worse. But there is more than one way out of the crisis, not just the austerity being pushed by the so-called "Troika" (International Monetary Fund (IMF), European Commission, and European Central Bank (ECB)). We need to look around a bit more, since—as they say on every flight—the nearest exit may not be right in front of us. Can an alternative catch hold? And, if so, will it be Keynesian or socialist?

The origins of the crisis are manifold: trade imbalances between Germany and Greece, the previous Greek government's secret debts (hidden with the connivance of Wall Street banks), the 2007 global economic crisis, and the flawed construction of the eurozone (see sidebar). As Greece's economic crisis has continued to deepen, it has created a social disaster: Drastic declines in public health, a rise in suicides, surging child hunger, a massive exodus of young adults, an intensification of exploitation (longer work hours and more work days per week), and the rise of the far right and its attacks on immigrants and the LGBT community. Each new austerity package brokered between the Greek government and the Troika stipulates still more government spending cuts, tax increases, or "economic reforms"—privatization, increases in the retirement age, layoffs of public-sector workers, and wage cuts for those who remain.

While there are numerous possible paths out of the crisis, the neoliberal orthodoxy has maintained that Greece had no choice but to accept austerity. The country was broke, argued the Troika officials, economists, and commentators, and this tough medicine would ultimately help the Greek economy to grow again. As Mark Weisbrot of the Center for Economic and Policy Research (CEPR) put it, "[T]he EU authorities have opted to punish Greece—for various reasons, including the creditors' own interests in punishment, their ideology, imaginary fears of inflation, and to prevent other countries from also demanding a 'growth option.'" By focusing on neoliberal solutions, the mainstream press controls the contours of the debate. Keynesian remedies that break with the punishment paradigm are rarely discussed, let alone socialist proposals. These may well gain more attention, however, as the crisis drags on without end.

Neoliberal Solutions

Despite the fact that 30 years of neoliberalism resulted in the worst economic crisis since the Great Depression, neoliberals are undaunted and have remained intent

Causes of Greece's Deepening Crisis

Trade imbalances. Germany's wage restraint policies and high productivity made German exports more competitive (cheaper), resulting in trade surpluses for Germany and deficits for Greece. Germany then used its surplus funds to invest in Greece and other southern European countries. As German banks shoveled out loans, Greek real estate boomed, inflation rose, their exports became less competitive, and the wealthy siphoned money abroad.

Hidden debt. To enter the eurozone in 2001, Greece's budget deficit was supposed to be below the threshold (3% of GDP) set by the Maastricht Treaty. In 2009 the newly elected Panhellenic Socialist Movement (PASOK) government discovered that the outgoing government had been hiding its deficits from the European authorities, with the help of credit default swaps sold to it by Goldman Sachs during 2002-06. The country was actually facing a deficit of 12% of GDP, thanks to extravagant military spending and tax cuts for (and tax evasion by) the rich.

Global crisis. When the 2007 global economic crisis struck, Greece was perhaps the hardest-hit country. Investments soured, banks collapsed, and loans could not be repaid. Debt-financed household consumption could no longer be sustained. Firms cut back on investment spending, closed factories, and laid off workers. Output has fallen 20% since 2007, the unemployment rate is now above 25%, (for youth, 58%), household incomes have fallen by more than a third in the last three years, and government debt has surpassed 175% of GDP.

The eurozone trap. Greece's government could do little on its own to rescue its economy. With eurozone countries all using the same currency, individual countries could no longer use monetary policy to stimulate their economies (e.g., by devaluing the currency to boost exports or stimulating moderate inflation to reduce the real debt burden). Fiscal policy was also weakened by the Maastricht limits on deficits and debt, resulting in tight constraints on fiscal stimulus.

on dishing out more of the same medicine. What they offered Greece were bailouts and haircuts (write-downs of the debt). While the country—really, the country's banks—got bailouts, the money flowed right back to repay lenders in Germany, France, and other countries. Very little actually went to Greek workers who fell into severe poverty. The bailouts invariably came with conditions in the form of austerity, privatization (e.g., water systems, ports, etc.), mass public-sector layoffs, labor-market "flexibilization" (making it easier to fire workers), cutbacks in unemployment insurance, and tax reforms (lowering corporate taxes and raising personal income and sales taxes). In sum, the neoliberal structural adjustment program for Greece shifted the pain onto ordinary people, rather than those most responsible for causing the crisis in the first place.

Austerity and internal devaluation

With steep cuts in government spending, neoliberal policy has been contracting the economy just when it needed to be expanded. Pro-austerity policy makers, however, professed their faith in "expansionary austerity." Harvard economists Alberto Alesina and Silvia Ardagna claimed that austerity (especially spending cuts) could lead to the expectation of increased profits and so stimulate investment. The neoliberals also hoped to boost exports through "internal devaluation" (wage cuts, resulting in lower costs and therefore cheaper exports). An economist with Capital Economics in London claimed that Greece needed a 30–40% decline in real wages to restore competitiveness. A fall in real wages, along with the out-migration of workers, the neoliberals suggested, would allow labor markets to "clear" at a new equilibrium. Of course, they neglected to say how long this would take and how many workers would fall into poverty, get sick, or die in the process.

Meanwhile, international financial capitalists (hedge funds and private equity firms) have been using the crisis as an opportunity to buy up state assets. The European Commission initially expected to raise €50 billion by 2015 from the privatization of state assets (now being revised downward to just over €25 billion through 2020). The magnitude of the fire sale in Greece is still five to ten times larger than that expected for Spain, Portugal, and Ireland. Domestic private companies on the brink of bankruptcy are also vulnerable. As the crisis drags on, private-equity and hedge-fund "vulture capitalists" are swooping in for cheap deals. The other neoliberal reforms—labor and pension reforms, dismantling of the welfare state, and tax reforms—will also boost private profits at the expense of workers.

Default and exit from the euro

Another possible solution was for Greece to default on its debt, and some individuals and companies actively prepared for such a scenario. A default would lift the onerous burden of debt repayment, and would relieve Greece of complying with all the conditions placed on it by the Troika. However, it would likely make future borrowing by both the public and private sectors more difficult and expensive, and so force the government to engage in some sort of austerity of its own.

Some economists on the left have been supportive of a default, and the exit from the euro and return to the drachma that would likely follow. One such advocate is

The Role of Goldman Sachs

Greece was able to "hide" its deficits thanks to Goldman Sachs, which had sold financial derivatives called credit-default swaps to Greece between 2002 and 2006. The credit-default swaps operated a bit like subprime loans, enabling Greece to lower its debts on its balance sheets, but at very high borrowing rates. Goldman Sachs had sales teams selling these complicated financial instruments not just to Greece, but to many gullible municipalities and institutions throughout Europe (and the United States), who were told that these deals could lower their borrowing costs. For Greece, the loans blew up in 2008-2009, when interest rates rose and stock markets collapsed. Among those involved in these deals included Mario Draghi (now President of the ECB), who was working at the Greece desk at Goldman Sachs at the time. While these sales generated huge profits for Goldman Sachs, the costs are now being borne by ordinary Greek people in the form of punishing austerity programs. (For more on Goldman Sachs's role, see part four of the PBS documentary "Money, Power, Wall Street.")

Mark Weisbrot, who has argued that "a threat by Greece to jettison the euro is long overdue, and it should be prepared to carry it out." He acknowledges there would be costs in the short term, but argues they would be less onerous "than many years of recession, stagnation, and high unemployment that the European authorities are offering." A return to the drachma could restore one of the tools to boost export competitiveness: allowing Greece to use currency depreciation to lower the prices of its exports. In this sense, this scenario remains a neoliberal one. (Many IMF "shock therapy" have included currency devaluations as part of the strategy for countries to export their way out of debt.)

The process of exit, however, could be quite painful, with capital flight, bank runs, black markets, significant inflation as the cost of imports rises, and the destruction of savings. There had already been some capital flight—an estimated €72 billion left Greek banks between 2009 and 2012. Furthermore, the threat of a Greek exit created fear of contagion, with the possibility of more countries leaving the euro and even the collapse of the eurozone altogether.

Keynesian Solutions

By late 2012, Keynesian proposals were finally being heard and having some impact on policymakers. Contrary to the neoliberal austerity doctrine, Keynesian solutions typically emphasize running countercyclical policies—especially expansionary fiscal policy (or fiscal "stimulus"), with deficit-spending to counter the collapse in private demand. However, the Greek government is already strapped with high deficits and the interest rates demanded by international creditors have spiked to extremely high levels. Additional deficit spending would require that the ECB (or the newly established European Stability Mechanism (ESM)) intervene by directly buying Greek government bonds to bring down rates. (The ECB has been lending to private banks at low rates, to enable the banks to buy public bonds.) In any case, a Keynesian approach ideally would waive the EU's deficit and debt limits to allow the Greek government more scope for rescuing the economy.

Alternatively, the EU could come forward with more grants and loans, in order to create employment, fund social-welfare spending, and boost demand. This kind of bailout would not go to the banks, but to the people who are suffering from unemployment, cuts in wages and pensions, and poverty. Nor would it come with all the other conditions the neoliberals have demanded (privatization, layoffs, labor-market reforms, etc). The European Investment Bank could also help stimulate new industries, such as alternative energy, and help revive old ones, such as tourism, shipping, and agriculture. In a European Union based on solidarity, the richer regions of Europe would help out poorer ones in a crisis (much as richer states in the United States make transfers to poorer ones, mostly without controversy).

Even some IMF officials finally recognized that austerity was not working. An October 2012 IMF report admitted that the organization had underestimated the fiscal policy multiplier—a measure of how much changes in government spending and taxes will affect economic growth—and therefore the negative impact of austerity policies. By April 2013, economists at UMass-Amherst found serious mistakes in research by Harvard economists Carmen Reinhart and Kenneth Rogoff, alleging that debt-to-GDP ratios of 90% or more seriously undermine future economic growth. Reinhart and Rogoff's claims had been widely cited by supporters of austerity for highly indebted countries. So yet another crack emerged in the pillar supporting austerity policies.

Keynesians have argued, contrary to the "internal devaluation" advocates, that the reduction in real wages just depressed aggregate demand, and made the recession deeper. Economists such as Nobel laureate Paul Krugman proposed that, instead, wages and prices be allowed to rise in the trade-surplus countries of northern Europe (Germany and the Netherlands). This would presumably make these countries' exports less competitive, at some expense to producers of internationally traded goods, though possibly boosting domestic demand thanks to increased wages. Meanwhile, it would help level the playing field for exporters in the southern countries in crisis, and would be done without the punishing reductions in real wages demanded by the Troika. The Keynesian solution thus emphasized stimulating domestic demand through fiscal expansion in both the northern and southern European countries, as well as allowing wages and prices to rise in the northern countries.

Signs pointing in this direction began to emerge in spring 2013, when some Dutch and German trade unions won significant wage increases. In addition, the Dutch government agreed to scrap its demands for wage restraint in some sectors (such as the public sector and education) and to hold off (at least until August) on its demands for more austerity. (Another €4.5 billion cuts had been scheduled for 2014, after the government spent €3.7 billion in January to rescue (through nationalization) one of the country's largest banks.)

Socialist Solutions

For most of the socialist parties in Greece and elsewhere in Europe, the neoliberal solution was clearly wrong-headed, as it worsened the recession to the detriment of workers while industrial and finance capitalists made out like bandits. Greece's Panhellenic Socialist Movement (PASOK) was an exception, going along with austerity, structural reforms, and privatization. (Its acceptance of austerity lost it significant support in the 2012 elections.) Other socialists supported anything that alleviated the recession, including Keynesian prescriptions for more deficit spending, higher wages, and other policies to boost aggregate demand and improve the position of workers. Greece's SYRIZA (a coalition of 16 left-wing parties and whose support surged in the 2012 elections) called for stopping austerity, renegotiating loan agreements, halting wage and pension cuts, restoring the minimum wage, and implementing a type of Marshall Plan-like investment drive. In many ways, these proposale resemble standard Keynesian policies—which have historically served to rescue the capitalist system, without challenging its inherent exploitative structure or vulnerability to recurrent crisis.

While Keynesian deficit-spending could alleviate the crisis in the short-term, who would ultimately bear the costs—ordinary taxpayers? Workers could end up paying for the corruption of the Greek capitalist class, who pushed through tax cuts, spent government funds in ways that mainly benefited themselves, and hid money abroad. Many socialists argued that the Greek capitalists should pay for the crisis, through increased taxes on wealth, corporate profits, and financial transactions, and the abolition of tax loopholes and havens. As SYRIZA leader Alexis Tsipras put it, "It is common knowledge among progressive politicians and activists, but also among the Troika and the Greek government, that the burden of the crisis has been carried exclusively by public and private sector workers and pensioners. This has to stop. It is time for the rich to contribute their share... ."

Slowly, the right-wing government began making gestures in this direction. In 2010, French finance minister Christine Lagarde had given a list of more than 2,000 Greeks with money in Swiss bank accounts to her Greek counterpart George Papaconstantinou, of the PASOK government, but Papaconstantiou sat on it and did nothing. But in the fall of 2012 the so-called "Lagarde list" was published by the magazine Hot Doc, leading to fury among ordinary Greeks against establishment political leaders (including the PASOK "socialists") who had failed to go after the tax dodgers. Another list of about 400 Greeks who had bought and sold property in London since 2009 was compiled by British financial authorities at the request of the current Greek government. In total, the economist Friedrich Schneider has estimated that about €120 billion of Greek assets (about 65% of GDP) were outside the country, mostly in Switzerland and Britain, but also in the United States, Singapore, and the Cayman Islands. The government also started a clamp down on corruption in past government expenditures. In the Spring of 2013, two politicians (a former defense minister and a former mayor of Thessaloniki, the country's second-largest city) were convicted on corruption charges.

Socialists have also opposed dismantling the public sector, selling off state assets, and selling Greek firms to international private equity firms. Instead of bailouts, many socialists have called for nationalization of the banking sector. "The banking system we envision," SYRIZA leader Alexis Tsipras announced, "will support environmentally viable public investment and cooperative initiatives.... . What we need is a banking system devoted to the public interest—not one bowing to capitalist profit. A banking system at the service of society, a banking system that serves as a pillar for growth." While SYRIZA called for renegotiating the Greece's public debt, it favored staying in the euro.

Other socialist parties have put forth their own programs that go beyond Keynesian fiscal expansion, a more equitable tax system, and even beyond nationalizing the banks. For instance, the Alliance of the Anti-Capitalist Left (ANTARSYA) called for nationalizing banks and corporations, worker takeovers of closed factories, and canceling the debt and exiting the euro. The Communist

Party of Greece (KKE) proposed a fairly traditional Marxist-Leninist program, with socialization of all the means of production and central planning for the satisfaction of social needs, but also called for disengagement from the EU and abandoning the euro. The Trotskyist Xekinima party called for nationalizing not just the largest banks, but also the largest corporations, and putting them under democratic worker control.

Those within the Marxist and libertarian left, meanwhile, have focused on turning firms, especially those facing bankruptcy, into cooperatives or worker self-directed enterprises. Firms whose boards of directors are composed of worker-representatives and whose workers participate in democratic decision-making would be less likely to distribute surpluses to overpaid CEOs or corrupt politicians and lobbyists, or to pick up and relocate to other places with lower labor costs. While worker self-directed enterprises could decide to forego wage increases or to boost productivity, in order to promote exports, such decisions would be made democratically by the workers themselves, not by capitalist employers or their representatives in government. And it would be the workers themselves who would democratically decide what to do with any increased profits that might arise from those decisions.

One Greek company that is trying to survive as a transformed worker cooperative is Vio.Me, a building materials factory in Thessaloniki. In May 2011 when the owners could no longer pay their bills and walked away, the workers decided to occupy the factory. By February 2013, after raising enough funds and community support, the workers started democratically running the company on their own. (They do not intend to buy out the owners, since the company owed the workers a significant amount of money when it abandoned the factory.) They established a worker-board, controlled by workers' general assemblies and subject to recall, to manage the factory. They also changed the business model, shifting to different suppliers, improving environmental practices, and finding new markets. Greek law currently does not allow factory occupations, so the workers are seeking the creation of a legal framework for the recuperated factory, which may enable more such efforts in the future. Vio.Me has received support from SYRIZA and the Greek Green party, from workers at recuperated factories in Argentina, as well as from academics and political activists worldwide.

Whither Europe and the Euro?

As Europe faces this ongoing crisis, it is also grappling with its identity. On the right are the neoliberal attempts to dismantle the welfare state and create a Europe that works for corporations and the wealthy—a capitalist Europe more like the United States. In the center are Keynesian calls to keep the EU intact, with stronger Europe-wide governance and institutions. These involve greater fiscal integration, with a European Treasury, eurobonds (rather than separate bonds for each country), European-wide banking regulations, etc. Keynesians also call for softening the austerity policies on Greece and other countries.

Proposals for European consolidation have inspired criticism and apprehension on both the far right and far left. Some on the far right are calling for exiting the euro, trumpeting nationalism and a return to the nation state. The left, meanwhile, voices concern about the emerging power of the European parliament in Brussels, with its highly paid politicians, bureaucrats, lobbyists, etc. who are able to pass legislation favoring corporations at the expense of workers. Unlike the far right however, the left has proposed a vision for another possible united Europe—one based on social cohesion and inclusion, cooperation and solidarity, rather than on competition and corporate dominance. In particular, socialists call for replacing the capitalist structure of Europe with one that is democratic, participatory, and embodies a socialist economy, with worker protections and participation at all levels of economic and political decision-making. This may very well be the best hope for Europe to escape its current death spiral, which has it living in terror of what the next stage may bring. ❑

Sources: Amitabh Pal, "Austerity is Killing Europe," Common Dreams, April 27, 2012 (commondreams.org); Niki Kitsantonis, "Greece Resumes Talks With Creditors," *New York Times*, April 4, 2013 (nytimes.com); Mark Weisbrot, "Where I Part from Paul Krugman on Greece and the Euro," *The Guardian*, May 13, 2011 (guardian.co.uk); Alberto F. Alesina and Silvia Ardagna, "Large Changes in Fiscal Policy: Taxes Versus Spending," National Bureau of Economic Research (NBER), October 2009 (nber.org); Geert Reuten, "From a false to a 'genuine' EMU," Globalinfo, Oct. 22, 2012 (globalinfo.nl); David Jolly, "Greek Economy Shrank 6.2% in Second Quarter," *New York Times*, Aug. 13, 2012; Joseph Zacune, "Privatizing Europe: Using the Crisis to Entrench Neoliberalism," Transnational Institute, March 2013 (tni.org); Mark Weisbrot, "Why Greece Should Reject the Euro," *New York Times*, May 9, 2011; Ronald Jannsen, "Blame It on the Multiplier," *Social Europe Journal*, Oct. 16, 2012 (social-europe.eu); Landon Thomas, Jr., and David Jolly, "Despite Push for Austerity, European Debt Has Soared," *New York Times*, Oct. 22, 2012; "German Public sector workers win above-inflation pay rise," Reuters, March 9, 2013 (reuters.nl); Liz Alderman, "Greek Businesses Fear Possible Return to Drachma," *New York Times*, May 22, 2012; Landon Thomas, Jr., "In Greece, Taking Aim at Wealthy Tax Dodgers," *New York Times*, Nov. 11, 2012; Rachel Donadio and Liz Alderman, "List of Swiss Accounts Turns Up the Heat in Greece," *New York Times*, Oct. 27, 2012; Landon Thomas, Jr., "Greece Seeks Taxes From Wealthy With Cash Havens in London," *New York Times*, Sept. 27, 2012; Niki Kitsantonis, "Ex-Mayor in Greece Gets Life in Prison for Embezzlement," *New York Times*, Feb. 27, 2013; Sam Bollier, "A guide to Greece's political parties," Al Jazeera, May 1, 2012 (aljazeera.com); Alexis Tsipras, "Syriza London: Public talk," March 16, 2013 (left.gr); Amalia Loizidou, "What way out for Greece and the working class in Europe," Committee for a Workers' International (CWI), March 19, 2013 (socialistworld.net); Richard Wolff, "Yes, there is an alternative to capitalism: Mondragón shows the way," *The Guardian*, June 24, 2012 (guardian.co.uk); Peter Ranis, "Occupy Wall Street: An Opening to Worker-Occupation of Factories and Enterprises in the U.S.," MRzine, Sept. 11, 2011 (mrzine.monthlyreview.org); viome.org.

Article 11.7

PROSPECTS FOR THE SPANISH LEFT

BY WILLIAM O. SAAS, JORGE AMAR, DAVID GLOTZER, AND SCOTT FERGUSON
November/December 2016

They are beautiful sights, the public squares of Madrid—open spaces, lush gardens, and sparkling fountains, all surrounded by striking architecture dating from the city's days as the seat of a global colonial empire. These ornate public spaces now serve as makeshift residences for a growing number of Spanish dispossessed. After nearly a decade of austerity, depression, chronic unemployment, and perpetual political submission to the dictates of the Troika (the International Monetary Fund, European Central Bank, and European Commission), thousands displaced from work and home are left with little choice but to seek refuge in the few parcels of public infrastructure that remain available to them.

Improvisation is the name of the game for members of the new Spanish precariat. At Madrid's main square, the Plaza Mayor, newly homeless citizens (some highly educated) rise early for work busking or selling scrap metal. Throughout the country, members of the growing reserve army of *ninis*—or "neither nors," the quarter of the young Spanish who are neither in school, nor employed, nor in training programs—forage for food to take home to their squatted apartments. *Los irrecuperables* ("unrecoverables"), the more than half of long-term unemployed Spanish over age 50, are meanwhile forced to figure out how to subsist on severely reduced pensions and the charity of their fellows.

The homeless, *ninis*, and *irrecuperables* are not alone in their plight. Indeed, stability and security elude even the employed *afortunados* ("lucky ones") in austerian Spain. Changes in Spanish labor law, first passed by the center-left (and resolutely neoliberal) Spanish Socialist Workers' Party (PSOE) and then expanded by the conservative People's Party (PP), have eroded workers' rights and enabled employers to seize an even larger share of national income. Wages and benefits are taking a beating, too. Total worker compensation fell from about €523 million in 2007 to less than €510 million in 2015. Even as unemployment has risen, total spending on unemployment benefits has fallen more than 25%. Temporary work is replacing traditional employment. The average length of a contract—formal contracts between employer and employee are legally required in Spain—fell from 77 days in 2008 to 57 by 2014, and part-time work constitutes one third of all labor contracts. Finally, the percentage of unpaid overtime rose from less than 40% in 2008 to over 55% in 2015—a sum equal to the lost income of approximately 87,000 full-time jobs.

Nearly 30% of the Spanish population is currently classified by the Unión General de Trabajadores (General Union of Workers, or UGT) as "at risk" of poverty. Any among them may consider joining the estimated 700,000 Spaniards who have fled the country to find marginal employment elsewhere. Most will opt to stay, however, knowing full well that that they are not welcome in other EU countries, and that their prospects would not improve by much in any of those countries, anyway.

What relief does the Spanish left have to offer a population so imperiled? The simple answer is: not much. On the one hand, the PSOE has consistently—if not exclusively—made things worse for Spain over the last decade. That the PSOE is presently in the throes of a slow and torturous death spiral is no consolation for the years of impoverishment and despair that resulted from the party's servile deference to the Troika's commands. On the other hand, the slick façade of the only-slightly-further-left Podemos makes poor cover for the purple party's own orthodox underbelly. In the face of all evidence to the contrary, Podemos leadership appears convinced that "balanced budgets" are the best remedy for Spain's economic ills. As recent elections have demonstrated, Spanish voters were less than inspired by Podemos' master plan to squeeze more euros out of domestic businesses and middle-class families in order to facilitate increases in public spending. A similar plan—to transcend austerity through more efficient tax collection—has clearly not worked out well for Syriza and the Greeks. Spaniards simply want—and deserve—better.

The far left coalition, the United Left (UL), would give it to them, were it in a position to do so. While Podemos' top economist Nacho Álvarez calls for better tax enforcement as the key to achieving a more symmetrical balance sheet, Eduardo Garzón, economic advisor to UL and researcher at the Fundación por la

---

The Jobs Guarantee

A "jobs guarantee" program is the best political tool for breathing new life into the Spanish economy. A proposal of this kind was presented to the Spanish parliament in 2014. Designed by Eduardo Garzón and presented to parliament by his brother, Alberto Garzón, the jobs guarantee program would have put a large portion of the ninis, irrecuperables, and the homeless back to work. As opposed to the current system, under which the last to be fired is the first to be hired, the Spanish jobs guarantee program sought to put most idle labor to work immediately, involving Spain's dispossessed in socially meaningful and adequately compensated communal projects. In accordance with MMT, meanwhile, financing for Spain's full employment economy would not be contingent upon tax revenues or government borrowing. Unlike the short-term and revenue constrained New Deal programs deployed in the United States during the 1930s, the Spanish jobs guarantee program should be financed through direct government authorization and appear as a fixed charge on the federal balance sheet.

Garzón's proposal suffered a resounding defeat in 2014. Deluded by the poor logic of the neoliberal consensus and a punishing phantom gold standard, opponents of the program ignored Garzón's arguments and voted against the bill without comment (here the Spanish saying, "no hay mayor desprecio que no hacer aprecio" or, there is no bigger contempt than not listening at all, is apt). It is also worth noting that, had the jobs guarantee been implemented under the aegis of the EU's budget rules, the policy's overall impact would have been severely limited by the fiscal straitjacket of Maastricht.

Europa de los Ciudadanos (Citizens' Europe Foundation), argues that a municipal jobs guarantee program is the only viable path to renewed Spanish prosperity. For Álvarez, the vital first steps to recovery are to "reduce the deficit more slowly" and to "broaden the tax base." For Garzón, deficits and taxes are secondary to the need for "construction of a new alternative economic model that puts the current economy at the service of the people." The disparity of ambition between the proposals of Álvarez and Garzón—an archaic and conservative accounting target for the former, a progressive full-employment agenda for the latter—is stark. Of the two, only one bears any real chance of achieving meaningful relief for the Spanish working class. Unfortunately, the force of Garzón's rejoinder to Álvarez's plan for functional-in-name-only finance is presently attenuated by UL's minority position in the Podemos-led Unidos Podemos ("United We Can") coalition, where the spirit of "sound finance" otherwise prevails unabated. Moreover, the very public conflict between Podemos' top officials—"number one" Pablo Iglesias and "number two" Íñigo Errejón—makes for splashier headlines than does news of disagreements within the coalition about how best to escape from austerity.

When one shifts focus from the public spectacle of political discord to the more vital behind-the-scenes debate over political economy, however, the prospects for the Spanish left look a lot more promising. Several major figures in Unidos Podemos, besides Garzón, do understand that the fiscal strictures forced upon Spain by the Troika institutions foreclose any hope for true economic recovery. Informed by the insights of Modern Monetary Theory (MMT), a select and well-placed few clearly see that monetary union without fiscal union is a tried-and-true recipe for endless austerity. They recognize that jobs and demand, not equilibrium and "confidence," are the key ingredients of economic well-being. Most importantly, they understand that the last best hope for Spain is to again become sovereign in its own currency.

The impending collapse of PSOE will leave masses of Spanish voters alienated and in search of alternatives to the newly formed PP-led government. While some voters might prefer the familiar feel of PP's austere embrace, it is a safe bet that many more will defect to the parties that make up the Unidos Podemos coalition. This is, we feel, a very promising development. But in order for a reinvigorated Unidos Podemos to follow through on its promise to deliver the Spanish working class from austerity, the coalition must finally disavow, without apology or regret, the utopian dream of a single-currency Europe.

The Story So Far

That the euro currency experiment has been an abject failure is a truism across the European left. Most non-centrist leftists recognize that what was sold as a means to achieve the dream of an open and unified Europe has in practice resulted in more deeply entrenched nationalism and still greater economic division. As Podemos leader Pablo Iglesias pithily summarized, "This Europe doesn't work. This Europe is dying."

Modern Monetary Theory*

Modern Monetary Theory (MMT) is a school of heterodox economic theory that describes how monetary systems operate in modern states. MMT's critical insight is that states that are sovereign in their own currency cannot ever run out of money, and so can always afford to purchase anything that is priced in their own currency. This is true for any state that does not "peg" the value of its currency to a metallic standard (like the gold standard) or other government currencies (like a "dollar peg"), but instead issues its currency by "fiat" and allows its value to "float." The only real spending constraints in such a system are 1) access to real resources and 2) concerns about inflation (though such concerns can be, and often are, overstated). Any additional constraints on domestic spending—e.g., a balanced budget rule—are artificial, political, and hence contestable.

Furthermore, MMT explains that taxation and public borrowing are both fiscal policy instruments designed to regulate the growth of the economy—not means for generating necessary revenue. This is because states that are sovereign in their own currency have no natural need to raise revenue. For this reason, MMT suggests that fiscal policy decisions ought always to be taken in service of the "public purpose." Typically, the public purpose is best served by the full employment of national resources, including and especially labor. Toward that end, MMT advocates conclude that a government-supported jobs guarantee is the optimum policy for full employment of national resources in a state with a sovereign monetary system. Such a program, they argue further, will function as both a price floor and an economic stabilizer. MMT advocates have long objected to the euro currency project on the grounds that the monetary union deprives EU states of the fiscal authority necessary to adequately provide for the care and employment of their citizens.

It is one thing to notice that Europe is dysfunctional and dying. It is quite another to identify precisely what is killing Europe and, following from that diagnosis, to do what is necessary to restore individual European nations to good health. While Iglesias and his cohort on the European further-left seem to grasp the severity of the pathology, their prescriptions for ailing European nations have so far been shockingly modest in scope and frustratingly palliative in nature. What's more, these prescriptions exhibit signs of contamination by the sorts of groupthink and denial that are endemic to the neoliberal European consensus. They have only extended Europe's suffering.

Spain's current case of chronic and intractable debt deflation—sky-high private debt levels and suppressed wages and pensions that make paying down private debts impossible—exemplifies neoliberalism's dead-end political-economic wisdom. Between 1998 and 2007, rapid expansion of private credit precipitated the tripling of property prices in Spain. When the global credit bubble burst in 2008, property prices crashed but private debt levels remained high. The next part of the story mirrors events in the United States: millions of people lost their homes, their jobs, and their access to easy credit. What separates Spain's experience from that of the United States, however, is that the Spanish government was not empowered to defend and stimulate its economy through proactive fiscal policy. Rather, because it is not sovereign in its own currency, Spain was forced to borrow €100 billion from the European Stability Mechanism to stop the collapse of its banks. The rules of the monetary union strictly prohibited the Spanish government from deficit spending to keep its citizens fed, housed, and employed. Meanwhile, the United States was able spend as needed by issuing Treasury bonds payable in its own currency (deficit spending).

The sustained annual deficits needed to get Spain out of its current depression likely exceed 9% of GDP—roughly three times the limit imposed by the EU. If Spain were to breach that limit, it could set in motion the EU's Excessive Deficit Procedure (EDP), an arbitrary law that would drain up to 0.2% of Spain's total economic output. The social and economic costs of a possible EDP fine are outstripped by the potential output currently being sacrificed in the name of budgetary balance, only underscoring the fickleness of the Troika's rules and the misguidedness of obedience to them. To make matters worse, the Spanish government cannot control the interest rates on its national debt. This leaves the Spanish economy almost entirely subject to the whims of both the international bond market and the supranational European Central Bank.

To be sure, of all the proposals to address Spain's debt deflation problem, Podemos' has been among the least terrible. Much like the budget plans of so-called "deficit doves" in the United States, Podemos' plan prescribes increased domestic spending in the near-term and balanced budgets over the long-term. To pursue the doves' path within the strictures of the EU is difficult if not impossible. To hear Podemos' Nacho Álvarez tell it, however, all that is needed for Spain to save its citizens and balance its budget is better and more consistent tax collection. Revenue gained through more effective tax collection could be used immediately to increase funding for vital social welfare programs. Over time, Álvarez argues, this process would have the salutary effect of bringing government revenues into balance with public expenditures.

This policy agenda has its heart in the right place, but it is irretrievably diluted by wrong-headed economic analysis. MMT's "deficit owls" will immediately notice the sources of error. First of all, there is little reason to believe that Álvarez's plan for more effective tax collection will work, so long as Spain remains in the euro currency union. This is because adequate tax collection in a free capital zone is nearly impossible without a supranational tax authority that is empowered to both enforce and collect. Otherwise it's entirely too easy for private citizens and corporations to shuffle their euros between EU countries without notice.

More importantly, the idea that governments are naturally revenue-constrained and so always ought to strive to balance their budgets is a debilitating economic myth. Typically, governmental revenue constraints are artificial and self-imposed. That is, revenue constraints are first and foremost political constraints. In the eurozone, the balanced budget political constraint was formally codified with the

Maastricht Treaty in 1992. Against the advice of numerous, ideologically diverse economists, the signatories of the Treaty entered into an economic system governed by what Scott Ferguson and Jorge Amar (two of the co-authors of this article) have recently called a "phantom gold standard." Like the gold standard of old, the EU's phantom standard functions to constrain the number of euros in circulation. Instead of precious metal, however, the Troika backs the euro with a capricious moralism. We will not allow your government to spend in excess of its current and anticipated revenues, the institutions protest, because to do so would be imprudent. It is unfortunate that millions must meanwhile starve and go without shelter, but such concerns are only incidental to the greater moral responsibility of the institutions to maintain euro-equilibrium.

The Way Forward

In order to escape its cycle of debt deflation, Spain must ultimately do what its counterparts on the European "periphery" have so far failed to do: exit the eurozone. To proceed otherwise—to continue to acquiesce to the destructive rules of the institutions—is to guarantee the continued immiseration of the Spanish working class.

It is time for leaders within Unidos Podemos to pledge, in no uncertain terms, to take the steps that are necessary to restore Spain to prosperity. The most controversial of these steps will be the Spanish Left-exit, or "lexit." Path-breakers in a lexit-oriented Unidos Podemos must anticipate and account for popular reluctance to depart the euro. With the example of UKIP's noxious campaign for Brexit fresh in their minds, some Spaniards will doubtless view Spanish lexit as an inherently reactionary proposal. In stark contrast with UKIP, however, a lexit-oriented Unidos Podemos will be able to supplement its proposal with a roadmap for a prosperous post-euro Spanish economy, as well as a leadership that is prepared to execute the requisite sharp left-turn.

The economic prospects of Spain in 2016 remain as dour as they were in 2014. Unlike 2014, however, today there is a critical mass inside the Unidos Podemos coalition that is ready to support a fresh and genuine alternative agenda for Spain. With the specter of a PP-led government looming on the horizon, it is likely that Iglesias and Unidos Podemos will soon be faced with a stark choice: stay the course and hope for change, or change the course and make a better future. ❏

Sources: A. Makris, "Stiglitz: Greece and Spain are 'in Depression,'" *Greek Reporter,* Oct. 17, 2012 (greece.greekreporter.com); "Homeless crisis hits Spain's educated elite," *The Local,* April 22, 2013 (thelocal.es); "The 'Ninis': no school, no job and no more bank of mum and dad?" *The Guardian,* June 6, 2016 (theguardian.com); Suzanne Daley, "Spain Recoils as Its Hungry Forage Trash Bins for a Next Meal," *New York Times,* Sept. 24, 2012 (nytimes.com); Nicolás Sarriés, "Los 'irrecuperables': el 52% de parados de muy larga duración tiene 50 años o más," Sabemos Digital, June 9, 2015 (sabemos.es); Government of Spain, Ministry of Employment and Social Security, "Trabajadores" (seg-social.es); "El derecho contra los precarios, de Adoración Guaman y Héctor Illueca en Público," Caffe Reggio,

Oct. 30, 2013 (caffereggio.net); Alejandro Bolaños, "Las rentas empresariales superan por primera vez a las salariales en España," *El País*, Feb. 17. 2012 (economia.elpais.com); Eurostat, Compensation of Employees (ec.europa.eu); Confederación Sindical de Comisiones Obreras, "El pare se reduce poque hay menos gente buscando empleo y por el umento del empleo estacional y a tiempo parcial" (ccoo. es); "Las horas extras no pagadas en España equivalen a 87.000 empleos a tiempo completo," *La Voz de Galicia*, Feb. 16, 2016 (lavozdegalicia.es); Unión General de Trabajadores, "La precarización del empleo y de los salarios lleva a la población a la pobreza," Jan. 19, 2015 (ugt.es); Amparo González-Ferrer, "La nueva emigración española," Laboratorio de alternativas (2013) (fundacionalternativas.org); "Alemania también expulsa a parados españoles," *El Plural*, May 21, 2014 (elplural.com); "Sánchez mantiene la batalla contra los críticos y convoca Congreso Extraordinario para noviembre," *Público*, Sept. 29, 2016 (publico.es); Philip Arestis and Malcolm Sawyer, "The Eurozone Balanced Budget Disaster," Triple Crisis blog, Nov. 27, 2013 (triplecrisis.com); Andrés Gil, "Unidos Podemos fracasa en el sorpasso a un PSOE que logra el peor resultado histórico en escaños," *El Diario*, June 27, 2016 (eldiario.es); Jorge Uxó and Ignacio Álvarez, "Is the end of fiscal austerity feasible in Spain?" Universidad de Castilla-La Mancha, Working Papers (DT 2016/2) (uclm.es); Tim Fernholz and Jason Karaian, "Ode on a Grecian Earn: Syriza's most radical plan for Greece? Collect taxes," *Quartz*, Feb. 9. 2015 (qz.com); Fundacion por la Europa de los Ciudadanos (europadelosciudadanos.net), Nacho Álvarez, "Las cuentas sí cuadran," *El País*, Feb. 22, 2016 (elpais.com); Eduardo Garzón, "La izquierda necesita aprender de la Teoría Monetaria Moderna," Saque de Esquina, July 25, 2016 (eduardogarzon.net); Gonzalo Cortizo, "Iglesias y Errejón enfrentan públicamente sus diferencias sobre la estrategia de Podemos," *El Diario*, Sept. 20, 2016 (eldiario.es); "MMT Primer," New Economic Perspectives (neweconomicperspectives. org); Alejandro Reuss, "European Social Democracy and the Roots of the Eurozone Crisis—Part 1: Monetary Union and Fiscal Disunion," *Dollars & Sense*, July/August 2016 (dollarsandsense.org); Sam Jones, "Spanish Socialists' week of turmoil not just down to Pedro Sánchez," *The Guardian*, Sept. 30, 2016 (theguardian.com); Sam Jones, "Pedro Sánchez insists he is still in charge of Spanish Socialist party," *The Guardian*, Sept. 29, 2016 (theguardian.com); "Encuentro de Pablo Iglesias con los círculos," *Público* (especiales.publico.es); Y. Varoufakis, S. Holland, and J.K. Galbraith, "A Modest Proposal for Resolving the Eurozone Crisis – Version 4.0," July 2013 (yanisvaroufakis.eu); William Mitchell, Eurozone Dystopia: Groupthink and Denial on a Grand Scale (Edward Elgar, 2015); Michael Hudson, "Democracy's Debt Ladder," Oct. 18. 2016 (michael-hudson.com); Podemos. Elecciones Generales 2016. Memoria Económica, Unidos Podemos (lasonrisadeunpais.es); Dylan Matthews, "You know the deficit hawks. Now meet the deficit owls," *Washington Post*, Feb. 19, 2012 (washingtonpost. com); L. Randall Wray, "Paul Samuelson on Deficit Myth," New Economic Perspectives, April 30, 2010 (neweconomicperspectives.org); Wynne Godley, "Maastricht and All That," London Review of Books, Oct. 8, 1992 (lrb.co.uk); Tim Congdon, "In Defence of Sterling" (timcongdon4ukip. com); Anealla Safdar, "Brexit: UKIP's 'unethical' anti-immigration poster," Al Jazeera, June 28, 2016 (aljazeera.com); "El Trabajo Garantizado," Fundación por la Europa de los Ciudadanos, June 8, 2016 (europadelosciudadanos.net); "It's Time for a LEXIT," Lexit Network (lexit-network.org); Marién Kadner, "Pablo Iglesias: 'Lo que tenemos claro es que este euro no sirve,'" *El País*, May 23, 2014 (politica.elpais.com); Joaquín Romero, "Podemos pide a Bruselas un mecanismo para suprimir el euro," *La Crónica Global*, Jan. 2, 2016 (cronicaglobal.elespanol.com); "Fort Apache Europa: ¿Game over?" HispanTV, Oct. 26, 2013 (youtube.com); Paul Mason, "Podemos: how Europe's political centre is being eaten by the radical left and nationalist right," *The Guardian*, Dec. 21, 2015 (theguardian.com);

Stephen Burgen, "Flat-pack policies: new Podemos manifesto in style of Ikea catalogue," *The Guardian*, June 9, 2016 (theguardian.com); "La decadencia de la profesión económica," *Voz Pópuli*, Aug. 24, 2016 (vozpopuli.com); "Frente al pensamiento gregario, un Plan B para España," *Voz Pópuli*, May 25, 2016 (vozpopuli.com); Lorenzo Marsili, "Miguel Urbán: 'No se tiene que hacer ningún esfuerzo más por el euro,'" *Diagonal*, Feb. 18, 2016 (diagonalperiodico.net); Eduardo Garzón, "Desmontando los mitos sobre la inflación y la creación de dinero," Saque de Esquina, Aug. 24, 2016 (eduardogarzon.net).

Chapter 12

RESISTANCE AND ALTERNATIVES

Article 12.1

KEEP IT IN THE GROUND

An alternative vision for petroleum emerges in Ecuador. But will Big Oil win the day?

BY ELISSA DENNIS
July/August 2010; Updated October 2013

In the far eastern reaches of Ecuador, in the Amazon basin rain forest, lies a land of incredible beauty and biological diversity. More than 2,200 varieties of trees reach for the sky, providing a habitat for more species of birds, bats, insects, frogs, and fish than can be found almost anywhere else in the world. Indigenous Waorani people have made the land their home for millennia, including the last two tribes living in voluntary isolation in the country. The land was established as Yasuní National Park in 1979, and recognized as a UNESCO World Biosphere Reserve in 1989.

Underneath this landscape lies a different type of natural resource: petroleum. Since 1972, oil has been Ecuador's primary export, representing 57% of the country's exports in 2008; oil revenues comprised on average 26% of the government's revenue between 2000 and 2007. More than 1.1 billion barrels of heavy crude oil have been extracted from Yasuní, about one quarter of the nation's production to date.

At this economic, environmental, and political intersection lie two distinct visions for Yasuní's, and Ecuador's, next 25 years. Petroecuador, the state-owned oil company, has concluded that 846 million barrels of oil could be extracted from proven reserves at the Ishpingo, Tambococha, and Tiputini (ITT) wells in an approximately 200,000-hectare area covering about 20% of the parkland. Extracting this petroleum, either alone or in partnership with interested oil companies in Brazil, Venezuela, or China, would generate approximately $7 billion, primarily in the first 13 years of extraction and continuing with declining productivity for another 12 years.

The alternative vision is the simple but profound choice to leave the oil in the ground. Environmentalists and indigenous communities have been organizing for years to restrict drilling in Yasuní. But the vision became much more real when President Rafael Correa presented a challenge to the world community at a September 24, 2007 meeting of the United Nations General Assembly: If governments, companies, international organizations, and individuals pledge a total of $350 million per year for 10 years, equal to half of the forgone revenues from ITT, then Ecuador will chip in the other half and keep the oil underground indefinitely, as this nation's contribution to halting global climate change.

The Yasuní-ITT Initiative would preserve the fragile environment, leave the voluntarily isolated tribes in peace, and prevent the emission of an estimated 407 million metric tons of carbon dioxide into the atmosphere. This "big idea from a small country" has even broader implications, as Alberto Acosta, former Energy Minister and one of the architects of the proposal, notes in his new book, *La Maldición de la Abundancia (The Curse of Abundance)*. The Initiative is a "punto de ruptura," he writes, a turning point in environmental history which "questions the logic of extractive (exporter of raw material) development," while introducing the possibility of global *"sumak kawsay,"* the indigenous Kichwa concept of "good living" in harmony with nature.

Sumak kawsay is the underlying tenet of the country's 2008 Constitution, which guarantees rights for indigenous tribes and for "Mother Earth." The Constitution was overwhelmingly supported in a national referendum, but putting the document's principles into action has been a bigger challenge. While Correa draws praise for his progressive social programs, for example in education and health care, the University of Illinois-trained economist is criticized for not yet having wrested control of the nation's economy from a deep-rooted powerful elite bearing different ideas about the meaning of "good living." Within this political and economic discord lies the fate of the Yasuni Initiative.

An Abundance of Oil

Ecuador, like much of Latin America, has long been an exporter of raw materials: cacao in the 19th century, bananas in the 20th century, and now petroleum. Shell discovered the heavy, viscous oil of Ecuador's Amazon basin in 1948. In the 1950s, a series of controversial encounters began between the native Waorani people and U.S. missionaries from the Summer Institute of Linguistics (SIL). With SIL assistance, Waorani were corralled into a 16,000-hectare "protectorate" in the late 1960s, and many went to work for the oil companies who were furiously drilling through much of the tribe's homeland.

The nation dove into the oil boom of the 1970s, investing in infrastructure and building up external debt. When oil prices plummeted in the 1980s while interest rates on that debt ballooned, Ecuador was trapped in the debt crisis that affected much of the region. Thus began what Correa calls "the long night of neoliberalism": IMF-mandated privatizations of utilities and mining sectors, with a concomitant decline of revenues from the nation's natural resources to the Ecuadorian people. By 1986, all of the nation's petroleum revenues were going to pay external debt.

After another decade of IMF-driven privatizations, oil price drops, earthquakes, and other natural disasters, the Ecuadorian economy fell into total collapse, leading to the 2000 dollarization. Since then, more than one million Ecuadorians have left the country, mostly for the United States and Spain, and remittances from 2.5 million Ecuadorians living in the exterior, estimated at $4 billion in 2008, have become the nation's second highest source of income.

Close to 40 years of oil production has failed to improve the living standards of the majority of Ecuadorians. "Petroleum has not helped this country," notes Ana Cecilia Salazar, director of the Department of Social Sciences in the College of Economics of the University of Cuenca. "It has been corrupt. It has not diminished poverty. It has not industrialized this country. It has just made a few people rich."

Currently 38% of the population lives in poverty, with 13% in extreme poverty. The nation's per capita income growth between 1982 and 2007 was only 0.7% per year. And although the unemployment rate of 10% may seem moderate, an estimated 53% of the population is considered "underemployed."

Petroleum extraction has brought significant environmental damage. Each year 198,000 hectares of land in the Amazon are deforested for oil production. A verdict is expected this year in an Ecuadorian court in the 17-year-old class action suit brought by 30,000 victims of Texaco/Chevron's drilling operations in the area northwest of Yasuní between 1964 and 1990. The unprecedented $27 billion lawsuit alleges that thousands of cancers and other health problems were caused by Texaco's use of outdated and dangerous practices, including the dumping of 18 billion gallons of toxic wastewater into local water supplies.

Regardless of its economic or environmental impacts, the oil is running out. With 4.16 billion barrels in proven reserves nationwide, and another half billion "probable" barrels, best-case projections, including the discovery of new reserves, indicate the nation will stop exporting oil within 28 years, and stop producing oil within 35 years.

"At this moment we have an opportunity to rethink the extractive economy that for many years has constrained the economy and politics in the country," says Esperanza Martinez, a biologist, environmental activist, and author of the book *Yasuní: El tortuoso camino de Kioto a Quito (Yasuní: The Tortuous Road from Kyoto to Quito)*. "This proposal intends to change the terms of the North-South relationship in climate change negotiations."

Collecting on Ecological Debt

The Initiative fits into the emerging idea of "climate debt." The North's voracious energy consumption in the past has destroyed natural resources in the South; the

South is currently bearing the brunt of global warming effects like floods and drought; and the South needs to adapt expensive new energy technology for the future instead of industrializing with the cheap fossil fuels that built the North. Bolivian president Evo Morales proposed at the Copenhagen climate talks last December that developed nations pay 1% of GDP, totaling $700 billion/year, into a compensation fund that poor nations could use to adapt their energy systems.

"Clearly in the future, it will not be possible to extract all the petroleum in the world because that would create a very serious world problem, so we need to create measures of compensation to pay the ecological debt to the countries," says Malki Sáenz, formerly Coordinator of the Yasuní-ITT Initiative within the Ministry of Foreign Relations. The Initiative "is a way to show the international community that real compensation mechanisms exist for not extracting petroleum."

Indigenous and environmental movements in Latin America and Africa are raising possibilities of leaving oil in the ground elsewhere. But the Yasuní-ITT proposal is the furthest along in detail, government sponsorship, and ongoing negotiations. The Initiative proposes that governments, international institutions, civil associations, companies, and individuals contribute to a fund administered through an international organization such as the United Nations Development Program (UNDP). Contributions could include swaps of Ecuador's external debt, as well as resources generated from emissions auctions in the European Union and carbon emission taxes such as those implemented in Sweden and Slovakia.

Contributors of at least $10,000 would receive a Yasuní Guarantee Certificate (CGY), redeemable only in the event that a future government decides to extract the oil. The total dollar value of the CGYs issued would equal the calculated value of the 407 million metric tons of non-emitted carbon dioxide.

The money would be invested in fixed income shares of renewable energy projects with a guaranteed yield, such as hydroelectric, geothermal, wind, and solar power, thus helping to reduce the country's dependence on fossil fuels. The interest payments generated by these investments would be designated for: 1) conservation projects, preventing deforestation of almost 10 million hectares in 40 protected areas covering 38% of Ecuador's territory; 2) reforestation and natural regeneration projects on another one million hectares of forest land; 3) national energy efficiency improvements; and 4) education, health, employment, and training programs in sustainable activities like ecotourism and agro forestry in the affected areas. The first three activities could prevent an additional 820 million metric tons of carbon dioxide emissions, tripling the Initiative's effectiveness.

Government Waffling

These nationwide conservation efforts, as well as the proposal's mention of "monitoring" throughout Yasuní and possibly shutting down existing oil production, are particularly disconcerting to Ecuadorian and international oil and wood interests. Many speculate that political pressure from these economic powerhouses was behind a major blow to the Initiative this past January, when Correa, in one of his regular Saturday radio broadcasts, suddenly blasted the negotiations as "shameful," and a threat to the nation's "sovereignty" and "dignity." He threatened that if the full package of international commitments is not in place by this June, he would begin extracting oil from ITT.

Correa's comments spurred the resignations of four critical members of the negotiating commission, including Chancellor Fander Falconí, a longtime ally in Correa's PAIS party, and Roque Sevilla, an ecologist, businessman, and ex-Mayor of Quito whom Correa had picked to lead the commission. Ecuador's Ambassador to the UN Francisco Carrion also resigned from the commission, as did World Wildlife Fund president Yolanda Kakabadse.

Correa has been clear from the outset that the government has a Plan B, to extract the oil, and that the non-extraction "first option" is contingent on the mandated monetary commitments. But oddly his outburst came as the negotiating team's efforts were bearing fruit. Sevilla told the press in January of commitments in various stages of approval from Germany, Spain, Belgium, France, and Switzerland, totaling at least $1.5 billion. The team was poised to sign an agreement with UNDP last December in Copenhagen to administer the fund. Correa called off the signing at the last minute, questioning the breadth of the Initiative's conservation efforts and UNDP's proposed six-person administrative body, three appointed by Ecuador, two by contributing nations, and one by UNDP. This joint control structure apparently sparked Correa's tirade about shame and dignity.

Correa's impulsivity and poor word choice have gotten him into trouble before. Acosta, another former key PAIS ally, resigned as president of the Constituent Assembly in June 2008, in the final stages of drafting the nation's new Constitution, when Correa set a vote deadline Acosta felt hindered the democratic process for this major undertaking. The President has had frequent tussles with indigenous and environmental organizations over mining issues, on several occasions crossing the line from staking out an economically pragmatic political position to name-calling of "childish ecologists."

Within a couple of weeks of the blowup, the government had backpedaled, withdrawing the June deadline, appointing a new negotiating team, and reasserting the position that the government's "first option" is to leave the oil in the ground. At the same time, Petroecuador began work on a new pipeline near Yasuní, part of the infrastructure needed for ITT production, pursuant to a 2007 Memorandum of Understanding with several foreign oil companies.

If the People Lead...

Amid the doubts and mixed messages, proponents are fighting to save the Initiative as a cornerstone in the creation of a post-petroleum Ecuador and ultimately a post-petroleum world. In media interviews after his resignation, Sevilla stressed that he would keep working to ensure that the Initiative would not fail. The Constitution provides for a public referendum prior to extracting oil from protected areas like Yasuní, he noted. "If the president doesn't want to assume his responsibility as leader...let's pass the responsibility to the public." In fact, 75% of respondents in a January poll in Quito and Guayaquil, the country's two largest cities, indicated that they would vote to not extract the ITT oil.

Martinez and Sáenz concur that just as the Initiative emerged from widespread organizing efforts, its success will come from the people. "This is the moment to define ourselves and develop an economic model not based on petroleum," Salazar says. "We have other knowledge, we have minerals, water. We need to change our consciousness and end the economic dependence on one resource." ❑

Resources: Live Yasuni, Finding Species, Inc. (liveyasuni.org); "S.O.S. Yasuni" (sosyasuni.org); "Yasuni-ITT: An Initiative to Change History," Government of Ecuador, (yasuni-itt.gov.ec).

Update

Declaring "the world has failed us," Ecuador's President Rafael Correa signaled the termination of the Yasuni ITT Initiative this past August. Citing a meager $116 million in pledges, he announced the decision to move forward with the Plan B that was always in the background: extraction of oil from the Ishpingo, Tambococha, and Tiputini fields in the eastern section of Yasuni National Park. The drilling will only impact 0.1% of the parklands, Correa contends, noting that the estimated value of oil in the targeted area has increased from $7 billion to $18 billion. Despite street demonstrations in Quito and Cuenca and calls for a national referendum, the National Assembly ratified Correa's action in October with legislation protecting indigenous communities and prohibiting drilling in an "untouchable zone" to be preserved as a wildlife sanctuary.

Correa, a U.S. trained economist, has consistently ridiculed "infantile" environmentalists, and is clearly most comfortable with a pragmatic economic development model of extractivism with equitable distribution of resources. Like his Bolivian counterpart Evo Morales, Correa has run afoul of indigenous communities and the environmental Left through efforts to transform the nation from exploited exporter of raw materials into savvy user of natural resources to fuel economic growth and social programs. Correa's critics say his government never wholeheartedly supported the Yasuni effort, and point to a growing Chinese political and economic influence. Since Correa's 2008 move to default on the nation's IMF debt, China has provided billions of dollars to Ecuador, with oil production pledged as repayment of some of that debt. China is also a key investor in Ecuador's oil industry, including links to ITT. —*Elissa Dennis*

Article 12.2

CHINA AND THE GLOBAL ECONOMY
Why China Must Shift from Export-Led Growth to Domestic Demand-Led Growth

BY THOMAS PALLEY
November/December 2005

O ver the last twenty years, China has undergone a massive economic transfor-mation. A generation ago, China's economy was largely agricultural; today, the country is an industrial powerhouse experiencing rapid economic growth. Now, however, many economists question the sustainability of China's development model. Ironically, this debate has been triggered by recent acceleration in China's growth, which exceeded 9% in both 2003 and 2004. Some analysts claim this acceleration is being driven by a private investment bubble and by misdirected state investment, posing the risks of inflation and a hard landing when the bubble pops.

China's development model is indeed unsustainable—but not for the reasons most economists suggest. It is not overinvestment or excessive growth that is the problem. Instead, it is China's impact on the global economy. China's export-led development model threatens to trigger a global recession that will rebound and hit China itself. In short, in the same kind of scenario that Keynes addressed in the 1930s, China has failed to develop the demand side of its economy, and so its massive production growth threatens to swamp a weakening demand picture world-wide, with potentially severe consequences for both China and its customers.

A Brief Review of China's Development Model

Broadly speaking, China's development model aims to reduce the size of the centrally planned economy and increase the size of market-based private-sector activity. The first step in this transition was taken with the historic 1979 reforms of the agricultural sector, which allowed small farmers to produce for the market. Since then, the government has allowed private-sector activity to spread more widely by removing controls on economic activity; at the same time, it is privatizing state-owned enterprises (SOEs) on a limited basis. This spread of market-centered activity has been accompanied by both external and internal capital accumulation strategies. The external strategy rests on foreign direct investment (FDI) and export-led growth. The internal strategy uses credit creation by state-controlled banks to fund SOEs and infrastructure investment.

Though FDI is small relative to total Chinese fixed asset accumulation, it serves a number of important functions. Construction and operation of foreign-owned plants has created employment. FDI has also brought capital goods and high technology into the country, and the inflow has been financed by foreign multinational companies (MNCs). Industrialization inevitably requires importing capital goods from developed economies. Most poor countries have borrowed to pay for these capital goods, which has constrained their growth and made them vulnerable to ever-fluctuating global currency markets. In China, FDI has been a form of self-financing development that short-circuits these foreign financing problems. Significantly, FDI has provided a key source of export earnings, since a significant portion of MNC output in China is exported. In 2004, MNCs provided 57% of total exports. These exports earnings have bolstered China's balance of payments and ensured external investor confidence.

Low-wage labor plus the advanced technology and capital that FDI has brought into the country have made China the world's low-cost manufacturing leader. With exports booming, foreign MNCs have been willing to continue building new plants in China. This has given rise to an anomalous situation in which low-income China has been a lender (in the form of its trade surplus) to the high-income United States. Normally, it is expected that high-income households save and lend to low-income households. However, there is a logic to this situation. Exports and a trade surplus (i.e., Chinese savings) are the price that China pays for getting foreign MNCs to invest there. For the Chinese government this is a deal worth striking, since China gains productive capacity, high technology, and jobs. It also gains foreign exchange from the trade surplus, which provides protection against the vagaries of the international economy.

This external capital accumulation strategy has been complemented by an internal strategy predicated on state-directed bank credit expansion. The state-owned banking system has been used to fund large industrial and infrastructure investment projects, as well as to maintain employment in unprofitable SOEs. This has helped support aggregate demand and avoid a precipitous collapse of employment in the SOE sector. With no alternative places to invest their money, Chinese savers have effectively been forced to finance these state investments; the government keeps interest rates low by fiat and thus controls the interest cost of these public investments.

External Contradictions: Limits to Export-Led Growth

Though highly successful to date, China's development strategy is ultimately fundamentally flawed. China has become such a global manufacturing powerhouse that it is now driving the massive U.S. trade deficit and undermining the U.S. manufacturing sector. This threatens the economic health of its major customer. China is putting pressure on the European Union's manufacturing sector, slowing economic growth there as well. The contradiction in China's model, then, is that China's success threatens to undermine the U.S. economy, which has provided the demand that has fueled that success.

China's trade surpluses with the United States have been growing rapidly for several years. In 2004, the United States' bilateral trade deficit with China was $162.0 billion, representing 38.8% of the U.S. trade deficit with all non-OPEC countries. The bilateral China deficit is growing fastest, too: by 30.5% from 2003 to 2004, compared to 16.8% growth in the non-China, non-OPEC trade deficit.

The U.S. trade deficit threatens to become a source of financial instability. More important, the deficit is contributing to the problems in manufacturing that are hindering a robust, investment-led recovery in the United States. There are two ways in which the trade deficit has hindered recovery. First, the deficit drains spending out of the U.S. economy, so that jobs are lost or are created offshore instead of at home. Using a methodology that estimates the labor content embodied in the deficit, economist Robert Scott of the Economic Policy Institute estimates that the U.S. trade deficit with China in 2003 represented 1,339,300 lost job opportunities. Using Scott's job calculations and assuming the composition of trade remained unchanged in 2004, the 2004 trade deficit with China of $162 billion represents 1,808,055 lost job opportunities.

Second, China's policies hurt U.S. investment spending through a range of channels. The draining of demand via the trade deficit creates excess capacity, which reduces demand for new capital. The undervaluation of China's currency makes production in China cheaper, and this encourages firms to both shift existing facilities to China and build new facilities there. Undervaluation also reduces the profitability of U.S. manufacturing and this reduces investment spending.

The U.S. economy is of course a huge economy and these China effects are small in terms of total investment. However, China is likely exerting a chilling effect at the margin of manufacturing investment, and it is at this margin where the recessionary impacts of investment decline have been and continue to be felt.

Together, these employment and investment effects risk tipping the U.S. economy back into recession after what has already been a weak expansion. If this happens, there will be significant adverse consequences for the Chinese economy, and for the global economy as a whole, since the U.S. economy is the main engine of demand growth that has been keeping the world economy flying. (Much is made of China as itself an engine of demand growth, particularly benefiting Japan. China is buying capital goods and production inputs from Japan. However, China's internal demand growth depends on the prosperity generated by exporting to the U.S. economy. In this sense, the U.S. economy is the ultimate source of demand growth; this demand growth is then multiplied in the global economy, where China plays an important role in the multiplier process.)

That's why China must replace its export-led growth strategy with one based on expanding domestic demand. China's people need to have the incomes and the institutions that will enable them to consume a far larger share of what they produce.

For the moment, thanks to continued debt-financed spending by U.S. households, China's adverse impact has not derailed the U.S. economy. China has therefore continued to grow despite the weak U.S. recovery from recession. But there are reasons to believe the U.S. economy is increasingly fragile—a Wile E. Coyote economy running on thinner and thinner air. The recovery has been financed by asset price appreciation, especially in real estate, which has provided collateral for the home-equity loans and other borrowing consumers have used to keep spending. This means the U.S. economy is increasingly burdened by debt which could soon drive the economy into recession. Once in recession, with private sector balance sheets clogged with debt taken on at current low interest rates and not open to refinancing, the United States would not have recourse to another recovery based on consumer borrowing and housing price inflation.

Policymakers, including those in China, tend to have a hard time grasping complex scenarios such as this one, where the damage to China is indirect, operating via recession in the United States. Now that it has become a global manufacturing powerhouse, China's export-led manufacturing growth model is exerting huge strains on the global economy. Until now, China has been able to free-ride on global aggregate demand. The strategy worked when Chinese manufacturing was small, but it cannot continue working now that it is so large. The difficulty is to persuade China's policymakers of the need for change now, when the model still seems to be working and the crash has not come.

Developing the Demand Side of the Chinese Economy

In place of export-led growth, China must adopt a model of domestic demand-led growth. Such a model requires developing structures, institutions, and economic relations that generate sustained, stable internal demand growth. This is an enormous task and one that is key to achieving developed-country status, yet it is a task that has received little attention. Economic theory and policy have traditionally focused on expansion of the supply side in developing countries. This is the core of the export-led growth paradigm, which emphasizes becoming internationally competitive and relying on export markets to provide demand and absorb increases in production. The demand side is generally ignored in the main body of development economics because economists assume that supply generates its own demand, a proposition known as Say's Law.

Nor are traditional Keynesian policies the right answer. Though Keynesian economics does emphasize demand considerations, it operates in the context of mature market economies in which the institutions that generate stable, broad-based demand are well established. For Keynesians, demand shortages can be remedied by policies that stimulate private-sector demand (e.g., lowering interest rates or cutting taxes) or by direct government spending. These policies address temporary failures in an established demand-generation process.

Developing countries, however, face a different problem: they need to build the demand-generation process in the first place. Application of standard Keynesian policies in developing countries tends to create excessive government deficits and promote an oversized government sector. Increased government spending adds to demand but it increases deficits, and it also does little to generate "market" incomes that are the basis of sustainable growth in demand. What is needed is a new analytic approach, one focused on establishing an economic order that ensures income gets into the hands of those who will spend it and encourages production of needed goods that have high domestic employment and expenditure multipliers. This can be termed "structural Keynesianism," in contrast with conventional "demand-side Keynesianism."

In China, then, the challenge is to develop sustainable, growing sources of noninflationary domestic purchasing power. This means attending to both the investment allocation process and the income allocation process. The former is critical to ensure that resources are efficiently allocated, earn an adequate rate of return, and add to needed productive capacity. The latter is critical to ensure that domestic demand grows to absorb increased output. Income must be placed in the hands of Chinese consumers if robust consumer markets are to develop. But this income must be delivered in an efficient, equitable manner that maintains economic incentives.

While banking reform is critical to improving China's capital allocation process, the greater challenge is to develop an appropriate system of household income distribution that supports domestic consumer markets. Investment spending is an important source of demand, but the output generated by investments must find buyers or investment will cease. Likewise, public-sector investment can be an important source of demand, but private-sector income must grow over time or else the government sector will come to dominate, with negative consequences.

With a population of 1.3 billion people, China has an enormous potential domestic market. The challenge is to distribute its rapidly growing income in a decentralized, equitable fashion that leaves work and production incentives intact. The conventional view is that markets automatically take care of the problem by paying workers what they are worth and that all income is spent, thereby generating the demand for output produced. In effect, the problem is assumed away. Indeed, to intervene and raise wages to increase demand would be to cause unemployment by making labor too expensive.

This conventional logic contrasts with Keynesian economics, which identifies the core economic problem as one of ensuring a level of aggregate demand consistent with full utilization of a nation's production capacity. Moreover, the level of aggregate demand is affected by the distribution of income, with worsened income distribution lowering aggregate demand because of the higher propensity to save among higher-income households. From a Keynesian perspective, market forces do not automatically generate an appropriate level of aggregate demand. Demand can be too low because of lack of confidence among economic agents that lowers investment and consumption spending. It can also be too low because the distribution of income is skewed excessively toward upper income groups.

In sum, for neoclassical economists, labor markets set wages such that there is full employment, and income distribution is a by-product that in itself has no effect on employment. For Keynesians, full employment requires an appropriate level of aggregate demand, which is strongly affected by the distribution of income.

The importance of income distribution for demand means that labor markets are of critical significance. Labor markets determine wages, and wages affect income distribution. The problem is that bargaining power can be highly skewed in favor of owners, leading to wages that are too low. This problem is particularly acute in developing countries. Trade unions are a vital mechanism for rectifying imbalances of bargaining power and achieving an appropriate distribution of income. Evidence shows that improved freedom of association in labor markets is associated with improved income distribution and higher wages.

Rather than representing a market distortion, as described in conventional economics, trade unions may correct market failure associated with imbalanced bargaining power. Viewed in this light, trade unions are the market-friendly approach to correcting labor market failure because unions set wages in a decentralized fashion. Though set by collective bargaining, wages can differ across firms with unions in more efficient firms bargaining higher wages than those at less efficient firms.

This contrasts with a government-edict approach to wage setting.

This suggests that a key priority for China is to develop democratic trade unions that freely bargain wages. Just as China is reforming its corporate governance and financial system, so too it must embrace labor market reform and allow free democratic trade unions. This is the market-centered way of establishing an income distribution that can support a consumer society. Outside of Western Europe, only the United States, Canada, Japan, South Korea, Australia and New Zealand have successfully made the transformation to mature developed market economies. In all cases this transformation coincided with the development of effective domestic trade unions. Free trade unions should also be supported by effectively enforced minimum-wage legislation that can also promote demand-led growth. China is a continental economy in which regions differ dramatically by level of development. This suggests the need for a system in which minimum wages are set on a regional basis and take account of regional differences in living costs. Over time, as development spreads and backward regions catch up, these settings can be adjusted with the ultimate goal being a uniform national minimum wage.

Lastly, these wage-targeted labor market reforms should be paired with the development of a social safety net that provides insurance to households. This will increase households' sense of confidence and security; with less need for precautionary saving, households can spend more on consumption.

These reforms raise the issue of wage costs. As long as China follows an export-led growth strategy, production costs will be paramount. This is because export-led growth forces countries to try to ever lower costs to gain international competitive advantage, thereby creating systemic downward pressure on wages. A domestic demand-led growth paradigm reverses this dynamic. Now, higher wages become a source of demand that strengthens the viability of employment. Capital must still earn an adequate return to pay for itself and entice new investment, but moderately higher wages strengthen the system rather than undercutting it.

Independent democratic trade unions are key to a demand-led growth model, as they are the efficient decentralized way of raising wages. However, independent unions are unacceptable to the current Chinese political leadership. That means China must also solve this political problem as part of moving to a domestic demand-led growth regime. ❑

This article is a shortened and revised version of "External Contradictions of the Chinese Development Model," Journal of Contemporary China, *15:46 (2006).*

Sources: Blecker, R.A. (2000), "The Diminishing Returns to Export-Led Growth," Council of Foreign Relations Working Group on Development; Palley, T.I. (2003), "Export-led Growth: Is There Any Evidence of Crowding-Out?" in Arestis et al. (eds.), *Globalization, Regionalism, and Economic Activity*, Edward Elgar; Palley, T.I. (2002), "A New Development Paradigm: Domestic Demand-Led Growth," *Foreign Policy in Focus* (www.fpif.org); Palley, T.I. (2005), "Labor Standards, Democracy and Wages: Some Cross-country Evidence," *Journal of International Development* 17:1-16; Hong Kong Trade & Development Council (www.tdctrade.com/main/china.htm).

Article 12.3

INTERNATIONAL LABOR STANDARDS

BY ARTHUR MacEWAN
September/October 2008

Dear Dr. Dollar:

U.S. activists have pushed to get foreign trade agreements to include higher labor standards. But then you hear that developing countries don't want that because cheaper labor without a lot of rules and regulations is what's helping them to bring industries in and build their economies. Is there a way to reconcile these views? Or are the activists just blind to the real needs of the countries they supposedly want to help?

—*Philip Bereaud, Swampscott, Mass.*

In 1971, General Emilio Medici, the then-military dictator of Brazil, commented on economic conditions in his country with the infamous line: "The economy is doing fine, but the people aren't."

Like General Medici, the government officials of many low-income countries today see the well-being of their economies in terms of overall output and the profits of firms—those profits that keep bringing in new investment, new industries that "build their economies." It is these officials who typically get to speak for their countries. When someone says that these countries "want" this or that—or "don't want" this or that—it is usually because the countries' officials have expressed this position.

Do we know what the people in these countries want? The people who work in the new, rapidly growing industries, in the mines and fields, and in the small shops and market stalls of low-income countries? Certainly they want better conditions—more to eat, better housing, security for their children, improved health and safety. The officials claim that to obtain these better conditions, they must "build their economies." But just because "the economy is doing fine" does not mean that the people are doing fine.

In fact, in many low-income countries, economic expansion comes along with severe inequality. The people who do the work are not getting a reasonable share of the rising national income (and are sometimes worse off even in absolute terms). Brazil in the early 1970s was a prime example and, in spite of major political change, remains a highly unequal country. Today, in both India and China, as in several other countries, economic growth is coming with increasingly severe inequality.

Workers in these countries struggle to improve their positions. They form—or try to form—independent unions. They demand higher wages and better working conditions. They struggle for political rights. It seems obvious that we should support those struggles, just as we support parallel struggles of workers in our own country. The first principle in supporting workers' struggles, here or anywhere else, is supporting their right to struggle—the right, in particular, to form independent unions without fear of reprisal. Indeed, in the ongoing controversy over the U.S.-Colombia Free Trade Agreement, the assassination of trade union leaders has rightly been a major issue.

Just how we offer our support—in particular, how we incorporate that support into trade agreements—is a complicated question. Pressure from abroad can help, but applying it is a complex process. A ban on goods produced with child labor, for example, could harm the most impoverished families that depend on children's earnings, or could force some children into worse forms of work (e.g., prostitution). On the other hand, using trade agreements to pressure governments to allow unhindered union organizing efforts by workers seems perfectly legitimate. When workers are denied the right to organize, their work is just one step up from slavery. Trade agreements can also be used to support a set of basic health and safety rights for workers. (Indeed, it might be useful if a few countries refused to enter into trade agreements with the United States until we improve workers' basic organizing rights and health and safety conditions in our own country!)

There is no doubt that the pressures that come through trade sanctions (restricting or banning commerce with another country) or simply from denying free access to the U.S. market can do immediate harm to workers and the general populace of low-income countries. Any struggle for change can generate short-run costs, but the long-run gains—even the hope of those gains—can make those costs acceptable. Consider, for example, the Apartheid-era trade sanctions against South Africa. To the extent that those sanctions were effective, some South African workers were deprived of employment. Nonetheless, the sanctions were widely supported by mass organizations in South Africa. Or note that when workers in this country strike or advocate a boycott of their company in an effort to obtain better conditions, they both lose income and run the risk that their employer will close up shop.

Efforts by people in this country to use trade agreements to raise labor standards in other countries should, whenever possible, take their lead from workers in those countries. It is up to them to decide what costs are acceptable. There are times, however, when popular forces are denied even basic rights to struggle. The best thing we can do, then, is to push for those rights—particularly the right to organize independent unions—that help create the opportunity for workers in poor countries to choose what to fight for. ❏

Article 12.4

EQUAL TREATMENT FOR IMMIGRANTS

BY ALEJANDRO REUSS
July 2013; Washington Spectator

In this age of mass migration, U.S. immigration policy has mixed relative openness to immigration (since 1965) with nativist hostility toward immigrants. On the state level, we have seen a wave of anti-immigrant legislation (like the Arizona "papers, please" law); on the federal level, the militarization of the U.S.-Mexico border coupled with spasms of workplace immigration raids. Recent reform proposals, including the bill passed by the Senate, have coupled "guest worker" provisions with still more military-police-prisons immigration enforcement. Nativist fantasies of walling off the United States, it is clear, are doomed to fail. Given the harm that such measures cause in both economic and human terms, moreover, it would be bad if they succeeded.

Immigration today is inextricably bound up with globalization. In fact, immigration *is* globalization. Just as surely as international trade, investment, and finance, the international movement of people connects different countries economically. The corporate-driven globalization under which we are living has helped drive mass immigration. First, the flood of agricultural imports from high-income countries has accelerated the decimation of small-farmer agriculture in low-income countries, and with it the exodus from rural areas. Second, imports of manufactured goods have also increased the allure of "first-world" lifestyles, and so created an additional spur to immigration from low-income to high-income countries.

Globalization in its current form, however, has been shaped by the wealthy and powerful to their own advantage. This is obvious when we compare the treatment of the international movement of capital to the international movement of people.

Under the guise of "equal treatment of investors in similar circumstances"—as put by the World Bank's *Guidelines on the Treatment of Foreign Direct Investment*—international trade-and-investment agreements have guaranteed corporations' ability to invest abroad without fear of unfavorable government intervention. A NAFTA tribunal, for example, notoriously decided against Mexico in a case where the Mexican government had blocked foreign investment in the form of a toxic-waste dump.

International agreements, in contrast, have varied dramatically in their treatment of international migration—the movement of people as opposed to the movement of capital. The European Union, for all its shortcomings, allows nearly unencumbered migration between member countries. NAFTA, on the other hand, has created a three-country zone where goods and capital can move with little restriction, but people face harsh barriers to migration.

The U.S.-Mexico border is one of the most militarized in the world—lined with razor-wire, armed patrols, and even drone aircraft—and undocumented immigrants live in constant peril of arrest and deportation. A recent article in *The Economist* paraphrases

UC San Diego economist Gordon Hanson on the results of U.S. immigration policy: "inflicting economic self-harm by spending so much to keep workers out." The self-harm hardly compares to that inflicted on undocumented migrants themselves.

We can see the operation of unequal power here in three ways.

First, undocumented immigrants lack political power. In addition to being denied formal political rights, like the vote, their insecure status poses an additional obstacle to legal social protest. On the other hand, the increasing significance of Latinos as an electoral constituency is a political counterweight. Many Latinos rightly see attacks on "illegal immigration" as thinly veiled attacks on them, so immigrant-bashing politicians risk an electoral backlash. That's why some Republicans are talking immigration reform now.

Second, labor wields far less political influence than capital. It is employers, not labor, who have gotten what they wanted from trade-and-investment agreements (mainly the ability to locate operations where labor costs are low and government regulation lax). While organized labor has not always championed immigrants' rights, U.S. unions have turned more pro-immigrant in recent years, especially as they have come to see immigrant workers as crucial to their own futures.

Third, global corporations have powerful governments on their side. The U.S. government fights for agreements protecting the interests of U.S.-based companies. The governments of many lower-income countries advocate in favor of their nationals abroad, but they have less muscle on the international political scene. Unsurprisingly, their efforts have been less successful.

Today, discrimination on the basis of national origin is a central principle of immigration law. Even though U.S. labor laws, on their face, cover all workers regardless of immigration status, everyone knows this is a fiction because undocumented immigrants' precarious status keeps them from reporting violations to the authorities.

Imagine, instead, that the contours of political power were reversed. Instead of untrammeled freedom for globetrotting corporations, we would have guarantees for people of the right to move, live, and work where they wish. Instead of the "equal treatment" for global investors under trade-and-investment agreements, we would have equal treatment for workers, regardless of nationality, wherever they worked. That would be good not only for immigrants, but also for workers in general, by reducing labor-market competition and strengthening workers' overall bargaining power. As the late legal scholar Anna Christensen put it, in the context of Europe, "Equal treatment of foreign and domestic workers ... is no threat to the position of domestic labor. If anything, the reverse is true."

That is a far cry from the current situation. Indeed, it is a far cry from the Senate bill, which includes still more money for coercive enforcement measures, plus guest-worker provisions that would leave immigrant workers largely at the mercy of their employers.

Equal treatment, however, is the immigration reform we need. ❏

Article 12.5

REMEMBERING THE "TOKYO NO"
When 21 Countries Defied the World Bank

BY ROBIN BROAD
January/February 2015

Fifty years ago last fall, at the 1964 World Bank annual meeting in Tokyo, 21 developing-country governments voted "no" on the convention to set up a new part of the World Bank Group where foreign corporations could sue governments and bypass domestic courts. It was to be called the International Centre for Settlement of Investment Disputes (ICSID). The 21 included all of the 19 Latin American countries attending, as well as the Philippines and Iraq.

The historic vote was dubbed "El No de Tokyo," or the "Tokyo No." It could well be the largest collective vote against a World Bank initiative ever. And perhaps the one time that all Latin American representatives voted "no."

So I write in part to toast that Tokyo No on its fiftieth anniversary. But I also write because it is time to recognize that the 1964 "no" vote has been vindicated by history.

What were the 21 voting against? Rather than paraphrase, let me turn to the then-representative of Chile, Félix Ruiz, speaking on behalf of the Latin American countries:

The legal and constitutional systems of all the Latin American countries that are members of the Bank offer the foreign investor at the present time the same rights and protection as their own nationals; they prohibit confiscation and discrimination and require that any expropriation on justifiable grounds of public interest shall be accompanied by fair compensation fixed, in the final resort, by the law courts.

The new system that has been suggested would give the foreign investor, by virtue of the fact that he is a foreigner, the right to sue a sovereign state outside its national territory, dispensing with the courts of law. This provision is contrary to the accepted legal principles of our countries and, de facto, would confer a privilege on the foreign investor, placing the nationals of the country concerned in a position of inferiority.

In short, the new investor/state dispute settlement system was both unnecessary and unfair.

The ICSID treaty went forward, despite the "no" votes. For the record, Brazil never joined, and in fact has never agreed to investor-state dispute settlement in any venue.

Those who follow the World Trade Organization (WTO) and its dispute resolution mechanism might note the irony: A fundamental rule of today's neoliberal push towards "ultra-globalization," as embedded in the WTO, is that a country's rules must treat foreign and domestic investors the same. As ICSID's existence shows, ultra-globalization proponents do not find it problematic to have foreign investors privileged over domestic investors.

The Tokyo No criticisms were prescient in terms of the track record of ICSID in the ensuing decades. ICSID moved center-stage in the wake of the neoliberal bilateral and multilateral trade and investment agreements that expanded starting in the 1980s. Forty years after ICSID's first case was filed in 1972, a record 48 new arbitration cases were added to ICSID's docket in 2012. To put this in perspective, the number of cases registered never reached five in any year between 1972 and 1996. Since 2003, the number has been over twenty every single year. The last three years for which data have been published, 2011-2013, have the three highest figures to date, with at least 37 cases registered each year. (See figure below.)

As the number of cases being brought before ICSID has ballooned, so too have the criticisms—mainly by sovereign states but increasingly by trade lawyers. The arguments are that ICSID rulings are: 1) increasingly biased in favor of investors over the state (sound familiar?), and 2) too narrow in their focus on "commercial" rights (that is, the private foreign investor) over broader "non-commercial" issues. Shouldn't the government of El Salvador, for example, have the right to protect its key watershed from the environmental ravages of gold mining? Indeed, shouldn't El Salvador be rewarded rather than sued at ICSID? And, why should the investor—as a non-state actor—get to sue the government, while other presumably key non-state actors such as the affected communities are not even allowed to listen to ICSID's often secret hearings, never mind participate equally? (OK: communities can submit amicus briefs—if they find a lawyer willing to write one on their behalf. But there is not even any assurance that such briefs will be read by the World Bank-certified tribunal members who preside over any given case.)

Indeed, as ICSID's case-load has expanded, the verbal criticism has been matched with action. Bolivia, Ecuador, and Venezuela—all part of the original Tokyo No— have left ICSID. South Africa is establishing a new investment law that allows foreign corporations to bring such claims only to domestic courts. India is conducting a review of its treaties in the face of several corporate lawsuits, and Indonesia has announced its intention not to renew its bilateral investment treaties. Australia declined to include

TOTAL NUMBER OF ICSID CASES REGISTERED, BY CALENDAR YEAR

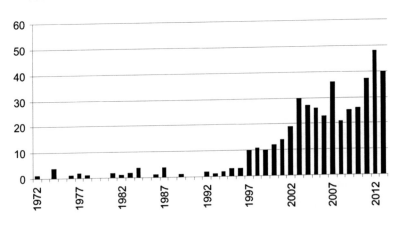

Note: Includes ICSID Convention Arbitration Cases, ICSID Additional Facility Arbitration Cases.

Source: The ICSID Caseload–Statistics (Issue 2014-2).

The "Tokyo No" Roll Call

There were 21 votes against ratifying the ICSID convention, including the 19 Latin American World Bank member countries. The countries voting no were: Argentina, Bolivia, Brazil, Chile, Colombia, Costa Rica, Dominican Republic, Ecuador, El Salvador, Guatemala, Haiti, Honduras, Iraq, Mexico, Nicaragua, Panama, Paraguay, Peru, Philippines, Uruguay, and Venezuela..

Sources: Antonio R. Parra, The History of ICSID (Oxford University Press, 2012); ICSID, Database of ICSID Member States (icsid.worldbank.org).

---

these corporate rights in the 2005 Australia-U.S. Free Trade Agreement. Recently leaked documents suggest that several of these governments are attempting to at least scale back investors' rights (and, thus, the power of ICSID) in the Trans-Pacific Partnership (TPP) trade deal. So, too, are countries in the European Union—notably France and Germany—voicing concerns about investor-state provisions.

But, wait: won't the global economy fall apart without such investor rights and its key venue ICSID? Won't foreign investment dry up? Well, actually, no. Case in point is Brazil, a leading host to foreign investment but, again, a country that has never accepted investor-state dispute settlement. To make a more general point: Foreign investors, if they believe they are making a risky investment, should simply rely on foreign risk insurance. And, like domestic investors, they have recourse to the relevant domestic courts in a given country.

There is increasing urgency to say "no" to ICSID. If the Trans Pacific Partnership (TPP) and the Transatlantic Trade and Investment Partnership (TTIP) are approved, as President Obama hopes, ICSID's case-load will mushroom further, thanks to the investor-state dispute settlement clauses currently in both drafts. And we can expect even more action in terms of investors' propensity to sue governments not just for "direct taking" via expropriation—the original purpose of ICSID—but also for "indirect taking" via environmental, social, and other regulations that might just impinge on a foreign investor's future ability to make profits by pillaging said resources.

So, a shout-out to those governments of the 21 countries who so rightly said "no" in Tokyo fifty years ago. Let's celebrate the 50th anniversary by urging current member governments to withdraw from this forum that undermines democracy, fairness, and the broader common good.

To borrow a slogan that seems apropos: Fifty years is enough. ❑

Sources: Antonio R. Parra, The History of ICSID (Oxford University Press, 2012); Andreas F. Lowenfeld "The ICSID Convention: Origins and Transformation" Georgia Journal of International and Comparative Law, (2009) 38, pp.47-62; Silvia Fiezzoni, "The Challenge of UNASUR Member Countries to Replace ICSID Arbitration," I, (2011) 2, pp. 134-144.

Article 12.6

EQUALITY, SOLIDARITY, SUSTAINABILITY

AN INTERVIEW WITH JAYATI GHOSH
January/February 2015

J*ayati Ghosh is a professor of economics at the Centre for Economic Studies and Planning, Jawaharlal Nehru University, in New Delhi, India. She is a member of the Executive Committee of International Development Economics Associates (IDEAs), a global network of economists devoted to developing "alternatives to the current mainstream economic paradigm as formulated by the neoliberal orthodoxy." In this wideranging interview, Professor Ghosh addresses major challenges of global economic development, environmental sustainability, and global solidarity: the transfiguration of the world capitalist economy today (along with the reproduction of structures like the division between the wealthy "core" and exploited "periphery"), the prospects for the transformation and revival of socialist movements, the difficulties and possibility of overcoming divisions within the working class at the national and global levels, and the way forward towards egalitarian and sustainable societies. —Eds.*

D&S: We are scarcely two decades removed from the supposed global triumph of capitalism, the death of socialism, and (maximum hubris) proclamations of the "end of history." And yet we're seeing a revival of socialist movements—what you have called the "emerging left in the emerging world." What are the key factors explaining this revival?

JG: I think it is now becoming more evident to most people across the world that global capitalism—especially in its current neoliberal manifestation—is not likely to deliver genuinely better material conditions, security, and justice. This is generally still a largely inchoate and diffuse sense of unhappiness with the state of things in many parts of the world. It is true that in some regions, like Latin America, there is a more developed sense of how neoliberal policies pushed the advance of aggressive and extremely unequal capitalist forces.

This emerging left has many features that distinguish it from the earlier, more centralizing and in some ways less socially sensitive left that characterized the second half of the 20th century in particular. For example, there is some rejection of top-down models of party organization which often distorted the idea of the Leninist vanguard, and greater respect for a plurality of opinions, even as many of these movements are more actively engaged in processes of electoral democracy. The language of human rights is explicitly used in these political formations, which in turn demands the recognition of a greater variety of identities that go beyond the class identities that were the standard form of division. So the rights of women, of indigenous communities, of marginalized groups within society in general, are more explicitly recognized. A specific concern regarding human interaction with nature is also an important element, tempering the earlier somewhat simplistic celebration of technology and human ingenuity, which was seen as trumping the requirements and rights of nature.

It is interesting that these features are to be found in new social and political movements in many parts of the world. They are found not just in Latin America, where they also were associated with some amount of political transformation and shifts in economic strategies, but also among movements in countries as far apart as Thailand, Spain, and South Africa.

D&S: The same does not seem to be true to nearly the same extent in the so-called "core" countries of Western Europe or North America. Why is that? And if the current crisis can't spark a profound questioning of capitalism, and discussion of alternatives to it, what can?

JG: It seems to me that in the core capitalist countries the left in every shape or form has taken a long time to recover from the existential blows delivered by the collapse of "socialism" in the Soviet Union and Eastern Europe, and the very market-oriented moves of Communist regimes in East Asia, including China and Vietnam. Interestingly, this blow has affected even those leftists who had rejected these models as not reflecting true socialism at all.

The social and political ascendancy of capitalism, despite its major recent crises and continuing inability to deliver either inclusive growth or social justice, is largely because of this sense that the alternative proved to be so apparently unpleasant and so different from original expectation. So there is some questioning of capitalism, but no real belief in a viable socialist alternative. This may be why the anger and resistance to the effects of the way capitalism functions is now finding expression in more right-wing responses, which are superficially anti-capitalist but essentially focused on symptoms of the problem and on blaming perceived "others," like immigrants.

D&S: A half century ago, the most influential radical view of economic "underdevelopment" focused on the dominance of industrial-manufacturing "core" economies over raw-materials-producing "periphery." Has that story changed in the current era of neoliberal globalization, with many developing countries moving out of mineral and agricultural exports and into export-oriented manufacturing (often "offshored")?

JG: Geographical and locational changes in productive structures do not negate the idea of "core" and "periphery" operating within capitalism. Global capitalism has, throughout its history, experienced such shifts.

First, despite the so-called shift in economic power between developed and "emerging" nations, the material differences between these countries remain very large. Second, the big engine of global manufacturing growth in the developing world, China, has emerged on the basis of a very different economic system, in which market forces have been shaped by the prevailing political and institutional relations, the control of a central party and the advantages of a broadly egalitarian system bequeathed by the Communist revolution. China's engagement with global markets therefore was on very different terms, unlike those of most primary product exporters. This has certainly enabled some productive relocation—but the idea that all other developing countries can follow a similar trajectory is misplaced. Even insertion into global value chains at lower levels can have the effects of perpetuating the unequal relations that propelled such insertion in the first place. Third, the production of underdevelopment is unfortunately not a process that has ended—it still persists, though sometimes in unlikely and unexpected ways. The core and periphery within the eurozone provides a striking example.

D&S: Another major aspect of radical economists' thinking about development in the "Third World" centered on the problem of the unequal distribution of wealth—especially the unequal ownership of agricultural land. Does the distribution of land remain a central issue in the global South? Has it declined in importance in more urbanized and non-agricultural regions?

JG: The idea that the distribution of wealth (including land) has become less important in contemporary capitalism is completely wrong. The talk of capitalism generating a new kind of productive system that relies on "knowledge" to transform material reality is similarly misleading. The rapacious exploitation of nature remains a central requirement of the capitalist system, and that in turn means that the need to control nature, to privatize it and make its ownership concentrated. This is actually true in all parts of the world, but in developing countries it is most directly evident.

Unequal control over land, water, and other resources is a huge impediment to real development for many reasons. Of course it has an adverse impact on agricultural productivity and the expansion of the home market, thereby impeding industrialization—but that is only one problem. It is significant that all the developing countries that have progressed in terms of industrial transformation, South Korea and China, for example, are those that experienced far-reaching land reforms including land redistribution at the start of the development project. Otherwise, landlordism creates not just economic obstacles but also socio-political impediments to industrialization and modernization, and allows the persistence of reactionary social features. India is a good example of this.

D&S: The ways that capitalism has linked together economies all over the world—trade in goods, international investment, international migration—directly pose the need for labor internationalism. Is it possible to develop the necessary kinds of labor solidarity when that means reaching across divides, say, between native and immigrant, or the workers of one country and with those of another country half a world away?

JG: It is obviously necessary for such bonds to be forged—it is even essential, because global forces cannot be fought only within nation states. But clearly such bonds are getting harder to forge. However, that is not only because of the material reality of physical differences and geographical distances. It is also—and possibly more crucially—because of changing perceptions of community, identity, oneness, and difference among various social groups. So workers from different countries see themselves as competing against one another in the struggle to keep their jobs and prevent their wages from falling.

A major role in this division across workers is unfortunately played by media, which wittingly (and sometimes unwittingly) transmits and disseminates a discourse in which workers of one country, region, or type are pitted against other workers, and in which they are then seen as the enemy that must be fought. This obfuscatory role played by the corporatized media is of course extremely useful for capitalism, for the agents of global finance and other large capital, because it succeeds in diverting and distracting from the real problems. Obviously, the left in different parts of the world has not just to express clearly the fallacies associated with such a position, but to think creatively about how to give that critique the widest possible traction and publicity.

D&S: How can we square development objectives—including a dramatic increase in standards of living in lower-income countries—with environmental sustainability? Is there a way to sustainably bring the entire world up to rich-country levels? Or should we also be imagining a massive global redistribution of income and wealth, equalizing per capita incomes of global North and South somewhere in the middle?

JG: In developing countries, the most important goals are to help people adapt to climate changes that we already see and to find ways of mitigation without burdening the poor or preventing their access to essential goods and services. This is important because, even in "emerging" economies, the development project is far from complete, with many millions—the majority of the people—excluded from the minimum conditions for a decent and secure life that ensures dignity and allows creativity. Bringing the vast majority of the developing world's population to anything resembling a minimally acceptable standard of living will involve extensive use of global resources. It will necessarily imply more natural resource use and more carbon emissions. So we have to reduce resource use and emissions elsewhere and in other activities, and re-orient growth in cleaner and greener directions.

In terms of economic strategy, this probably requires policies at several different levels. To start with, the orientation of economic policies and public perception must shift away from the single-minded obsession with GDP growth. For this to happen, it is necessary to develop a set of quantifiable measures of genuine human progress, based as far as possible on objective criteria describing conditions of life (not GDP), which can be regularly estimated and monitored to hold governments and other agents accountable.

Ways of production must change. In agriculture it would be necessary to promote actively the viability of sustainable food production with small holder cultivation that can cope with the greater incidence of climate variability. It is also necessary to reduce and regulate corporate power in food and other productive industries, as well as in finance, so that undesirable forms of consumption and production are not promoted or perpetuated. For all production, the shift from carbon-based production to renewable energy-based activities needs to be encouraged.

The ways in which we organise our physical conditions of life and work also need to change. This can include focussing on urban planning and management that reduces resource use and deals better with waste of all kinds; and emphasising clean, efficient and affordable public transport systems rather than allow polluting and congesting private transport systems. Clearly, protecting and nurturing dwindling water resources and preventing privatized over-exploitation of this and other key gifts of nature is essential.

This is not possible without a simultaneous attack on the growing inequality evident in most societies. Income and asset inequalities generate unsustainable consumption patterns among the privileged and create the desire for them among others. This has to be reduced by using explicitly redistributive measures, fiscal incentives such taxes and subsidies, patterns of public spending more directed to improving conditions of worse-off groups, and improvement of the conditions of work through better regulation and protection of wage workers and the small self-employed.

At the global level, this also requires fighting the monopoly of knowledge and control over technology created by the regime of intellectual property rights and ensuring greater access to relevant "green" technologies to developing countries. And this in turn is part of a broader need to resist and control international trade and investment patterns that create incentives for over-exploiting people and nature.

D&S: The problems we face are not going to be solved overnight, and certainly the world is not going to be transformed overnight. What do you think are the most important changes that we need to start making now, though, to see a world more like the one we want—more egalitarian, democratic, cooperative, and sustainable— forty or fifty years from now?

JG: For me, the desired goal for an ideal society would be one in which some things that you cannot control—where you are born, what you are born as, the family into which you are born—do not affect your basic conditions of life—having a secure home; peace and security; access to nutritious food and other basic requirements for good health; access to education; opportunities for work, leisure, self-expression, and social participation.

This would not mean putting an end to all social and cultural differences, because after all, that is what makes life interesting. But it would mean that your life chances are not fundamentally different because of accidents of birth. So if you are born as a girl of a minority ethnic group in a rural area of a poor region, you would still have access to minimum conditions of life and opportunities for developing your capabilities that are not too different from a boy born in a well-off household of a dominant social group in an affluent society. This would obviously require a certain organization of both economy and society.

To begin with, it would mean that economic arrangements would not be oriented around the simple expansion of aggregate incomes and profits as the most significant goals. It is actually irrational to be obsessed with GDP growth. Consider just one example: a chaotic, polluting, congested, and frustrating system of privatized urban transport generates much more GDP than a clean, efficient, affordable, and "green" system of public transport. This in turn means that other goals would matter: reasonable living conditions for all, development of people's capabilities and space for their creativity, decent employment opportunities, safe and clean environments.

Access to the essentials of life—food, water, basic housing, and so on—would not be determined by the ability to pay but treated as human rights, made available to all in an affordable way. Ensuring this does not mean eliminating market forces altogether. Rather, market forces that help in achieving these goals would be encouraged, while those that operate to reduce standards of living and quality of life of ordinary people would be regulated, restricted, or even abolished.

Extreme inequalities would not be tolerated. Systems of taxation and distribution, as well as methods of monitoring and regulating pay and other returns, would ensure that material differences between people did not grow too large. Social discrimination and exclusion of all kinds would be actively discouraged and sought to be done away with. In addition, in these economic and social arrangements there would be much greater social respect for nature. Economic activities would be monitored and assessed for the damage they do to nature, with a focus on reducing this as much as possible.

All this means that governments would obviously be much more important. So they would have to be more genuinely democratic, transparent, and accountable, and adjust policies to changing conditions. There would be more people's voice and participation in the decisions that affect their lives. Governments would respect both the collective rights and concerns of groups and communities as well as the individual rights of all citizens. For these to be possible within one country, it would be necessary for international political and economic arrangements to support the possibility of such societies emerging and being sustained, without the threat of destabilizing trade and capital flows or military aggression.

At least some of these goals are not so hard to achieve, after all. And for the more ambitious goals, it only requires more people everywhere to share them and strive to achieve them. ❑

CONTRIBUTORS

Frank Ackerman, a founder of *Dollars & Sense,* is a senior economist at Synapse Energy Economics in Cambridge, Mass. His extensive publications on economics and the environment are available at frankackerman.com.

Jorge Amar is a Spanish economist, president of Asociación por el Pleno Empleo y la Estabilidad de Precios (Full Employment and Price Stability Association), and a doctoral candidate in applied economics at the Universidad Valencia. Recently, Amar served as economic advisor for Spain's Unidad Popular party.

David Bacon is a journalist and photographer covering labor, immigration, and the impact of the global economy on workers.

Dean Baker is co-director of the Center for Economic and Policy Research.

Sarah Blaskey is a freelance journalist from Madison, Wisc. whose work has also appeared in CounterPunch, Truth-Out and other publications.

James K. Boyce is a professor of economics at the University of Massachusetts-Amherst and co-director of the Political Economy Research Institute (PERI) Program on Development, Peacebuilding, and the Environment.

Sasha Breger Bush is a lecturer at the Josef Korbel School of International Studies at the University of Denver and author of *Derivatives and Development* (Palgrave Macmillan, 2012).

Robin Broad is a Professor of International Development at the School of International Service, American University.

Roger Bybee is a Milwaukee-based writer on labor issues who has contributed frequently to Dollars & Sense, The Progressive, Working In These Times (workingin-thesetimes.com), and Z Magazine. He also teaches Labor Studies at the University of Illinois and Penn State..

John Cavanagh is the Director of the Institute for Policy Studies in Washington, D.C.

C.P. Chandrasekhar is a professor of economics in te School of Social Sciences at Jawaharlal Nehru University.

Alan Cibils is an Argentine economist and Professor of Political Economy at the Universidad Nacional de General Sarmiento in Buenos Aires, Argentina.

Anita Dancs is an associate professor of economics at Western New England University.

Elisa Dennis is a consultant to nonprofit affordable housing developers with Community Economics, Inc., in Oakland, Calif.

Nina Eichacker (co-editor of this book) is a lecturer in economics at Bentley University.

Gerald Epstein is a professor of economics and co-director of the Political Economy Research Institute (PERI) at the University of Massachusetts Amherst.

Scott Ferguson is an assistant professor of humanities and cultural studies at the University of South Florida. He is also a Research Scholar at the Binzagr Institute for Sustainable Prosperity. His essays have appeared in CounterPunch, Naked Capitalism, and Flassbeck Economics International.

Elizabeth Fraser is an intern scholar at the Oakland Institute.

Gerald Friedman is a professor of economics at the Univeristy of Massachusetts-Amherst.

Phil Gasper teaches at Madison College and writes a column for *International Socialist Review.*

Jayati Ghosh is a professor of economics at the Centre for Economic Study and Planning at Jawaharlal Nehru University.

David Glotzer is a valuation analyst at Solidifi, and freelance writer whose background is in economics and mathematics. His writings have appeared in CounterPunch, Investig'Action, Strategic Culture Foundation, and Young Progressive Voices.

Jesse Griffiths is the director of the European Network on Debt and Development (Eurodad).

Jim Hightower is a national radio commentator, writer, public speaker, and author of *Swim Against The Current: Even A Dead Fish Can Go With The Flow* (Wiley, 2008). He was twice elected Texas Agriculture Commissioner.

Marie Kennedy is professor emerita of Community Planning at the University of Massachusetts-Boston and visiting professor in Urban Planning at UCLA. She is a member of the board of directors of Grassroots International.

David Kotz is a professor of economics at the Univeristy of Massachusetts-Amherst and author of *The Rise and Fall of Neoliberal Capitalism*.

José A. Laguarta Ramírez is a scholar-activist and educator born in San Juan, Puerto Rico and trained in anthropology, law, and comparative politics. His recent doctoral dissertation from the CUNY Graduate Center explores the 2010-2011 University of Puerto Rico student strike against austerity.

Arthur MacEwan, a founder of *Dollars & Sense*, is professor emeritus of economics at the University of Massachusetts-Boston and is a *D&S* Associate. **John Miller** is a member of the *Dollars & Sense* collective and teaches economics at Wheaton College.

John Miller is a member of the *Dollars & Sense* collective and teaches economics at Wheaton College.

Anuradha Mittal is founder and director of the Oakland Institute in Oakland, Calif. She is an internationally renowned expert on trade, development, human rights, and agriculture issues.

William G. Moseley is a professor of geography at Macalester College in Saint Paul, Minn.

Jawied Nawabi (co-editor of this book) is a professor of economics and sociology at CUNY Bronx Community College and a member of the *Dollars & Sense* collective.

Immanuel Ness is a professor of political science at Brooklyn College-City University of New York. He is author of *Immigrants, Unions, and the New U.S. Labor Market* and editor of *WorkingUSA: The Journal of Labor and Society*.

Evita Nolka is a political theorist from Greece.

Thomas Palley is an economist and the author of *Financialization: The Economics of Finance Capital Domination* (Palgrave Macmillan, 2013).

James Petras is an advisor and teacher for the Rural Landless Workers Movement in Brazil and an activist-scholar working with socio-political movements in Latin America, Europe, and Asia.

Robert Pollin teaches economics and is co-director of the Political Economy Research Institute at the University of Massachusetts-Amherst. He is also a *Dollars & Sense* Associate.

Alejandro Reuss (co-editor of this book) is co-editor of *Dollars & Sense* and an instructor in labor studies at the University of Massachusetts-Boston.

Patricia M. Rodriguez is an assistant professor of politics at Ithaca College.

William O. Saas is is an assistant professor of rhetoric at Louisiana State University. His work has appeared in *symplokē* and *Rhetoric & Public Affairs*.

Helen Scharber is an assistant professor of economics at Hampshire College.

Chris Sturr (co-editor of this book) is co-editor of *Dollars & Sense*.

Chris Tilly is director of the Institute for Research on Labor and Employment and professor of urban planning at UCLA and a *Dollars & Sense* Associate.

Junji Tokunaga is an associate professor in the Department of Economics, Dokkyo University, Saitama, Japan.

Marie Trigona is an independent journalist based in Buenos Aires. She is also a member of Grupo Alavío, a direct action and video collective.

Marjolein van der Veen is an economist. She has taught economics in Massachusetts, the Seattle area, and the Netherlands.

Ramaa Vasudevan is an assistant professor of economics at Colorado State University.

Mark Weisbrot is an economist and co-director of the Center for Economic and Policy Research (www.cepr.net) in Washington, D.C.

CPSIA information can be obtained
at www.ICGtesting.com
Printed in the USA
FFOW05n2314030117

9 781939 402288